EARLY CHILD DEVELOPMENT IN THE FRENCH TRADITION

Contributions From Current Research

EARLY CHILD DEVELOPMENT IN THE FRENCH TRADITION

Contributions From Current Research

Edited by

André Vyt
University of Ghent–NFSR
Belgium

Henriette Bloch
École des Hautes Études–CNRS
Paris

Marc H. Bornstein
National Institute of Child Health and Human Development
Bethesda, Maryland

 LAWRENCE ERLBAUM ASSOCIATES, PUBLISHERS
1994   Hillsdale, New Jersey   Hove, UK

Lawrence Erlbaum Associates, Inc., Publishers
365 Broadway
Hillsdale, New Jersey 07642

Library of Congress Cataloging-in-Publication Data

Early child develpment in the French tradition : contributions from
current research / edited by André Vyt, Henriette Bloch, Marc H.
Bornstein.
    p.   cm.
    Includes bibliographical references and indexes.
    ISBN 0-8058-1193-1
    1. Perception in children—France. 2. Perceptual-motor processes .
  3. Social interaction in children. 4. Language acquisition.
  I. Vyt, André. II. Bloch, Henriette. III. Bornstein, Marc H.
  BF723.P36E17   1994
  155.4'0944—dc20   93-43363
                                              CIP

Books published by Lawrence Erlbaum Associates are printed on acid-free paper,
and their bindings are chosen for strength and durability.

Printed in the United States of America

10 9 8 7 6 5 4 3 2 1

Contents

Preface

With the exception of the embrace of Piagetian theory after World War II by Anglophone psychology, modern Francophone research in the domain of human development has not become well known worldwide.

The work of a new generation of developmental theorists and experimentalists continues to shape important and original lines of thinking and research in France, Canada, and other French-speaking countries, and to contribute unique perspectives on perception, cognition, and communication. Paris, Montreal, and Geneva have provided continuous fruitful soil for research in human development, generating philosophical schools, research institutes, and eminent scientists. These cities have functioned as cradles for scientific study and still attract international meetings and conferences on child development.

Scientific concepts and research traditions are not only embedded in a paradigm, but also in a culture and in a language. The present volume testifies to the great number of refreshing ideas and heuristic paths that contemporary research in the French tradition offers an international audience. It brings together original contributions, written by researchers from different Francophone countries, to give a full account of the French tradition, including not only Piagetian paradigms, but also the concepts of Henri Wallon and other more recent authors. These contributions provide the reader with a fuller understanding of current French research practice and theory. Each chapter summarizes and interprets work on a given topic and makes explicit the context of Francophone philosophical and theoretical traditions in which the empirical advances are embedded.

This volume is divided into four sections. In the first, sensorimotor behavior and perceptuocognitive functioning are examined from different viewpoints. The second section focuses on sociocognitive development in both infancy and early childhood. The third section presents communicative and linguistic issues from a variety of areas of study, such as preverbal communication, lexical and meta-linguistic development, and the acquisition of phonology. The last section incorporates interactional sources of development over a range of different contexts, such as parent–infant interaction, day care, and school. Each section ends with commentaries written by scientists working on the same topics in other parts of the world. Together, these essays fully and faithfully represent modern French scientific perspectives toward understanding the many facets of mental growth and development of the young child.

Editing a volume with more than 20 contributors requires close coordination and collaboration. From conceptualization to finalization of the volume, we have continuously focused on a coherent frame to provide the reader with an anthology of today's Francophone developmental psychology. It would be a serious underestimation, however, to see this volume as the exhaustive collection of all the best Francophone researchers. Even a volume with as many chapters as this one is not voluminous enough to embrace all Francophone scientists working in the field of developmental psychology. Readers should, therefore, not view this volume as an index of Francophone researchers today, but rather as an overview of research and thinking, trying to cover the broad range of topics as they are studied in the French tradition.

We would like to express our thanks to all the contributors and commentators. Further, we would also like to offer our sincere appreciation to all who supported this project and stimulated us by providing ideas, by pointing out themes of study, and by encouraging our endeavor to fill a gap in the internationalization of developmental research.

André Vyt
Henriette Bloch
Marc H. Bornstein

List of Contributors

Teresa Blicharski Laboratoire de Psycho-Biologie de l'Enfant, Université de Toulouse le Mirail, Toulouse, France.

Henriette Bloch Laboratoire de Psycho-Biologie de l'Enfant, Ecole des Hautes Etudes–CNRS, Paris.

Marc H. Bornstein National Institute of Child Health and Human Development, National Institutes of Health, Bethesda, Maryland.

Peter Bryant Department of Experimental Psychology, University of Oxford, UK.

André Bullinger Faculté de Psychologie et des Sciences de l'Education, Université de Genève, Switzerland.

George E. Butterworth School of Psychology, University of Sussex, Brighton, UK.

Bettye Caldwell Child Development and Education, Arkansas Children's Hospital, Little Rock, Arkansas.

Bénédicte de Boysson-Bardies Laboratoire de Psychologie Expérimentale, Ecole des Hautes Etudes en Sciences Sociales–CNRS, Paris.

Christine Deruelle Laboratoire de Neurosciences Fonctionnelles–CNRS, Marseille, France.

Scania de Schonen   Laboratoire de Neurosciences Fonctionnelles–CNRS, Marseille, France.

Stephan Desrochers   Département de Psychologie, Université de Montréal, Canada.

Annie Deprels-Fraysse   CREPCQ, U.F.R. de Psychologie et des Sciences de l'Education, Université de Provence, Aix-en-Provence, France.

Elisabeth Fivaz-Depeursinge   Département Universitaire de Psychiatrie Adulte, Université de Lausanne, Switzerland.

Jean Claude Fraysse   CREPCQ, U.F.R. de Psychologie et des Sciences de l'Education, Université de Provence, Aix-en-Provence, France.

Jean Emile Gombert   Laboratoire d'Etudes des Acquisitions et du Développement, Université de Bourgogne, Dijon, France.

Thérèse Gouin Décarie   Département de Psychologie, Université de Montréal, Canada.

Susan A. Graham   Department of Psychology, Concordia University, Montréal, Canada.

France Gravel   Laboratoire d'Ethologie Humaine, Université du Québec à Montréal, Canada.

Pierre Hallé   Centre d'Etudes des Processus Cognitifs et du Langage, Ecole des Hautes Etudes en Sciences Sociales–CNRS, Paris.

Florence Labrell   Laboratoire de Psychologie du Développement et de l'Education de l'Enfant, Université René Descartes Paris V–CNRS, Paris.

Roger Lécuyer   Laboratoire de Psychologie du Développement et de l'Education de l'Enfant, Université René Descartes, Paris.

Gerard Malcuit   Laboratoire d'Etude du Nourisson, Université du Québec à Montréal, Canada.

Jacqueline Nadel   CNRS URA, Université de Poitiers, France.

Hanuš Papoušek   Strassbergerstrasse 43, Munich, Germany.

Mechthild Papoušek   Institute for Social Pediatrics, University of Munich, Germany.

Marie Germaine Pêcheux   Laboratoire de Psychologie du Développement et de l'Education de l'Enfant, Université René Descartes, Paris.

Blaise Pierrehumbert   Service Universitaire de Psychiatrie de l'Enfant et de l'Adolescent, Université de Lausanne, Switzerland.

Andrée Pomerleau   Laboratoire d'Etude du Nourisson, Université du Québec à Montréal, Canada.

Diane Poulin-Dubois   Department of Psychology, Concordia University, Montréal, Canada.

Marc A. Provost   Département de Psychologie, Université du Québec à Trois-Rivières, Canada.

Hellgard Rauh   Institute of Psychology, Free University of Berlin, Germany.

Marcelle Ricard   Département de Psychologie, Université de Montréal, Canada.

Philippe Rochat   Department of Psychology, Emory University, Atlanta, Georgia.

Tibie Rome-Flanders   Département d'Orthophonie et Audiologie, Université de Montréal, Canada.

Colette Sabatier   Laboratoire d'Etude du Nourrisson, Université de Rennes, France.

Elizabeth Spelke   Department of Psychology, Cornell University, Ithaca, New York.

Arlette Streri   Laboratoire de Psychologie du Développement et de l'Education de l'Enfant, Université René Descartes, Paris.

Marcel Trudel   Laboratoire du Développement, Université du Québec à Abitibi-Tamissquemingue, Canada.

Christiane Vandenplas-Holper   Unité de Psychologie du Développement Humain, Université Catholique de Louvain-la-Neuve, Belgium.

Paul van Geert   Department of Developmental Psychology, University of Groningen, The Netherlands.

André Vyt   Department of Developmental and Personality Psychology, University of Ghent–NFSR, Belgium.

1

An Introduction to Francophone Research and Thinking in Developmental Psychology

Henriette Bloch
Ecole Pratique des Hautes Etudes—CNRS

Andre Vyt
University of Ghent—NFSR

Marc H. Bornstein
National Institute of Child Health and Human Development

PARIS AND THE BEGINNINGS OF FRANCOPHONE DEVELOPMENTAL SCIENCE

The seminal notions that have emerged from French-language publications in the area of human development, and that form what can be termed the "French tradition," are, of course, not solely French. Although they emerged in Paris in the early part of the 20th century, and made Paris one of the most stimulating centers for developmental science, they have always been international. (After World War II, the Genevan School for Piagetian research took on a more important role, and Montreal began attracting a growing number of research teams.) For more than 50 years—between 1882, when Jean Martin Charcot won over the Academy of Sciences, and 1937, when he described hysteria and the XIth International Congress of Psychology was held in honor of Pierre Janet—Paris was home to the brightest constellation of developmental psychologists of that era. During this period, Paris was the meeting place for Sigmund Freud and James Mark Baldwin, who both attended Charcot's lectures at the Salpétrière Hospital. Later, Baldwin, Henri Wallon, and Jean Piaget spent time together when Piaget began to work under the direction of Theodore Simon, Alfred Binet's main collaborator. It was the Sorbonne that housed the *Ecole Pratique des Hautes Etudes,* which gathered in one place all the contemporary research in psychology: Binet's laboratory was directed by Henri Piéron in 1912, and was site of the first chair of child psychology, which was created for Baldwin in 1913 and later passed on to Wallon, when Baldwin retired in 1929. These developmental psychologists maintained constant contact with researchers in other fields and at other institutions. Every 2 weeks, many took part in the scientific session of the French Society of Psychology, which was open to other sciences such as biology, sociology, linguistics, philosophy, and history. From the outset, then, French developmental psychology was part of a broad common network incorporating other disciplines. Nothing comparable could be found in other Francophone cities at that time: In Geneva, genetic psychology was dominant under Edouard Claparède, but it was relatively isolated. In Louvain, development retained the personal interest of Albert Michotte, but was viewed as merely a component of general psychology without any unique importance.

The crucial ingredient in the success that was achieved was not geography, however, but a common goal. At this time, French thought was pervaded by Positivism and was also influenced by the writings of Claude Bernard. Nascent genetic psychology professed a cautious opinion regarding Positivism, but it was encouraged to adhere to experimental laws set down by Claude Bernard. It is this that prompted Baldwin to assert, as early as 1895, that scientists who study development must do more than conduct good observations. He suggested they go beyond the "sophisticated cogitations of the adult" to become "psychologists of the nursery" and focus attention on the "clumsy movements of the infant" (Baldwin, 1902, p. 413). Above all, they needed to build theories: "Give us theories", he proclaimed, "more theories, yet more theories" (Baldwin, 1905, p. 192). His appeal was heeded by Wallon and by Piaget, who were guided to search for general laws and processes of development rather than for mechanisms of specific mental functions. According to Baldwin, both Wallon and Piaget placed themselves in an evolutionary perspective, and viewed the study of child development as psychobiology, with a meaning similar to the one Hall and Oppenheim (1987) defined only recently. The notions they derived from biology were characteristic of this orientation: *accommodation,* used by Baldwin to account for "circular reactions"; *assimilation,* strongly associated with Piaget; and *maturation,* expanded on simultaneously by both Wallon and Gesell. Obviously, this choice of orientation distanced these European developmentalists from Behaviorism and prompted the epithet of "mentalists," which they were not.

Such theoretical positions distracted Wallon and Piaget from psychometry, although they were both involved in the development of psychodiagnostic tools. The young Piaget originally came to Paris in 1919 to participate in an extensive revision of the Binet–Simon Scale of Intelligence. This provided him with an opportunity to observe a large sample of children and to talk with them. These observations served as the source of Piaget's first paper in psychology, which was devoted to the development of the notion of "part of a whole," and published in 1921. Wallon and Piaget both benefitted from the work of Binet. They adhered to his method of questioning children and adopted some of his views on the development of logical thinking. They did not, however, follow Binet's interest in individual differences, and they never accepted psychometrical reductionism.

Rather, Wallon and Piaget appear to have been influenced more by Janet's ideas. Janet's impact on French developmental psychology can be seen in the notion of the *hierarchical architecture of behavior,* in which different levels of nervous control harmonize in the normal adult. Developmentalists hypothesized that this harmony was shaped over time and that ontogenetic studies could not only reveal the successive strata of the architecture and its pathological dissociations, but also could point to their diachronic links or *filiation.* This orientation led Wallon and Piaget to emphasize general organization over local constellations of responses, and to entertain the notion of invariant features across time, rather than transitory instantaneous adjustments. The concept of structure is foreshadowed by this approach, and was to take on different forms in Wallon's and Piaget's formulations. For both Wallon and Piaget, development proceeded by integrative succession of general organizations, qualitatively different from each other, such that development could not be truly represented as cumulative improvement. This was in sharp contrast with the psychometric approach. Within this frame, their views of the diachronic process diverged: It was considered less linear in Wallon's theory than in Piaget's. Wallon (1941) considered the onset of a structure as a shift from a preceding dominant and antagonistic orientation, which he called the principle of *functional alternation.* Piaget considered a structure to be an *equilibrated state* covering the components of the preceding organization.

Piaget remarked at Wallon's death that, as researchers, they could be seen as quite complementary. Piaget focused his work on cognition; Wallon explored both the affective and the cognitive aspects of activity. Notwithstanding their different foci, their views on early development now appear closer than has generally been thought: Both considered that the achievement of a first structure of thinking is attained halfway through the second year of life, when by acting and perceiving the infant elaborates means–ends relations. This allows the infant to move and act within a homogeneous space and to consider objects in the external environment independent of the actor. Their methods disconcerted experimentalists, who favored a psychology of measurement, because both Piaget and Wallon combined open questioning of the child with controlled situations and experimental manipulations, and because they did not use statistics.

First Wallon, then gradually Piaget, and finally (if indirectly) Baldwin influenced French developmental psychology through their lectures and writings far beyond the "golden" prewar era, and even beyond their deaths (Wallon died in 1962, Piaget died in 1980). Wallon's transactionalist ideas *avant-la-lettre* provided firm ground for studies in parent–infant interaction, but because of neglect in this area of study, it was some time before researchers revisited the issue with sufficiently large samples (e.g., Lézine, 1955, 1964). The research policies of successive French governments focusing on the effects of day care at a time when increasing numbers of women began to work inhibited fundamental research on parent–infant interaction. In the meantime, Piaget divided his time between Geneva and Paris. In 1952, he accepted a part-time but permanent position at the University of Paris as an invited professor, a position he held until 1966. His lectures had a direct impact on entire generations of future psychologists, among them some contributors to this book. After the war, he founded the *Centre d'Epistemologie Génétique* in Geneva, which attracted, over the years, scientists from every part of the world including, of course, many French researchers. Up to his last years, Piaget participated in the French scientific forum. Many of his books and all the volumes from the Centre were originally brought to press by Parisian publishers.

During that time, neither Wallon's nor Piaget's dominant influence was seriously challenged by new ideas coming from different philosophical streams. The phenomenology defended by Maurice Merleau-Ponty and the existentialist ideas, which changed the *Weltanshauung* of many people and put Jean-Paul Sartre in the spotlight, had no substantial effect on developmental psychology. The first major influence from other disciplines after World War II came with advances in brain neurophysiology and with new techniques of behavioral investigation in the 1960s.

It was and still is a feature of the French tradition to be attentive and open to external contributions. Eliane Vurpillot, for example, introduced J. J. Gibson's theses on perception and Eleanor Gibson's ideas on differentiation in cognitive development to the French scientific community. René Zazzo kept close ties to Arnold Gesell and the so-called "naturalistic" studies, and later introduced Bowlby, Winnicott, and Harlow to his students in a booklet called *L'Attachement* (1974).

INTERNATIONAL INFLUENCES

Jean Piaget is undoubtedly one of the most important theoreticians in developmental studies even today. Whatever the relative contributions of non-Piagetian psychology, Piaget established the framework for infant development for French-language psychology. All work in infant development was to be interpreted within the Piagetian system of stages and mechanisms of development. That this system was essentially the only reference for discussing these mechanisms was clear at the 1954 European meeting on the notion of developmental stages.

In the early 1950s, however, Piagetian theory was still under-assimilated in the United States and English-speaking Canada. As Ricard et al. (this volume) point out, this is readily explained by a number of factors. It was the last volume of Piaget's trilogy that was the first to be translated into English, namely *Play, Dreams, and Imitation in Childhood* (1945/1951). This work could not be fully understood without the knowledge of *The Origins of Intelligence in Children*

(1936/1952) and *The Construction of Reality in the Child* (1937/1954), which were translated only later. Also, Piaget used a lexicon of scientific concepts from other fields of study in a highly idiosyncratic way, which further distanced outsiders. Comparable misunderstandings, fostered by problems in interpretation, also occurred with the introduction of psychoanalysis into Anglo Saxon schools of thought: The German term *Triebe* was translated simply as *instincts,* a notion that was unacceptable in French schools of psychoanalysis. Beyond the language barrier between French and English, Piaget had used the clinical method (without any statistical measures) at a time when experimental psychology was resorting more and more to statistical formalization. Even today, the term *Piagetian* is as idiomatic as Freudian or Pavlovian.

While Piaget became more and more prominent on the international stage, Baldwin was underevaluated or ignored—Boring (1929/1957) called him a philosopher—and Wallon received scarcely any attention outside French-speaking countries. His compliance with dialectical materialism—despite his being very critical of Marxism as a total philosophical position—implied a belief that people and nature could not be studied as isolated elements; that was in agreement with some American ideas about education. Moreover, Wallon kept to the Darwinian notion of the living milieu—rather than just objects or stimuli—being the primary setting of influence for human development (Bloch, 1993). His socio-constructivistic view of the development of self–other differentiation influenced René Spitz in the latter's search for an interpretation of infant reactions to maternal loss (Spitz & Wolf, 1946).

CONTEMPORARY FRANCOPHONE RESEARCH

A tradition of research in developmental psychology can develop by identifying basic ideas, methods, or schools of thought or by focusing on specific age periods or domains of behavior. A basic feature of Francophone research is that it centers mainly on early childhood, and more specifically on infancy and its sensorimotor organization and cognition (see, e.g., Bloch, 1990). Other areas of research are far from excluded, however. Here we briefly review the contributions of the four different sections in this volume.

Structuralist and Functionalist Views of Mental Functioning

Jean-Jacques Rousseau's work on education, first published in 1762, is widely recognized as having paved the way for a specific French scientific approach to child development by introducing the view that infants are qualitatively different from adults. He, and later Claparède, postulated a set of fundamental principles about the development of behavior. The law of *genetic succession,* the notion of orderly and qualitatively different stages in development, and the law of *functional autonomy*, which emphasizes organization, adequateness, and adaptivenes of behavior at the various stages of child development, became cornerstones of Piagetian theory and of the structuralistic approach to cognitive development.

As de Schonen and Deruelle remark (chap. 3), it has become obvious that the emergence of a new cognitive ability in infants cannot be accounted for simply by the functional onset of action by a group of neurons that have remained silent up to that point. We must discover how learning mechanisms and neural maturation cooperate and are correlated with age-related behavioral changes.

Rochat and Bullinger (chap. 2) have revised our approach to sensorimotor organization by examining dynamic interaction among physiological maturation, posture, and functional action. Bodily posture is both a scaffolding canalization and also a burden, in the case of postural immaturity. Several studies have revealed new sensorimotor patterns when natural biomechanical constraints on the child are lifted, as demonstrated by Grenier's innovative neuropediatric technique (see Amiel-Tison & Grenier, 1980). Also, infants adjust their posture according to regularities in the environmental circumstances they experience and adjust their functional activity according to what position they are in. A clear example, cited by the authors, is the instinctual behavior of sucking, which is shaped by early feeding experiences (Alegria & Noirot, 1982; Bullinger & Rochat, 1984).

De Schonen and Deruelle (chap. 3) introduce a neuropsychological approach to perceptual-cognitive development in examining hemispheric lateralization processes in pattern and face recognition. As they note, it was only quite recently that interest developed in hemispheric differences in how patterns and objects are processed in infancy. Alongside this biologically oriented approach, the need to examine perceptual and attentional processes in a multifaceted way, purely from the perspective of a functional behavior-context analysis, is clearly demonstrated by Malcuit and Pomerleau (chap. 4). In critically examining different explanatory models that have been proposed to explain attention, these authors conclude that the study of attention in infants suffers from *conceptual overextension*, as practically all attentional processes are explained with reference to a single information-processing model inspired by Sokolov (1963). They underscore the importance of analyzing the functions of behaviors and the nature of external stimuli when accounting for these processes.

In chapter 5, on sensorimotor behavior and cognition, Lécuyer and Streri adopt a similar stance with regard to a holistic and functional view of perception, action, and cognition, arguing that the three are tightly and reciprocally related to one another. The authors explore this relation by examining intermodal perception, which illustrates perceptual relations involving a cognitive activity, and categorization, which exemplifies a cognitive activity that is highly influenced by perceptual context. As these authors contend, despite the fact that Francophone developmental psychology for a long time incorporated a certain reticence toward data that did not fit the Piagetian framework, studies from French researchers clearly demonstrate that intelligent activity occurs before the Piagetian starting point of coordination of sensorimotor schemes. An alternative constructivism was founded on an epistemology that assigns less importance than Piagetian theory did to activity and more to what the infant can learn by observation from others (Lécuyer, 1989).

Social-Cognitive Development and Induction of Cognitive Strategies

Another research team that strived to remain sensitive to Piagetian ideas while maintaining an openness of mind toward new theoretical and methodological approaches, was formed in Montreal. Gouin Décarie and her colleagues (chap. 8) have enriched Piagetian concepts by combining them with such topics as the development of affectivity and infant socialization, focusing on the field now known as social cognition. In their chapter on socio-cognitive development, Ricard, Gouin Décarie, Desrochers, and Rome-Flanders investigate relations between social referencing and the Piagetian notion of causality, extending other well-known research in which cognitive aspects of social referencing were analyzed into the context of general referential behaviors of the infant.

Chapters 10 and 11 by Fraysse and Desprels-Fraysse and by Vandenplas-Holper, respectively, are embedded in a very strict Piagetian framework; they reflect the influence of the Genevan school in a very salient way. Since the late 1970s, researchers have tried to test the constructs of equilibration, assimilation, and accommodation, which have only a theoretical status in Piaget's theory. Experimental intervention studies, inducing socio-cognitive conflict in preschool children, relate process-oriented variables to effects in cognitive operational thought. In different studies (e.g., Doise & Mugny, 1981; Gilly, 1989; Inhelder, Sinclair, & Bovet, 1974; Perret-Clermont, 1979), various procedures, used according to the objectives of the *méthode clinique,* tried to activate assimilatory and accommodatory schemes in children by inducing cognitive conflict. Vandenplas-Holper's chapter exemplifies this clinical format of studying cognitive processes, and she addresses this process-oriented approach with other microgenetic approaches. In a similar way, Fraysse and Desprels-Fraysse provide an overview of characteristics of Vygotskian-like research on cognitive-strategy induction and on learning, critically examining the research paradigms used and their role in questioning certain aspects of Piaget's theory.

A prominent socio-cognitive development in infancy is the emergence of self-awareness and awareness of others. Vyt (chap. 9) deals with some heretofore neglected confounding, influential factors in the insular paradigm of self-recognition studies in infancy, a major way that self-awareness and symbolic functioning have been operationalized. In a critical examination, the author discusses what self-recognition studies have to say about self-awareness and underlying learning processes, arguing that visual self-recognition tasks may present a good paradigm to study specific visual sensorimotor information processing, but perhaps do not always indicate self-awareness or symbolic functioning. Self-recognition is a complex process influenced by a number of variables; the experience of contingency in the simultaneity of movement in mirror conditions is but one. Nevertheless, this kind of experience appears to be an important cue in early self-discovery.

Communicative and Linguistic Development

In examining the process of evolving states of self–other differentiation, Nadel (chap. 14) stresses the importance of emotional expressiveness and its role in prelinguistic communication. Affective symbiosis resulting from emotional sharing, durable reciprocal attention, and imitation, and tonic (i.e., motor-postural) adjustments between infant and parent develop the basis for healthy growth.

Although Wallon focused on nonverbal components of communication and their relation to social cognition, Piaget was more involved in a search for basic cognitive structures in children apart from questions about communicative abilities. According to Piaget, language plays a major role in the child's representation of the world and is a manifestation of the semiotic function, the ability to process information on a representational, as opposed to an action, level (Piaget, 1937/1954). Language is, however, considered an expression of underlying cognitive maturational processes rather than a vehicle for, or determinant of, cognitive development.

Studies have demonstrated correspondences between specific cognitive achievements and particular aspects of language. Poulin-Dubois and Graham (chap. 16) review evidence for a relation between early lexical acquisition of object words and categorization abilities. Their research clearly suggests that the development of categorization skills constrains the acquisition of meaning of object words during the second year of life. On the issue of speech development, de Boysson-Bardies and Hallé (chap. 15) claim that vocal production and articulatory performance can be molded from a very young age by structured linguistic inputs furnished by the ambient language. In their chapter, they use systematic comparisons of the course of evolution of pre-speech and first-speech productions of infants from different linguistic backgrounds to gain insights on this point. According to their *interaction hypothesis,* an alternative to traditional models like the structuralist one of Jakobson (1941/1968), early interaction between experience and biological endowment plays a crucial role in the evolution of phonetic organization. In a fascinating array of studies, de Boysson-Bardies and Hallé provide appealing evidence for this view.

Finally, Gombert (chap. 17) shows the usefulness of distinguishing between epilinguistic and metalinguistic behaviors: *Epilinguistic* behavior takes place outside the conscious monitoring of one's linguistic processing; *metalinguistic* behavior occurs on a conscious level. Using Karmiloff-Smith's (1986) model as a reference point, Gombert postulates four successive phases in the metalinguistic development in young children. The author contends that prior to the mastery of reading and writing, which provide impulses to metalinguistic development (see, e.g., Morais, Cary, Alegria, & Bertelson, 1979), other factors may also play a crucial role in triggering the development of metalinguistic awareness. Within a neo-Piagetian functionalist approach, different contextual and organismic issues are posited that modulate the structural framework of an orderly succession of stages in cognitive and metalinguistic development, being held for a long time as characteristic of French developmental research.

Interactional Sources of Development

Socio-emotional development is a relatively recent concern among French researchers outside of the psychoanalytic tradition. Despite the introduction of attachment theory by René Zazzo (1974), and the important work of Daniel Stern (1985) on the infant–caregiver bond, no real Francophone tradition in this area or in the area of clinical developmental psychology has been established. It was only in the early 1980s that French researchers and clinicians working on infant development founded the *Groupe Francophone du Développement Psychologique de l'Enfant Jeune,* with a deliberate focus on parent–infant interaction.

Pêcheux and Labrell, in chapter 20, discuss a series of studies that give new insight into specific ways that mothers' focusing behavior relates to their infants' developing attention and into the specifics of fathers' play with toddlers. According to these authors, Cartesian doubt is at work in the French way of thinking, and French skepticism colors efforts to capture objectively the essence of parent–infant interaction in normative "data." In the same vein, Pierrehumbert and Fivaz-Depeursinge (chap. 21) stress the necessity of looking "beyond the dyad" to address interactional processes. They describe how relationships in the family are constructed within a triadic context and how age-related changes in the family exert an influence on interpersonal organization.

In a chapter concerned with representation and communicative processes in the social construction of early temperament, Blicharski, Gravel, and Trudel (chap. 24) propose to extend the traditional way temperament has been conceptualized. Early temperamental traits were traditionally linked to hypothesized differences in underlying constitutional dispositions and primary physiological processes. They were thought of as affective components of infant personality in terms of maturational variation in emerging CNS processes (Wallon, 1934). Tonicomotor behavioral styles were considered to be the core of differentiation of early temperament (Malrieu, 1952) and were even used to predict later cognitive and social adjustment. Within the general Wallonian principle of experiential canalization, these authors investigate family environment as a potential source of constraint and facilitation of children's early social styles and individual development.

A special child-rearing context, which is thought to have a canalizing influence on child development, especially on social competencies, is the organization of day-care settings. One of the first attempts to deal with the day-care topic and to compare development of day-care and home-care children originated in France with studies by Irène Lézine (1955). Today, it is a topic of French research within a truly international interest (e.g., Balleyguier, 1991). Rather than stressing the influence of day care *per se,* Provost (chap. 22) focuses on qualitative discontinuities between day care and home, and between day care and kindergarten, as potential influences on social adjustment in preschoolers. The assumption can be made that such discontinuity may disrupt the development of young children, and that in this discontinuity perceptions of kindergarten teachers regarding day-care–reared children can exert a crucial influence (Baillargeon & Betsalel-Presser, 1988), possibly in the sense of self-fulfilling prophecies. Perceptions of parents, of course, are always crucial. Conceptions about parenting and cultural differences in child-rearing attitudes may instigate certain parenting styles, and thus indirectly influence the development of child competencies. These are dealt with by Sabatier in chapter 23, on parenting knowledge and parenting styles. More specifically, she analyzes important differences in educational attitudes and styles among various ethnic groups and in diverse Francophone cultures.

CONCLUSION

As one sees in many scientific fields, increasing worldwide collaboration and communication have tended to foster unification and standardization of methods and concepts in developmental science. Contemporary developmental psychologists in French-speaking countries do not see themselves as radically different from their colleagues in other parts of the world. They, like others, are fascinated by infant and child capabilities and interested in the growing body of data on development. Because French psychologists have been schooled within a particular historical and theoretical framework, however, they have remained attentive to the need to provide a unique background to their work. The contributions in this volume, therefore, bring some of this background to the fore.

Commentaries to each section of this volume, written by eminent scientists working in other (non-Francophone) parts of the world, highlight the basic features and striking peculiarities of Francophone research, but also point out its commonalities with other international work. The commentaries by George Butterworth, Elizabeth Spelke, Peter Bryant, Marc Bornstein, Hanus and Mechthild

Papoušek, Paul van Geert, Bettye Caldwell, and Hellgard Rauh provide a broad range of perspectives on this vast territory of research. Research in developmental psychology in a specific country or culture can be characterized by its historical roots, ideological influences, social policy, and prototypical themes of study, but also by more peripheral aspects: by the choice of illustrations for its book covers, by the style of presentation, or even by the culturally determined molds of what are seen as important tools in development, such as day care, school arrangements, and even toys. One can infer from them some basic cultural views on parenting and education, just as one can experience vividly the maternal nurturing aspect in Morisot's tableau of *Le berceau*.

References

Alegria, J., & Noirot, E. (1982). On early development of oriented mouthing in neonates. In J. Mehler, M. Garrett, & E. Walker (Eds.), *Perspectives on mental representation* (pp. 389–398). Hillsdale, NJ: Lawrence Erlbaum Associates.

Amiel-Tison, C., & Grenier, A. (1980). *Evaluation neurologique du nouveau-né et du nourrisson* [Neurological examination of the neonate and the baby]. Paris: Masson.

Baillargeon, M., & Betsalel-Presser, R. (1988). Effets de la garderie sur le comportement social et l'adaptation de l'enfant: Perceptions des enseignantes de la maternelle [Effects of day-care on social behavior and adaptation of the infant: Perceptions of day-care and kindergarten teachers]. *Revue Canadienne de l'Etude de la Petite Enfance, 2,* 91–98.

Baldwin, J. M. (1902). *Le développement mental chez l'enfant et dans la race* (2nd. ed.). [Mental development in the infant and in the human race]. Paris: Griard et Brière.

Baldwin, J. M. (1905). *Développement et évolution* [Development and evolution]. Paris.

Balleyguier, G. (1991). French research on day care. In E. C. Melhuish & P. Moss (Eds.), *Day care for young children: International perspectives* (pp. 27–45). London: Routledge.

Bloch, H. (1990). Status and function of early sensorimotor coordination. In H. Bloch & B. I. Bertenthal (Eds.), *Sensorimotor organization and development in infancy and early childhood* (pp. 163–178). Dordrecht, Netherlands: Kluwer Academic Publishers.

Bloch, H. (1993). Sociabilité & développement cognitif: Leur relation écologique chez Wallon [Sociability and cognitive developments: Their ecological linkage in Wallon's thinking]. *Enfance, 47,* 59–63.

Boring, E. G. (1957). *A history of experimental psychology.* New York: Appleton-Century-Crofts. (Original work published 1929)

Bullinger, A., & Rochat, P. (1984). Head orientation and sucking response by newborn infants. *Infant Behavior and Development,* 7(Special ICIS Issue), 55.

Doise, W., & Mugny, G. (1981). *Le développement social de l'intelligence* [The social development of intelligence]. Paris: Interéditions.

Gilly, M. (1989). The psychological mechanisms of cognitive constructions: Experimental research and teaching perspectives. *International Journal of Educational Research, 13,* 605–621.

Hall, W. G., & Oppenheim, R. W. (1987). Developmental psychobiology: Prenatal, perinatal, and early postnatal aspects of behavioral development. *Annual Review of Psychology, 38,* 91–128.

Inhelder, B., Sinclair, H., & Bovet, M. (1974). *Apprentissage et structures de la connaissance* [Learning and structure of knowledge]. Paris: P.U.F.

Jakobson, R. (1968). *Child language, aphasia and phonological universals* (transl. A. Keiler). The Hague: Mouton. (Original work published 1941)

Karmiloff-Smith, A. (1986). From meta-processes to conscious access: Evidence from metalinguistic and repair data. *Cognition, 23*, 95–147.

Lécuyer, R. (1989). *Bébés astronomes, bébés psychologues: L'intelligence de la première année* [Infants as astronomers, infants as psychologists: Intelligence in the first year of life]. Brussels: Mardaga.

Lézine, I. (1955). L'enfant dans le milieu de la crèche [The infant in the day-care setting]. *Revue Internationale de psycho-pedagogie belge, 3*, 240–250.

Lézine, I. (1964). *Psycho-pédagogie du premier âge* [Infant psychopedagogy]. Paris: Presses Universitaires de France.

Malrieu, P. (1952). *Les émotions et la personnalité de l'enfant* [Child emotions and personality]. Paris: Vrin.

Morais, J., Cary, L., Alegria, J., & Bertelson, P. (1979). Does awareness of speech as a sequence of phonemes arise spontaneously? *Cognition, 7*, 323–331.

Perret-Clermont, A. N. (1979). *La construction de l'intelligence dans l'interaction sociale* [The construction of intelligence in social interaction]. Berne: Lang.

Piaget, J. (1951). *Play, dreams, and imitation in childhood* (C. Gattagno & F. M. Hodgson, trans.). New York: Norton. (Original work published 1945)

Piaget, J. (1952). *The origins of intelligence in children* (M. Cook, Trans.). New York: International Universities Press. (Original work published 1936)

Piaget, J. (1954). *The construction of reality in the child* (M. Cook, Trans.). New York: Basic Books. (Original work published 1937)

Rousseau, J. J. (1964). *Emile ou de l'éducation*. Paris: Richard. (Original work published 1762)

Sokolov, E. N. (1963). *Perception and the conditioned reflex*. New York: Macmillan.

Spitz, R. A., & Wolf, K. M. (1946). Anaclitic depression. *Psychoanalytic Study of the Child, 2*, 313–342.

Stern, D. N. (1985). *The interpersonal world of the infant*. New York: Basic Books.

Wallon, H. (1934). *Les origines du caractère chez l'enfant* [The origins of character in children]. Paris: Boivin.

Wallon, H. (1941). *L'Evolution psychologique chez l'enfant* [The psychological development in the infant]. Paris: Armand Colin.

Zazzo, R. (1974). *L'Attachement* [Attachment]. Neuchatel: Delachaux et Niestlé.

SENSORIMOTOR DEVELOPMENT AND PERCEPTION

2 Posture and Functional Action in Infancy

Philippe Rochat
Emory University

André Bullinger
Université de Genève

Jean-Jacques Rousseau's work on education, first published in 1762, is widely recognized as having been a revolutionary influence that paved the way to the scientific approach to child behavior and development. Kessen (1965) suggested that Rousseau's *Emile, ou de l'Éducation* (1911) is at the origin of child study as a specific discipline of knowledge. Aside from influencing the establishment of a new discipline, Rousseau's essays on education contain a set of fundamental principles that inspired, and eventually shaped, Francophone perspectives on child development. Claparède (1912) recognized in the Emile of Rousseau critical issues and fundamental principles that dictated his views of child development. The principles included the law of *genetic succession,* which posits orderly stages in development, and the law of *functional autonomy,* which emphasizes the appropriateness of the child's behavior at the various stages of development. The law of functional autonomy refers to the achievements and organizations that are specific to each period of development and is in sharp contrast to the view that children are merely miniature or unfinished adults. Principles of genetic succession and functional autonomy became the cornerstones of Piaget's theory.

The concept of stage and the law of functional autonomy can be viewed as trademarks of past and present Francophone approaches to child development. These principles are commonly taken for granted in the Francophone perspectives, and viewed as necessities of development. By contrast, Anglophone perspectives and theories often question these principles, in particular the empirical grounds and heuristic power of theories that conceive development as a discontinuous progression through an orderly succession of stages and organizations (Brainerd, 1978). In the tradition of Binet, Piaget, and Wallon, Francophone perspectives assume that child behavior and development are marked by both quantitative and qualitative changes. Qualitative changes express "revolutions" or radical transformations characterizing the transition from one stage of development to another (Mounoud, 1976, 1984). Development is characterized by different types of organization at particular moments of developmental time, these organizations expressing qualitatively different "psychologies" that are linked by the law of genetic succession or *developmental filiation*. Piaget's theory of cognitive development is prototypical of such view, specifying the organization of various stages of development and providing a qualitative demarcation of successive levels and periods in development. Within this perspective, the primary task of developmental psychologists is to account for the nature and specificity of child behavior at each particular stage of development, trying to unveil the principles of the transitions among them.

This chapter is an attempt to integrate the major developmental problem of posture and functional action in infancy. Empirical observations suggest that posture and functional action interact in a way unique to infants. It is proposed that an important aspect of the functional autonomy attached to the infancy period is the rapid development of posture and its impact on action development.

POSTURAL CONSTRAINTS AND ACTION IN INFANCY

The lack of postural control is a major constraint of early development. It determines infant behavior and places a formidable burden on the execution of basic acts young infants are prepared to perform immediately after birth. Orienting, sucking, grasping, and the rudiments of reaching and communication, require effort and external body support that are hard to imagine and are easily taken for granted by the healthy adult caretaker or by the student of infancy. When orienting toward a stimulus by turning his or her head toward its source, an infant is faced with the risk of rolling over. At around 4 months of age, when infants begin to reach for visible objects, they are at risk of falling forward. At this age, they still lack the basic ability to maintain a sitting position without external body support. The lack of muscular control that will eventually enable the individual to overcome, counteract, and use the force of gravity, creates a primordial constraint on infant behavior. During infancy, a major developmental achievement is the maintenance of overall body balance and dynamic posture as the scaffolding of functional action. This development culminates with the conquest of verticality and the ability to locomote, which expand the zones of functional action and give infants access to new environmental resources.

In general, any movement pattern is a complex whole that integrates posture and action. The postural aspect of movement refers to the integrity of the whole body while a specific action is carried out. Observation tells us that movement and posture are not controlled separately, but are tightly integrated into what Reed (1990) called *dynamic posture*. Accumulated evidence shows the importance of studying posture and action in relation to one another rather than separately, as is commonly done (Rochat & Senders, 1991). Considering that human infants have a relatively extended period of postural immaturity, and that postural development parallels progress in the skilled control of action, the question of how posture and action interact in development is of profound importance. A central question of early development is how progress in the control of posture relates to the development of functional action in infancy. *Functional action* is defined here as goal-oriented behavior (e.g., sucking to ingest food; transporting an object to the mouth for feeding or for oral/haptic exploration; reaching for an object to grasp it; and moving eyes, head, and trunk to track a visual target).

Infancy research has revealed that from birth, infants are capable of performing actions of remarkable complexity and organization (see E. J. Gibson & Spelke, 1983; Thelen & Fogel, 1986). Such early behaviors include head orientation to sound (Muir & Field, 1979), visual tracking of moving targets (Bullinger, 1977), and hand extension toward a visible moving object (von Hofsten, 1982). The revelation of precocious competence, however, depends on external body support provided by the experimenter to the young infant, compensating for lack of postural control and, particularly, for lack of head and neck control (Bower, 1989). These procedures suggest that proper postural support is essential for a clear manifestion of early behavior, yet we lack empirical facts regarding the relation between postural development and early behavior.

Virtually from birth, infants learn to overcome and also to use gravitational force to perform movements that are part of functional action patterns. With growing control over posture, they free themselves from external body supports, opening up new possibilities of action and exploration. Experiments with animal and human infants suggest a release of coordinated action under supportive posture conditions. Thelen and Fisher (1983) showed that synergistic movements of the legs, seen in newborn stepping, are restored in 1- and 3-month-old infants by submerging their legs in water, a condition that supports the infant and compensates for a low muscle-to-fat ratio. Gustafson (1984) studied pre-locomoting infants placed in a baby walker, and showed that the postural support and mobility provided by the walker is associated with spontaneous reorganization of exploratory activities into more mature patterns.

These observations provide evidence that posture and its control play an important role in the development of skilled action. Progressive control over posture is a potential releaser of action. Conversely, lack of postural control limits the capabilities for action. Pediatricians, proposing a new neurobehavioral assessment of the newborn and the young infant, reported remarkable clinical observations on the relation between posture and action in early development (Amiel-Tison, 1985; Grenier, 1980, 1981). These observations demonstrate the importance of posture and its control in the emergence of sensorimotor skills early in development, in particular the effect of posture on motor behavior and the level of attention in neonates.

By holding the neonate's head firmly in the trunk's axis, Grenier and Amiel-Tison were able to elicit the visuomotor coordination of reaching toward an object lying on a table. According to the authors, the apparent sensorimotor clumsiness and the obligatory responses of the neonate are linked to poor neck control. When experimentally provided with adequate postural support to remedy their "neck impotence," neonates revealed striking sensorimotor aptitudes. These observations demonstrate the inseparability of posture and action from birth, such that postural immaturity emerges as a major constraint in the expression and development of precocious functional actions (i.e., pre-reaching). Further demonstration that postural development is a major determinant of functional action in infancy is based on three bodies of observations—sucking, looking, and reaching—is presented next.

POSTURE AND SUCKING IN NEONATES

Recent investigations reveal that the variety of sensorimotor responses displayed by the neonate moments after birth are integrated and organized, rather than independent and juxtaposed. Studies show that coordinated activities of hands and mouth can be observed in infants only a few hours old. Butterworth and Hopkins (1988) observed episodes in which neonates opened their mouths in anticipation of the contact of hand brought straight toward the oral zone. Rochat, Blass, and Hoffmeyer (1988) observed that hand–mouth coordination at birth was under the control of certain stimulus conditions: Following the administration of a drop of sucrose, neonates doubled the duration and frequency of manual contacts with their mouth. Newborns' heart-rate responses appeared to be correlated with the visual appearance and disappearance of an object moving in front of them (Bullinger, 1977). Further evidence of an intermodal unity organizing different sensorimotor systems at birth are provided by research on head orientation to sounds (Clifton, Morrongiello, Kulig, & Dowd, 1981) and pre-reaching behavior in very young infants (Bower, Broughton, & Moore, 1972; Trevarthen, 1984; von Hofsten, 1982).

In general, these observations suggest that the control of early behavior is relative to a broad intermodal organization orchestrating the early sensorimotor repertoire. They support a molar view of infant action that must be approached as constrained by complex motor synergies and multiple connections among sensorimotor modalities (Bullinger, 1983; Thelen & Fogel, 1986).

From birth, infants display various body postures (Peiper, 1962). These postures reflect different internal and emotional states, as well as an adaptation to physical properties of the environment (Prechtl & Beintema, 1964; Wallon, 1942/1970). Within hours after birth, infants adjust their posture according to the regularities of the environmental circumstances they experience. Alegria and Noirot (1982) have shown that within the first three feeding sessions following birth, neonates orient their mouthing in the direction of a human voice. Furthermore, these authors report that breast-fed newborns orient their mouthing toward the right or left, depending on the source of a voice, whereas the bottle-fed infants orient their mouthing essentially in accordance with the usual location of the caretaker holding them during feeding.

To further assess the precocious integration between posture and oral response in the neonate, we conducted a study in which non-nutritive sucking rate was assessed in relation to two independent measures: head orientation and previous feeding experience (breast or bottle; Bullinger & Rochat, 1984). Two empirical questions guided this study. The first was whether newborn sucking response varied according to head orientation. The second was whether the potential head orientation effect depended on the type of previous feeding experience that imposed either unique head orientation to the infant (bottle-feeding) or alternating head orientation (breast-feeding). A group of 24 full-term healthy newborns with a postnatal age range from 44 to 94 hours were tested. Half were breast-fed and half were bottle-fed 2 to 3 hours before testing. A standard-bottle rubber nipple connected to an air pressure transducer allowed polygraphic recording of the negative pressure variations applied to the nipple. Neonates were securely seated in a 45° reclined infant seat facing a white circular background. The experimenter stood behind the seated infant and introduced the nipple into the infant's mouth for five successive trials of 1 min each. The trials consisted of one baseline trial, followed by three experimental trials, then followed by one more baseline trial. At the beginning of each trial, the experimenter changed and stabilized the infant's head in one particular orientation relative to its torso, following an assigned experimental order. The first and last trials served as baselines to assess the stability of response across testing. Head orientation was the same for the two baselines, and was systematically changed (right, left, center) during test trials.

Initial results showed an overall effect of head orientation on the rate of sucking. In general, the newborns tended to show a decrease in the rate of sucking response when their heads were oriented to the left. When we analyzed the data for the breast-fed and bottle-fed infants separately, however, the results indicated a decrease in sucking in the left head orientation only for the bottle-fed infants. Further analyses revealed that of the 12 bottle-fed infants, 8 sucked maximally with their heads oriented at center, and 4 sucked most with their heads oriented to the right, whereas none favored the left orientation. By contrast, 3 breast-fed infants showed maximum rate of sucking with their heads oriented to the right, 3 did so with a left orientation, and 6 sucked most rate with their heads centered. This observation suggests a bias toward the center and right head orientation for the group of bottle-fed infants only. A right and center head orientation corresponds to what bottle-fed infants experienced during the few feeding sessions they had had, assuming that the caretaker held the bottle with the right hand (as most would be expected to do).

In summary, these results indicate that, from birth, there is an interaction between posture and sucking as part of an overall body engagement. Analogous to the observations reported by Alegria and Noirot (1982), sucking engagement moments after birth is shaped by first feeding experiences, with each newborn picking up the postural invariants attached to the particular circumstances of his or her feeding.

From a theoretical point of view, an important feature of infant behavior at the onset of development is an overall or synergistic bodily engagement (Bullinger, 1981). This account of global (undifferentiated) behavioral engagement in the neonate is common in classic Francophone views on development. Newborns are described as experiencing their body as a totality (de Ajuriaguerra, 1969). Wallon (1985) suggested that early synergistic mobilization is at the origin of the progressive emergence of skilled action, and Piaget (1936/1952) described newborn behavior as "a total reaction of the individual" (p. 27). In support of this view, the observations just reported demonstrate the relation between posture and sucking. Further support can be found in the recent findings of Buka and Lipsitt (1991), who showed that the rate and strength of non-nutritive sucking coincides with the synchronous variations in grasping, breathing, and cardiac activities. Bullinger (1991) proposed that this synergistic engagement provides redundancies and functional regularities among the various sensorimotor systems. He suggested that at the beginning of development, the gleaning of these functional invariants orients infant behavior and feeds action schemes. Bullinger (1983) argued that as development progresses, infants' behavior shows a decrease in synergies; these are replaced by ways of functioning that are differentiated and spatially oriented.

POSTURE AND VISUAL EXPLORATION
IN YOUNG INFANTS

The interdependence of posture and vision is evident immediately after birth, when neonates start to move their eyes and show their first visual responses to the world. Immediately after birth, when ambient light hits the neonate's retina, ocular motricity is highly perturbed. In the dark, or in a dimly illuminated environment, neonates reveal organized oculomotricity and saccades covering large portions of the visual field, corresponding to ambient exploration (Haith, 1980). Ambient exploration becomes focal when newborns encounter contrast to look at, focusing on the edges of two-dimensional configurations presented to them. Newborns' visual activity shows orientation and appears readily coordinated with audition. Haith has demonstrated that in the dark, newborns tend to orient their ocular saccades in the direction of an invisible sound source. A few days after birth, the perturbation manifested in the light diminishes, and they start to systematically track objects, and show ambient and focal exploration of configurations' edges, somehow attracted by the zones of sharp contrast in the stimuli. This attraction and basic orientation of early visual exploration has been interpreted as the expression of mechanisms that yield maximum cortical stimulation (Bullinger, 1991; Haith, 1980). Once the eyes of the newborn are focused on one defined zone, focal exploration occurs in small-amplitude saccades that cross back and forth over the edge of the configuration, optimizing cortical stimulation. These observations indicate that from birth, visual response is not random, but rather organized, oriented, and attuned to particular aspects of the optical environment. Again, a basic constraint on the expression of this precocious visual functioning is the control of posture. The developmental account of young infants' postural engagement while tracking a visual target moving in front of them demonstrates this point (Bullinger, 1977, 1981, 1989).

The overall body postures adopted by young infants when visually tracking and exploring a visual event or configuration can be either symmetrical or asymmetrical. Casaer (1979) described the Asymmetric Tonic Neck Posture (ATNP) as a privileged postural state in which the young infant appears focused and oriented as regards the physical and human environment. Bullinger (1991) observed that in this posture, the young infant's gaze is more stable, and the extended hand, facing the infant sideways, offers a privileged target for visual exploration. Bullinger also noted that when the newborn is seated in a symmetrical posture, head aligned at center, head control is reduced, and the infant appears to huddle up, showing increased oral activity, such as spitting and tongue protrusion. Breathing appears to accelerate and is sometimes blocked for prolonged periods, providing a temporary "pneumatic" tonic state that compensates for the lack of postural support and control.

Asymmetrical postures, by contrast, anchor the young infant, providing stability and bearing points from which progress in the integration of posture and visual action can take place. When infants are solicited to change posture as they track a visual target, an interesting development is observed. Immediately after birth, it is the postural state in which infants find themselves that determines the spatial limits of their tracking. When the object exits the portion of the visual field the infant can attend to, he or she tends to wedge back to the stable and asymmetrical posture he or she was in at the beginning of the tracking motion. Once stabilized in this original posture, the infant appears to engage in intense visual scanning, although no objects are present in the visual field. Posture is not yet totally enslaved to visual events, which explains why caretakers often place themselves in particular locations of the infant's visual field to facilitate stimulation and social interaction.

As development unfolds, vision plays an increased role in determining postural adjustments, and in "shaping" the infant's overall body posture (Wallon, 1970). By the 2nd month, the whole body posture is associated with visual tracking activities. The various postures adopted by the infant are now strictly dependent on the spatial location of the visual target. When the target-object is in the left hemifield and the infant is sitting in a well-supporting seat, the infant's trunk tends to lean to the right with his or her head turned to the left. Movement of the target-object toward the right hemifield causes the infant to move into the reverse posture (leaning to the left with the head turned to the right). At this age, visual tracking is accompanied by a phasic opposition in the lateral movements of the trunk and the moving target-object. At the extreme locations in the right- or left-hemifield of the target-object, the infant manifests asymmetrical posture in the form of ATNP (Bullinger, 1989).

By 3 months, visual tracking by the infant appears to mobilize essentially head movements only, the stabilized trunk becoming the bearing point of the overall visual pursuit. The upper limbs do not participate anymore in the visual tracking, and this progress sets the hands free to capture and manipulate objects.

An important aspect of these developmental observations is the fact that at early stages, infants manifest difficulties in attending visually and stabilizing posturally the median portion of the visual field. When tracking an object, the young infant shows instability of posture and destabilization of gazing while moving through the median plane. This instability and destabilization is present until the infant masters the dissociation of head and trunk movements (A. Roucoux, Culée, & M. Roucoux, 1983). Bullinger (1991) has proposed that this dissociation is an important prerequisite for the development of eye–hand coordination, described extensively in the infancy literature.

The interaction between posture and vision in early development is evident in observations demonstrating that changes in the head posture of the young infant has a significant impact on the mapping of his or her visual space. Bullinger and Jouen (1983) showed that babies aged 10 and 20 weeks demonstrate a differential sensibility for peripheral detection when they are placed with the head at midline, or with it turned 45° to the right or 45° to the left relative to the shoulder line. According to the procedure that was used, in each posture the infants fixated one point at the center of their visual field for each particular posture in which they were placed. Once the baby was staring at the central fixation point, a mobile was moved from either the right or the left periphery of the visual field starting at about 135°, and moving toward the center. The dependent measure used to assess peripheral detection was the moment the infants stopped fixating at the center point and made the first saccade in the direction of the mobile. In general, the results showed that the field of peripheral detection expands with age. Furthermore, the younger group of infants showed that, although their overall field of peripheral detection was reduced compared to the older infants (approximately 50°, compared to approximately 60°), the left and right hemifields were homogeneous in all three postural conditions. By contrast, when the older infants were placed in either the left or center head posture, their field of peripheral detection was biased to favor the right hemifield (i.e., higher detection when the target-object was coming from the right). In the right head posture, like in the younger infants, they showed homogeneity between the left and right hemifields. This differential effect of posture on peripheral detection in 10- and 20-week-old infants was interpreted by Bullinger and Jouen as the expression of emerging laterality, as the visual field of the infant was becoming progressively calibrated in reference to the dominant hand to determine the perceived limits of the visual periphery. Accordingly, this would account for the right-hemifield bias that older infants manifest in their peripheral detection.

If posture interacts with focal vision and in particular with the ability of the infant to track objects in the environment, there is also good evidence that sensitivity to peripheral visual flux controls for postural adjustment in the young infant and even the newborn (Butterworth & Hicks, 1977; Jouen, 1984). From an early age, presentation of a flux at the periphery of the visual field causes tonic responses and postural adjustment of the infant's head and trunk. Peripheral vision contributes from the onset of development to the control of posture. It plays a crucial role in orienting the infant and in allowing it to adaptively tense the overall body in response to various events, such as the self-motion of perceived self-acceleration and -deceleration. From the onset of development, peripheral vision plays an important role in the regulation of posture and contributes to the emergence and control of basic skills, such as visually guided reaching, control of head movements in tracking, control of sitting and standing posture, and eventually of locomotion (Bullinger, 1991).

In summary, from the earliest age, posture plays a role in the determination of visual behavior, and vision appears to be linked to the control of posture. Recent observations on reaching in infancy and on the relation of this basic action to postural development, further illustrate the functional link between posture and action early in development.

POSTURE AND REACHING IN INFANCY

As mentioned, from birth infants demonstrate propensities to bring the hand in contact with objects in the environment (Trevarthen, 1974; von Hofsten, 1982). By 4 months, infants start to reach systematically and successfully to objects presented in their space of prehension (White, Castle, & Held, 1964). They continue to develop their ability to reach during the first year, demonstrating increased anticipation (von Hofsten & Ronnqvist, 1988), and the ability to use cues other than visual to guide their hands successfully toward an object in the dark (Clifton, Rochat, Litovsky, & Perris, 1991). Parallel to this well-documented development, the end of the first trimester is marked by a major achievement of sensorimotor development, the first conquest of verticality expressed by the emergence of the *self-sitting posture* (at about 6 months, according to the Bayley motor scale).

The emergence of self-sitting, together with the ability to generate lateral and rotation movements of the trunk without losing balance, marks the beginning of what André-Thomas and de Ajuriaguerra (1948) called the construction of a *bodily axis,* which allows upper limbs and hands to explore and manipulate objects, freed from having to maintain posture and balance. Around the time infants develop a self-sitting ability, they also appear to develop fine haptic exploration of objects and differential functioning of the hands (i.e., fingering, Rochat, 1989). The numerous mainstream studies on early eye–hand coordination have overlooked this important aspect of development and, in particular, three important components of infant reaching: (a) postural development, (b) coordination between the hands, and (c) coordination of the upper limbs and trunk (Rochat & Senders, 1991).

In a recent series of studies, we investigated further the impact of emerging self-sitting ability on the development, at about 6 months, of infant reaching and object manipulation (Rochat, 1992; Rochat & Goubet, 1993). This research effort was aimed at broadening the study of early eye–hand coordination in the context of dynamic posture. In particular, infant reaching and its development were approached as an overall body engagement, including the relative coordination of arm, hand, and torso movements during the reach act.

The particular aim of a first study was to document the relative coordination between hands in infant reaching as a function of postural condition, and self-sitting ability (Rochat, 1992). In this study, two groups of 5- to 8-month-old infants, either able to sit (sitters) or yet unable to sit on their own (non-sitters) were videotaped while reaching for objects in four different posture conditions that provided the infants with varying amounts of body support: seated, reclining, prone, and supine. The approach phase of the hands before their first contact with the object was microanalyzed. In particular, the relative alignment of the hands in relation to the object, as well as changes in distance between the hands as they approached the object were computed in a series of frame-by-frame analyses. These analyses revealed a clear difference in the type of manual engagement of non-sitter and sitter infants as they reach for the object. In general, non-sitter infants tended to reach with both hands forward, demonstrating synergistic movements of the hands toward midline, in what was tentatively typified as a "crabbing" motion of the upper limbs. This clearly synergistic and symmetrical bimanual reach was expressed predominantly in the well-supported postural conditions (reclining, supine, and prone), but not when non-sitters were placed in the upright seated-posture condition. In this latter condition, infants were constrained to reach with one hand forward to prevent falling forward. In the seated condition, non-sitter infants typically reached with one hand and tended to throw the other one backward to maintain balance and counteract the forward weight shift.

These results indicate that non-sitter infants are highly dependent on the postural conditions that determine their overall body engagement in reaching. In particular, although young infants appear to be inclined to reach for objects first with both hands forward, in less stable conditions they are forced to change their pattern of action to avoid the risk of falling to the ground. This result illustrates a potentially important feature of the impact of postural immaturity and postural development as a factor in behavioral changes in infancy. Regarding the group of sitter infants, 80% of their reaches were one-handed in all postural conditions. These results indicate that posture is an important factor in determining the morphology of reaching in the non-sitters but not in the sitter infants, who manifested increased posture independence.

It appears that with growing control over self-sitting ability, infants become one-handed reachers, regardless of posture. From a developmental perspective, these results also suggest that postural development might play an important role in breaking the original symmetrical and synergistic use of the hands in reaching, contributing to the emergence of a more differentiated functioning of the hands (Rochat, 1989; Rochat & Senders, 1991). It is interesting to note that a transition from a bimanual to a unimanual organization is not specific to the reach act. A developmental analysis shows an analogous progression in the movement of an object to the mouth by 2- to 5-month-old infants (Rochat, 1993; Rochat & Senders, 1991). This transition may be a general feature of early action development.

In another study, a group of sitter and non-sitter infants were compared for their overall body engagement in reaching. In particular, the coordination among the hand(s), arm(s), and trunk in reaching was assessed and compared between sitters and non-sitters (Rochat & Goubet, 1993; Rochat & Senders, 1990). Infants were placed in an upright infant seat resting on a platform supported by a central axle, allowing movement in the forward and backward direction relative to the infant (as in a seesaw). The movement was constrained by two spring scales, one placed under each end of the platform. After appropriate calibration, this simple device allowed each shift of the infant's center of gravity to be translated into weight gain observable on the forward scale supporting the platform. In this study, frame-by-frame scoring was aimed at the *co-analysis* of center-of-gravity shifts and movements of the upper limbs during the approach phase of infants' reaching (i.e., changes in weight shift, nose-to-object distance, and hand(s)-to-object distance during the 2 sec preceding contact with the object, at a rate of 5 images/sec). In general, results illustrate striking differences in the reaching of non-sitter and sitter infants. The majority of non-sitters (10 of 12), showed an independence between the reaching of the hand and the leaning of the trunk. By contrast, half of the sitter infants (6 of 12) showed remarkable coordination between the trunk and hand(s) in reaching. Analyses of individual reaches showed that, typically, the reaching hands of non-sitter infants move independently of any trunk movement. Their reaches appear to engage the hands and upper limbs, but not the trunk (i.e., there was no shifting of weight, and no reduction of nose-to-object distance). By contrast, the approach phase of half the sitter infants demonstrates a remarkable coordination of reaching and leaning. These sitter infants manifest an unmistakable coordinating (synergistic) action of upperlimbs and trunk. Further statistical analyses comparing values of the different measures, 2 sec prior to contact with the object and at the moment of contact, confirm these results (Rochat & Goubet, 1993).

In a follow-up study (Rochat & Goubet, 1993), a group of non-sitter infants were tested using the same procedure and allowing the co-analyses of upper-limb(s) and trunk movements in reaching. Non-sitter infants were provided with varying amount of hip support while sitting. Inflatable cushions were placed on each of the infants' sides, at hip level. These cushions were connected to a hand pump and a manometer allowing systematic control of the pressure applied on the infants' hips. Infants were filmed while reaching with no pressure applied on their hips, with medium pressure (20 mmHg) and with high pressure (40 mmHg). The rationale behind this design and procedure was to simulate in non-sitter infants the kind of support they will self-generate when they are able to sit on their own. In particular, the question was whether providing hip support would make non-sitter infants reach like sitter infants in coordinating movements of the upperlimbs and trunk. Results confirmed that non-sitter infants do indeed tend to resemble sitter infants in engaging their trunk while reaching as a function of increased hip support. This study demonstrates that the coordination between reaching and leaning is controlled by postural support provided to the non-sitter infant. External body support is potentially a releaser of complex and organized action in the young infant. These results are congruent with the clinical observations reported by Amiel-Tison and Grenier (1986), demonstrating pre-reaching activity and enhanced attention in seated newborns provided with neck support.

The same study also illustrates the freeing of the upper limbs and hands associated with the emergence of self-sitting ability at around 6 months of age. It demonstrates the potential changes in the interaction between the infant and the environment as a function of landmark progress in postural development. Specifically, emerging sitting ability is shown to be accompanied by drastic changes in infants' hand use as they reach, grasp, and explore objects. In this study, 5- to 7-month-old infants were presented with a display of 15 attractive balls attached to a curved board that paved the infant's prehensile space. The center of the board was aligned with the infant's shoulders, the infant sitting in a well-supporting upright infant seat. The experimenter presented the board to a distance of 30 cm in front of the infant for free play with the detachable balls. Three groups of infants were tested. A group of 10 non-sitters, a group of 10 sitters, and a group of 10 "near-sitters" who could sit on their own for up to 30 sec but only while leaning forward with their hands on the floor or leaning against their legs. Analyses of the free interaction of the infants with the display and successive reaches to the balls showed a clearly different pattern of hand use among the groups of infants. Infants demonstrated an expansion of their prehensile space and increased balance in the use of hands as a function of increasing sitting ability. In particular, analysis of the first ball touched by the infant indicates that non-sitter infants tended preferentially to contact balls that were at the center of the board, whereas near-sitters and sitters expanded their first contact with balls that were increasingly at the periphery of the board. Analysis of hand-use in

contacting the balls on the display indicated that non-sitter infants used predominantly one hand (i.e., the majority the right hand), crossing midline if necessary
to contact a contralateral ball.

Because of their lack of postural control, non-sitters tended to lean against the
side of the seat, constraining one of the hands. In general, they showed more
crossing of midline with the contralateral hand. By contrast, near-sitter and sitter
infants appeared straighter in their seats. This verticality is accompanied by an
equally distributed use of right and left hand to contact ipsilateral balls on the
board. Bruner (1973) described the "invisible midline barrier" demonstrated by
7-month-old infants, who tend not to cross the midline of prehensile space with
the contralateral hand. He viewed this phenomenon as a sign of a differential
functioning of the hands, each becoming specialized in attending the ipsilateral
hemifield of prehensile space. Our observations suggest that postural development has a role to play in the emergence of this phenomenon, illustrating some of
the consequences of the constitution of the bodily axis and its impact on the
infant's manual action (André-Thomas & de Ajuriaguerra, 1948).

POSTURE, FUNCTIONAL ACTION, AND THE INFANT'S
ECOLOGICAL SELF

Overall, the observations reported here demonstrate that posture is an important
control variable in early development and in the expression of functional action
in infancy. They demonstrate the functional link between posture and action at
the origin of development. Newborns are shown to suck preferentially in postures that correspond to their first few feeding experiences. Peripheral detection
and visual tracking by young infants depend on their posture and the relative
degree of postural control they have achieved. The development of self-sitting is
accompanied by important changes in overall body engagement in reaching, as
well as in the morphology of object manipulation and exploration.

In these observations, posture is treated as an independent variable, measuring its effects on the expression of functional action in early development. This
does not mean that the functional link between posture and action in infancy is
exclusively a one-way phenomenon. Evidence shows that young infants, even
before they can sit and locomote, demonstrate postural adjustments when presented with peripheral optic flow (Butterworth & Hicks, 1977; Jouen, 1984) and
objects looming toward them (Ball & Tronick, 1971; Caroll & Gibson, 1981). At
the level of exploration, 5- to 6-month-old infants presented with a sounding
object in the dark, were reported to perform large trunk and head movements in
an apparent effort to localize the object in auditory space (Clifton, Perris, &
Bullinger, 1991). In all, these observations demonstrate that from the outset of
development, posture and functional action are mutually dependent and interact
with one another.

From birth, the function attached to posture is not merely reducible to global bodily adjustments or anti-gravitational reactions. Indeed, when neonates and young infants manifest postural changes, it is not simply in response to perturbation but is also to orient, position, and direct their perceptual systems in ongoing interactions with objects, people, or events in the environment. The anti-gravitational and directional positioning (i.e., orienting) functions attached to the postural system (Paillard, 1971) are manifest from birth. The orienting function attached to the neonate's postural system underlies the necessity of considering posture, perception, and action as inseparable phenomena.

From birth, posture is dynamic and an integral part of the perception–action cycle. Postural development and postural constraints attached to the infancy period have to be understood within this context. Infants manifest from an early age remarkable perceptual and cognitive abilities (E. J. Gibson & Spelke, 1983; Spelke, 1991), but future development of these abilities, and the development of functional action in particular, is linked to progress in the development of posture. The sensorimotor systems newborns are equipped with—including visual, auditory, haptic, and vestibular systems—are functioning and attuned to particular features of the environment. Neonatal behavior is best described as a global engagement, in the sense that from the start of development the various sensorimotor systems are organized to function in synergy (Bullinger, 1981).

Furthermore, a central aspect of this organization that has been extensively demonstrated in recent years, is the fact that newborn behavioral organization is pre-oriented and attuned. Newborns, for example, demonstrate preference for their mothers' voice over that of a female stranger, and in general prefer high-pitched over low-pitched speech contours (De Casper & Spence, 1991). They prefer sharp visual contrast and dynamic displays over less contrasted and static visual configurations (Haith, 1980). They show a robust propensity to recover visual interest to a display that contains novelty (Fantz, 1963). These propensities have been fruitfully exploited by students of infancy to unveil precocious perceptual and cognitive competencies.

The newborn's synergistic functioning and the orientation and attunement of this functioning to particular features of the environment are sources of redundant information from which infants can extract invariants. Take, for example, a newborn laying supine in her bassinet, with eyes open and head oriented to the left. This infant hears a sound to her right and turns her head in that direction. This behavior has been extensively demonstrated only hours after birth (Clifton et al., 1981; Muir & Field, 1979; Weiss, Zelazo, & Swain, 1988). This action, which is accurately oriented in space, provides the infant with a complex covariation in the parameters of vestibular, tactile, proprioceptive, visual, and auditory stimulation. Furthermore, this covariation occurs in relation to an identical event in the environment: a particular sound with a particular address in space. Suppose, now, that the sound the baby heard came from a novel colorful music box that was placed on the right side of the bassinet. This covariation would result in a reinforcing visual consequence, eventually enhancing the probability of its repetition.

This simple example illustrates that the original synergistic nature of sensorimotor functioning, when combined with the rudimentary attunement of this organization to particular features of the environment, is a sufficient condition for providing the infant with regularities, invariants, and information about addresses in space. Recent studies with infants suggest an analogous role of invariant structure in perception and in the control of movement. Neisser (1985) proposed that infants are born with the ability to detect amodal invariants he characterized as "abstract spatio-temporal structures that can be embodied in more than one kind of stimulation" (p. 107). If Neisser is correct, then the interaction between the various sensorimotor systems and particular environmental events must indeed constitute the primary source of the rapid progress characterizing early development in general, and, early perception, cognition, and the development of skilled actions, in particular.

The act of perceiving the environment provides information that specifies both the environment and the observer that scans this environment (J. J. Gibson, 1979). When visually tracking a moving target, or when orienting to a sound, young infants learn as much about their body and what it affords for action as they learn about the environmental event that causes them to move. Bullinger (1981) proposed that the body of the infant is an object to be known, like any other object in the environment. By perceiving and acting, infants construct representations, or *schemata,* of their body that enable them to accomplish complex acts requiring great precision and anticipation. Neisser (1991) proposed that, based on information specifying directly their immediate situation in the environment, infants form what he called an *ecological self.* The ecological self is based on self-perception and the information specifying the point of observation of an observer. It pertains to how an observer perceives himself or herself while interacting with the environment. Research shows, for example, that from birth, infants are capable of manipulating their sucking responses to enhance a visual stimulus (Siqueland & DeLucia, 1969) or to trigger a particular voice or speech sound (DeCasper & Fifer, 1980; Eimas, 1982). This precocious ability to recognize the perceptual consequences of their own actions is part of the ecological self infants construct early in development.

CONCLUSION

Based on the observations presented in this chapter, the ecological self of the infant should not be restricted to the knowledge infants have of their immediate situation in the environment. The ecological self must also include knowledge about the resources of the environment and the resources of the body and what they afford for functional action at a particular moment of development (i.e., called the body's *efficiencies*). This knowledge about the body's efficiencies must be constantly revised in the course of perceptual, postural, and action development, as infants start to reach, roll, crawl, sit, and locomote. Postural development is an important determinant of the ecological self. Prior to the development of self-sitting and the construction of a bodily axis as a referential system for the organization of functional action infants adopt postures shaped by preadapted tonic bodily configurations, such as the ATNP described by Casaer (1979). These postures are biologically determined and serve as the original bearings used by neonates and young infants to perform actions, such as visual tracking. By the 3rd month, infants develop actions that are scaffolded by a bodily axis emerging from postural development and viewed as actively constructed by the infant (Bullinger, 1981).

This conceptualization has proved to be useful in early clinical interventions and in establishing new therapeutics for various sensorimotor handicaps (Bullinger, 1992). For example, tonic mobilization is enhanced in hypotonic infants by stimulating their right or left visual hemifield. Such lateral stimulations have shown to stimulate interactions between these infants and their environment, fostering major development. Systematic postural manipulation and efforts to provide infants with bodily support is used successfully for the tonic mobilization of hypotonic infants. Without these supports and manipulations, these infants fall back in a median posture in which they collapse forward in their seat, generating actions that revolve exclusively around the mouth. The success of such clinical interventions illustrate further the importance of posture and its relation to functional action. Posture is indeed the necessary scaffolding of early functional action.

Thus, the observations presented in this chapter demonstrate that posture, perception, and functional action form three inseparable phenomena. Their interaction needs to be viewed as a primary determinant of infant behavior and development.

ACKNOWLEDGMENTS

Appreciation is expressed to Dr. Julie Schweitzer for her comments on this chapter. This chapter was written while the authors were supported by Grant No. 11-28725.90 from the Swiss National Science Foundation (F.N.S.), and by a grant from the National Institute of Mental Health, No. 2RO3MH50385-01, awarded to Philippe Rochat.

REFERENCES

Alegria, J., & Noirot, E. (1982). Early development of oriented mouthing activity in neonates: Early development of differences related to feeding experiences. In J. Mehler, M. Garrett, & E. Walker (Eds.), *Perspectives on mental representation* (pp. 389–398). Hillsdale, NJ: Lawrence Erlbaum Associates.
Amiel-Tison, C. (1985). Pediatric contribution to the present knowledge on the neurobehavioral

status of infants at birth. In J. Mehler & R. Fox (Eds.), *Neonate cognition: Beyond the blooming buzzing confusion* (pp. 365–380). Hillsdale, NJ: Lawrence Erlbaum Associates.

Amiel-Tison, C., & Grenier, A. (1986). *Neurological assessment during the first year of life.* New York: University Press.

André-Thomas, A. S., & de Ajuriaguerra, J. (1948). *L'axe corporel, musculature et innervation* [Body axis, muscle structure and innervation]. Paris: Masson.

Ball, W. A., & Tronick, E. Z. (1971). Infant responses to impending collision: Optic and real. *Science, 171,* 818–820.

Bower, T. G. R. (1989). *The rational infant: Learning in infancy.* New York: Freeman & Co.

Bower, T. G. R., Broughton, J. M., & Moore, M. K. (1970). The coordination of visual and tactual inputs in infants. *Perception & Psychophysics, 8,* 51–53.

Brainerd, C. J. (1978). The stage question in cognitive-developmental theory. *The Behavioral and Brain Sciences, 2,* 173–213.

Bruner, J. S. (1973). Skill in infancy. In J. M. Anglin (Ed.), *Beyond the information given: Studies in the psychology of knowing* (pp. 241–308). New York: Norton & Co.

Buka, S. L., & Lipsitt, L. P. (1991). Newborn sucking behavior and its relation to grasping. *Infant Behavior and Development, 14,* 59–67.

Bullinger, A. (1977). Orientation de la tète du nouveau-né en présence d'un stimulus visuel [Orientation of the newborn's head in the presence of a visual stimulus]. *L'année Psychologique, 2,* 357–364.

Bullinger, A. (1981). Cognitive elaboration of sensorimotor behaviour. In G. Butterworth (Ed.), *Infancy and epistemology: An evaluation of Piaget's theory* (pp. 173–199). Brighton: The Harvester Press.

Bullinger, A. (1983). Space, the organism and objects: Their cognitive elaboration in the infant. In A. Hein & M. Jeannerod (Eds.), *Spatially oriented behaviour* (pp. 215–222). Berlin: Springer-Verlag.

Bullinger, A. (1989). Espace corporel et espace visuel: Leur coordination dans les débuts du développement [Bodily space and visual space: Their coordination at the origins of development]. *Annales de Réadaptation et de Médecine Physique, 32,* 511–522.

Bullinger, A. (1991). Vision, posture et mouvement chez le bébé: Approche développementale et clinique [Vision, posture and movement in infancy: A developmental and clinical approach]. In F. Jouen & A. Henocq (Eds.), *Du nouveau-né au nourrisson: Recherche fondamentale et pediatrie* (pp. 47–63). Paris: Presses Universitaires de France.

Bullinger, A. (1992). La prise en charge précoce d'enfants à risques [Early intervention with infants born at risk]. *Psychoscope, 1,* 28–29.

Bullinger, A., & Jouen, F. (1983). Sensibilité du champ de detection périphérique aux variations posturales chez le bébé [Relation between the field of peripheral detection and postural variations in the young infant]. *Archives de Psychologie, 51,* 41–48.

Bullinger, A., & Rochat, P. (1984). Head orientation and sucking response by newborn infants [Special issue]. *Infant Behavior and Development, 7*(7), 55.

Butterworth, G. E., & Hicks, L. (1977). Visual proprioception and postural stability in infancy: A developmental study. *Perception, 6,* 255–262.

Butterworth, G. E., & Hopkins, B. (1988). Hand–mouth coordination in the new born. *British Journal of Developmental Psychology, 6,* 303–314.

Caroll, J. J., & Gibson, E. J. (1981, April). *Differentiation of an aperture from an obstacle under conditions of motion by three-month-old infants.* Paper presented at the meetings of the Society for Research in Child Development, Boston, MA.

Casaer, P. (1979). *Postural behaviour in newborn infant* (Clinics in Developmental Medicine, No. 72). London: W. Heinemann Medical Books.

Claparède, E. (1912). J. J. Rousseau et la conception fonctionelle de l'enfance [J. J. Rousseau and the functional conception of childhood]. *Revue de Métaphysique et de Morale, 20,* 391–416.

Clifton, R. K., Morrongiello, B. A., Kulig, J. W., & Dowd, J. M. (1981). Newborns' orientation toward sound: Possible implications for cortical development. *Child Development, 52,* 833–838.

Clifton, R. K., Perris, E. E., & Bullinger, A. (1991). Infants' perception of auditory space. *Developmental Psychology, 27,* 187–197.

Clifton, R. K., Rochat, P., Litovsky, R., & Perris, E. (1991). Object representation guides infants' reaching in the dark. *Journal of Experimental Psychology: Human Perception and Performance, 17,* 323–329.

de Ajuriaguerra, J. (1969, July). *L'enfant et son corps* [The child and his/her body]. Paper presented at the First Latino-American Conference of Child Psychiatry, Punta del Este, Uruguay.

De Casper, A. J., & Fifer, W. P. (1980). Of human bonding: Newborns prefer their mothers' voice. *Science, 208,* 1174–1176.

De Casper, A. J., & Spence, M. J. (1991). Auditory mediated behavior during the perinatal period: A cognitive view. In M. Weiss & P. Zelazo (Eds.), *Newborn attention: Biological constraints and the influence of experience* (pp. 142–176). Norwood, NJ: Ablex.

Eimas, P. D. (1982). Speech perception: A view of the initial state and perceptual mechanisms. In J. Mehler, M. Garrett, & E. Walker (Eds.), *Perspectives on mental representation: Experimental and theoretical studies of cognitive processes and capacities* (pp. 339–360). Hillsdale, NJ: Lawrence Erlbaum Associates.

Fantz, R. L. (1963). Pattern vision in newborn infants. *Science, 140,* 296–297.

Gibson, E. J., & Spelke, E. S. (1983). The development of perception. In J. H. Flavell & E. Markman (Eds.), *Handbook of child psychology: cognitive development* (4th ed.). (Vol. 3, pp. 1–76). New York: Wiley.

Gibson, J. J. (1979). *The ecological approach to visual perception.* Boston: Houghton-Mifflin.

Grenier, A. (1980). Révélation d'une expression motrice différente par fixation manuelle de la nuque [Manifestation of a different motoric expression by manual fixation of the neck]. In A. Grenier & C. Amiel-Tison (Eds.), *Evaluation neurologique du nouveau-né et du nourrisson* (pp. 557–561). Paris: Masson.

Grenier, A. (1981). "Motricite libérée" par fixation manuelle de la nuque au cours des premières semaines de la vie ["Freed motricity" by manual fixation of the neck in the course of the first weeks of life]. *Archives Francaises de Pediatrie, 38,* 557–561.

Gustafson, G. (1984). Effects of the ability to locomote on infants' exploratory behaviors: An experimental study. *Developmental Psychology, 20,* 397–405.

Haith, M. M. (1980). *Rules that babies look by: The organization of newborn visual activity.* Hillsdale, NJ: Lawrence Erlbaum Associates.

Jouen, F. (1984). Visual–vestibular interactions in infancy. *Infant Behavior and Development, 7,* 135–145.

Kessen, W. (1965). *The child.* New York: John Wiley.

Mounoud, P. (1976). Les révolutions psychologiques de l'enfant [The psychological revolutions of the child]. *Archives de Psychologie, 44,* 103–114.

Mounoud, P. (1984). A point of view on ontogeny. *Human Development, 27,* 329–334.

Muir, D., & Field, J. (1979). Newborn infants orient to sounds. *Child Development, 50,* 431–436.

Neisser, U. (1985). The role of invariant structures in the control of movement. In M. Frese & J. Sabini (Eds.), *Goal directed behavior: The concept of action in psychology* (pp. 97–108). Hillsdale, NJ: Lawrence Erlbaum Associates.

Neisser, U. (1991). Two perceptually-given aspects of the self and their development. *Developmental Review, 11,* 197–209.

Paillard, J. (1971). Les determinants moteurs de l'organisation spatiale [Motor determinants of spatial organization]. *Cahiers de Psychologie, 14,* 261–316.

Peiper, A. (1962). Reflexes de posture et de mouvements chez le nourrisson [Postural and movement reflexes in the young infant]. *Revue de Neuropsychiatrie Infantile, 10,* 511–530.

Piaget, J. (1952). *The origins of intelligence in children* (M. Cook, Trans.). New York: International Universities Press. (Original work published 1936)

Prechtl, H. F. R., & Beintema, D. J. (1964). *The neurological examination of the full-term newborn infant* (Clinics in Developmental Medicine, No. 12). London: Spastics International Medical Publications, with Heinemann; and Philadelphia: Lippincott.

Reed, E. S. (1990). Changing theories of postural development. In M. Woollacott & A. Shumway-Cook (Eds.), *The development of posture and gait across lifespan* (pp. 3–24). Columbia: University of South Carolina.

Rochat, P. (1992). Self-sitting and reaching in 5–8 month old infants: The impact of posture ond its development on early eye–hand coordination. *Journal of Motor Behavior, 24,* 210–220.

Rochat, P. (1993). Hand–mouth coordination in the newborn: Morphology, determinants, and early development of a basic act. In G. J. P. Savelsbergh (Ed.), *The development of coordination in infancy* (pp. 265–288). Amsterdam: Elsevier Science Publishers.

Rochat, P., Blass, E. M., & Hoffmeyer, L. B. (1988). Oropharyngeal control of hand–mouth coordination in newborn infants. *Developmental Psychology, 24,* 459–463.

Rochat, P., & Goubet, N. (1993). *Development of sitting and reaching in 5–6-month-old infants.* Manuscript under review.

Rochat, P. (1989). Object manipulation and exploration in 2- to 5-month-old infants. *Developmental Psychology, 25, 6,* 871–884.

Rochat, P. & Senders, S. J. (1990, April). *Sitting and reaching in infancy.* Paper presented at the 7th International Conference on Infant Studies, Montreal.

Rochat, P., & Senders, S. J. (1991). Active touch in infancy: Action systems in development. In M. J. Weiss & P. R. Zelazo (Eds.), *Infant attention: Biological constraints and the influence of experience* (pp. 412–442). Norwood, NJ: Ablex.

Roucoux, A., Culée, C., & Roucoux, M. (1983). Development of fixation and pursuit of eye movements in human infants. *Behavioural and Brain Research, 10,* 133–139.

Rousseau, J. J. (1911). *Emile ou de l'éducation* [Emile, or On Education]. Barbara Foxley (Trans.). London: Dent. (Original work published 1762)

Siqueland, E. R., & DeLucia, C. A. (1969). Visual reinforcement of non-nutritive sucking in human infants. *Science, 165,* 1144–1146.

Spelke, E. S. (1991). Physical knowledge in infancy: Reflections on Piaget's theory. In S. Carey & R. Gelman (Eds.), *The epigenesis of mind: Essays on biology and cognition* (pp. 133–170). Hillsdale, NJ: Lawrence Erlbaum Associates.

Thelen, E., & Fisher, D. M. (1983). The organization of spontaneous leg movements in newborn infants. *Journal of Motor Behavior, 15,* 353–377.

Thelen, E., & Fogel, A. (1986). Toward an action-based theory of infant development. In J. J. Lockman & N. L. Hazen (Eds.), *Action in social context: Perspectives on early development* (pp. 23–64). New York: Plenum Press.

Trevarthen, C. (1974). Biodynamic structures, cognitive correlates of motive sets and the development of motives in infants. In W. Prinz & A. F. Sanders (Eds.), *Cognition and motor processes* (pp. 327–351). Berlin: Springer-Verlag.

Trevarthen, C. (1974). The psychobiology of speech development. In E. H. Lenneberg (Ed.), *Language and brain: Developmental aspects* (pp. 570–585). Neurosciences Research Program Bulletin, Nr. 12. Boston: Neurosciences Research Program.

von Hofsten, C. (1982). Eye–hand coordination in newborns. *Developmental Psychology, 18,* 450–461.

von Hofsten, C., & Ronnqvist, L. (1988). Preparation for grasping an object: A developmental study. *Journal of Experimental Psychology: Human Perception and Performance, 14,* 610–621.

Wallon, H. (1970). *De l'acte a la pensée: Essai de psychologie comparée* [From act to thought: An essay in comparative psychology]. Paris: Collection Champs Flammarion. (Original work published 1942)

Wallon, H. (1985). La maladresse [Unskillfulness]. *Enfance*, Nr. 7, 72–84.

Weiss, M. J., Zelazo, P. R., & Swain, I. U. (1988). Newborn response to auditory stimulus discrepancy. *Child Development, 59,* 1530–1541.

White, B. L., Castle, P., & Held, R. (1964). Observation on the development of visually directed reaching. *Child Development, 35,* 349–364.

3

Pattern and Face Recognition in Infancy: Do Both Hemispheres Perceive Objects in the Same Way?

Scania de Schonen
Christine Deruelle
Laboratoire de Neurosciences Cognitives—CNRS

The various neural networks of the infant brain do not all become functional at the same rate. Some parts of the brain begin to function before birth, and others later on. Investigating the relationships between emerging behaviors and maturational neural events can, therefore, be most instructive. In some respects, this approach to the neural basis of behavior, despite some methodological difficulties, is similar to the neuropsychological approach to adult patients with brain lesions. The double dissociations between emerging behaviors and neural maturational events correspond to the double dissociations studied in adult patients between the localization of lesions and between behavioral deficits. It has become obvious however, that the emergence of a new cognitive ability in an infant cannot be accounted for simply by the functional onset of action of a group of neurons that has remained silent up to that point. Other kinds of neural events very similar or even identical to those underlying adult learning processes are probably involved in the developmental mechanisms. Discovering how learning mechanisms and neural maturation cooperate and are correlated with age-related behavioral changes is the main aim of this developmental approach.

Generally speaking, there exist many different ways of conceiving of the type of filiation between two behaviors that emerge successively in the course of an infant's development. We lack the necessary criteria, however, for deciding whether or not the emergence of a particular competence at a given age depends on the prior acquisition of another type of behavior acting as an "ancestor" (Bresson, 1976; Bresson & de Schonen, 1979). One of the ways of determining the possible filiation between two successively emerging competencies consists of examining the neuronal events correlated with the behavioral acquisitions in question. If the emergence of the latter of the two behaviors requires the maturation of neuronal networks, which become functional only after those responsible for the earlier behavior, our conclusions will naturally be quite different from those to be drawn if the onset of the later competence is controlled by the same neuronal networks as those governing the earlier competence (for discussion of topics of this kind, see also Johnson & Morton, 1991). Considerable progress would be achieved in our understanding of cognitive development if we were able to say, for example, which neuronal systems deal with face perception during the first week after birth, and which do so during the subsequent months (de Schonen, 1989; Johnson, 1990; Johnson & Morton, 1991).

Contrary to the double dissociations studied in adult neuropsychology, the gaps in infants' maturation patterns from one behavior to another, and from one neuronal structure to another, are part of a normal and functional process. The fact that specific sets of neurons are not yet functioning, or that specific abilities are not yet acquired, is part of the normal process of development and may even play a decisive role in shaping and timing the course of forthcoming developmental events (Bresson & de Schonen, 1979; de Schonen & Bresson, 1983), if only by simply filtering the environmental stimuli, for example. In addition, the lack of maturity of some parts of the cortex at birth probably gives various environmental factors a nonnegligible part in shaping the organization of the neuronal networks, even though the role of these factors may be completely defined and anticipated in the working principles of the neuronal networks and their maturational timing (see, e.g., Greenough, Black, & Wallace, 1987; Singer, 1987). This was the general framework within which we first began to study the differences in the way the two hemispheres process visual patterns and faces, and the interhemispheric interactions occurring in infancy.

The two cerebral hemispheres are known to differ in some of their functional aspects in adults. Some of the differences between the hemispheres are to be found in most people, whereas others vary considerably from one individual to another. Studies of the development of these functional differences and of interhemispheric interactions can throw considerable light on the mechanisms involved in the functional specialization of the neuronal tissue and its plasticity.

The data obtained so far on the development of hemispheric specialization during the first few months of life have shown that the left hemisphere (LH) has an advantage over the right hemisphere (RH) in perceiving speech sounds a few months after birth (for a review, see Witelson, 1987), and one study even reports this finding from the age of one week (Bertoncini et al., 1990). Other data on hemispheric specialization have been provided by studies on handedness, which have shown that manual asymmetry develops at an early age, although some of the studies have suggested that handedness might be better described as due to different functional specializations of each hand than as the mere superiority of one hand over the other (Bresson, Maury, Pieraut-Le Bonniec, & de Schonen, 1977; de Schonen, 1977; Flament, 1976; Peters, 1983; Ramsay, 1983; Trevarthen, 1986; Wallon, Evart-Chmieniski, & Sauterey, 1958; G. Young,

Segalowitz, Misek, Corter, & Trehub, 1983, for a review). The status and role of interhemispheric communications were not touched on, however, either in the studies on the early LH specialization for speech sound perception or in those on the development of handedness.

Apart from a few studies (Best, Hoffman, & Glanville, 1982; Davidson & Fox, 1982; Fox & Davidson, 1987, 1988; Lewis, Maurer, & Kay, 1978; Segalowitz & Chapman, 1980), it was only quite recently that interest began to develop in the activities in which the RH specializes, and in the differences between the two hemispheres' visual modes of processing patterns and objects during infancy. The way in which these differences develop used to be simply inferred from what was known about children (as opposed to infants) and about adults with perinatal brain damage who had been tested long after the age of a few months. This sometimes gave rise to the idea that the hemispheric differences in visual pattern processing merely stemmed from the hemispheric language acquisition differences. Rothbart, Posner, and Boylan (1990) suggested, for instance, that the LH advantage for perceiving the local aspects of a pattern (as opposed to the global aspects) might not be innate, but might develop with age along with the ability to read and write. This was certainly an interesting conjecture, but it needed to be tested experimentally. As we show further on, the experiments we carried out led to a very different to account of the mechanisms underlying the specialization of the neuronal tissue than that suggested by Rothbart et al.

Some of the main questions we have been dealing with in our investigations are as follows:

• Is the adult RH advantage for some aspects of face processing (for reviews, see Benton, 1980; Ellis & Young, 1989; Hécaen & Albert, 1978; Moscovitch, 1979; A. W. Young, 1983) already present in infants when they begin to recognize individual faces? Or is this aspect of adult functional brain asymmetry simply the outcome of intervening developments, such as the increasing commitment of the available LH neural space to language-related activities?

• If the RH does have an early advantage for face recognition, does this involve only the processing of faces or does it include visual patterns in general?

• If differences do exist in the way the two hemispheres process visual patterns, does a time lag occur between the onsets of the two processing devices?

• At a more general level, can the functional differences between the two hemispheres' modes of visual pattern processing be correlated with differences between the maturational rhythms of homologous regions? The maturational lags between homologous brain regions in the two hemispheres might generate differences as to how the neuronal networks are organized on both sides, as well as a differential sensitivity to prenatal and postnatal environmental factors.

• Do any detectable traces of the limited visual capacities characteristic of infants during the first few months of life persist in the adult visual processing modes?

• How are the interhemispheric communication systems set up and developed?

In what follows, we shall attempt to come up with some partial answers to some of these questions, and where no definite answers are yet possible, to make a few speculations.

HEMISPHERIC SPECIALIZATION IN FACE PROCESSING

Recognition of Faceness

At birth, infants are already endowed with some ability to recognize human faces (Goren, Sarty, & Wu, 1975; Morton & Johnson, 1991). From the age of 3 months, both hemispheres are able to recognize and categorize stimuli that resemble faces, or *faceness*. Infants aged 12 to 26 weeks were required to recognize the patterns representing human faces among a set of scrambled face patterns. No two face-like or non–face-like patterns were the same. The recognition task procedure, which was incorporated in an operant conditioning paradigm, was run in each visual hemifield separately, so that the stimuli would be conveyed to one hemisphere at a time as is done in adult experiments (for further details see de Schonen & Bry, 1987).

Once the learning criterion was reached in one visual field, the subject immediately underwent the same learning task in the contralateral visual field in order to check whether or not interhemispheric communication had taken place. This method of testing interhemispheric transfer, by measuring learning economy, is commonly used in animal experiments to test the functioning of the corpus callosum (see, e.g., Doty, Ringo, & Lewine, 1986).

The results of this experiment showed that faceness recognition is equally possible in the left visual field–right hemisphere (LVF–RH) and in the right visual field–left hemisphere (RVF–LH) from the age of 12 weeks. Although each hemisphere is able to categorize faceness independently, what has been learned in one hemisphere does not begin to be transferred to the other before the age of 19 weeks.

Individual Face Recognition

What about infants' ability to recognize familiar faces and distinguish individual faces from each other? On the basis of the available data, infants acquire the ability to recognize a familiar person's face on a photograph at about 4 months (Barrera & Maurer, 1981), which shows that they are already equipped at this stage with a sophisticated face-processing system that can cope with the differences between photography and real objects. Well before reaching this age, however, they already have some individual face recognition ability. The results of three different studies have shown that around the third or fourth day of life, infants look at their mother's face for longer than a stranger's (Bushnell, Sai, & Mullin, 1989; Fields, Cohen, Garcia, & Greenberg, 1984; Pascalis, de Schonen, Morton, Fabre-Grenet, & Deruelle, 1993). During the first two months or so, however, features such as the hairstyle and coloring seem to be the main cues used by infants to recognize individuals (see a review by Flin & Dziurawiec, 1989). The face-processing system that operates after the age of 3 months may, therefore, differ from that available to younger infants (for a discussion of the topic, see Johnson & Morton, 1991).

Is the individual face recognition 4-month-olds exhibit in their ability to recognize a familiar face on a photograph (Barrera & Maurer, 1981), controlled by one hemisphere more than by the other, as it is in adults? De Schonen, Gil de Diaz, and Mathivet (1986) tested the ability of infants aged 4 to 9 months to recognize their mothers' face when it was presented very briefly to either the RVF–LH or the LVF–RH.

Each infant was shown color slides of his or her mother's and a stranger's face. One subject's mother's face served as the stranger's face for another subject. The photographs were taken in such a way that the discrimination between faces could be based only on physiognomic features. The faces were projected, as in the human faceness recognition study, to the right or left of the central fixation point. Subjects in the 4- to 6-month-old group were exposed to each stimulus for 350 msec, those in the 7- to 9-month old group viewed the stimuli for 250 msec (for further details, see de Schonen et al., 1986; de Schonen & Mathivet, 1990).

The measure of interest was the latency between the stimulus onset and the beginning of the ocular saccade produced in response to the stimulus. After a few trials, the latency of the response to the mother's face became significantly shorter than that to the stranger's face. The infants can, therefore, be said to have "recognized" their mothers in this situation. This selective decrease in the latency, which occurred in response to the stimulus of the mother, took place only in the LVF–RH, and not in the RVF–LH. Neither motor bias (de Schonen, Mac-Kenzie, Maury, & Bresson, 1978) nor differences in visual acuity or attention could account for this difference between the two visual fields, so the RH can be said to have had an advantage over the LH in recognizing—or at least reacting to—a two-dimensional picture of the mother's face. The RH reacts more quickly and/or more consistently and spontaneously (i.e., in the absence of any specific instructions) than the LH to a familiar face.

The results of another study suggested that this RH advantage is not restricted to the mother's face. The RH was again found to have an advantage when the stimulus was a photograph of a stranger's face with which the subjects were briefly familiarized (de Schonen et al., 1986, Exp. 2). The RH advantage for recognition of, or reactivity toward, faces therefore includes faces on photographs with which infants have become familiar.

The reason the LH did not react more differentially to the two types of stimuli in these experiments may have been not so much that it is unable to recognize individual faces, but rather that it is simply not spontaneously geared to reacting under these particular conditions to a familiar face, or to reacting differentially to different faces. This is why we used an operant conditioning technique (the same as that used in the faceness category recognition study described earlier) with the 4- to 9-month-olds as a means of inciting each hemisphere to respond differently to the mother's versus a stranger's face (de Schonen & Mathivet, 1990). Here, stimuli consisting of the mother's face and a stranger's face were prepared as in the mother-recognition experiment; they were also presented at the same distance from central fixation and for the same duration as in this experiment.

The results again showed that the LVF–RH had a considerable advantage for distinguishing between mother and stranger stimuli. Moreover, the boys' results differed from those of the girls. None of the boys reached criterion in the RVF–LH, whereas 25% of the girls did. A similar sex-related factor was found to operate in the earlier studies on familiar face recognition (de Schonen et al., 1986; Gil de Diaz, 1983), where the male population was found to be more strongly lateralized than the females. In the present study, the relationship between the degree of hemispheric asymmetry and the subjects' sex does not seem to vary between the age of 4 and 10 months. We were, therefore, not dealing here with a temporary difference, such as that described by Gwiazda, Bauer, and Held (1989; Held, 1989), for example, in their studies of stereopsis.

Interhemispheric Communication

The last point to emerge from these studies was the fact that no sign of interhemispheric transfer was observed in these infants, contrary to what was observed in the faceness recognition study. Although the LH is able to recognize the human face at this age, it does not score very high on familiar face recognition and does not seem to be able to use the information about faces that is learned by the RH.

Taken together, these results led to the following conclusions: First, both hemispheres develop a visual faceness-recognition system somewhere between birth and 3 months, but only one hemisphere is able to process an individual face efficiently at this age. The RH advantage for recognizing physiognomies from photographs probably develops at the age of 3 to 4 months, which is the age at which infants acquire this competence. One might think that the LH might identify the stimuli on the basis of nonphysiognomic elements by processing them in the same way as it would any other pattern; the data, however, show that this is not what actually occurred. At this age, the left hemisphere's faceness recognition system might orient the infant's attention toward activities such as lip-reading and the audio-visual processing of speech sounds, rather than toward identifying individual faces. This leaves us with the following alternative: Either a single hemisphere, usually the right, is able to develop a fast and efficient system for processing individual faces, or both hemispheres are able to develop such a system, but the system matures at an earlier age in the RH than in the LH.

The data presented argue against the hypothesis that the RH advantage for face recognition observed in adults might be due to the increasing amount of LH space being committed to language learning from about age 2. On the other hand, it seems quite plausible that those parts of the LH that receive visual and auditory afferents may be wholly engaged in speech-sound processing such as lipreading. The amount of neural tissue involved in an activity is not necessarily positively correlated with the degree of sophistication of a competence. More neuronal tissue may even be engaged in the processing of speech sounds at this age than is subsequently. Our data prove that if the RH lateralization of face processing has any connection with the fact that the left hemisphere is committed to language processing, the mechanism involved cannot be due to a competition, starting around 2 years of age, in which the face-recognition processes in the LH are gradually replaced by language-related activities (for discussion of these questions, see de Schonen & Mathivet, 1989; Turkewitz, 1989a, 1989b). Our data support the idea that in adults, the RH and LH abilities to recognize individual faces probably do not involve the same mechanisms.

Second, at the age of 9 months, the RH's ability to recognize individual faces from photographs is not yet usable by the LH. This lack of transfer may contribute toward stabilizing the hemispheric specializations. On the other hand, the fact that information about faceness does undergo transfer and that both hemispheres can recognize and categorize faceness, suggest that individual face recognition and species face recognition may not involve the same neuronal networks (de Schonen, 1989). Johnson and Morton (1991) also concluded that faceness recognition and individual face recognition might be separate systems in infants aged between birth and 3 months.

Finally, the fact that the degree of lateralization was found to differ between boys and girls without any difference being observed between their performance levels suggests that the neuronal organization may differ between the two sexes as early as the first year of life.

HOW FACE SPECIFIC IS THE RH-PROCESSING ADVANTAGE?

Both Right and Left Hemispheres are Able to Process Patterns

The RH advantage for individual face recognition that emerges during the first year of life may result from a more general RH advantage for complex pattern processing, either because the neuronal networks involved in pattern processing become functional in the RH before they do in the LH (see de Schonen & Mathivet, 1989 for discussion of this point), or because the RH has a general advantage for pattern processing. Another possible explanation is that because attentional requirements are dealt with by the right hemisphere (Posner & Petersen, 1990), split-visual-field tasks may be performed better by the RH than by the LH when they involve more than simply recognizing faceness.

Deruelle and de Schonen (1990, 1991) have shown that in infants aged 4 to 9 months, the both hemispheres process visual patterns, but they process different aspects of these patterns. In one situation, subjects were shown two geometrical designs very schematically representing a face, differing only in the shape of the elements standing for the eyes (Fig. 3a). The second situation involved patterns composed of the same elements, but they were arranged arbitrarily and with no vertical symmetry (Fig. 3b). The stimuli were presented as in the experiments already described. The first aim of this study was to determine whether the LH's inability to recognize individual faces was due to a general pattern-processing deficit in comparison with the RH, in which case it would be equally incompetent in both situations. It turned out that the two hemispheres are, in fact, equally able to learn to recognize the patterns in Fig. 3b. The LH disadvantage in individual face processing is therefore not attributable to a disadvantage in processing patterns in general.

Contrary to what might have been expected, the RH was found to score less well on learning the patterns in Fig. 1a than on the arbitrary patterns in Fig. 1b, and less well than the LH on the patterns in Fig. 3a. That the RH did poorly with the symmetrical patterns in Fig. 3a but not with the patterns in Fig. 3b shows that this hemisphere is sensitive to the overall arrangement of the components. One

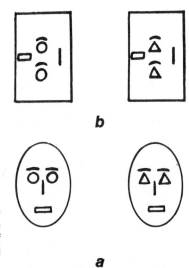

FIG. 3.1.   The two pairs of stimuli: (a) face-like patterns and (b) arbitrary patterns. Each of the two pairs was discriminable on the basis of whether the stimulus contained a pair of small circles or a pair of triangles.

might hypothesize that some configural aspects of shapes (here, the relevant configural feature may be either the similarity to a face or only the fact of symmetry) may prevent the RH from processing the components of the pattern, whereas the LH mode of processing may be better adapted to processing these local components. In individual face recognition, the RH advantage may, therefore, stem from its processing of configural aspects and differences. In the situation shown in Fig. 1a, the difference between the circles and the triangles standing for the eyes may not have been sufficiently obvious to be detected by the RH configural processing system. The difference between the RH's performances in the two situations suggests that RH processing is not always blind to local differences in patterns, but is only when the pattern configuration is face-like or has some symmetry.

Here again, no interhemispheric transfer was found to have occurred in either situation. These data, along with the finding that information about faceness undergoes interhemispheric transfer at a very early age, suggest that the transfer of information about the faceness categorization task may not be directed by the corpus callosum but by an interhemispheric subcortical pathway. It is also possible that faceness categorization (classifying patterns as faces and nonfaces) may not be a cortical activity. On the basis of a study on human faceness recognition in newborn infants and babies aged 1 and 2 months, Johnson (1990) has likewise concluded that the faceness recognition system involves neuronal structures different from those responsible for recognizing individual faces around the age of 2 months. The fact that the two systems continue to be dissociated after this age might indicate that at least some aspects of the earliest systems subsist despite the subsequent emergence of other, functionally linked, systems.

Lastly, the lack of transfer observed in our study points to the conclusion that during at least the first 9 months of life, infants acquire two different sets of representations about objects, which are not necessarily integrated with each other.

The LH is therefore not handicapped for pattern processing in comparison with the RH, but, rather, the two hemispheres process visual patterns differently. Rothbart et al. (1990) have argued that the orientation of attention may be controlled by the RH in infants from the age of 6 months on. The results of the study we have just described cannot be accounted for by this hypothesis, because they suggest, instead, that different types of processing may take place in the two hemispheres.

Configural and Local Processing Modes

The question has been raised as to whether the configural pattern processing mode operates before the local mode, or *vice versa* as the infant develops. Due to discrepancies in the data available on this topic, it is difficult to decide one way or the other (see review by Dodwell, Humphrey, & Muir, 1987). A recent study has shown, however, that at around the age of 3 months, infants become able to process information about both the global and the local aspects of a pattern (Ghim & Eimas, 1988).

Deruelle and de Schonen (1993) and de Schonen and Deruelle (1991a) attempted to find out whether the RH is systematically at a disadvantage when analyzing local components of symmetrical well formed patterns, or whether its disadvantage occurs exclusively with face-like and face processing. Using a procedure similar to that described in the previous experiments, infants aged 4 to 9 months learned to recognize and discriminate between the two patterns in Fig. 3.2a, which differ in the spatial position of one internal element and between the two patterns in Figure 3.2b, in which the shapes of the local components differed. The results indicate that the RH was more successful than the LH in the first situation, whereas the LH performed better in the second. In other words, local differences not affecting the spatial relationships among the components were perceived better by the LH, whereas a change affecting the location of a component of the pattern was detected more clearly by the RH.

These data are in agreement with those by Ghim and Eimas (1988) concerning the contemporaneous nature of the two modes of processing. Our results, however, show that different neuronal networks are involved. Each of the two hemispheres seems to pick up a different class of visual information from the surroundings without any coordination being possible in the age groups investigated here. Because the two modes of processing are set up at such an early age and

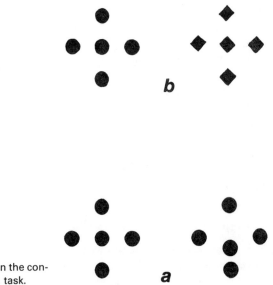

FIG. 3.2.   The stimuli used (a) in the configural task and (b) in the local task.

involve separate neuronal substrates, it seems unlikely that they reflect the conclusions of a central decision-maker regarding the best way of analyzing a
pattern. Our data further argue against the hypothesis by Rothbart et al. (1990)
that the lateralization of the processing of local aspects within the LH is a side-
product of learning to read. The LH advantage in local processing is based on a
neural organization that operates long before the child learns to read.

Van Kleeck and Kosslyn (1989) have proposed that one of the characteristics
of RH processing in adults is the ability to disentangle the various components of
a pattern provided that the way these components are embedded in the pattern fit
the "good form" rules. According to this proposal, the RH should not be at a
disadvantage when presented with the situations in either Fig. 1a or Fig. 2b.
During the first year at least, the good form pattern seems to induce the RH to use
a mode of processing that neglects the shape of the local components, even when
they are assembled in conformity with the good form rules.

To make categorical distinctions between configural, global processing on the
hand and local processing on the other hand is obviously to oversimplify the subtle differences between the various possible modes of processing, which might
be more aptly described in other terms. Exactly what the characteristics of the
different possible modes of pattern processing are is a major problem, which remains to be solved.

During the first year of life, the RH advantage for individual face recognition
may, therefore, involve configural rather than component processing. The existence of this preferential mode in the RH does not necessarily mean that the RH
is incapable of working on the local aspects of a pattern, however: The RH is as
efficient as the LH in discriminating between two patterns on the basis of the
shape of some of their components when the patterns do not constitute a good
form. The limitations and advantages of RH processing suggest the existence of
two pattern processors within the RH. One processor may be sensitive to good
forms, and when this processor is triggered, the local components may not be
processed as such. The other processor may operate when no good forms are
detected. This might mean that until at least 9 months of age the RH does not
perceive a pattern as a configuration unless this pattern is a good form. Non–
good-form patterns may be perceived as a collection of smaller patterns but not
as a configuration.

The LH disadvantage for individual face recognition might be due to the fact
that local processing is not the appropriate mode for this type of recognition task.
Processing the complex features of a face one by one might take too long to be
efficient in an experimental situation such as ours.

Based on the results of our experiment again, it seems unlikely that learning
was transferred from one hemisphere to the other. The coordination between the
local and global aspects of some patterns thus seems to be as limited as if the
infants were acquiring two sets of pattern representations that had nothing in

common. One might, therefore, wonder what happens to the pattern processing with the advent of interhemispheric transfer, when the two modes can be combined. One might also wonder how an infant links together the various representations he or she builds up about a person's face and the movements it makes (when expressing emotion, speaking, etc.) when these representations reflect each hemisphere's separate mode of processing.

SPECULATIONS ON THE POSSIBLE MECHANISMS OF PERCEPTUAL HEMISPHERIC SPECIALIZATION

What then are the main factors that lead to the two hemispheres developing different visual perceptual abilities? That is, what developmental mechanisms contribute to implementing the specialization programs? The environment is one factor liable to affect an infant's cortical organization and specialization, because the cortex is relatively immature at birth. Several authors have shown that visual experience influences the development of some aspects of the visual cortical neuronal organization (for a review on the cat primary visual cortex, see, e.g., Fregnac & Imbert, 1984). De Schonen and Mathivet (1989) drew up a scenario where endogenous and environmental factors combine and result in the different face-processing competencies of the left and right hemispheres.

The Possible Role of Early Limitation in the Infant's Vision

According to this scenario the RH system for processing individual faces and complex patterns might become functional before the LH system. The other possibility is that the infant's arousal system may act primarily in the RH. Contrary to what Rothbart et al. (1990) argued, this asymmetry of arousal effects may be a shaping factor only with visual events and only during the period between birth and 3 months. During this 3-month period when the RH system becomes functional (or is more strongly activated by the arousal system), infants' visual capacities are still rather restricted, partly because they involve pathways that are sensitive only to the low spatial frequencies (see Atkinson & Braddick, 1989; Banks & Dannemiller, 1987; Banks, Stephens, & Hartmann, 1985; Held, 1989). The individual face-recognition system may become stabilized on the basis of this coarse visual information. The conjunction of these two maturational events (the time gap between right and left maturation, and the various rates of maturation of the elementary visual capacities) may give rise to two separate hemispheric modes of processing patterns.

This scenario might lead one to expect that the adult RH might have an advantage, for example, in dealing with the information about faces which is conveyed by low spatial frequencies. Sergent (1983, 1985, 1989) has, in fact, suggested that the adult RH advantage in face processing may be based on its capacity to process low spatial frequencies. When tested directly in adults, this hypothesis has sometimes been confirmed and sometimes ruled out (Christman, 1990; Fiorentini & Berardi, 1984; Kitterle, Christman, & Hellige, 1990; Michimata & Hellige, 1987; Sergent, 1987; Szelag, Budohoska, & Koltuska, 1987). The conjecture that the difference between the two hemispheres' face-processing modes might involve several factors—including a difference between the relatively elementary visual mechanisms at work—has, to our knowledge, not yet been convincingly disproved.

Might the infant's limited visual abilities during the first two or three months of life constitute a factor favoring the RH's advantage for processing the configural aspects of a good form pattern? There is room for some speculation (de Schonen & Deruelle, 1991b) about the possible links between the processing of stimuli of low spatial frequency and the processing of the configural aspects of patterns. In the case of a low-pass visual system, some patterns or objects, such as faces, may be matched and recognized more frequently if they are perceived in terms of their configural aspects rather than their local ones, which are liable to show more variation from one occurrence to another. With a low-pass visual system, the representations involving some configural aspects of an individual face may yield a positive correlation with the various occurrences of this face more frequently (despite its possible variations) than other types of representation. Representations resulting from the local processing of the same face might not have as much chance of minimizing omissions and recognition errors, because the variations among the representations would be greater, and it would not be possible to correlate them with each other or with new occurrences of the same face. This would result in the storage and coding of objects (such as faces) being carried out on the basis of their configural aspects. Conversely, in the case of other types of objects, events, or visual scenes, it might be the local aspects that most frequently give rise to positive correlations between the various occurrences, and hence to a more efficient and frequently used system of memorization.

On the other hand, when the visual system becomes able to process the medium and high spatial frequencies, the LH neuronal networks capable of processing complex patterns might also begin to be functional. If the LH matures later than the RH, the time lag between the onset of low spatial frequency processing and that of the other frequency ranges might be shorter than what we see in the RH. Furthermore, the organization of the surrounding neuronal networks might have reached a more advanced stage than had been attained when these events took place in the RH. These differences may contribute to stabilizing differing modes of processing in the two hemispheres. The RH, despite the development of high-spatial-frequency processing, may conserve neural networks involved in processing patterns and faces on the basis of low spatial frequencies with a configural mode. The early visual limitations, together with the time lag between right and left maturation rates, could favor the use of configural representations of objects and faces versus a local mode; nevertheless, these factors cannot be at the origin of the two processing modes, nor can they explain why the RH is constrained to process configural aspects with good form patterns but not with nonsymmetrical patterns (Fig. 1). We, therefore, suggest that other perceptual mechanisms may also play a role in the development RH processing.

The existence of a sex-related factor in determining the degree of hemispheric lateralization in individual face recognition (in the two studies in which the familiar face was that of the mother, and the study that used a familiarized stranger) suggests that infants' brains may be organized differently in males and females. No such sex-related difference was found in the experiments that used the patterns in Figs. 3.1 and 3.2. Because of this difference in lateralization, the developmental history of the neural networks involved in face processing cannot be assumed to be identical to the developmental history of the neural networks involved in processing patterns other than faces, even though the two systems have some mechanisms in common.

Functional Cortical Maturation

Little evidence is available so far regarding the heterochrony of cortical maturation between the two hemispheres. A few data (see Geschwind & Galaburda, 1985; Rosen, Galaburda, & Sherman, 1987; Simonds & Scheibel, 1989) argue in favor of the idea that some parts of the RH mature faster than their LH counterparts. Even quite small time lags between the two maturational rates can lead to different patterns of synaptic organization being selected and subsequently stabilized. A neuronal network apparently can take anything from a few minutes to a few days to become stabilized (Buisseret, Gary-Bobo, & Imbert, 1978; Fifkova, 1985; Fifkova & Van Harreveld, 1977; Schechter & Murphy, 1976; Singer, 1987). Behavioral studies involving the use of EEG, evoked potential (ERP) and positron emission tomography (PET) studies on human infants have shown that changes correlated with cortical maturation take place at various times in various parts of the cortex (Best et al., 1982; Chugani & Phelps, 1986; Crowell, Jones, Kapunai, & Nakagawa, 1973; Harwerth, Smith, Duncan, Crawford, & von Noorden, 1986; Thatcher, Walker, & Giudice, 1987). The possibility should therefore not be ruled out that after birth, when visual experience becomes capable of modulating the organization of neuronal patterns, there may be maturational lags between homologous networks of the cortex in the right and left hemispheres (for further details about a scenario along these lines, see de Schonen, 1989; de Schonen & Mathivet, 1989; Turkewitz, 1989a, 1989b). Furthermore, the variability of the maturational lags might partly account for the sex difference in the degree of lateralization found in infants. A PET study is now being carried out with $H_2{}^{15}O$ (Tzourio et al., 1992). From this study, we hope to be able to determine some of the changes that take place during functional maturation in the brains of infants aged 2 to 4 months while they are engaged in cognitive activities. This particular period seems to be when numerous events in the functional maturation of the brain occur.

CONCLUSION

The fact that the two hemispheres become specialized at a very early age in different modes of processing that prefigure some of the differences found in adults does not rule out the possibility that other systems of processing may develop at a later stage. In particular, when the interhemispheric transmission of information becomes possible, a new kind of processing will develop in addition to the separate kinds that existed up to that point. Developments during the first month of life might provide the framework for future abilities while demarcating territories and neuronal networks in such a way as to guide the emergences of other new systems. Whatever the case may be, the very occurrence of these early specializations shows that during the first months of life, the brain is not just a homogeneous blob capable of a single kind of visual learning.

Our attempt to correlate maturational cerebral events with the emergence of perceptual abilities obviously suffers from a lack of factual knowledge. Our scenario has the advantage of providing a possible explanation as to how the two hemispheres become differently specialized and why the plasticity observed after early lesions tends to vary depending on the type of competence involved.

REFERENCES

Atkinson, J., & Braddick, O. (1989). Development of basic visual functions. In A. Slater & G. Bremner (Eds.), *Infant development* (pp. 7–41). Hove and London: Lawrence Erlbaum Associates, Ltd.

Banks, M. S., & Dannemiller, J. L. (1987). Infant visual psychophysics. In P. Salapatek & L. Cohen (Eds.), *Handbook of infant perception* (Vol. 1, pp. 115–184). Orlando: Academic Press.

Banks, M. S., Stephens, B. R., & Hartmann, E. E. (1985). The development of basic mechanisms of pattern vision: Spatial frequency channels. *Journal of Experimental Child Psychology, 40,* 501–527.

Barrera, M. E., & Maurer, D. (1981). Recognition of mother's photographed face by the three-month-old infant. *Child Development, 52,* 714–716.

Benton, A. L. (1980). The neuropsychology of facial recognition. *American Psychologist, 35,* 176–186.

Bertoncini, J., Morais, J., Bibeljac-Babic, R., McAdams, S., Peretz, I. P., & Mehler, J. (1990). Dichotic perception and laterality in neonates. *Brain & Language, 37,* 591–605.

Best, C. T., Hoffman, H., & Glanville, B. B. (1982). Development of infant ear asymmetries for speech and music. *Perception & Psychophysics, 31,* 75–85.

Bresson, F. (1976). Inferences from animal to man: Identifying behavior and identifying functions. In M. Von Cranach (Ed.), *Methodological problems in ethology* (pp. 319–342). The Hague: Mouton.

Bresson, F., & de Schonen, S. (1979). Le développement cognitif: Les problèmes que pose aujourd'hui son étude [Current issues in cognitive development]. *Revue de Psychologie Appliquée*, *29*, 119–127.

Bresson, F., Maury, L., Pieraut-LeBonniec, G., & de Schonen, S. (1977). Organization and lateralization of reaching in infants: An instance of dissymetric functions in hand collaboration. *Neuropsychologia*, *15*, 311–320.

Buisseret, P., Gary-Bobo, E., & Imbert, M. (1978). Ocular motility and recovery of orientational properties of visual cortical neurons in dark-reared kittens. *Nature 272*, 816–817.

Bushnell, I. W. R., Sai, F., & Mullin, J. T. (1989). Neonatal recognition of the mother's face. *British Journal of Developmental Psychology, 7*, 3–15.

Christman, S. (1990). Effects of luminance and blur on hemispheric asymmetries in temporal integration. *Neuropsychologia, 28*, 361–374.

Chugani, H. T., & Phelps, M. E. (1986). Maturational changes in cerebral function in infants determined by FDG positron emission tomography. *Science, 231*, 840–842.

Crowell, D. H., Jones, R. H., Kapunai, L. E., & Nakagawa, J. K. (1973). Unilateral cortical activity in newborn humans: An early index of cerebral dominance? *Science, 180*, 205–208.

Davidson, R. J., & Fox, N. A. (1982). Asymmetrical brain activity discriminates between positive and negative affective stimuli in human infants. *Science, 218*, 1235–1237.

Deruelle, C., & de Schonen, S. (1990, August). *Visual pattern processing by the right and left hemisphere: A developmental study.* Poster presented at the Fourth European Conference of Developmental Psychology, Stirling, Scotland.

Deruelle, C., & de Schonen, S. (1991). Hemispheric asymmetries in visual pattern processing in infancy. *Brain & Cognition, 16*, 151–179.

Deruelle, C., & de Schonen, S. (1993). Hemispheric asymmetry in pattern processing by infants: Local shape and position processing. Manuscript submitted for publication.

de Schonen, S. (1977). Functional asymmetries in the development of bimanual coordinations in human infants. *Journal of Human Movements Studies, 3*, 144–156.

de Schonen, S. (1989). Some reflections on brain specialisation in faceness and physiognomy processing. In A. Young & H. D. Ellis (Eds.), *Handbook of research on face processing* (pp. 379–389). Amsterdam: North-Holland.

de Schonen, S., & Bresson, F. (1983). Données et perspectives nouvelles sur les débuts du développement [Recent ideas and studies in early development]. In S. de Schonen (Ed.), *Le développement dans la première année* (pp. 13–26). Paris: Presses Universitaires de France.

de Schonen, S., & Bry, I. (1987). Interhemispheric communication of visual learning: A developmental study in 3- to 6-month-old infants. *Neuropsychologia, 25*, 601–612.

de Schonen, S., & Deruelle, C. (1991a, August). *Configurational and componential visual pattern processing in infancy.* Poster presented at the 14th European Conference on Visual Perception, Vilnius. (*Perception, 20* [Special issue], 123 [Abstract])

de Schonen, S., & Deruelle, C. (1991b). Spécialisation hémisphérique et reconnaissance des formes et des visages chez le nourrisson [Hemispheric specialization in face and pattern processing by infants]. *L'Année Psychologique, 91*, 15–46.

de Schonen, S., Gil de Diaz, M., & Mathivet, E. (1986). Hemispheric asymmetry in face processing in infancy. In H. D. Ellis, M. A. Jeeves, F. Newcombe, & A. Young (Eds.), *Aspects of face processing* (pp. 199–208). Dordrecht, Netherlands: Martinus Nijhoff.

de Schonen, S., MacKenzie, B., Maury, L., & Bresson, F. (1978). Central and peripheral object distances as determinants of the effective visual field in early infancy. *Perception, 7*, 499–506.

de Schonen, S., & Mathivet, E. (1989). First come first served: A scenario about development of hemispheric specialization in face recognition during infancy. *European Bulletin of Cognitive Psychology (CPC), 9*, 3–44.

de Schonen, S., & Mathivet, E. (1990). Hemispheric asymmetry in a face discrimination task in infants. *Child Development, 61*, 1192–1205.

Dodwell, P. C., Humphrey, G. K., & Muir, D. W. (1987). Shape and pattern perception. In

P. Salapatek & L. Cohen (Eds.), *Handbook of infant perception* (Vol. 2, pp. 1–79). New York: Academic Press.

Doty, R. W., Ringo, J. L., & Lewine, J. D. (1986). Interhemispheric mnemonic transfer in macaques. In F. Leporé, M. Ptito, & H. H. Jasper (Eds.), *Neurology and neurobiology* (Vol. 17, pp. 269–279). New York: A. R. Liss.

Ellis, H. D., & Young, A. W. (1989). Are faces special? In A. W. Young & H. D. Ellis (Eds.), *Handbook of research on face processing* (pp. 1–26). Oxford: North-Holland.

Fields, T., Cohen, D., Garcia, R., & Greenberg, R. (1984). Mother–stranger discrimination by the newborn. *Infant Behavior and Development, 7,* 19–26.

Fifkova, E. (1985). A possible mechanism of morphometric changes in dendritic spines induced by stimulation. *Cellular and Molecular Neurobiology, 5,* 47–63.

Fifkova, E., & Van Harreveld, A. (1977). Long lasting morphological changes in dendritic spines of granular cells following stimulation of the enthorinal area. *Journal of Neurocytology, 4,* 211–230.

Fiorentini, A., & Berardi, N. (1984). Right-hemisphere superiority in the discrimination of spatial phase. *Perception, 13,* 695–708.

Flament, F. (1976). *Coordination et prévalence manuelles chez les nourrissons* [Handedness and cooperation between the two hands in infancy]. Paris: CNRS Editions.

Flin, R., & Dziurawiec, S. (1989). Developmental factors in face processing. In A. W. Young & H. D. Ellis (Eds.), *Handbook of research on face processing* (pp. 335–378). Oxford: North-Holland.

Fox, N. A., & Davidson, R. J. (1987). EEG asymmetry in response to approach of a stranger and maternal separation in 10-month-old infants. *Developmental Psychology, 23,* 223–240.

Fox, N. A., & Davidson, R. J. (1988). Patterns of brain electrical activity during facial signs of emotions in 10-month-old infants. *Developmental Psychology, 24,* 230–236.

Fregnac, Y., & Imbert, M. (1984). Development of neuronal selectivity in primary visual cortex of cat. *Physiological Review, 64,* 325–434.

Geschwind, N., & Galaburda, A. M. (1985). Cerebral lateralization: Biological mechanisms, associations, and pathology. I. A hypothesis and a program for research. *Archives of Neurology, 42,* 428–459.

Ghim, H. D., & Eimas, P. D. (1988). Global and local processing by 3- and 4-month-old infants. *Perception & Psychophysics, 43,* 165–171.

Gil de Diaz, M. (1983). Asymetrie fonctionnelle hemispherique et reconnaissance d'un visage chez le nourrisson [Functional hemispheric asymmetry in familiar face recognition in infancy]. Unpublished doctoral dissertation, Université d'Aix–Marseille, France.

Goren, C. C., Sarty, M., & Wu, P. Y. K. (1975). Visual following and pattern discrimination of face-like stimuli by newborn infants. *Pediatrics, 56,* 544–549.

Greenough, W. T., Black, J. E., & Wallace, C. S. (1987). Experience and brain development. *Child Development, 58,* 539–559.

Gwiazda, J., Bauer, J., & Held, R. (1989). From visual acuity to hyperacuity: A 10-year update. *Canadian Journal of Psychology, 43,* 109–120.

Harwerth, R. S., Smith, E. L., III, Duncan, G. C., Crawford, M. L. J., & von Noorden, G. K. (1986). Multiple sensitive periods in the development of the primate visual system. *Science, 232,* 235–237.

Hécaen, H., & Albert M. (1978). *Human neuropsychology.* New York: Wiley.

Held, R. (1989). Development of cortically mediated visual processes in human infants. In C. Von Euler, H. Forssberg, & H. Lagerctantz (Eds.), *Neurobiology of early infant behaviour:* Proceedings of an International Wallenberg Symposium. (pp. 155–172). London: The MacMillan Press.

Johnson, M. H. (1990). Cortical maturation and the development of visual attention in early infancy. *Journal of Cognitive Neuroscience, 2,* 81–95.

Johnson, M. H., & Morton, J. (1991). *Biology and cognitive development: The case of face recognition*. Oxford: Blackwell.

Kitterle, F. L., Christman, S., & Hellige, J. B. (1990). Hemispheric differences are found in the identification, but not the detection, of low versus high spatial frequencies. *Perception & Psychophysics, 48,* 297–306.

Lewis, T. L., Maurer, D., & Kay, D. (1978). Newborns' central vision: Whole or hole? *Journal of Experimental Child Psychology, 26,* 193–203.

Michimata, C., & Hellige, J. B. (1987). Effects of blurring and stimulus size on the lateralized processing of nonverbal stimuli. *Neuropsychologia, 25,* 397–407.

Morton, J., & Johnson, M. H. (1991). Conspec and conlern: A two-process theory of infant face recognition. *Psychological Review, 98,* 164–181.

Moscovitch, M. (1979). Information processing and the cerebral hemispheres. In M. S. Gazzaniga (Ed.), *Handbook of behavioral neurobiology, Vol. 2* (pp. 379–446). New York: Plenum Press.

Pascalis, O., de Schonen, S., Morton, J., Fabre-Grenet, M., & Deruelle, C. (1993). Mother's face recognition in neonates: a replication of Bushnell, Sai and Mullin's study and an extension. Manuscript submitted for publication.

Peters, M. (1983). Differentiation and lateral specialization in motor development. In G. Young, S. Segalowitz, C. M. Corter, & S. Trehub (Eds.), *Manual specialization and the developing brain* (pp. 141–160). New York: Academic Press.

Posner, M. I., & Petersen, S. E. (1990). The attention system of the human brain. *Annual Review of Neuroscience, 13,* 25–42.

Ramsay, D. S. (1983). Unimanual hand preference and duplicated syllable babbling in infants. In G. Young, S. Segalowitz, C. M. Corter & S. Trehub (Eds.), *Manual specialization and the developing brain* (pp. 161–176). New York: Academic Press.

Rosen, G. D., Galaburda, A. M., & Sherman, G. F. (1987). Mechanisms of brain asymmetry: New evidence and hypothesis. In D. Ottoson (Ed.) *Duality and unity of the brain* (pp. 29–36). New York: Plenum Press.

Rothbart, M. K., Posner, M. I., & Boylan, A. (1990). Regulatory mechanisms in infant development. In J. T. Enns (Ed.), *The development of attention: Research and theory* (pp. 47–66). Oxford: North-Holland.

Schechter, P. B., & Murphy, E. H. (1976). Brief monocular visual experience and kitten cortical binocularity. *Brain Research, 109,* 165–168.

Segalowitz, S. J., & Chapman, J. S. (1980). Cerebral asymmetry for speech in neonates: A behavioral measure. *Brain & Language, 9,* 281–288.

Sergent, J. (1983). The role of the input in visual hemispheric processing. *Psychological Bulletin, 93,* 481–512.

Sergent, J. (1985). Influence of task and input factors on hemispheric involvement in face processing. *Journal of Experimental Psychology: Human Perception and Performance, 11,* 846–861.

Sergent, J. (1987). Failures to confirm the spatial-frequency hypothesis: Fatal blow or healthy complication? *Canadian Journal of Psychology, 41,* 412–428.

Sergent, J. (1989). Structural processing of faces. In A. W. Young & H. D. Ellis (Eds.), *Handbook of research on face processing* (pp. 57–91). Oxford: North-Holland.

Simonds, R. J., & Scheibel, A. B. (1989). The postnatal development of the motor speech area: A preliminary study. *Brain & Language, 37,* 42–58.

Singer W. (1987). Activity-dependent self-organization of synaptic connections as a substrate of learning. In J. Changeux & M. Konishi (Eds.), *The neural and molecular bases of learning* (pp. 301–336). New York: Wiley.

Szelag, W., Budohoska, W., & Kotulska, B. (1987). Hemispheric differences in the perception of gratings. *Bulletin of the Psychonomic Society, 25,* 95–98.

Thatcher, R. W., Walker, R. A., & Giudice, S. (1987). Human cerebral hemispheres develop at different rates and ages. *Science, 236,* 1110–1113.

Trevarthen, C. (1986). Form, significance and psychological potential of hand gestures of infants. In J.-L. Nespoulos, P. Perron, & A. R. Lecours (Eds.), *The biological foundations of gestures: Motor and semiotic aspects* (pp. 149–202). Hillsdale, NJ: Lawrence Erlbaum Associates.

Turkewitz, G. (1989a). Face processing as a fundamental feature of development. In A. Young & H. D. Ellis (Eds.), *Handbook of research on face processing* (pp. 401–404). Amsterdam: North-Holland.

Turkewitz, G. (1989b). A prologue to the scenario of the development of hemispheric specialization: Prenatal influences. *European Bulletin of Cognitive Psychology (CPC), 9,* 135–140.

Tzourio, N., de Schonen, S., Mazoyer, B., Bore, A., Pietrzyk, U., Bruck, B., Aujard, Y., & Deruelle, C. (1992). Regional cerebral blood flow in two-month-old alert infants. *Society for Neuroscience Abstracts, 19,* 1121.

van Kleeck, M. H., & Kosslyn, S. M. (1989). Gestalt laws of perceptual organization in an embedded figures task: Evidence for hemispheric specialization. *Neuropsychologia, 27,* 1179–1186.

Wallon, H., Evart-Chmieniski, E., & Sauterey, R. (1958). Equilibre statique, équilibre en mouvement: Double latéralisation [Lateralization of static and dynamic control of body posture]. *Enfance, Nr. 1,* 1–29.

Witelson, S. F. (1987). Neurobiological aspects of language in children. *Child Development, 58,* 653–688.

Young, A. W. (1983). *Functions of the right cerebral hemisphere.* New York: Academic Press.

Young, G., Segalowitz, S., Corter, C. M., & Trehub, S. (Eds.). (1983). *Manual specialization and the developing brain.* New York: Academic Press.

4

A Functional Analysis of Visual Fixation, Habituation, and Attention in Infancy

Gérard Malcuit
Andrée Pomerleau
Laboratoire d'Étude du Nourrisson

Evidence of integrated cognitive activity in infants has been deduced from the ways they allocate their attention to specific aspects of the environment (Colombo & Mitchell, 1990). Attention has been described as a multifaceted phenomenon, probably involving more than one psychological process and more than one neural mechanism (Posner & Boies, 1971). The processes of attention are considered as accomplishing a two-fold function. First, they enhance and facilitate the intake of information contained in the stimulus that happens to catch the infant's attention at a particular moment. This information is then used to guide the infant's activity. This function coincides with the orienting response. Through a generalized system, including central, motor, and autonomic components, this "What is it?" response optimizes the reception of afferent input and its central processing (Graham & Clifton, 1966). Depending on the function of the event, action will follow. The second function of the attentional processes is that it permits the infant to selectively turn his or her perceptual apparatus toward the most salient stimuli (salient at this very moment, and under these prevalent circumstances) among the many events competing for attention. When certain stimuli are interpreted as having no (or no more) significance for the ongoing activity, or when their power to maintain attention becomes eroded, the infant may focus his or her receptors on other stimuli. In the normal ecology of the infant, these two functions—intake enhancing and selectivity—interact in a constant manner.

Although still at an incomplete level of maturation, infants' sensory systems can apprehend a variety of stimuli, which, in turn, offer many response opportunities, even though the infants' response systems are as yet not perfectly functional. Given the quantity of internal and external events to which they are exposed, infants would be overwhelmed if they were not equipped to shut off certain stimuli and to selectively direct their attention to others. A first level of filtering can be found in the defense responses (Graham & Clifton, 1966), which serve to reduce the impact of stimuli that might interfere with the ongoing activity. At the second level, attention is determined by the attentional selectivity process. Infants are more attracted by certain types of stimuli because these stimuli possess an unconditional eliciting capacity based on their physical features and their being specifically attuned to the characteristics of infants' sensory systems (Banks & Salapatek, 1983). Infants' attention is triggered not solely because of a fit between selected stimuli characteristics and some prewired perceptual dispositions, but also because of the functional value of the stimuli in the infants ongoing activity. This functional value is thought to be acquired during the infants' transactions with their environment. The activation of attention is studied in terms of the attention-getting process. Within this dimension, it is important to determine which characteristics—of the stimulus, of the infant, and of their interaction in a given context—are the most suited to the capturing attention and to accounting for its transformations with time or with repeated exposure. Moreover, the infant must be able to maintain or to terminate the attention given to a particular stimulus. This function coincides with the attention-holding and attention-terminating dimensions (Cohen, 1972; Sigman, 1988). In spite of the theoretical importance attributed to this third dimension of withdrawal and reorientation of attention, little research has been directed toward identifying the factors responsible for it. Once again, with respect to attention-holding and attention-terminating, we need to determine what factors—at the level of the stimulus (e.g., novelty and complexity), the child, and their interaction within particular contexts—can account for variations in the speed with which attention is withdrawn from a stimulus.

Complexity is not easy to quantify and has not always been the best predictor of attention (Kaplan, Werner, & Rudy, 1990). A number of researchers base their predictions solely on the physical properties of stimuli and their fit with infants' sensory-perceptual systems (Banks & Salapatek, 1983). Consequently, they have come to conclude that cognitive processes may not play as large a role in early infant attentional dynamics as has generally been assumed (Dannemiller & Banks, 1983; Kaplan et al., 1990).

Although stimulus energy and selective receptor adaptation might explain some of the variation in attentional responses, it is questionable as an exclusive interpretation (Ackles & Karrer, 1991). We argue here for a more cognitive conception of attention. To the extent that it takes into consideration the acquired significance or functional value of contextual elements, our analysis of infant attention stresses the role of psychological processes. We consider it important to specify what a task requires of the infant (by the implicit demands of our experimental contexts), and the role of the contextual elements to which the infant has to attend. The process of habituation affords partial resolution of these topics.

Infants' responsiveness and interest in a stimulus declines with its repetition, as the stimulus no longer has any salience (biological or psychological) for their ongoing activities. Conversely, infants will continue to pay attention to a stimulus that has acquired a signaling value, and will maintain their attention longer on a stimulus that has a high degree of either attractiveness *or* usefulness in guiding their activities. It is, therefore, essential to evaluate the variables involved in the habituation process.

HABITUATION AND ATTENTION

Habituation is the preferred tool for studying attention from birth to 6 months of age. Habituation procedures generate measures of change in infants' (physiological or behavioral) responses to the repetitive presentation of an unchanging stimulus. Both physiological and behavioral responses are assumed to reflect the contributions of attentional processes. The organism learns to inhibit nonessential responding to an initially response-eliciting stimulus that has been experienced as having no particular significance—that is, no signalizing or other function—for the organism's ongoing activity in the present context (Malcuit & Pomerleau, 1985; Malcuit, Pomerleau, & Lamarre, 1988). The habituation of the orienting response aptly shows that the organism has acquired enough information about the functional significance (or lack of it) of the stimulus. The subsequent recovery of attention to a novel stimulus confirms that active inhibition of responses to a particular stimulus had indeed occurred. The ability to distribute attention selectively and to determine rapidly where and when it is to be redirected is a necessary prerequisite for optimal transactions with the environment, as well as for the acquisition of new behaviors (Fagen & Ohr, 1990).

The majority of infancy researchers explain the reduction in attention to the habituated stimulus by resorting to a schemata-comparator model inspired by the theoretical neurological model of Sokolov (1963). Aside from minor variations, the explanations proposed share basic assumptions (Dunham, 1990). One is the *construction* of a mental representation of the novel stimulus, which improves at each of its presentations. There is then assumed to be a *comparator* apparatus, which decides when a match between the internal schema and the external stimulus has been accomplished. Attention to the stimulus is inhibited when the match is achieved. This model of construction and comparison is in line with the computer analogy, but it is far too general to account for the observed phenomena of infant attention. Above all, we need to know what is required of infants when we study their attentional responses. For comparison to take place, it is necessary that the result of this comparison serves in guiding the activity. For instance, one stimulus configuration may signalize something, whereas a different configuration conveys no signal whatsoever. The infant's behavior will vary in accordance with these functional values. The former may not maintain the infant's attention for a long time if its function is to signal the infant to engage in some other activity or if the infant must discriminate rapidly between these configurations. On the other hand, the pattern with no significance may well be fixated on for a long time if it is the most interesting one in a context with very little competition. Whether or not it is necessary to engage the entire comparator machinery in order to answer the "What is it?" question of an incoming stimulus, rests on the valence of this stimulus within a given context.

The study of infant attention is determined, in part, by methodological constraints. Attention is usually assessed in tasks implicating the visual modality. The dependent variables are most often measures of infants' looking activity. Beyond theoretical considerations of the privileged status of vision in processing sensory information during this period of development, one can easily conceive of why the study of infants' attention is predominantly the study of infants' visual attention. By observing and recording where and for how long an infant looks, we obtain a good index of the direction and distribution of his or her attention. Such facility for assessing the various dimensions of attention is not to be had with audition, the other modality with a privileged status during the first period of an infant's life. Researchers have been able to assess attention triggered by auditory stimuli, the attention-getting dimension, by means of head-turning responses (e.g., Tarquinio, Zelazo, Gryspeerdt, & Allen, 1991), through behavioral inhibition of all other irrelevant forms of activity (e.g., Birns, Blank, Bridger, & Escalona, 1965), or by resorting to physiological indices, mostly the phasic cardiac responses (e.g., Richards, 1989). Measuring the attention-holding dimension is more complicated, however. A measure of duration analogous to looking time does not easily find its equivalence in the auditory modality. Occasionally, researchers have relied on the coupling of auditory stimuli with a visual target (e.g., Julien, Pomerleau, Feider, & Malcuit, 1983), but it then becomes difficult to decide whether the infant is attentive to the auditory or the visual aspect of the stimulus. In research presently in progress, we evaluate the relation between the allocation of attention given to visual and auditory stimuli presented in successive sessions. Behavioral indices of sustained attention to the auditory stimulus are not obvious. The many difficulties encountered with audition, as well as with other sensory modalities, have precluded the study of the *maintenance* of attention outside the visual modality.

VISUAL EXPLORATION AND SUSTAINED ATTENTION

The study of the factors that explain the maintenance of visual attention has remained within the theoretical model originally conceived for the study of the habituation of orienting responses (i.e., the attention-getting dimension). As a corollary, there has been an overextension of concepts of the habituation paradigm. This tendency to proceed from the study of the habituation of orienting responses to the study of the persistence (or lack of it) of attention is particularly evident in the use of the infant control procedure (Horowitz, Paden, Bhana, & Self, 1972). We have argued elsewhere (Malcuit et al., 1988) that it is preferable to consider the maintenance of attention as reflecting something other than the interplay of a comparison process used to explain the habituation of an orienting response. In studying the duration of attention directed at a particular event and its changes over time, one is working on exploratory and operant behaviors within a choice context. The stimulus is looked at for as long as its capacity to attract attention remains at a higher level than that of other stimuli present in the setting. This capacity to *sustain,* as well as to *attract* attention, does not depend solely on the complexity of building up a mental schema. By making the infant-control procedure the paradigm of choice for evaluating infants' information processing capacities within a schemata-comparator model, one has treated non-sustained attention (conceived as a rapid speed of information processing) as a cognitive capacity continuous with later intelligence (Bornstein & Sigman, 1986). No one will deny that a more efficient information processing system is a more intelligent system, because the first of these terms is becoming a synonym for the latter, but is maintenance of attention really always and only this kind a cognitive activity? It may not be when we analyze the variables called into play in an infant-control procedure, and take into consideration findings from learning experiments, from sustained attention tasks, or from variants of these procedures.

It is necessary to be precise about what behaviors are most likely to occur in our experimental contexts and what may be the function of their constituent elements. In infant-control procedures, by implicitly asking infants to process a visual stimulus presented repeatedly, we assume that they face a task of construction-comparison. One can also conceive of the infant as being placed in a choice situation in which his or her attention is held by the most salient elements of the setting. The infant may look at the target or elsewhere. We have reduced the probability of the latter, however, by making the setting drab and by limiting the possibilities for other behaviors. The stimulus itself is chosen to be moderately interesting, and hence likely to be conducive to the infant's eventual loss of interest. The infant's attention is solicited by the elicitation of an orienting response via the projection of the stimulus. The most probable response is to turn the head in the direction of the incoming stimulus and to examine it. The stimulus' functional value is that of triggering an orientation, of signaling that there is something to be looked at, and of reinforcing the maintenance of attention, depending on its intrinsic characteristics and its eventual acquired value. To assure that the infant remains on the task for a certain time, the stimulus must not be too simple. In a situation where the stimulus is highly monotonous, it could be a sign of intelligent behavior to try to do anything rather than remain on the task. Because attending to visual stimuli is related to a relatively immobile stance, it so happens that the less receptive infants end up in the attrition group (Wachs &

Smitherman, 1985). The infant's attention depends on variables other than those related to the implicit demands to process information. We therefore need to identify what other processes are active during visual exploration and what can explain the inter- and intraindividual variations in visual fixation.

A close examination of the literature reveals that researchers vary in their interpretations of the duration of looking according to the procedures they use. In experiments on operant learning with 3- to 4-month-old infants, Hayes, Ewy, and Watson (1982) reported a positive relation between the duration of visual attention to noncontingent visual stimuli during baseline and learning performance. Only the infants who spent *more time* looking at the luminous display showed reliable evidence of learning. Infants who shifted to low looking time from the first to the fifth minute of baseline failed to learn. The authors concluded that infants' capacity to maintain their attention on the stimulus prepares them to analyze the contingencies in the environment. The visual display was evidently more attractive than most of the static visual stimuli used in infant-control situations, thus creating an implicit demand for persistent or sustained attention.

To capture this type of attention, Ruff (1990) proposed the following measures, each associated with its own experimental context: looking time in habituation tasks (Cohen, 1972), focused attention in exploratory tasks (Ruff, 1986), and space-focused looking in vigilance tasks (Ruff, Capozzoli, Dubiner, & Parrinello, 1990). In spite of the commonality of attention-holding dimensions (and its measurement through duration of looking) in these procedures, there are variations in the task demands, the procedural arrangements, and the functional values of the elements comprising each task. In exploratory and infant-control tasks, the explicit aim is to assess the same processes. In both tasks, infants are induced to look at stimuli for as long as they want. They control the onset and offset of their sustained attention by turning their visual fixation on and off the stimuli, but there are two diametrically opposed and rarely explicitly discussed, interpretations of the same looking measures. According to the interpretation found in infant-control studies, the shorter the periods of fixation, the more efficient the information processing (Bornstein, 1988). According to the interpretation found in exploration studies, on the other hand, the persistence of attention reflects efficiency in the mode of intake and use of information (Ruff, 1986). There are, however, two main differences between these tasks: the age range within which each task is predominantly used and the elements of the experimental context. In infant-control studies, the target age concentrates around 4 months, an age at which the exploration of the environment proceeds mainly through the visual modality, as the infant is not yet capable of coordinated reaching and grasping of objects presented at a distance. In exploration studies, the infants used are older and are capable of acting on stimuli. The experimental contexts are likewise construed so as to correspond to the different age ranges. In infant-control studies, the stimuli are usually two-dimensional and moderately attractive. The experimental setting and its elements in no way support a prolonged engagement with the stimuli. In exploration studies, the stimuli are three-dimensional objects, designed to elicit a variety of exploratory behaviors of greater persistence. In other words, everything is done to make the stimuli to be attended attractive, salient, and motivating and to provoke a range of attention-related activities (i.e., visual *and* tactile exploration).

In these studies, an infant who looks at an object is scored as being engaged in visual attention up to the time when he or she begins to touch the objects and to explore them (tactile exploration). Thus, taking into consideration the infants' age, one may consider that those who limit their activities to looking at the objects without touching them are in some way not acting appropriately. Although it is possible that infants who do not engage rapidly in some form of active exploration might be cognitively less advanced than infants who do, many other variables can also account for this more contemplative activity, ranging from motivational variables to previous learning experiences. Ruff (1990) interpreted these latencies as reflecting the initiation of a process distinct from attention holding. Latency is said to represent the time necessary to activate attention and the information gathering system. This period would bring into play various subprocesses, which, for the author, represent "pre-attentive" processes. It seems hardly economical to label an infant's looking at an object without touching it as pre-attentive, just because the experimental task implicitly requires more active exploration.

The other context for studying sustained attention in infants is described as a *vigilance task* (Ruff et al., 1990), perhaps overextending the concept. In a vigilance task, the organism is in a state of preparation for detecting signals so as to be able to react adequately. In Ruff et al.'s task, 5- and 11-month-old infants were induced to look at the location of a previously seen, but now absent, event: The durations of infants' visual fixations at locations where a puppet entered and exited were measured. The infants spent 21% of the intervals in "sustained attention." One cannot claim, however, that sustained attention during these intervals was information processing in the usual sense, because during these intervals there was no stimulus to be processed. In this context, the duration of looking is seen as an index of the quality of cognitive functioning. Still, one ought to analyze these various task demands and the elements they contain. Attentiveness in these different contexts is not under the control of the same variables, and does not have the same consequences on the behaviors and events that follow.

Some studies also present inconsistencies in the interpretation of results, as a consequence of their exclusive appeal to the traditional model of information processing. As an illustration, consider two studies—Laplante, Zelazo, and Gauthier (1989) and Stack, Laplante, and Zelazo (1991)—that relied on sequential visual stimuli (Zelazo & Kearsley, 1982). These stimuli are thought to be more compelling than static stimuli and, consequently, are expected to elicit higher levels of attention, and more attractive stimuli are more apt to reinforce the maintenance of visual exploration (Malcuit et al., 1988). The authors, however, considered these stimuli as more complex, in the sense that they would slow down the rate at which internal representations of events can be formed. In support of this assertion, they reported a positive correlation between the usual duration measures of looking at static two-dimensional stimuli and three-dimensional mobile stimuli. Thus, according to the authors, the correlation implies that the measures derived from the two types of stimuli are measures of similar processes. Following the two main arguments of the model—stimulus complexity and cognitive maturity—one would expect that a more complex stimulus, being more difficult to match than a simple one, would hold the infants' visual attention longer; in addition, such a complex stimulus should be processed faster by infants who have a more mature information-processing system. Sigman, Beckwith, Cohen, and Parmelee (1989), for example, reported that premature infants fixate a visual target longer (i.e., habituate more slowly) than full-term infants, but in Stack et al.'s study (1991), Down syndrome (DS) infants were found to spend proportionally less time looking at the mobile three-dimensional stimuli than normal controls. Moreover, the mean duration of the first look before turning away on each trial was much shorter among DS infants than among controls. On the basis of the model's explanation of looking durations, one should conclude that DS infants have better information-processing capacities or else question the schemata-comparator model. Stack et al. (1991) concluded that DS infants showed "depressed attention." DS infants have poorer information-processing ability because of lower levels of attention. It is difficult not to agree with this assertion, but then the model that explains everything no longer explains anything. What sense is to be made out of shorter durations of looking time indicating depressed attention and poorer information-processing ability in one case, and more focused attention and more efficient information processing in other cases, on the basis of the same measures of looking time? To consider attention in every case where it is estimated by means of visual fixations under the general rubric of information processing (with or without the additional analogy of construction-comparison), while avoiding to specify more precisely the functional-contextual variables involved and their relations to the visual fixation behaviors, lacks explanatory power.

ATTENTION IS MORE THAN WHAT WE MEASURE

The duration of attention directed at a visual stimulus does not have the same interpretation in the various tasks in which it is studied. One way to escape this difficulty is to claim that attention time is different from looking time. It would be difficult to claim otherwise. Posner and Rothbart (1981) had already criticized the rather simplistic but, in practice, widely accepted assumption that infants' ocular fixations on a stimulus were a direct index of their attention. As already discussed, the bulk of infancy research is centered on visual attention because orienting and maintaining the visual apparatus on the target is a necessary (although not a sufficient) condition for attending to it. Nevertheless, infants may well have their eyes riveted to a stimulus without really being attentive to it. According to Lécuyer (1989), the term *attention* should be reserved for moments when the infant is effectively engaged in information processing. Thus, an infant who fixates a target for a long fixation in an infant-control task and who would be described as a slow habituator would be an infant whose attention fluctuates. Even though his or her looking may be sustained, only a small portion of this looking time would be spent processing information. In contrast, an infant who fixates for a shorter period (a fast habituator) should have a better capacity to sustain attention. Such an infant would be able to extract the information contained in a stimulus rapidly and efficiently.

This point of view, although seductive, presents two problems. First, the term *attention* should not be reserved only for those occasions when there is information processing. To be attentive to something does not always mean "to process information," in the sense of template construction and comparison. The second problem is more important: If attention time does not equal looking time, then how can one measure attention? One solution consists of adding other behavioral indices to the criteria for defining attention. For instance, Ruff (1986) defined the concept of *focused attention* by what she called "examining behavior": an intent expression on the face, concentration, and inspection, the fingering and turning of the object. Because tactile manipulation is the most important of the elements constituting the behavior of examining this definition may well apply only to tasks in which objects have to be manipulated by infants who are *necessarily* older (i.e., over 25 weeks). This method was adopted in Yarrow et al.'s research (1983). Evidently, this definition is inapplicable to research with younger infants, who only do visual exploring, as in the infant-control procedure. Another solution consists of adding physiological measures to the behavioral ones. Cardiac activity may be used, because variations in heart rate have some relationship to attention (Pomerleau & Malcuit, 1980). Richards (1989) uses the term *sustained attention* in relation to infants' cardiac responses with deep deceleration, although phasic cardiac responses (i.e., orienting responses) are involved. As such, cardiac responses do not have the function of indicating the level of attention or the quality of information processing (Malcuit & Pomerleau, 1985). In short, there is no simple solution. What needs to be done is to determine the characteristics and requirements of the task, in parallel with the developmental level of the infant. This choice of analyzing the functions of attention forms the basis of our experimental approach, which we present in the final section.

The emphasis on the schemata-comparison model of information processing in research on the development of cognitive abilities is found, particularly, in studies with infants from birth to 6 months old. The study of cognitive processes has been biased toward the study of receptive rather than enactive processes

(Bloom, 1990). The organism is more and more conceptualized as a simple transmission line rather than as a user of stimulation. Because babies seem drawn to examine certain noninteractive stimuli, the belief appears justified that they are well suited for research contexts in which they are presented with visual stimulations they can only look at. In this kind of context, behaviors such as head turning and visual fixation are of interest because they indicate attention, and attention means that the infant is engaged in information processing.

The importance attributed to this propensity for being absorbed (for a certain period of time) by external stimuli and to the relative absence of overt behaviors during the time of intense attending, reinforces the notion of a purely perceptual organism, engaged in encoding, constructing, and comparing representations. The baby's intelligence thus appears perceptual rather than sensorimotor, because his or her perceptual capacities are more developed than his or her motor capacities. As a consequence, in order to study the ways in which infants process information, it is necessary to reduce motor noise as much as possible. To this end, researchers have tried to develop procedures to assess infants' cognitive abilities "that distinguish mental activity, defined more appropriately as central information processing, from confounding performance measures, namely, expressive/communicative behaviors" (Zelazo, 1989, p. 95). This makes it possible to obtain measures of specific mental abilities independent of the organism's other systems. Information processing ability cannot stand alone, however. As Richelle (1987) pointed out, the organism is not only a machine for perceiving and representing information, but is also one that performs actions. Taking in and processing information makes sense when we take into account the behaviors that make possible and modulate these cognitive activities. The need for information is understood by considering the behaviors that these cognitive activities lead up to. The age of the infants and the type of tasks one presents them with can partly explain this bias in favor of a psychology of afferent processes. The greater importance attributed to overt exploration—manipulation and goal-directed behaviors—in defining attention in older infants leads to a less "receptive" and "perceptual" conception of attention and of the cognitive activities it permits. Nevertheless, this has not yet led to a conception that avoids treating attention as an individual trait characteristic still too detached both from the variables inherent in the task producing it and from the functional significance of the elements that compose it. This brings us to a discussion of the arguments that substantiate this position and to a presentation of facts that demonstrate the necessity of taking other elements into consideration.

The interpretation that duration of attention directed toward a stimulus is an indication of the time required to process the informational content of the stimulus seems to be validated by the observation of shorter looking times with increasing age and longer looking times with increasing levels of complexity. We note that the age range for verifying the first part of this statement is rather narrow. Before 2 months, it is difficult to have infants perform a standard infant-control task, and after 6 months, they get bored quickly and can no longer tolerate the task. It is evident that the infants' behavioral repertoire determines to a large extent how attention is studied. Before the baby is able to control the alternation and maintenance of visual fixation, researchers usually use auditory stimuli (a still more "receptive" sensory system). When infants succeed in acting on the stimuli, and their behavioral repertoire becomes large enough to enable them to modify or terminate the task, this receptive-contemplative characteristic of the infant-control procedure must be abandoned in favor of tasks requiring more active exploration. Hence, the hypothesis on the relation between age and speed of processing can only be tested with infants between the ages of 2 and 6 months. Published data are not numerous. We have argued elsewhere (Malcuit et al., 1988) that this reduction in looking time is better explained by the fact that, as infants advanced in age, the stimuli were less apt to retain their attention within these contexts, than by reference to infants' greater information processing capacities. The stimuli lose their capacity to reinforce attention because other stimuli or other activities become more competitive in this choice context, but this in itself does not settle the problem. One can always suppose that the stimuli get boring because they are too simplistic, because the processing demands are insufficient (Creighton, 1984), or because only the less advanced infants can be satisfied with the information coming from 2 × 2 checkerboards (DeLoache, Rissman, & Cohen, 1978). We always come back to the implicit demand made by researchers that babies "process the information" contained in a stimulus and, in corollary fashion, to the idea that the more information there is, the longer it takes to process and hence the longer the time infants need to attend to the stimulus. Whenever this association is not borne out by the facts, it is claimed that the information cannot be processed at a given age, or is too easy at another (Cohen, 1988), or that the infants show depressed attention (Stack et al., 1991). In short, a stimulus is looked at longer than another if it is more difficult or has more elements to be processed, and it loses the capacity to sustain attention after all its content has been processed, at which time the infant can then proceed to the next stimulus. Any alternative explanation, such as the reinforcement value the stimulus has for the infant in the particular context, must, therefore, also appeal to information processing (Cohen, 1988).

THE IMPLEMENTATION OF A FUNCTIONAL ANALYSIS

A functional explanation of infant attention is not devoid of criticisms. One concerns the circularity that is attributed to the approach: Whatever attracts and maintains the infant's attention the most is the most reinforcing (Cohen, 1988). A second refers to the difficulty, if not the impossibility, of empirically testing the model's propositions. How can we increase the reinforcement value of a stimulus without simultaneously increasing the number of elements to be processed? At this level, each of the competing models runs into what appears to be a tautology in its capacity to explain the capture and maintenance of attention. Following Lécuyer's (1989, p. 112) demonstration, for the information processing model, a complex stimulus maintains the infant's attention longer because it contains a greater quantity of information to be processed; according to a two-process model, this is because the complex stimulus, by virtue of its own physical characteristics (and those of the infant) is more potent in arousing the infant's interest; and, following the functional approach, this is because the stimulus has a greater reinforcement value. To break out of this vicious circle, it is necessary to show how these explanations differ, other than by the labels they attach to the underlying construct. In other words, a stimulus with a high value for reinforcing attention has to be better characterized than simply by the fact that it is looked at longer; it must be described as something that requires more processing time because it is more complex.

Even though the explanations of complexity in terms of the contrast sensitivity function of a spatial frequency analysis (cf. Banks & Salapatek, 1983), the quantity of information to be processed (Bornstein, 1988), or the reinforcement value (Pomerleau & Malcuit, 1983) sometimes refer to the same reality, they differ as to the factors they invoke. Other things being equal, one can enhance or lower the reinforcement value of a stimulus for maintaining attention within a given context by changing the number of information elements to be processed on a particular physical dimension (e.g., the number of squares on a checker-board). In the first place, the relationship between the level of stimulus complexity thus defined and its capacity to capture attention and sustain infants' visual exploration is not linear (Kaplan et al., 1990). Secondly, it has been demonstrated that certain stimulus characteristics can elicit and sustain more visual activity than others because of physical features of the stimulus, as such, and because of their interactions with the infant's visual system (Banks & Salapatek, 1983). Hence, the reinforcement value of a stimulus (in the sense of its intrinsic capacity to attract and maintain looking behavior) does not *necessarily* have to be explained in terms of a schemata-comparator model. At this first level of analysis of the intrinsic characteristics of stimuli, it is therefore possible to define the impact of a given stimulus on the measured parameters of infant attention independently of the quantity of information to be processed. It is not sufficient to look only at stimulus characteristics and their match with the infant's sensory systems to explain why the stimulus is a good elicitor and reinforcer of attention. Within this context, one should also consider the functional relation the stimulus has to the infant, depending on its particular valence, which is determined by the task requirements and acquired through the infant's previous experiences. In this sense, because it makes reference to the significance or value of events derived from experience (and, thus, the formation of representations and the contribution of memory processes), the functional approach cannot be seen as basically antinomical to a cognitivist approach to attention. An experimental demonstration of the relevance of a functional model would consist in showing that an identical stimulus—defined by an identical number of elements to be treated and having a stable biological valence—may differ in its capacity to capture and retain attention, depending on the functional values it acquires through the demands and constraints inherent in the context and following the experience of the infants. This is what we attempted to do in two recent studies.

In the first study (Malcuit, Bastien, & Pomerleau, in preparation) using 4-month-old infants, we were interested in the process by which attention is triggered and in its differential habituation, depending on the functions of the eliciting stimulus. In the classic visual attention studies, after the infant's gaze is focused on a luminous target, a stimulus is projected peripherally. This produces an orienting response in the direction of the stimulus (the attention-getting dimension). Having oriented his or her receptors toward the stimulus, the infant is now in front of a picture that may be more or less attractive to explore (attention-holding dimension). With repetition, the eliciting stimulus comes to have confounded functions. First, it may preserve its initial function of unconditional orienting trigger. A stimulus lighting up all of a sudden, within a context where there are few stimuli competing for attention, may maintain for a certain time its capacity to elicit visual orientation in its direction. Second, it acquires the function of a discriminative stimulus. The event seen in the periphery comes to signal that, if one turns in its direction, there is something to be looked at. Finally, the stimulus has a synchronous reinforcement function on looking activity. In an infant-control procedure, the same stimulus is used for triggering head turns, and for signaling and reinforcing visual exploration. As pointed out by Lécuyer (1988), the event can also inform the baby that he or she has mastered the task. As the baby turns his or her head toward and away from the stimuli, slides appear and disappear. Although we consider this operant repetitive game very plausible, our focus is on the reinforcement value of the *maintenance* of attention within each trial. At different successive moments, the same stimulus fulfills three functions: eliciting orientation, signaling the possibility of looking at a visual pattern, and reinforcing its exploration. These three functions are confounded in the usual procedure, and it was our aim to separate them.

To this end, we submitted 48 four-month-old infants to three experimental conditions. In the first, the visual stimulus had only a triggering function: a stimulus of short duration (2 sec) was presented. Half the infants saw a 4 × 4, the other half an 8 × 8 checkerboard. In the second condition, one or the other checkerboard was presented and continued to be visible as long as the infant looked at it. In this infant-control condition, the stimulus fulfilled the eliciting, signaling, and reinforcing functions. In the third condition, one or the other checkerboard was presented for 2 sec; then, visible only after the first orientation toward it, another attractive stimulus (an animated cartoon) was projected in a more peripheral location for as long as the infant looked at it. In this condition, the checkerboard had an eliciting and a signaling function; the event that reinforced the maintenance of attention was different.

We found that when the eliciting function was isolated, the orienting response gradually became habituated. In the first condition, the percentage of infants who turned their heads in response to the stimulus decreased over the 12 presentations, and was significantly lower than that of infants in the other conditions. Infants in the third condition showed even more orienting than those in the second condition, although the stimulus was of short duration (as in the first condition) rather than continuous (as in the second). Moreover, only in this third condition, where the function of signaling an interesting event was present, did we find an increase of orientations over successive presentations. The 8 × 8 checkerboard (considered more complex) elicited a higher percentage of orienting responses than did the 4 × 4 checkerboard for infants in the first two conditions, but not for those in the third. The functional value of signaling appears more important than its complexity in a situation where one or the other type of stimulus signals the opportunity to observe an attention-maintaining event. There was no decrease in the duration of looking at the animated cartoon over trials, confirming its high reinforcement value. The complexity and functional value of the stimulus induced other interesting effects when, after 12 habituation trials, we presented a novel stimulus (attention recovery) and reintroduced the first stimulus afterward (dishabituation). In the first two conditions only, we found the complexity effect. The percentage of infants orienting to the novel stimulus increased from the final two habituation trials when the novel stimulus was the 8 × 8 checkerboard, but decreased in the case of a change from the 8 × 8 to the 4 × 4 checkerboard. Conversely, the effect of dishabituation was more marked with the return of the more complex stimulus than the inverse. The impact of complexity was stronger than the impact of novelty, and the effect of immediate contrast appeared more important than the effect of sensitization. None of these effects is seen in the third condition. There there was no differential effect of habituation, of response to novelty nor of dishabituation as a function of stimulus complexity. The percentage of orienting responses remained uniformly high regardless of the complexity level of the stimulus.

We also computed the latency of head turning from the onset of stimulation to the moment when the infant's gaze reached the checkerboard (or its location, when the stimulus had already disappeared). Only the latencies of the third group showed a decrease over trials. The relation between complexity and speed of responding appeared in those infants for whom the eliciting-signalizing stimulus was the same as the reinforcing stimulus. In this condition of the infant-control procedure, the latencies were longer for the 4 × 4 as compared to the 8 × 8 checkerboard, but they remained uniformly rapid when both checkerboards elicited and signaled the occasion to look at a more interesting stimulation, as in the third condition. Hence, the affirmation that pattern complexity has an effect on attention-getting (Cohen, DeLoache, & Rissman, 1975) needs to be qualified and made more precise. In contrast to the effect of complexity obtained for the orienting responses, no effect of this factor was noted on the maintenance of fixation for infants in the second condition. For both the simple and the complex stimuli, a decrease in looking time was observed over trials, but recovery of attention to novelty and dishabituation were found only in those infants who had received the 4 × 4 checkerboard during habituation. When they were presented with the 8 × 8 checkerboard, they increased their fixation times, which remained high when the 4 × 4 pattern was reintroduced in the dishabituation phase. None of this happened with the infants who had first seen the more complex pattern. It seems that it is a phenomenon of recovery of interest in visual exploration produced by an increase in complexity more than a phenomenon of response to novelty following schemata comparison.

In a second study (with C. Carpenter), which is still in progress, we have also varied the functional value of a visual stimulus (an 8 × 8 checkerboard). Our starting point was the two processes involved when infants pay attention to a stimulus: orienting their sensory apparatus toward the stimulus and looking at it. Attention can be elicited by a stimulus that appears suddenly, as in most habituation studies, or by a stimulus that is already present in the infants' sensory environment. In either case, it is by orienting their receptors focally on the stimulus that the stimulus may become the object of their attention. In order to separate the operant and respondent processes, one can imagine a condition in which the head turn effectively makes the stimulus appear. This operant may or may not be signaled. A discriminative stimulus can indicate the occasion for a head turn to be reinforced by the appearance of a stimulus. Such conditions make precise the role of operant and respondent variables in head-turning responses. The attending behavior used in this study is an operant process synchronously reinforced by an ecological stimulus. It is by assigning different values to this stimulus and by observing ensuing variations in the maintenance of attention that we can depart from competing explanations. We have thus created four conditions, to which we have assigned four groups of 16 four-month-old infants. Condition 1 is a classic infant-control procedure. There is one stimulus fulfilling the three functions of eliciting head turning, signaling the occasion of reinforcement, and synchronously reinforcing visual exploration. Condition 2 is a situation in which the stimulus is constantly present. There is no sudden eliciting stimulus; the stimulus has a discriminative and a synchronous reinforcing function. In Condition 3, the stimulus appears if and only if the infant turns his or her head toward an illuminated surface. There is no sudden eliciting stimulus, but there is a discriminative stimulus different from the reinforcing one. Condition 4 is a free-operant situation. The checkerboard appears if and only if the infant turns his or her head in the direction of a nonsignaled point in space. There is neither a sudden eliciting nor a discriminative stimulus.

Preliminary results indicate that a constantly present stimulus, without a sudden appearance, is looked at the least (i.e., it reinforces visual inspection for the shortest period). When it is the infants' behaviors that make the checkerboard appear, whether these operants are signaled or not, the peaks of fixation are of the longest durations, as are the mean looking times at each fixation. These two duration parameters attain values more than twice as high as those observed in the situation where the checkerboard is constantly present; those in the infant-control procedure occupy an intermediate position.

Each session lasted 4 minutes following the first visual fixation on the checkerboard. Dividing the session into three blocks of equal duration, we observed that, although the number of turns remained equal and relatively stable in the three blocks for Conditions 1 and 2, there was a linear increase across blocks for the two operant conditions. This is an indication of operant learning. Although the peaks and the mean durations in looking times decreased linearly over blocks of durations and blocks of trials among all groups, they were always superior in the two operant conditions.

Two observations follow from these results. First, the decrease in duration of attention parameters with repeated trials reflects the weakening of the checkerboard's reinforcement value on visual exploration. It may also be that they reflect habituation in the sense of the schemata-comparison model. The infants looked for briefer and briefer periods because there was less template construction work to be done. As revealed by the second observation, however, the durations of visual exploration vary according to the characteristics of the stimulus. A stimulus that appears suddenly as a consequence of a particular behavior seems to be more potent in sustaining attention than a stimulus that is always present or a stimulus whose sudden appearance triggers attention. There are intuitive reasons for expecting different amounts of attention to be triggered and sustained by contingent and noncontingent stimuli. One would expect more attention to be given to contingent stimuli. A contingent stimulus should produce more intense and habituation-resistant orienting behavior, which is then reduced once the infant has mastered the contingency (H. Papousek & M. Papousek, 1984). In contrast, Millar (1975), and Millar and Schaffer (1972) suggested that infants will more readily habituate to contingent stimuli because contingent stimuli become progressively redundant for them. Because these interpretations apply to data derived from different experimental contexts, it is difficult to make a clear-cut decision in favor of one or the other. Apparently, a baby may look at a stimulus contingent on a specific behavior more than at a stimulus already present in the context. When the experimental situation becomes a problem-solving task ("What makes this checkerboard appear all of a sudden?"), then the presentation of the checkerboard becomes a reinforcer of head turning, providing information about what actions are relevant to produce the stimulation, rather than being a reinforcer of sustained attention. We might then expect an increase in the rate of head turns and a decrease in the duration of looking. Under these conditions, the stimulus comes to confirm that the two events are interrelated, one being dependent upon the other, but the stimulus needs not be explored or processed further. There is still ample room left for studying differences in orienting and attending behaviors induced by stimuli whose functional value is experimentally manipulated. This is the direction to be taken by our research in the coming years.

CONCLUSION

The study of attention in infants seems to suffer from conceptual overextension. The triggering of attention by incoming stimuli and its waning with their repeated presentation, as well as the maintenance of attention on particular events and its termination with their persistent presentation, are all explained with reference to a single information-processing model of template construction and comparison, derived from Sokolov's theoretical model (1963). The same model is called on to explain the maintenance of visual exploration in 2- to 4-month-old infants and the visual exploration and tactile manipulation of objects in older infants, although the persistence of attention, as defined in these two types of experiments, is interpreted in opposite ways. By being too general, this model loses its explanatory power and cannot adequately cover the multiple dimensions of attention in the various contexts where it is elicited. We insist on the importance, for developmental psychology, of studying the habituation of orienting responses, that is, the process by which attention is triggered and becomes differentially habituated by repetitive presentation of stimuli whose value may vary from neutral to feedback functions. Exposure to new stimuli no doubt constitutes a considerable part of infants' experiences in their everyday life. Learning to continue to respond only to significant events, and to inhibit responding to nonimportant or neutral events, represents a cognitive ability that deserves to be analyzed more thoroughly.

On the other hand, the maintenance of attention on a continuously present stimulus is more adequately conceived as an operant behavior (visual exploration activity) synchronously reinforced by the event to which the infant attends. Some events are more potent than others in reinforcing the maintenance of visual attention alone or active exploration with hands and mouth, because of some of their properties and because of individual characteristics of the infants. Among the many properties of a stimulus, its processing load, as exemplified by the complexity continuum, may be one determining factor of sustained attention in certain contexts, but it is not the only factor in most contexts. Specific physical features of stimuli and their fit with infants' sensory systems also participate in the capture and maintenance of attention, but, most importantly, we need to take into consideration the significance or functional value of stimuli on infants' ongoing activity. By defining the task demands and the functional value of the various elements these tasks include, we may determine why a stimulus differentially maintains attention or is more habituation-resistant. These stimulus properties interact with infants' particular modes of behaving, which are not restricted to differential information-processing capacities. They can be interpreted, among other possibilities, as different ways to explore the environment due to past experience or individual predispositions, as infants' sensitivity to various settings, or as particular ways of entering into contact with novel events. Attention and habituation should be analyzed in terms of the functional significance of the context elements and of infants' characteristics.

ACKNOWLEDGMENTS

We gratefully acknowledge the support of research grants from the Natural Sciences and Engineering Research Council of Canada and from the Université du Québec à Montréal. We also wish to thank Helga Feider for her comments and assistance in the English version of this paper, and our graduate students, Christian Bastien, Christian Carpenter, Joane Normandeau, and Michelle Sala, for their stimulating contributions.

REFERENCES

Ackles, P. K., & Karrer, R. (1991). A critique of the Dannemiller and Banks (1983) neuronal fatigue (selective adaptation) hypothesis of young infant habituation. *Merrill–Palmer Quarterly, 37*, 325–334.

Banks, M. S., & Salapatek, P. (1983). Infant visual perception. In P. Mussen (Series Ed.) & M. M. Haith & J. J. Campos (Vol. Eds.), *Handbook of child psychology: Vol. 2. Infancy and developmental psychobiology* (4th ed., pp. 435–572). New York: Wiley.

Birns, B., Blank, M., Bridger, W. H., & Escalona, S. K. (1965). Behavioral inhibition in neonates produced by auditory stimuli. *Child Development, 36*, 639–645.

Bloom, K. (1990). Selectivity and early infant vocalization. In J. T. Enns (Ed.), *The development of attention: Research and theory* (pp. 121–136). Amsterdam: Elsevier Science Publishers.

Bornstein, M. H. (1988). Answers to three prominent questions about habituation. *European Bulletin of Cognitive Psychology, 8*, 531–538.

Bornstein, M. H., & Sigman, M. D. (1986). Continuity in mental development from infancy. *Child Development, 57*, 251–274.

Cohen, L. B. (1972). Attention-getting and attention-holding processes of infant visual preferences. *Child Development, 43*, 869–879.

Cohen, L. B. (1988). The relationship between infant habituation and infant information processing. *European Bulletin of Cognitive Psychology, 8*, 445–454.

Cohen, L. B., DeLoache, J. S., & Rissman, M. W. (1975). The effect of stimulus complexity on infant visual attention and habituation. *Child Development, 45*, 611–617.

Colombo, J., & Mitchell, D. W. (1990). Individual differences in early visual attention: Fixation time and information processing. In J. Colombo & J. Fagen (Eds.), *Individual differences in infancy: Reliability, stability, prediction* (pp. 193–227). Hillsdale, NJ: Lawrence Erlbaum Associates.

Creighton, D. E. (1984). Sex differences in the visual habituation of 4-, 6- and 8-month-old infants. *Infant Behavior and Development, 7*, 237–249.

Dannemiller, J., & Banks, M. (1983). Can selective adaptation account for early infant habituation? *Merrill-Palmer Quarterly, 29,* 151–158.

DeLoache, J. S., Rissman, M. W., & Cohen, L. B. (1978). An investigation of the attention-getting process in infants. *Infant Behavior and Development, 1,* 11–25.

Dunham, P. (1990). Temporal structure of stimulation maintains infant attention. In J. R. Enns (Ed.), *The development of attention: Research and theory* (pp. 67–85). Amsterdam: Elsevier Science Publishers.

Fagen, J. W., & Ohr, P. S. (1990). Individual differences in infant conditioning and memory. In J. Colombo & J. Fagen (Eds.), *Individual differences in infancy: Reliability, stability, prediction* (pp. 155–191). Hillsdale, NJ: Lawrence Erlbaum Associates.

Graham, F. K., & Clifton, R. K. (1966). Heart-rate change as a component of the orienting response. *Psychological Bulletin, 65,* 305–320.

Hayes, L. A., Ewy, R. D., & Watson, J. S. (1982). Attention as a predictor of learning in infants. *Journal of Experimental Child Psychology, 34,* 38–45.

Horowitz, F. D., Paden, L., Bhana, K., & Self, P. (1972). An infant control procedure for studying infant visual fixations. *Developmental Psychology, 7,* 90.

Julien, D., Pomerleau, A., Feider, H., & Malcuit, G. (1983). Temporal and content variations as determinants of infants' visual control of verbal stimulations. *Developmental Psychology, 19,* 366–374.

Kaplan, P. S., Werner, J. S., & Rudy, J. W. (1990). Habituation, sensitization, and infant visual attention. In C. Rovee-Collier & L. P. Lipsitt (Eds.), *Advances in infancy research (Vol. 6,* pp. 61–109). Norwood, NJ: Ablex.

Laplante, D., Zelazo, P. R., & Gauthier, S. (1989, April). *Normal, moderate and high-risk infant attention to sequential and static visual stimuli.* Paper presented at the meeting of the Society for Research in Child Development, Kansas City, MO.

Lécuyer, R. (1988). Please, infant, can you tell me exactly what you are doing during a habituation experiment? *European Bulletin of Cognitive Psychology, 8,* 476–480.

Lécuyer, R. (1989). *Bébés astronomes, bébés psychologues. L'intelligence de la première année* [Infants as astronomers, infants as psychologists: Intelligence in the first year of life]. Liège: Mardaga.

Malcuit, G., & Pomerleau, A. (1985). Le rythme cardiaque [The cardiac rhythm]. In P. M. Baudonnière (Ed.), *Étudier l'enfant de la naissance à 3 ans: Les grands courants méthodologiques actuels* (pp. 9–32). Paris: CNRS Editions.

Malcuit, G., Bastien, C., & Pomerleau, A. (in preparation). *Habituation of the orienting response to stimuli of different functional values in 4-month-old infants.*

Malcuit, G., Pomerleau, A., & Lamarre, G. (1988). Habituation, visual fixation and cognitive activity in infants: A critical analysis and attempt at a new formulation. *European Bulletin of Cognitive Psychology, 8,* 415–440.

Millar, W. S. (1975). Visual attention to contingent and non-contingent stimulation in six- and nine-month-old infants. *Psychological Research, 37,* 309–319.

Millar, W. S., & Schaffer, H. R. (1972). The influence of spatially displaced feedback on infant operant conditioning. *Journal of Experimental Child Psychology, 14,* 442–453.

Papousek, H., & Papousek, M. (1984). Learning and cognition in the everyday life of human infants. In J. S. Rosenblatt, C. Beer, M.-C. Busnel, & P. J. B. Slater (Eds.), *Advances in the study of behavior* (Vol. 14, pp. 27–61), New York: Academic Press.

Pomerleau, A., & Malcuit, G. (1980). Development of cardiac and behavioral responses to a three-dimensional toy stimulation in one- to six-month-old infants. *Child Development, 51,* 1187–1196.

Pomerleau, A., & Malcuit, G. (1983). *L'enfant et son environnement. Une étude fonctionnelle de la première enfance* [The infant and his environment. A functional analysis of the early infancy]. Brussels: Mardaga; Québec: Presses de l'Université du Québec.

Posner, M. I., & Boies, S. J. (1971). Components of attention. *Psychological Review, 78*, 391–408.

Posner, M. I., & Rothbart, M. K. (1981). The development of attentional mechanisms. In H. E. Howe & J. H. Flowers (Eds.), *Nebraska symposium on motivation* (pp. 1–52). Lincoln, NB: University of Nebraska Press.

Richards, J. E. (1989). Sustained visual attention in 8-week-old infants. *Infant Behavior and Development, 12*, 425–436.

Richelle, M. (1987). Les cognitivismes: Progrès, régression ou suicide de la psychologie [The cognitivisms: Progress, regression or a psychological suicide]. In M. Siguan (Ed.), *Comportement, cognition, conscience: La psychologie à la recherche de son objet* (pp. 181–199). Paris: Presses Universitaires de France.

Ruff, H. A. (1986). Components of attention during infants' manipulative exploration of objects. *Child Development, 57*, 105–114.

Ruff, H. A. (1990). Individual differences in sustained attention during infancy. In J. Colombo & J. Fagan (Eds.), *Individual differences in infancy: Reliability, stability, prediction* (pp. 247–270). Hillsdale, NJ: Lawrence Erlbaum Associates.

Ruff, H. A., Capozzoli, M., Dubiner, K., & Parrinello, R. (1990). A measure of vigilance in infancy. *Infant Behavior and Development, 13*, 1–20.

Sigman, M. (1988). Infant attention: What processes are measured? *European Bulletin of Cognitive Psychology, 8*, 512–516.

Sigman, M., Beckwith, L., Cohen, S. E., & Parmelee, A. H. (1989). Stability in the biosocial development of the child born preterm. In M. H. Bornstein & N. A. Krasnegor (Eds.), *Stability and continuity in mental development. Behavioral and biological perspectives* (pp. 29–42). Hillsdale, NJ: Lawrence Erlbaum Associates.

Sokolov, E. N. (1963). *Perception and the conditioned reflex.* New York: Macmillan.

Stack, D. M., Laplante, D., & Zelazo, P. R. (1991, August). *Four-month Down syndrome infants' attention to sequential visual stimuli.* Paper presented at the meeting of the American Psychological Association, San Francisco, CA.

Tarquinio, N., Zelazo, P. R., Gryspeerdt, D. M., & Allen, K. M. (1991). Generalization of neonatal habituation. *Infant Behavior and Development, 14*, 69–81.

Wachs, T. D., & Smitherman, C. H. (1985). Infant temperament and subject loss in a habituation procedure. *Child Development, 56*, 861–867.

Yarrow, L. J., McQuiston, S., MacTurk, R. H., McCarthy, M. E., Klein, R. P., & Vietze, P. M. (1983). Assessment of mastery motivation during the first year of life: Contemporaneous and cross-age relationships. *Developmental Psychology, 19*, 159–171.

Zelazo, P. R. (1989). Infant–toddler information processing and the development of expressive ability. In P. R. Zelazo & R. G. Barr (Eds.), *Challenges to developmental paradigms: Implications for theory, assessment and treatment* (pp. 93–122). Hillsdale, NJ: Lawrence Erlbaum Associates.

Zelazo, P. R., & Kearsley, R. B. (1982). Memory formation for visual sequences: Evidence for increased speed of processing with age [Abstract]. *Infant Behavior and Development, 5* (Special issue), 263.

5 How Should Intelligence Be Characterized in the Infant?

Roger Lécuyer
Arlette Streri
Université René Descartes

The historical importance of tests in the American psychology of infant intelligence has been highlighted in an excellent way in a volume edited by Michael Lewis (1976/1983). Early American infant psychology was marked by the influence of Arnold Gesell, who, 20 years after Alfred Binet, was the first to produce an adaptation of Binet-type tests to the very special case of infants. In French-language psychology, during this same period, the Swiss Jean Piaget was becoming the most influent psychologist and the main reference for the description of the first steps of human intelligence. Piaget worked in Binet's laboratory, but, in the American empiricist tradition, Gesell was much more the true heir of Binet than the rationalist Piaget.

In the United States, Gesell and his successors studied and defined intelligence through tests. Their careful description of infants' development, however, produced a body of knowledge about infants that led to a dead end for both general and specific reasons. Psychology based on tests was used to investigate the mechanisms of intelligence from the beginning of the 20th century (and somewhat later for infant tests), but it has lost most of it heuristic value today. This general reason is linked to specific reasons concerning the purpose of infants' tests and their failure to predict later intelligence. This lack of predictive power was known as early as the 1930s (Bayley, 1933, 1949) and prompted test authors to take contradictory stances. Although they did not claim that their tests were measures of intelligence, both research on the predictivity of tests or items and the development of new tests were actively pursued. Test authors took the position that infant intelligence developed discontinuously, and that the acquisition of language was the watershed that hindered predictions of later intelligence from infant "intelligence." Nevertheless McCall (1981) entitled a paper on the

75

topic "Early predictors of later IQ: The search continues." Since the 1960s, American research on cognitive psychology in the infant has not focused primarily on infant intelligence as measured by tests, but there is a continuous link between the traditional orientations in intelligence measurement and the use of new techniques for the same purpose, between Bayley and the Fagan test of infant intelligence.

French-language psychology was long dominated by a feeling shared by most of Piaget's disciples, and probably by Piaget himself, that their psychology, because it was less empirical and more theoretical than American psychology, was much more accurate, in particular in the area of infant cognitive development. In retrospect, there is a striking contrast between most publications on infants in the 1930s and Piaget's *La naissance de l'intelligence chez l'enfant* (The origins of intelligence in childhood), which came out in 1936. Whatever the relative contribution of non-Piagetian psychology (from Gesell, and from Wallon in France), Piaget truly established the framework for infant development in French-language psychology for at least 40 years. All work in infant development was to be interpreted within the Piagetian system of stages and mechanisms of development.

Nevertheless, beyond or despite differences in approaches and theoretical underpinnings, Europe and the United States shared some common beliefs on infant intelligence. The most obvious was the importance of sensorimotor development and sensorimotricity in infant cognitive functions. What prompted this consensus? The answer is essentially methodological. Test builders and stage builders alike could only observe what they could observe in the infant, and their observations drew, necessarily, on infant motor activity. Motor activity was the sole part of the test battery that could be measured objectively from the first months, and the term "sensorimotor intelligence" reflects an assessment of cognitive development through motor performance. Activity plays a crucial role in Piaget's theory of learning and the development of intelligence. Activity must produce a transformation of the environment to be efficient. Thus, motor activity is the precondition for acquisition of the basic concepts that structure the infant's cognitive world. For Piaget, the infant is a young scientist who must produce variations in the world to understand it. Hence, the portrait of the infant as sketched by both these psychologies is paradoxical, because the infant is described as, and in fact is, an immature organism whose motor performance is very poor, whose intelligence is indeed "sensorimotor". The infant must rely on this inefficient system to understand its world. The consequence is that most of the infant's basic cognitive abilities will be acquired gradually and will only be consolidated at the end of the sensorimotor period, at the end of the second year.

The revolution in infant cognitive psychology was to take place in the United States in the early 1960s. Rather than being based on a new theoretical approach to infant intelligence, the innovation was Fantz's new method of studying infant perception. Fantz's first experiments (1958, 1961, 1963) had modest goals, and were devised to investigate figure preferences in young infants. The method was very powerful, and enhancements of his technique led rapidly to the familiarization–novelty preference method and then to the habituation–dishabituation paradigm. Operant conditioning and high-amplitude sucking measures were also decisive in some domains. The word "revolution" is not too strong here, because these new methods immediately expanded the limited knowledge of infant perception of that time and rapidly modified conceptions of *infant cognition,* the term that was becoming more frequent at time. At the same time, the concept of *intelligence* was used preferentially to refer to "what is tested."

There was rapid acceptance, in both the United States and the United Kingdom, (where Bower's work was fundamental: see Bower, 1974/1982), of these new data, which convinced even the most skeptical. In French-language developmental psychology, however, there was much more reticence, because most of the new "data" contradicted Piaget's theory, and did not fit into the Piagetian framework. This led to a period of complete rejection, followed by a new period that has lasted up to the present day. Two totally incompatible positions have emerged: One defends the infant's precocious cognitive competencies, as revealed by recent evidence, whereas the other views the development of infant intelligence within the framework of Piagetian theory. After the extended era when this theory was the most heuristic in infant cognitive psychology, and perhaps in psychology as a whole, it became a barrier to understanding in infant cognition.

No overview of current evidence for infant intelligence is presented here (see Lécuyer, 1989). We simply examine the bases of this methodological revolution and its main consequences as regards the general picture we currently have of infant intelligence. First, this shift can be characterized by the changeover from observation to experimentation. This is obviously true, but is not to the point. The more fundamental difference between current and previous methods is that existing methods practically never draw on infant motor activity, and when motor activity is the observed response, it is a mature motor response.

Another major characteristic of current experimental techniques is that most tap perceptual activities. This was true for Fantz's methods, and is still the case for most current studies. Cognitive activity is inferred from perceptive activity. Of course, cognitive activity cannot be directly observed and is always inferred, but what is instructive in the history of infant studies is that perceptual activities were not originally seen as a means of accessing cognitive functioning. Rather, despite their aim to merely explore perceptual activities *per se,* early studies rapidly shifted to descriptions of intelligent activities. This shift was motivated by the fact that, in the first months of life, infants must organize the first level of information processing, that is, information intake. The combination of sensory immaturity and the invasion of sensory information makes perception a difficult cognitive problem. Because of innate perceptual capacities, and the rapid development of their efficiency, infants can organize their environment, which is closely tied to perception. This tight and reciprocal relation between perception and cognition is the assumption we explore through two examples: intermodal perception, which illustrates perceptual relations involving a cognitive activity, and categorization, which is an example of a cognitive activity that is highly influenced by its perceptual context.

INTERMODAL PERCEPTION AND INTELLIGENCE IN INFANCY

The multimodal perception of an object is the ability to perceive different information extracted by the sensory modes in a unified manner in order to conceive the object as a unitary and stable entity in time and space. This ability is remarkable, because properties of objects, such as shape and texture, are specified in strikingly different ways in the two modalities, and other properties, such as color, weight, and temperature, are specific to one modality. Intermodal perception is the complex ability to abstract and exchange information between different modes. What are the origins of this capacity? A series of studies was addressed to this question for a brief period of time.

Since the 1940s, intermodal perception has been evidenced in infants aged 6 months and older (Bryant, Jones, Claxton, & Perkins, 1972; Bushnell, 1982; Ruff & Kohler, 1978; see Rose & Ruff, 1987 and Streri, 1993, for reviews). However, these studies do not completely address the old philosophical issue of unity or separation of the sensory modes at birth. In 6-month-old infants, coordination between vision and prehension is well established. Infants reach for seen objects and transport handled objects to view. Intermodal transfer, thus, might be due to the infant's new ability to explore an object bimodally and the coordination of schemas, as described by Piaget (1936). Two studies (Gibson & Walker, 1984; Meltzoff & Borton, 1979), however, have shown that 1-month-old infants recognize visually an object that they have previously explored orally without seeing it. Transfer depended on perception of object texture (Meltzoff & Borton, 1979) and substance (Gibson & Walker, 1984). To our knowledge, there have been no studies on intermodal transfer in the newborn, but these latter two studies suggest that an amodal perception exists in very young infants, as postulated by Gibson (1969).

In all these studies, two questions remain unanswered. First, although intermodal transfer has been shown to exist in 1-month-old infants from orality to vision, does it exist from manual to visual exploration in very young infants? The manual system has two remarkable functions (Hatwell, 1986): a perceptual function and a motor function. When serving the perceptual function, the hand abstracts and processes information about object properties. When serving the motor function, the hand transports objects, makes tools, destroys, or constructs.

The two functions of the hand do not appear at the same age in infants. Studies have demonstrated that the perceptual function of the hand is present in neonates (Rochat, 1987) and in 2-month-olds (Streri, 1987). This ability improves in the older infants (see Streri, 1993, for a review). The motor function seems to appear later, in about 4–5-month-old infants, when the coordination between vision and prehension is becoming established. Second, in all studies, intermodal transfer has been shown from touch to vision, but transfer from vision to touch has not been studied. If amodal perception exists in very young infants, transfer between sensory modes should be expected in both directions. Our studies attempted to answer these two questions. We investigated intermodal transfer from touch to vision and from vision to touch in 2- and 4-month-old infants, before there is coordination between vision and prehension.

Perception of Object Properties and Intermodal Transfer: An Intelligent Ability?

The process of intermodal transfer, from vision to touch or from touch to vision, usually takes place in two phases: a familiarization phase in the first modality and a test phase in the second modality. This procedure is complex, and subjects need to process information in four steps:

1. Information is extracted and processed in the first modality.
2. This information is retained.
3. New information is processed in the second modality.
4. After a comparison of the two forms of information, there should be recognition.

Are young infants able to accomplish this?

In two studies (Streri, 1987; Streri & Milhet, 1988), we investigated amodal perception in 2-month-old infants by testing intermodal transfer, both from touch to vision and from vision to touch. In these experiments, infants tactually or visually explored several small, simple wooden objects, such as a ring versus a disk, a square versus a square with a hole, and a flower versus a star. Two methods were used: an habituation procedure and a matching procedure. Habituation and discrimination between objects were shown in 2-month-old infants in both the visual and the haptic modes (Streri, 1987). Thus, the infants were able to handle and manipulate the objects without visual control and to discriminate different shapes of objects.

Intermodal transfer has been observed in these 2-month-old infants from touch to vision, but not from vision to touch (Streri, 1987; Streri & Milhet, 1988). One possible explanation for this asymmetry can be found in the complexity and elaborateness of the representation that young infants construct when they explore objects with their hands and when they look at objects: Visually derived representations of objects may be more elaborate and more accurate than tactually derived representations. At 2 months, the visual system is biologically more developed than the tactual system (Banks & Salapatek, 1983; Vurpillot, 1972). Moreover, the motor control of the hand appears to be less efficient at processing information because of the predominant grasping reflex (Twitchell, 1970).

Studies of visual perception in infants have provided evidence that the mechanisms of object perception take a representation of the three-dimensional (3D) surface layout as input and do not operate on lower level representations of retinal elements and relations (Kellman, Gleitman, & Spelke, 1987; Kellman, Spelke, & Short, 1986; Spelke, 1990). No similar data exist on tactual perception in infancy. Do infants operate on lower level representations of tactually explored objects? If such is the case, then the lack of reversible transfer might be explained in the following manner. Visually derived representations of objects are elaborate and three-dimensional, whereas tactually derived representations of objects are simpler and of lower dimensionality, perhaps a two-dimensional (2D) sketch (see Marr, 1982). Moreover, it may be more difficult to recognize the lower level components of a high-level representation than it is to recognize the high-level structure implicit in a lower level representation, because normal perceptual processing proceeds in the latter direction, from lower to higher levels (see Marr, 1982; Pinker, 1984). A series of studies (Streri & Molina, 1994) investigated this hypothesis by simplifying and reducing the dimensionality of the information presented to the visual mode. In these experiments, infants were presented 3D objects tactually, and were presented 2D silhouettes visually. Only object contours and surfaces were specified in the silhouette pictures. We investigated intermodal transfer from tactual solid objects to their visual pictures and from vision to touch with the same displays. These experiments provided strong evidence for an intermodal transfer from solid objects to their silhouettes and from silhouettes of objects to the objects themselves. Thus, for infants, the visual perception of a 2D silhouette apparently corresponds to a tactual perception of a solid object, whereas the visual perception of a solid object does not appear to correspond to a tactual perception of the same object. This finding was predicted by the levels of processing hypothesis but does not support the hypothesis of prerequisite amodal perception.

Other studies of 4–5-month-old infants (Streri & Pêcheux, 1986) have investigated intermodal transfer from touch to vision and from vision to touch. The findings provided evidence for transfer from vision to touch but not from touch to vision. Thus, the visual perception of a solid object appears to correspond to a tactual perception of the same object 2 months later than in Streri's (1987) experiments. The hypothesis that the tactual perception of an object does not correspond to the visual perception of the same object is an unconvincing account of the lack of transfer from touch to vision. An alternative explanation is that, at the start of coordination between prehension and vision, the motor function of the hand is predominant at 4–5 months and could interfere with the perceptual function. These hypotheses were investigated in two experiments conducted in the tactual mode without visual control (Streri, 1993; Streri & Pineau, 1988). In the first experiment, which employed a tactual habituation procedure, 5-month-old infants were able to discriminate between a sphere and a cube. In the second experiment, infants were presented with a display composed of a music box with a crank handle. Either the sphere or the cube was glued to the handle. In the tactual familiarization phase, infants had to turn the crank handle for 80 seconds. Subsequently, in the tactual test phase, infants were presented with the sphere and the cube. The results showed no discrimination between the two object shapes. Thus, movement constrained by the display plays a major role in information intake during fine manipulation of object shapes.

Most studies have investigated intermodal transfer of object shape, but sometimes objects are complex and are composed of several components. Are infants able to tactually detect these different component parts of an object and recognize these parts visually? Pineau and Streri (1990) designed an experiment to test these issues in 4-month-old infants. The object was composed of three parts: a diamond and two rings. The diamond was located either in the middle, between the two rings, or on the right or left side. The infants were presented with these displays in a tactual intramodal transfer and in an intermodal transfer situation from touch to vision. The findings showed that infants discriminated the different locations of the diamond tactually and that there was intermodal transfer of these locations. Thus, 4-month-old infants are able to detect small differences in an object tactually and to recognize them in a visual display.

Few studies have investigated intermodal transfer of specific information to one modality (Gibson & Walker, 1984). We recently investigated intermodal transfer of the difference between the weights of two objects (Milhet & Streri, 1991). In this study, 2- and 4-month-old infants were presented with two objects, one in each hand. The objects were identical in shape and texture, but had either the same weight or different weights. After tactual habituation with a display, the infants were visually presented with two displays in alternation. The visual objects were the same as the tactual objects. When the weights were equal, the infants were presented with a balance system in equilibrium; when the weights were different, the infants were presented with an unbalanced display, in which the heavier object was lower than the lighter one (see Fig. 5.1). The data indicate that the 2- and 4-month-old infants were able to discriminate between the different displays and to recognize visually the display corresponding to the one they had previously felt. Thus, young infants are able to establish a relationship between the tactual displays presented in the habituation phase and the visual displays presented in the test phase. This ability is remarkable, because tactual

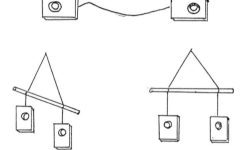

FIG. 5.1. Tactual and visual displays for experiments on haptic exploration of objects weights and intermodal transfer (from Milhet & Streri, 1991).

and visual information are obviously different. This finding suggests that weakly equal or different pressures on the two hands are sufficient for detecting information about object weight and for transfering this information visually.

Overall, these studies on intermodal transfer provide strong evidence that very young infants are able to process different information about objects, such as shape, texture, small component parts of an object, and weight, in the four steps described earlier. These findings suggest that object properties in very young infants are perceived by a relatively central mechanism (Spelke, 1990). Moreover, young infants are able to establish a relationship between a tactual event and a visual event: This behavior also reveals the existence of intelligence mechanisms that are independent of perception. All these studies investigated felt and seen information of the surface layout. What happens when objects are partly occluded?

Apprehending Objects by Touch

Research on object perception in infancy began with studies of visual perception of partly occluded objects (Kellman & Spelke, 1983). Like adults, 4-month-old infants were found to perceive a center-occluded object as a complete and continuous unit if the visible surfaces of the object moved together in depth, vertically or laterally. Infants did not perceive the complete object when visible surfaces were stationary. These studies provided evidence that motion specifies object unity to infants, but that static configurational properties do not.

A series of studies (Streri & Spelke, 1988, 1989) dealt with object perception in the tactual mode. The experiments investigated whether infants perceive the unity and boundaries of objects under the same conditions when they feel objects as when they see them. Four-month-old infants held two spatially separated rings, one in each hand, under a cloth that blocked their view of the rings and of the space between them. In different conditions, the rings could either be moved rigidly together (as they were connected to each other by a rod) or could be moved independently (as they were connected by elastic). The infants were found to perceive the two moved-together rings as a single unit and the two moved-independently rings as two distinct objects. Perception was unaffected by the configurational properties of the ring displays.

All these findings suggest that perceiving objects may be more closely linked to intelligence or thinking about the physical world than to perceiving the immediate environment (Spelke, 1990).

CATEGORIZATION AS AN INTELLIGENT ACTIVITY

Categorization, which is defined as the organization or structuration of knowledge, may be regarded as the prototype for intelligent activity. The issue that arises immediately, however, is that of level, and the relations between a given level and the age at which infants and children master a category or a system of categories.

In the infant, the most precocious examples of what had been called "categorization" concern vowel sounds (Eimas, Siqueland, Jusczyk, & Vigorto, 1971) and colors (Bornstein, 1981, 1983). There is a commonality between these two examples: categorization consists of processing as discontinuous a continuously varying physical stimulus. Is the concept of "categorization" appropriate to this form of digitalization? This mode of processing may, in fact, be sensorial, implying that no cognitive construction is involved. The second level of categorization is illustrated by experiments of Bomba and Siqueland (1983) and Quinn (1987). Infants were familiarized with variations on a regular shape, which was never presented. They were then tested with that shape or a new variation of it, as opposed to a different shape or a variation of a new figure. Three-month-olds proved to be able to differentiate the new shape from variations on the old one. This is a genuine example of categorization, because the stimuli were differentiated, and an organization of shared dimensions and differences between stimuli was required to produce responses, as shown by the authors' data. However, the categorization capacity evidenced is limited in that stimuli were simple geometric shapes (square, triangle, diamond) composed of 12 black dots. The basic shape, considered to be the prototype, is the simplest to code in each category, and, above all, there was little irrelevant information.

In older infants—in particular, 10-month-olds who have been tested more frequently—data indicate that infants at this age can categorize abstract properties, such as faces or features represented in photographs and even in drawings (Strauss, 1979; Strauss & Curtiss, 1981, 1984). In the case of Fagan's (1976, 1979) experiments, the categories tested and the gender of the person whose photograph was presented have necessarily been learned before the experiment, because infants see male and female faces in ordinary environments. What was tested was the existence of a prior category. In Strauss's (1979) figures, however, there is some doubt as to what had been learned prior to or in the situation. Thus, what is usually tested in the 10-month-old infants is a complex capacity to organize their environment, requiring memorized knowledge and the ability to relate this knowledge and the figures presented. This is not the case in younger infants. In most of the experiments, what is evidenced is the capacity to learn a new category. Thus, the capacities of 6-month-olds differ considerably from those observed in younger and older infants. For this reason, we decided to study infants' categorization capacities (a) with simpler pictures than drawings of faces, which necessarily imply a representation of the presented face (Kestenbaum & Nelson, 1990), and (b) in a context where both relevant and irrelevant information was presented and where learning a category implied constructing the relations between the different features of the stimuli presented.

In one series of experiments (Lécuyer & Poirier, in press) the category to learn was a figure composed of four elements (see Fig. 5.2a). Each of the elements had three colors. The arrangement of the elements was modified across category stimuli and in some experiments, the shape of the elements or surface differed as well (see Fig. 5.2b). An habituation with an infant control procedure was used. After habituation, infants were presented with two series of tests alternating a new category picture and a picture out of the category. Three indices were used to

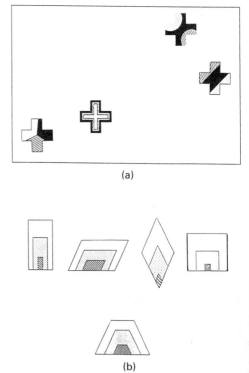

(a)

FIG. 5.2. Examples of figures used to test a categorization capacity based on (a) number of elements (from Lécuyer & Poirier, in press), and on (b) figure cuts (from Lécuyer, 1991).

(b)

measure categorization: (a) the difference in looking times between the last habituation trials and the out-of-category stimulus (novelty reaction), (b) the difference between the stimuli in and out of category during the test, and (c) the difference in looking durations between the last habituation trials and the test stimulus in category. In three conditions, categorization was obtained in 3- and 5-month-old infants. No novelty reaction was observed for a figure composed of three elements. Further, infants' fixation durations differed between these two figures. When the shape of the elements was held constant during the familiarization phase (four circles), a novelty reaction was also observed for new elements (four ovals). Thus, young infants are apparently able to code two different properties of a category and to discriminate noncategory members on the basis of two features of the category (number and shape of elements) that are taken into account simultaneously.

In a second series of experiments (Lécuyer, 1991), the category stimuli presented were simple geometric figures (square, rectangle, parallelogram, diamond). Each figure was composed of three identically shaped component figures of decreasing size and differing color. These three figures were arranged concentrically around the base of the largest component. After familiarization, two test figures were presented in alternation: the category figure (a trapezoid) and a modified version of the first stimulus of the series. In one experiment, it was rotated 180° so that the cuts were on the top; in another experiment, the three component configurations were moved to become concentric about the center of the largest component. In both cases, categorization was observed. In the two series of experiments, it is the structure of the figures that appears to be crucial. When the component figures were moved from the edge to the center of the main figure, categorization appeared to be more difficult than when they were moved from the bottom to the top. Thus, abstraction activity is tightly connected to perceptual activity.

These experiments suggest that 3- to 5-month-olds have a capacity to abstract common properties in a series of multi-dimensional stimuli, when some of the features presented are irrelevant. This is of major importance because out of the laboratory, what infants have to categorize is always composed of relevant and irrelevant features. This same capacity is also involved in intermodal transfer situations where infants must select relevant information and eliminate irrelevant ones. Thus, infants demonstrate a capacity of organization of their environment that can be termed intelligent.

INTELLIGENCE IN THE INFANT: NEW PERSPECTIVES

Given the data outlined here and our interpretation of them, how can intelligence in the infant best be characterized? One response to this question comes from the relations between perception and cognitive activities. Intermodal relations were initially viewed as confusion between information processing from different sensory modes. The concept of amodal perception (Gibson, 1969) draws on this assumption. This approach of intermodality may appear to be parsimonious, but the asymmetries of transfer observed in the 2- and 5-month-olds seriously challenge this hypothesis, because performances are not equivalent. Rather, intermodal perception should be viewed as a relation between two representations: the visually and tactually derived representations of objects. From this point of view, it is an intelligent activity.

The issue is reversed for categorization. Categorization has always been seen as an intelligent activity, and the real question is to define what constitutes categorization in infants' responses. In other words, what criteria successfully differentiate a categorization response from one that is not? Unfortunately, these criteria are difficult to define. Categorization develops continuously, and the premises of categorization probably emerge early in infancy, because categorization is linked to perceptual organization. Although no clear line can be drawn between before and after the acquisition of an organized capacity, unambiguous conditions can be presented to infants. The data from studies of this type demonstrate an early intelligent organizational activity in infants.

Let us return to our considerations on early theories of intelligence, in particular, Piagetian theory. The evidence presented here conflicts with the assumption that intelligent behavior emerges as the result of the acquisition of coordination between vision and prehension and the possibilities for transformation of the environment they provide to the infant. Are intermodal transfer and categorization (among other capacities) innate competencies? Does intelligence appear in the first months of life? And what exactly is innate versus developing during this period? There are no simple answers to these questions, but it is obvious now that the nativist point of view was overextended. As Piaget, as well as others, argued, perception is an active process, and as an activity can be a powerful way to learn about the environment without producing any transformation on it. Piaget was probably right in seeing the infant as a scientist, but the infant becomes one earlier than Piaget supposed. Before being an experimental scientist, the infant is an observational scientist. As long as he or she is unable to transform the object he or she wants to study, the infant observes the transformation produced in and by the environment.

Consider the case of object permanence and identity. From the first days of life, infants are confronted with a fascinating puzzle. Various events always appear at the same time or successively, but always in the same order. If you cry, something moves in your direction. It is large and produces noises. After that, you can see a jerky object (the caretaker) producing and modulating the same kind of sounds. The smell is the same, too, and you feel you are being touched on both sides. Then your entirely immobile visual field changes quickly and you feel you have been moved. You receive a flow of sensation from all modalities.

As you move, things disappear behind others, but sometimes appear again. Because this experience is repetitive, a question comes to your mind: Maybe the big thing that comes to you, the moving scene that comes afterward, these smells, these sounds, these touching sensations, these movements that cause rapid changes in the world, is not only the result of your crying, but the result of a unique (but immensely powerful) object. A daring hypothesis, but one that is borne out by everyday life.

Infants' everyday lives provide them with opportunities to realize that an object may disappear partially or completely and appear again, simply by being moved and to see spatial relations between objects. They have chances to feel the permanence of this cognitively (and affectively) interesting object, too, from caregivers who are the source of most of the changes infants experience. Studies about mothering demonstrate that adults' attitudes and behavior are organized in such a way that they provide the infant with the best opportunities to observe regularities in changes in their environment and, hence, provide redundancy in the information the infants can process.

Caregivers are not only objects to perceive and a source of variations in the environment, but are also the first object on which and by which infants can be efficient and produce a transformation of the environment. Piaget produced an arbitrary effect after one of his infants was pulling a ribbon. When the infant pulled the ribbon again, Piaget wrote that the infant had a magico-phenomenist view of causality (Piaget, 1937); but by doing that, Piaget was doing exactly what parents do when they play with infants. He was not studying magico-phenomenist causality, but allowing infants to have an impact on their environment. A causality conception is realistic if the caregiver is included in the causality chain. When do infants conceive of this chain? Parents give them this opportunity very early on.

CONCLUSION

The consequences of the series of studies described in this chapter can be summarized very simply: First, the main difference between old and new conceptions of infant intelligence lies in the role of sensorimotricity. It is a commonplace to stress human infant immaturity, but this immaturity is much more motor than sensory and cognitive. Second, built-in mechanisms have been put forward too quickly to explain infants' early performance: The groundwork for a new constructivism has been laid by recent data that demonstrate that there is improvement in cognitive performance in the first months of life. Furthermore, this new constructivism is founded on an epistemology that assigns less importance to activity than Piagetian theory did and more to observation and perhaps contemplation. In addition, the role and impact of the upbringing given by parents in the acquisition of basic physical laws is still to be explored. Finally, thought does not develop along a concrete-to-abstract trajectory, but from abstract to more abstract, simply supported by the concrete.

REFERENCES

Banks, M. S., & Salapatek, P. (1983). Infant visual perception. In P. Mussen (Series Ed.) & M. M. Haith & J. J. Campos (Vol. Eds.), Handbook of child psychology: Vol. 2. *Infancy and developmental psychobiology* (pp. 435–571). New York: Wiley.

Bayley, N. (1933). *The California First Year Mental Scale.* Berkeley: University of California Press.

Bayley, N. (1949). Consistency and variability in the growth of intelligence from birth to 18 years. *Journal of Genetic Psychology, 75,* 165–196.

Bomba, P. C., & Siqueland, E. R. (1983). The nature and structure of infant form categories. *Journal of Experimental Child Psychology, 35,* 294–328.

Bornstein, M. H. (1981). Psychological studies of color perception in human infants: Habituation, discrimination and categorization, recognition and conceptualization. In L. P. Lipsitt (Ed.), *Advances in infancy research* (Vol. 1, pp. 1–40). Norwood, NJ: Ablex.

Bornstein, M. H. (1983). A descriptive taxonomy of psychological categories used by infants. In C. Sophian (Ed.), *Origins of cognitive skills* (pp. 313–338). Hillsdale, NJ: Lawrence Erlbaum Associates.

Bower, T. G. R. (1982). *Development in infancy.* San Francisco: W. H. Freeman. (Original work published 1974)

Bryant, P. E., Jones, P., Claxton, V., & Perkins, G. H. (1972). Recognition of shapes across modalities by infants, *Nature, 240,* 303–304.

Bushnell, E. W. (1982). Visual–tactual knowledge in 8-, 9½- and 11-month-old infants. *Infant Behavior and Development, 5,* 63–75.

Eimas, P. D., Siqueland, E. R., Jusczyk, P. W., & Vigorto, J. (1971). Speech perception in infants. *Science, 171,* 303–306.

Fagan, J. F. (1976). Infant' recognition of invariant features of faces. *Child Development, 47,* 627–638.

Fagan, J. F. (1979). The origins of facial pattern recognition. In M. Bornstein & W. Kessen (Eds.), *Psychological development from infancy: Image to intention* (pp. 83–113). Hillsdale, NJ: Lawrence Erlbaum Associates.

Fantz, R. L. (1958). Pattern vision in young infants. *Psychological Record, 58,* 43–47.

Fantz, R. L. (1961). The origin of form perception. *Scientific American, 204,* 66–72.

Fantz, R. L. (1963). Pattern vision in newborn infants. *Science, 140,* 296–297.

Gibson, E. J. (1969). *Principles of perceptual learning and development.* New York: Appleton-Century-Crofts.

Gibson, E. J., & Walker, A. (1984). Development of knowledge of visual–tactual affordances of substance. *Child Development, 55,* 453–460.

Hatwell, Y. (1986). *Toucher l'espace* [Touching space]. Lille: Presses Universitaires de France.

Kellman, P. J., Gleitman, H., & Spelke, E. S. (1987). Object and observer motion in the perception of objects by infants. *Journal of Experimental Psychology: Human Perception and Performance, 13,* 586–593.

Kellman, J. J., & Spelke, E. S. (1983). Perception of partly occluded objects in infancy, *Cognitive Psychology, 15,* 483–524.

Kellman, P. J., Spelke, E. S., & Short, K. (1986). Infant perception of object unity from translatory motion in depth and vertical translation. *Child Development, 57,* 72–86.

Kestenbaum, R., & Nelson, C. A. (1990). The recognition and categorization of upright and inverted emotional expressions by 7-month-old infants. *Infant Behavior and Development, 13,* 497–511.

Lécuyer, R. (1989). *Bébés astronomes, bébés psychologues: L'intelligence de la première année* [Infants as astronomers, infants as psychologists: Intelligence in the first year of life]. Brussels: Mardaga.

Lécuyer, R. (1991). La catégorisation de figures géométriques chez des bébés de 5 mois [The categorization of geometric figures by 5-month-old babies]. *Archives de Psychologie, 59,* 143–155.

Lécuyer, R., & Poirier, C. (in press). Categorization in five-month-old infants. *International Journal of Psychology.*

Lewis, M. (Ed.). (1983). *Origins of intelligence* (2nd ed.). New York: Plenum. (Original work published 1976)

Marr, D. (1982). *Vision: A computational investigation into the human representation and processing of visual information.* San Francisco: W. H. Freeman.

McCall, R. B. (1981). Early predictors of later IQ: The search continues. *Intelligence, 5,* 141–147.

Meltzoff, A. N., & Borton, R. W. (1979). Intermodal matching by human neonates. *Nature, 282,* 403–404.

Milhet, S., & Streri, A. (1991). Haptic perception of weights and intermodal transfer in infancy. Unpublished manuscript.

Piaget, J. (1936). *La naissance de l'intelligence chez l'enfant* [The origins of intelligence in the infant]. Neuchâtel: Delachaux & Niestlé.

Piaget, J. (1937). *La construction du réel chez l'enfant* [The construction of reality in the infant]. Neuchâtel: Delachaux & Niestlé.

Pineau, A., & Streri, A. (1990). Intermodal transfer of spatial arrangement of the component parts of an object in infants aged 4–5 months. *Perception, 19,* 795–804.

Pinker, S. (1984). Visual cognition: An introduction. 1. *Cognition, 18,* 1–64.

Quinn, P. C. (1987). The categorical representation of visual pattern information by young infants. *Cognition, 27,* 145–179.

Rochat, P. (1987). Mouthing and grasping in neonates: Evidence for the early detection of what hard or soft substances afford for action. *Infant Behavior and Development, 10,* 435–449.

Rose, S. A., & Ruff, H. A. (1987). Cross-modal abilities in human infants. In J. D. Osofsky (Ed.), *Handbook of infant development* (pp. 318–362). New York: Wiley.

Ruff, H. A., & Kohler, C. J. (1978). Tactual–visual transfer in six-month-old infants. *Infant Behavior and Development, 1,* 259–264.

Spelke, E. S. (1990). Principles of object perception. *Cognitive Science, 14,* 29–56.

Strauss, M. S. (1979). Abstraction of prototypical information by adults and 10-month-old infants. *Journal of Experimental Psychology: Human Learning and Memory, 5,* 618–632.

Strauss, M. S., & Curtis, L. E. (1981). Infant perception of numerosity. *Child Development, 52,* 1146–1152.

Strauss, M. S., & Curtis, L. E. (1984). Development of numerical concepts in infancy. In C. Sophian (Ed.) *Origins of cognitive skills* (pp. 131–155). Hillsdale, NJ: Lawrence Erlbaum Associates.

Streri, A. (1987). Tactile discrimination of shape and intermodal transfer in 2- to 3-month-old infants. *British Journal of Developmental Psychology, 5,* 213–220.

Streri, A. (1991/1993). Seeing, reaching, touching: The relations between vision and touch in infancy. London: Simon and Schuster. [Original work published in French, 1991]

Streri, A., & Milhet, S. (1988). Equivalences intermodales de la fome des objets entre la vision et le toucher chez les bébés de 2 mois [Intermodal matching of objects shape between vision and touch in 2-month-old infants]. *L'Année Psychologique, 88,* 329–341.

Streri, A., & Molina, M. (1994). *Visual–tactual and tactual–visual transfer between objects and pictures in 2-month-old infants. Perception* (in press)

Streri, A., & Pêcheux, M. G. (1986). Cross-modal transfer of form in 5-month-old infants. *British Journal of Developmental Psychology, 4,* 161–167.

Streri, A., & Pineau, A. (1988, April). *Cognitive and motor functions of the hand.* Paper presented at the 10th International Conference on Infant Studies, Washington, DC.

Streri, A., & Spelke, E. S. (1988). Haptic perception of objects in infancy. *Cognitive Psychology, 20,* 1–23.

Streri, A., & Spelke, E. S. (1989). Effects of motion and figural goodness on haptic object perception in infancy. *Child Development, 60,* 1111–1125.

Twitchell, T. E. (1970). Reflex mechanisms and the development of prehension. In K. Connoly (Ed.), *Mechanisms of motor skill development* (pp. 25–38). New York: Academic Press.

Vurpillot, E. (1972). *Les perceptions du nourrisson* [Perception in the infant]. Paris: Presses Universitaires de France.

6 Sensorimotor Development and Perception From Francophone Perspectives: An Appreciation

George Butterworth
University of Sussex

Of all branches of scientific psychology, developmental psychology is the one most indebted to the French tradition. In the final analysis, the roots of the Francophone tradition may have much in common with the Anglophone, through developmental explanation based in evolutionary epistemology, yet their styles of explanation differ in important ways. The English empiricist tradition somehow elevates data over theory, whereas the strength of the Francophone tradition is that it demands more attention to the theoretical consequences of empirical enquiry. The French tradition, more synthetic and holistic, has regularly generated important and unexpected new discoveries, as chapters in this section attest.

Rochat and Bullinger, in their chapter, illustrate beautifully the particular theoretical quality of the Francophone perspective. It is not obvious to someone brought up in the empiricist tradition that one's own body constitutes an object of knowledge to be acquired in development. In fact, at one time, the empiricist approach reduced the fact of embodiment to mindless behaviorism. Rochat and Bullinger reintegrate the body with the mind in their examination of the influence of posture as a fundamental determinant of development. They argue that the integration of posture with action, into functional systems, is fundamental to a proper understanding of the origins of development.

Take, as an example, the fact that the head of the newborn baby is disproportionately larger than the body; it occupies as much as 30% of the total body volume (by comparison with only 10% in the adult), yet very few investigators have realized that this exercises a major biomechanical constraint on the expression of early behavior. Lacking control over his or her head, the infant cannot make much use of whatever degree of eye–hand coordination may be present at birth. Supporting the weight of the infant's head, as in the neurological examination of Amiel-Tisson and Grenier (1985), liberates the motor system to reveal that there is, indeed, an innate eye–hand coordination, although it ordinarily remains unexpressed. Synergistic stepping movements may also be liberated in early infancy, if the heavy legs of the infants are given appropriate support (Thelen & Fisher, 1982).

Rochat and Bullinger use such examples to make the imaginative theoretical suggestion that, in normal development, gaining control over posture will ordinarily enable the expression of a basic repertoire of innately coordinated actions. The starting point for development need not be characterized in terms of primitive reflexes; there also exist complex coordinations, which await control over posture for their expression. Further support for this position comes from infants whose postural development is delayed. Infants whose hips must be placed in plaster casts because of congenital malformations are delayed in acquiring autonomous control of sitting. One consequence of lack of control over the hips and trunk, which provide a stable platform for reaching, is delay in the development of reaching (Kohen-Raz, 1977).

An additional implication is that posture is integral to emotional expression and social development, where the infant "molds" his or her body to that of the caregiver. Rochat and Bullinger review evidence for such postural integration from very early in life, in the differences in spontaneous orientation of the mouth and head in breast- or bottle-fed babies. Universal human postures, such as the asymmetrical tonic neck reflex (ATNR), which can be observed from the 28th gestational week through the 8th month of postnatal life, are of particular theoretical interest. This is a pattern of coordinated muscular activity in which the arm and leg on the side to which the head is turned are extended, and the opposite arm and leg are flexed.

Rochat and Bullinger comment on the "anchoring" quality of this posture in visual tracking. With the acquisition of postural control, there is a dissociation of the head and trunk from the hand and arm in the development of visually guided reaching. Their argument for the fundamental importance of the ATNR postural synergy can be profitably extended to explain the origins of handedness. Rochat (1989) showed that when 3-month-olds are given support at the trunk their natural tendency is to reach bilaterally toward an object to bring it to the mouth. He suggests that unilateral handedness may emerge through the complementary roles of the arms ensuring balance while reaching, with the dominant hand moving forward to grasp the object and the nondominant arm moving backward, as a counterbalance (Rochat and Stacy, 1989). On this view, the ATNR posture provides a developmental substrate for subsequent visually guided reaching and manual prehension, which in turn takes over species-typical right-hand dominance.

Handedness and early communication can also be linked to mechanisms of posture. The ATNR is thought to predict whether the baby will be right- or left-handed, according to the spontaneous orientation of the head and arm when the baby is lying supine. The typical head orientation, to the right in the majority of babies, may be responsible for the fact that mothers almost always pick up and hold their infant in the left hand (Harris & Fitzgerald, 1982). This preference for left-arm cradling—from 60% to 75% of spontaneous holding—occurs in nulliparous females, in males, and even among female preschoolers lifting a doll (Saling & Bonnert, 1983; Saling & Tyson, 1981). Butterworth and Hopkins (1993) have argued that it is possible that the left-hand holding preference is closely connected with face-to-face contact and communication. Given the predominant right headturning preference of the newborn, through the ATNR, carrying on the left arm would maximize the opportunity for face-to-face contact and socioemotional communication from birth onward. This hypothesis is also consistent with our knowledge of hemispheric specialization for language and speech (Papoušek, 1991). In summary, Rochat and Bullinger are absolutely correct to emphasize the fundamental importance of postural control to our understanding of development in infancy.

The question posed by de Schonen and Deruelle in their chapter is whether pattern and face recognition are perceived in the same way by each of the cerebral hemispheres. These authors advocate a developmental neuroscientific approach that rests heavily on the differential specialization for language in the left hemisphere and spatial processing in the right hemisphere. Their developmental evidence suggests that perceiving faceness per se is not lateralized, but that recognition of familiar faces shows a right-hemisphere advantage. Their data suggest, however, that face perception by the left hemisphere may be implicated in language-specific aspects of perceptual processing, such as lip reading. This analysis seems very reasonable, and it certainly illustrates how a developmental analysis can complement adult neuropsychological data on face perception and recognition.

Additional data that might be revealing, especially about the relationship between face recognition and face perception, concerns the dynamics of face perception. In studies using photographic images, the animated properties of the face are lost, yet there is evidence that some aspects of visual information processing of faces in newborns depends on the dynamics of the visual display (Vinter, 1986). If the technique described by de Schonen and Deruelle, of presenting faces to the left or right visual field, could be extended to dynamic displays, this might allow further progress in determining the relative advantage of the right and left hemispheres with unfamiliar and familiar faces. The hypothesis that could be tested is as follows. There may be a developmental transition between early face perception, which may depend on information carried in the dynamics of stimulation, and later face recognition, which may be based on the static or stored products of the perceptual process. Furthermore, it is possible that speech-specific perception of the auditory–visual dynamics may be centered in the left hemisphere.

A special point of interest in sensorimotor development is the characterization of action in the neonate, especially as it relates to subsequent cognitive development. Both Piaget and Wallon emphasized the role of active movement in sensorimotor coordination. The question is whether coordinations arise as a result of motor activity in development. A number of well-known demonstrations, such as when adults adapt to spatial displacement produced by prismatic goggles, suggest that the calibration of the sensorimotor system may be assisted by active movement (Hay & Brouchon 1972). However, such studies may simply reveal the limits of plasticity of an already existing coordination, rather than being a model for the establishment of the initial sensorimotor coordination during ontogeny. Evidence on this point comes from Bullinger's (1990) studies of the effects of the sonic guide with congenitally blind infants. After an initial period of practice with such a device, infants are able to make use of the auditory information provided by the sonic guide. They are able both to define reaching space and to control posture using the exteroceptive auditory flow, similarly to the way sighted infants use visual information. Of course, mastering the sonic guide takes time, but the fact that the auditory information is isomorphic to that normally obtained through vision is actually strong evidence that activity is not responsible for establishing the link between perception and action. Rather, activity facilitates the detection of the dynamic information available in the auditory stream.

The characterization of the initial sensorimotor state is far from clear. Given the prevalent assumption that development begins from reflex action, it is interesting to read Dewey's (1896) criticism of the reflex arc concept. Dewey complained that the dualism of sensory stimulus and reflex response insufficiently displaced the older dualism of body and soul. He argued that sensory stimulation, central connections, and motor responses should not be viewed as separate entities, but as divisions of labor within a single unit of perception and action. The complaint made by Dewey about the rigidity of the reflex arc concept might well be made of contemporary accounts of the neonatal origins of development. It remains commonplace to dismiss the initial state of organization as "merely reflexive," with little analysis of the status of this explanation. As Dewey argued, and as contemporary psychologists such as Gibson (1966) have stressed, perception lies within action, it is not an external stimulus to action. The study of spontaneous motor behavior, especially as revealed in studies of fetal movement, is likely to yield a much more complex view of the initial state of motor organization in the neonate. De Vries, Visser, and Prechtl (1984), using ultrasonic scanning, listed 15 different kinds of movement patterns in 15-week-old fetuses. Could these movement synergies be the fundamental building blocks for behavior? It seems likely that an analysis, in dynamic systems terms, of the repertoire of basic motor synergies and their perceptual links will move the field on to a more satisfactory account of the initial state of development (Butterworth, 1990; Thelen, 1990).

REFERENCES

Amiel-Tisson, C., & Grenier, A. (1985). *La surveillance neurologique au cours de la premiere année de la vie* [The neurological examination during the first year of life]. Paris: Masson.

Bollinger, A. (1990). Posture control during reaching. In H. Bloch & B. I. Bertenthal (Eds.), *Sensory-motor organizations and development in infancy and early childhood* (pp. 263–272). Dordrecht: Kluwer.

Butterworth, G. E. (1990). On reconceptualising sensorimotor development in dynamic systems terms. In H. Bloch & B. I. Bertenthal (Eds.), *Sensory-motor organizations and development in infancy and early childhood* (pp. 57–74). Dordrecht: Kluwer.

Butterworth, G. E., & Hopkins, B. (1993). Origins of handedness in human infants. *Developmental Medicine and Child Neurology, 35*(2), 177–184.

DeVries, J. I. P., Visser, J. H. A., & Prechtl, H. F. R. (1984). Fetal motility in the first half of pregnancy. In H. F. R. Prechtl (Ed.), Continuity of neural functions from prenatal to postnatal life. Oxford: Blackwell.

Dewey, J. (1896). The reflex arc concept in psychology. *The Psychological Review, 4,* 357–370.

Gibson, J. J. (1966). *The senses considered as perceptual systems.* London: George, Allen & Unwin.

Harris, L. J., & Fitzgerald, H. (1982). Postural orientation in human infants: Changes from birth to three months. In G. Young, S. J. Segalowitz, C. Corter, & S. Trehub (Eds.), *Manual specialization and the developing brain* (pp. 285–304). New York: Academic Press.

Hay, L., & Brouchon, M. (1972). Analyse de la reorganisation des coordinations visuo–motrices chez l'homme. [Analysis of the reorganization of visuo–motor coordination in man]. *Ann. Psychol.* (Paris) *72,* 25–38.

Kohen-Raz, R. (1977). *Psychobiological aspects of cognitive growth.* New York: Academic Press.

Papoušek, H. (1991). Toward hemispheric specialization during infancy: Manual skills versus acquisition of speech. In H. E. Fitzgerald, B. M. Lester, and & M. W. Yogman (Eds.), *Theory and research in behavioral pediatrics* (pp. 209–215). New York: Plenum.

Rochat, P. (1989, April). Sitting and reaching in infancy. Paper presented at the meeting of the Society for Research in Child Development, Kansas City, MO.

Rochat, P., & Stacy, M. (1989, April). *Reaching in various postures by 6- and 8-month-old infants: The development of mono-manual grasp.* Paper presented at the meeting of the Society for Research in Child Development, Kansas City, MO.

Saling, M., & Bonnert, R. (1983). Lateral cradling preferences in female preschoolers. *The Journal of Genetic Psychology, 142,* 149–150.

Saling, M., & Tyson, G. (1981). Lateral cradling preferences in nulliparous females. *The Journal of Genetic Psychology, 139,* 309–310.

Thelen, E. (1990). Coupling perception and action in the development of skill: A dynamic approach. In H. Bloch & B. I. Bertenthal (Eds.), *Sensory-motor organization and development in infancy and early childhood* (pp. 39–56). Dordrecht: Kluwer.

Thelen, E., & Fisher, D. M. (1982). Newborn stepping: An explanation for a "disappearing reflex." *Developmental Psychology, 18,* 760–775.

Vinter, A. (1986). The role of movement in eliciting early imitation. *Child Development, 57,* 66–71.

7 Developing Knowledge: Diverse Perspectives and Common Themes

Elizabeth S. Spelke
Cornell University

The chapters in this section demonstrate, I believe, that research on early development from French-language countries is as rich and diverse as the field as a whole. The first two chapters exemplify one source of diversity. De Schonen and Deruelle view the human infant primarily as a neural system growing in interaction with its immediate environment: Their research illustrates how the study of developing perceptual and cognitive capacities and the study of the developing human brain illuminate one another. Rochat and Bullinger, in contrast, view the human infant as an organism that acts adaptively at every point in development and grows in harmony with its environment: Their research illustrates how an ecologically oriented study of development can shed light on the origins and nature of complex actions. Within biology, mechanistic and ecological approaches are complementary, and the same is likely to be true in psychology. This diversity of perspectives stands to enrich our understanding of the growing child's capacities to perceive, act, and reason.

The remaining two chapters exemplify two contrasting approaches to the development of knowledge. Whereas Lécuyer and Streri focus on early-developing perceptual capacities as a foundation for knowledge, Malcuit and Pomerleau focus on early-developing capacities to attend and to learn. Both approaches take controversial stands concerning such issues as the relation between knowledge and perception, the role of action in the development of knowledge, and the nature of the learning processes by which knowledge grows. Psychologists from all theoretical perspectives may agree, however, that the studies described in these chapters increase considerably our understanding of perception, attention, and learning. The study of knowledge is sure to benefit from this increased understanding.

Do any common themes emerge from these chapters? Perhaps revealing my own perspective and predilections, I see three.

1. *Structure and interaction.* The mind of a human newborn is not undifferentiated and equipotential but consists of distinct structures with distinct functions. Human behavior, at any age, results from the interaction of these structures. The difficult tasks for developmental psychology are to discover the initial structures that constitute the infant's core capacities, to analyze the interactions among these structures that result in the infant's overt actions on his or her environment, and to probe the events by which these structures and interactions emerge and change.

Because neither the elementary structures of the mind nor the interaction of such structures is known in advance, the task of developmental psychology is extremely difficult. Nevertheless, the research described in these chapters provides instructive examples of how progress can be made. Consider, for example, de Schonen and Deruelle's (1991) use of laterality tasks, Streri's (1991) use of intermodal transfer tasks, and Lécuyer's (1991) use of categorization tasks to shed light on the representations and processes underlying object recognition. Consider, also, the ingenious studies reviewed by Rochat and Bullinger, teasing apart basic action capacities through the study of interactions between action and posture. As a final example, Malcuit and Pomerleau show how careful task manipulations can begin to dissect the complex component processes that underlie an apparently simple act of looking. Psychologists have developed a repertoire of tools for probing the structures and processes underlying infants' functioning.

2. *Early competence and developmental continuity.* Until recently, most students of early development stressed the differences between infants and adults and the radical changes that occur over the course of postnatal growth. Human action was thought to progress from rigid reflexes to coordinated, intentional acts; human perception was thought to change from meaningless sensation to meaningful apprehension; human knowledge was thought to progress from an initial void to an array of concepts and beliefs. In different ways, all the authors in this section appear to reject this view. Rochat and Bullinger argue for a new view of action development, in which human action is seen as flexible and intentional from its beginnings. The remaining authors exemplify a different approach to perception, in which the infant is seen as a perceiver from birth. This theme also has emerged, in part, because of the astute observations and inventive research of these investigators and their colleagues. Consider, in particular, Rochat and Goubet's (1992), and Amiel-Tison and Grenier's (1986) studies, which demonstrate how coordinated actions can emerge when postural constraints are minimized; de Schonen and Bry's (1987) studies of initial abilities to categorize a visual display as a face; and Lécuyer's (1992) studies of early categorization of number. Although these investigators do not deny the existence or importance of developmental change, they stress the invariance of certain psychological capacities over the course of development. From the beginning of

life, humans appear to perceive, to act, and to reason; these invariant capacities serve as foundations for growth and change.

3. *Developmental psychology and cognitive science.* The third theme was stressed by Piaget, and before him by Rousseau and Descartes. By studying the development of children, one sheds light not only on development and on children, but on human nature itself. For example, the student of face perception in infancy may illuminate the processes and representations by which humans perceive faces as adults; the student of neonatal reaching may learn about mature, skilled action; the student of infant numerical concepts may shed light on mature mathematical concepts and mathematical reasoning and even on the nature and history of formal mathematics (Piaget, 1980). The study of early development serves as a valuable tool for increasing knowledge in psychology and cognitive science.

Studies of infants may provide an especially useful tool for understanding human action, perception, and reasoning, for two reasons that relate to the preceding themes. First, if human psychological capacities depend on essentially modular mechanisms, those mechanisms may be easier to discern at an early point in development, before they are organized into complex routines and mimicked by overlearned skills. Second, if human development is underpinned by invariant capacities to act, to perceive, and to reason, then those capacities may be revealed more clearly in infants than in older children or adults, for whom they are overlaid by a vast array of acquired abilities. In the mind of the infant, we may see a reflection of the adult mind: a reflection that is distorted and impoverished, but that may reveal the outlines of human intelligence.

REFERENCES

Amiel-Tison, C., & Grenier, A. (1986). *Neurological assessment during the first year of life.* New York: Oxford University Press.

de Schonen, S., & Bry, I. (1987). Interhemispheric communication of visual learning: A developmental study of 3- 6-month-old infants. *Neuropsychologia, 25,* 601–612.

de Schonen, S., & Deruelle, C. (1991). Spécialisation hémisphérique et reconnaissance des formes et des visages chez le nourrisson. *L'Année Psychologique, 91,* 15–46.

Lecuyer, R. (1991). La catégorisation de figures géométriques chez des bébés de 5 mois [The categorization of geometric figures by 5-month-old babies]. *Archives de Psychologie, 59,* 143–155.

Lécuyer, R. (1992, July). *About categorization of geometric figures in the 5- and 3-month-old infant.* Paper presented at the International Congress of Psychology, Brussels, Belgium.

Piaget, J. (1980). Comments on the impossibility of acquiring more powerful cognitive structures. In M. Piatelli-Palmarini (Ed.), *Language and learning: The debate between Piaget and Chomsky.* Cambridge, MA: Harvard University Press.

Rochat, P., & Goubet, N. (1992). *Postural development and reaching.* Manuscript submitted for publication.

Streri, A. (1991). *Voir, atteindre, toucher: Les relations entre la vision et le toucher chez le bébé.* Paris: Presses Universitaires de France.

II SOCIOCOGNITIVE DEVELOPMENT

8

From "Cold-Blooded" Cognition to Socio-Cognitive Development

Marcelle Ricard
Thérèse Gouin Décarie
Stephan Desrochers
Tibie Rome-Flanders
Université de Montréal

In 1954, the *Congrès international de psychologie scientifique* held its annual meeting in Montréal. Piaget was one of the guest speakers, and during his stay, his first in the province of Québec, he met the few developmental psychologists who worked at the relatively new Department of Psychology of the University of Montréal. Piaget, who never learned to speak English, was delighted to find a nucleus of researchers who were already familiar with his work and . . . who spoke French.

From that time on, he made regular visits to the department, which he affectionately called *mon petit Genève* (my little Geneva), and his influence on some colleagues was deep rooted and long lasting. This influence was reflected as early as 1962, in works by Laurendeau and Pinard, such as *La pensée causale,* followed by *Les premières notions spatiales de l'enfant* in 1968. The studies of Pinard and his co-workers cover a 25-year span (see Bouffard-Bouchard & Pinard, 1988; Lefebvre-Pinard & Pinard, 1985). These Piagetian scholars were (and still are) working in what has been labeled "cold-blooded" cognition (Butterworth & Light, 1982, p. xi).

In the early 1950s, Piagetian theory was still under-assimilated in the United States and in English-speaking Canada. Especially with respect to the sensorimotor period, this under-assimilation and the difficult process of accommodation that followed are quite understandable and readily explained. First, Piaget's main books on infancy (1936/1952, 1937/1954, 1945/1951) were originally written in French, and it was the last volume of this trilogy that was translated to English first, with the subtitle becoming the title; that is, *La formation du symbole chez l'enfant* became *Play, Dreams, and Imitation in Childhood,* a more attractive but misleading title. Besides, this work could not be fully understood without the knowledge of *The Origins of Intelligence in Children* (1936/1952) and *The Construction of Reality in the Child* (1937/1954), which were translated only later. Second, Piaget, as mentioned by Anthony (1957), was a borrower of genius: He used terms that were familiar to scientists (mostly in biology and physics), but he infused them with a meaning that was his and his alone, so that words, such as *adaptation, reversibility, stage, schema,* and *equilibrium,* required some reinterpretation. This reinterpretation led many psychologists initially to consider Piaget a philosopher rather than a genuine child psychologist. Third, Piaget did, in fact, vigorously maintain that he was not a child psychologist and that his unique concern had always been epistemology, stressing repeatedly that his monumental work on infancy, childhood, and adolescence had been only a *détour,* a by-product (Piaget, 1970). Finally, Piaget never used statistics: He believed that one good observation was worth a thousand statistics. At a time when experimental psychology was acquiring the status of a scientific discipline by resorting more and more to statistical formalization, such a stance was anathema, so much so that many psychologists in North America who referred to Piaget's theory in the 1950s often did so with more than a modicum of condescending tolerance.

At the University of Montréal, the seminal influence of Piagetian ideas and perspectives led to the creation of the *Laboratoire de la première enfance* (Early Infancy Laboratory) and to the onset of a series of infancy researches. Even though the framework and main concerns of these researches have been of Piagetian inspiration, we also strived to keep a constant sensitivity and openness of mind toward the new theoretical and methodological approaches put forward by the booming contemporary research in infant psychology. This led us not only to pay close attention to some neo- or even anti-Piagetian perspectives emerging in the field of infant cognition, such as the Bowerian and Brunerian theories (see Ricard, 1983; Rome-Flanders & Ricard, 1992; Simoneau & Gouin Décarie, 1979), but also to try to enrich our Piagetian concerns by combining them with such topics as the development of affectivity (Gouin Décarie, 1962/1965, 1978) and, most of all, various aspects of the process of infant socialization (Gouin Décarie, 1972/1974, 1980; Gouin Décarie & Ricard, 1982; Ricard, 1989, 1993; Ricard & Gouin Décarie, 1989; Solomon & Gouin Décarie, 1976). Thus, our research concentrated more and more in the field now called social cognition, which has become—as the following works illustrate—our main, yet not unique, concern.

THE ORIGINS OF THE PERSON–OBJECT DÉCALAGE AND THE DEVELOPMENT OF OBJECT IDENTITY

Within Piaget's theory, the notion of décalage (be it vertical or horizontal) has a considerable heuristic value. One of the best known and most intriguing décalages appears at the sensorimotor level of intelligence and is related to the object concept. Piaget (1937/1954) stated that the development of the object concept does not proceed at the same pace with respect to all objects in the infant's environment, and although he studied this acquisition only in reference to inanimate objects, he wrote that "persons obviously constitute the most easily substantified sensory pictures perceived by the child" (p. 5). In other words, he presumed that, of all the elements that constitute the child's early environment, persons were the first to be "conceived as substantial, independent of the self, and firm in existence even though they do not directly affect perception" (p. 5).

This décalage was experimentally tested for the first time by Saint-Pierre (1962; see also Gouin Décarie, 1966), but almost from the outset, the cognitive basis of the phenomenon and its universality were challenged. Some researchers, though admitting the existence of the person–object décalage, traced its origins to variables that were of an affective or motivational nature. Bell's (1970) initial work on the subject was followed by numerous studies (see Ricard, 1986) indicating that the infant had a tendency to perform better on object permanency tasks when the social objects were figures of attachment or when the nonsocial objects were familiar or preferred toys. Nevertheless, this tendency was not empirically confirmed, and researchers, such as Jackson, Campos, and Fischer (1978) rejected not only the attachment hypothesis, but the very existence of the décalage: They considered it to be an artifact associated with the experimental procedure or the result of mere familiarity. In their study, however, they did note a slight décalage in favor of the mother compared with an unfamiliar inanimate object.

Both variables, attachment and familiarity, are indissolubly linked to the infant's prior experiences with his or her environment. Ricard (1986) attempted to assess the role of a third variable that is a major property of the objects themselves: their mobility or immobility. She asked the following question: Could the basis of the person–object décalage be the result of a difference in the rate of acquisition of the concept of object *identity* when related to the person as compared to the physical object?

In a previous cross-sectional study of 60 infants, prompted by the stimulating work of researchers and theorists such as Bower and Moore (see Bower, 1974; Moore, 1974; Moore, Borton, & Darby, 1978; Wishart, 1979), Ricard (1983) designed a series of five identity tasks and proposed a set of rules governing the acquisition of object identity in infants between the ages of 5 and 15 months (see also Ricard & Gouin Décarie, 1983). From there, Ricard (1986) assumed that an object that moves autonomously, because of its frequent transformations from stationary to mobile state, and its repeated changes of apparent features, would be at the origin of more cognitive conflicts between the infant's identity rules than an inanimate object. The mobile object should, therefore, be conceived of as identical to itself, whatever the spatiotemporal changes it underwent, *before* the motionless object, and such a décalage between mobile and immobile objects in the acquisition of the notion of identity could be at the root of the person–object décalage relative to permanency.

To test this hypothesis, the following experiment was devised using two sets of objects. The mobile objects were a toy train that moved along an elliptical track, and a remote-controlled car that moved along an 8-shaped track. The immobile objects were a ball-launcher in the shape of a gun, and a trapezoidal insect trap. Prior to the experimental tasks, each infant was familiarized with all four objects, which were displayed simultaneously in a row where the immobile and moving objects alternated position.

The five identity tasks consisted of (a) a reorientation of the object; (b) a stationary disappearance; (c) a substitution; (d) a mobile disappearance, followed by the reappearance of a different object; and (e) a mobile disappearance, followed by the reappearance of a featurally similar object. For all of the tasks, the infant had to recognize that the object remained the same despite the spatiotemporal transformation it underwent. These five tasks were administered to 15 infants (8 boys and 7 girls) using all four objects.

Two independent observers, working from videotapes, recorded the subjects' responses on pre-established scales made up of the possible responses to each task, in an ascending order related to the level of comprehension of object identity (Ricard, 1983). For example, in response to the reorientation task, the infant could take the untransformed object, or take the transformed object, or reproduce the transformation, and so on.

The basic prediction was not confirmed by the data: In none of the five experimental tasks did the infants show more advanced identity behaviors when presented with the two objects they knew as mobile than with the two objects they had never seen in motion.

In order to insure that these results were not merely an artifact of the low power of the measurement procedure (identity tasks), the infants were also administered standardized, conventional object permanence tasks, using the same four objects. Again, the differences in the behaviors of the subjects when presented with the two categories of objects were not significant.

Thus, the results of this study did not support the existence of a mobile–immobile object décalage in the development of the concept of identity. One could argue that, at 9 months, the infants were not able to discriminate between the two types of objects, but our subjects' visual behavior during the familiarization period clearly revealed that such was not the case: The infants were much more interested in the mobile objects than in the motionless ones. Therefore, if one accepts the amount of looking directed at an object as an index of familiarization, short-term familiarity did not facilitate the infants' performance on either the identity or the object permanence tasks.

These negative results are probably best explained by the fact that the encounter with these mobile and immobile objects was a very brief one. Such a short exposure might not have yielded a sufficient quantity of cognitive conflict in reference to the basic identity rules to allow a significant difference in the level of mastery of the identity notion as related to the two categories of objects. More important, this study could neither confirm nor disconfirm the possible role played by the autonomous mobility of the person versus the immobility of the physical object in the person–object décalage. The experimental design, of course, was rather artificial: By using only nonsocial objects, this study did what Piaget did in his analysis of the object concept, even though it is obvious that mobility as a property of a person is very different from the provoked autonomous mobility of an object that is usually stationary.

It was partly this inability to account for the person–object décalage in terms of mere stimulus-related variables that eventually led to a reexamination of our approach and to the study of the infant's differential reactions to people and things in a wider, more social-cognitive perspective (Ricard & Gouin Décarie, 1989; Ricard, 1991). It may be that the person–object décalage, instead of being a matter of "cold-blooded" cognition, could be an aspect of the infant's whole experience with each category of stimuli and events, as reflected in the spontaneous strategies he or she uses to become familiar with them.

THE DEVELOPMENT OF CAUSALITY AND THE EMERGENCE OF SOCIAL REFERENCING

Since the 1980s, social referencing has become an important research topic, not only for infancy researchers but also for the growing number of psychologists interested in the child's acquisition of a theory of mind (Bretherton, 1991; Poulin-Dubois & Schultz, 1988; Wellman, in press). For the time being, however, no clear and unanimous definition of such a major phenomenon is available.

For Boccia and Campos (1983), social referencing refers to "the tendency of an individual to *seek out* [italics added] and use the emotional information in facial, vocal or gestural expression of another to help determine how to behave toward an object or an event in the environment" (p. 2). Although this stricter definition is the one used in a certain number of studies (Clyman, Emde, Kempe, & Harmon, 1986; Klinnert, 1984; Sorce, Emde, Campos, & Klinnert, 1985), other researchers, such as Feinman (1983), believe that social referencing "can be instrumental as well as affective, verbal as well as non-verbal, and *imposed* [italics added] as well as voluntarily solicited" (p. 470). This is a broader definition, on which a large portion of the recent research is also based (Feinman & Lewis, 1983; Gunnar & Stone, 1984; Hornik & Gunnar, 1988; Hornik, Risenhoover, & Gunnar, 1987).

Whatever the differences of opinion, however, all agree that social referencing, even if it can also be found in adults, has its roots in infancy and is a normal socio-cognitive process by which the infant, at a certain stage, tries to make sense of an event or an object that is otherwise ambiguous or beyond its own intrinsic appraisal capabilities (Klinnert, Campos, Sorce, Emde, & Svejda, 1983).

In addition to the two essential components of social referencing—the ambiguity of the situation and the uncertainty it provokes—other aspects have been investigated, such as the relationship between social referencing and attachment (Bradshaw, Goldsmith, & Campos, 1987; Dickstein, Thompson, Estes, Malkin, & Lamb, 1984) and between social referencing and temperament (Bradshaw et al., 1987; Feinman & Lewis, 1983; Feinman, Roberts, & Morissette, 1986). These studies have yielded mixed results, probably due to the fact that the methods and the subjects' ages varied greatly from one to the other.

The cognitive aspects of social referencing have also been analyzed, but mostly in the limited context of other referential behaviors of the infant, such as pointing (Boccia & Campos, 1983; Hoffman-Wilde & Rothbart, 1985; Hornik & Gunnar, 1986) and the appearance of the infant's first words (Hoffman-Wilde & Rothbart, 1985). Here again, the findings are difficult to interpret.

At this point of our understanding of the phenomena, one might appropriately ask: Are there some fundamental mental acquisitions that are needed before the infant can seek out or effectively use the information transmitted by others? Some studies (Evans & Tomasello, 1986; Klinnert et al., 1983) explicitly suggested that social referencing should appear during Stage V of the development of sensorimotor intelligence (Piaget, 1936/1952), that is, when the infant "comes to understand that one environmental event is related to or predicts something about another environmental event" (Klinnert et al., 1983, p. 75). It is within this framework that the second study presented here was carried out by Desrochers (Desrochers, Ricard, Gouin Décarie, & Allard, in press), who wished to investigate the relationship between social referencing and the acquisition of the Piagetian notion of causality.

According to Piaget (1936/1952, 1937/1954), the infant, starting from an entirely egocentric conception of causal relations and a feeling of omnipotence, gradually discovers the possibility that objects and persons around him or her not only can act as causal agents, responsible for events that occur independently of his or her own will, but also that they obey certain physical rules that are seldom violated.

In the younger child, the illusions peculiar to the egocentric point of view produce a sense of magical power or omnipotence and consequently make him or her unaware of the uncertainty associated with an ambiguous situation. When the infant reaches Stages V and VI of the notion of causality, however, the newly discovered autonomy of persons and objects should make him or her vulnerable to unusual objects and events. An ambiguous situation is, by definition, a situation that arouses perplexity, because it does not allow clear-cut predictions. Therefore, on reaching this stage in the understanding of causality, the infant in such a situation should turn more frequently to the adult in order to know how to behave adequately.

After Piaget described the evolution of the notion of causality in his first two books on sensorimotor development, especially in chapter 3 of *The Construction of Reality in the Child* (1937/1954), his detailed observations were operationalized to create a number of scales that assess the child's understanding of causality through a series of tasks (Goulet, 1972/1974; Mehrabian & Williams, 1971; Uzgiris & Hunt, 1975). Using some of these tasks and creating others, Desrochers' longitudinal study attempted to analyze, in 25 babies who were seen at 6, 9, 12, 15, and 18 months, the relationship likely to exist between social referencing and the development of the notion of causality in infancy.

To provoke social referencing, five stimuli were selected on the basis of their reliability to elicit attention and uncertainty in infants aged 6 to 18 months. They were: (a) a helium-inflated balloon, resembling a black spider and emitting an intermittent owl's cry; (b) a dancing King Kong with moving arms and lips, activated by a noise; (c) a robot moving laterally; (d) a stuffed owl placed in a glass box and spinning slowly; and (e) a soft mannequin of a 3-year-old child lying supine on the floor and emitting an intermittent song. Each subject saw a different object at each session.

Only the following sequence of behaviors was scored as social referencing: (a) The infant looks at the unfamiliar object with an expression of perplexity, surprise, or circumspection (see Young & Gouin Décarie, 1977), and then (b) turns deliberately to the mother and looks at her face for at least 1 second. The infant's eyes must not rest on any other object in the lab (camera, windows, lights) between (a) and (b). It was felt that this strict criterion would allow differentiation between social referencing and other types of social looking (Clyman et al., 1986). It was only *after* referencing to the mother that the infant received a positive message from her: She smiled, said "How nice," and leaned toward the object.

The causality scale, consisting of nine tasks and using ordinary toys similar to those required by other scales (Goulet, 1972/1974; Uzgiris & Hunt, 1975), was administered after the social referencing situation. The method of coding the infant's responses was the same as that of Uzgiris and Hunt (1975), but the criteria of Goulet (1972/1974) were used to assess the stage reached by each subject.

The first clear-cut finding of this study was that social referencing is a relatively rare phenomenon in infants between 6 and 18 months of age. It was observed in the course of only 38 sessions of a total of 125, and only 76 instances of social referencing could be coded. Five infants never consulted their mothers when placed in any of the five ambiguous situations.

Such scarcity is not as surprising as it may seem, considering our very strict criterion (see Allard, Ricard, Gouin Décarie, & Desrochers, 1993). Hornik and Gunnar (1988) also found that reference looks occurred during only 4.8% of their coding intervals, the probability increasing when mothers provided unsolicited information (contrary to our situations, where the mother had to wait for the infant to look at her before giving any information), and 16% of their sample never referenced.

Even though social referencing was rare in our sample, the number of subjects showing it at least once at the different age levels did indicate some evolution. Between 9 and 12 months, especially, this number increased significantly.

Results on the causality scale showed that the sequential order of the stages of causality reached by our subjects did correspond to the one observed by Piaget (1937/1954). From one age level to the next, every infant either moved from one stage to a more advanced one, or simply remained at the same stage. No inversion in the order of acquisition was observed.

Because of the presence of this fixed order, age was seen as an important factor in the development of causality. All sessions in which subjects were attributed inferior causality levels (Stages III or IV) were the first ones (6 and 9 months), and most of the sessions in which subjects were attributed superior causality levels (Stages V or VI) were the later ones, when the infants were 12, 15, or 18 months. It was interesting that every infant attained Stage V by the 12-month session.

Here, again, there was a significant jump in cognitive level between the ages of 9 and 12 months. By 1 year of age, every infant had progressed from an understanding of causality that was mainly magical and phenomenistic to the more mature concept of objective and spatialized causality.

Thus, some important similarities between the evolution of social referencing and the development of causality were revealed. On both dimensions, the last quarter of the 1st year appeared as a turning point, where the likelihood of an infant actively seeking out information from the mother not only increased, but was also paralleled by the infant's entering superior levels of causal understanding. In other words, it seemed that the infants became so aware of the ambiguity of the situations that they had to turn to their mothers in an attempt to relieve their uncertainty only when they had gained sufficient mastery of causality (typical at least of Stage V).

Recently, some authors (Bretherton, 1991; Wellman, in press) have suggested that social referencing is a phenomenon that implicitly reveals a certain capacity of "mind-reading," or some intersubjectivity of the spirit (Stern, 1985). It would be interesting to continue exploring whether there are, indeed, links among social referencing, causality, and the very first steps in the development of a theory of mind.

SOCIAL GAMES AND THE DEVELOPMENT OF LANGUAGE

In the preface of his book *Studies in Cognitive Growth*, which he dedicated to Piaget, Bruner (1966) wrote, "Many points of disagreement are nevertheless minor by comparison with the points of fundamental agreement we share with professor Jean Piaget. This volume would have been impossible without his monumental work. His genius has founded modern developmental psychology" (p. xv).

In spite of this apparently unmitigated expression of admiration for Piaget, Bruner repeatedly stressed that the major sources of inspiration for his ingenious hypotheses and empirical studies were, rather, Freud, Vygotsky, and Chomsky (see Bruner, 1983). At one time, Bruner considered himself a "Piagetian revisionist." On being told about this, Piaget remarked to the senior author: "There is only one Piagetian revisionist: Piaget . . . " (J. Piaget, personal communication, 1970).

In fact, there is obviously a fundamental disagreement between Piaget and Bruner in their views of how the mind begins and, especially, of how language begins. Despite the fact that Piaget considered social interactions to be one of the factors intervening in the growth of intelligence—along with maturation, actions upon objects, and the process of equilibrium (Piaget & Inhelder, 1966)—he made infancy an exception. Even though he asserted that, from birth on, there exists a complex kind of relationship between mental and affective development (Piaget, 1954/1981; Gouin Décarie, 1978), he still seemed to believe that social interactions have little influence (if any) on the early growth of intelligence: "During the sensorimotor period preceding language acquisition, we cannot yet speak of the socialization of intelligence . . . . Sensorimotor imitation does not influence intelligence; rather it is a manifestation of intelligence. As for the emotional contacts of the baby with his surroundings (smiles, etc.), these are not interactions that affect the intelligence as such" (Piaget, 1967, pp. 155–156).

In this context, one can well understand the following assertion by Bruner: "The world is a quiet place for Piaget's growing child. He is virtually alone in it . . . . He begins his journey egocentrically and must impose properties on the world that will eventually be shared with others. But others give him little help. The social reciprocity of infant and mother plays a very small role in Piaget's account of development" (Bruner, 1983, p. 38).

In contrast, the world is a very busy and noisy place for Bruner's growing child. People (especially mothers) talk, listen, follow requests, and make requests themselves. They indicate things by pointing and labelling, and, in a way, they organize the world in accordance with the clues given by the infant. This "scaffolding" role of the mother is crucial in the development of language in infancy.

It was around 1966 that Bruner turned from the study of the pre-operational child to that of the infant. His hypotheses on games and language development, which prompted the last study presented here, originated (to the best of our knowledge) some 10 years later, at the Harvard Center for Cognitive Studies, and are now well known in the French world, thanks, in part, to Deleau (1983, 1990).

According to Bruner (1975), language is a specialized extension of cooperative action, and "it is the infant's success in achieving joint action that virtually leads him into language" (p. 6). Moreover, early social games are the framework and the best illustration of this joint action. They constitute the basis for three main aspects of language development: semantics, syntax, and pragmatics.

Most of the empirical research done by Bruner and his co-workers on this subject consists of studies limited to a small number of infants (Bruner, 1975, 1977; Bruner & Ninio, 1978; Bruner & Sherwood, 1975; Ratner & Bruner, 1977). It was in order to verify more systematically the possibility of a relationship between game-playing skills and the linguistic competence of the infant that the following longitudinal study was carried out at our laboratory by Rome-Flanders (1989).

Twenty-five infants were observed every 3 months from age 6 months to 18 months, and again at 24 months, playing a ball game and a game of peek-a-boo with their mothers as they would at home. The dependent measures consisted, first, of the frequencies of game-relevant gestures emitted by each infant in the two 3-minute game sessions. For the peek-a-boo game, these game-relevant gestures consisted of (a) hiding a doll, and (b) uncovering it, with or without the mother's help. For the ball game, they consisted of (a) catching and (b) returning the ball, with or without mother's help. The infants' vocal responses—that is, their positive, negative, and neutral vocalizations—were also coded, as were a variety of facial expressions, such as disinterest, surprise, perplexity, interest, and smiles. In addition, a certain number of combined behaviors were found to be pertinent in the study of the evolution of games and were, therefore, noted. These were: anticipatory behaviors, teasing, searching, requesting a turn, and generating modification.

To test the infants' linguistic development, the Receptive Expressive Emergent Language Test (Bzock & League, 1980) was used for the first five age levels (6, 9, 12, 15, and 18 months), and the Reynell (1977) test of linguistic abilities was administered at 24 months.

As hypothesized by Bruner, the analysis of the data revealed significant changes in game-playing skills between 6 and 24 months. The infants progressed from an absence of participation and autonomous actions (the subjects frequently requesting their mothers' help), to autonomous game-relevant behaviors and an awareness of the rules of the game that finally allowed some of them to try to introduce modifications in the course of the game.

Interestingly, the rate of development of game-playing skills was different from one game to the other. The rules of the ball game, whose structure is relatively simple, were mastered earlier than those of peek-a-boo. In light of this result, we conclude that universal age norms should not be attached to the evolution of game-playing behaviors or to the various levels of comprehension of rules. Given a baseline, the rate of development seems to be as much a function of the particular game at hand as of the infant who is playing. Therefore, any study of game-playing skills in infancy should take into careful consideration the type of game used to assess the subjects' behaviors and abilities.

A second, more specific aspect of Bruner's theory, was also confirmed. In their longitudinal study of two boys playing peek-a-boo with their mothers, Ratner and Bruner (1977) observed an important development in the vocal behavior of these infants during game episodes (see also Bruner & Sherwood, 1975). When they discovered the right rhythm of the game, the boys began to vocalize at certain precise junctures in the sequences, and this gradual timing of vocalization was interpreted by the authors as revealing a growing awareness of the reciprocity of roles and of the rules of the game. The analysis of this specific aspect in our study (Rome-Flanders & Ricard, 1992) confirmed this evolution of a gradual coordination of vocalizations, not only in the peek-a-boo game, but also in the ball game.

The third finding was rather disappointing: The ranking of the subjects based on their game-playing skills in each game, at each age level, when compared to their rank order on the two linguistic tests, failed to show any significant relationship between competence in the games and language abilities. This is in accord with the findings of Rubin, Fein, and Vanderberg (1983), who were also unable to find a clear-cut relationship between social and linguistic skills in infants. Still, they considered this lack of precise correspondence as inconclusive evidence for the independence of these two variables. We agree with them. In Rome-Flanders' study, the number of rounds in which each infant participated was not measured, and the development of sharing of agency was not systematically traced. These behaviors might have yielded a correspondence.

Moreover, if the results of this last study did not directly support Bruner's initial hypotheses, they are not in opposition with his revised account of his theory on the relationship between early social interaction and language. Rather than viewing nonlinguistic competence as a direct precursor of the structure of language, Bruner (1981, 1983) has more recently suggested that the systems of language "are autonomous problem spaces that, how ever much their conquest may be aided by nonlinguistic knowledge or external support from others, must be mastered on their own" (1983, p. 28). It would seem that if there is a Brunerian revisionist today, it is Bruner himself.

CONCLUSION

The research interests of our lab seem to have come full circle, back to the "construction of reality," but it is not the reality simply of a world of objects that the infant must arrange in space, time, and causal relationship that now challenges the research team. It is, rather, the construction of the *social* reality, that is, the complex psychological world of persons. In becoming a "psychologist" as well as an "astronomer" in the first year, as Lécuyer (1989) put it, the infant has already laid down the foundations of what will become, at about 3 years of age, his or her first theories of mind.

ACKNOWLEDGMENTS

Research presented in this paper was supported by grants from the Social Sciences and Humanities Research Council of Canada, and by the Fonds FCAR of the Québec Government.

REFERENCES

Allard, L., Ricard, M., Gouin Décarie, T., & Desrochers, S. (1993). *Looking at the mother: A longitudinal study of the information-gathering process of social referencing.* Manuscript submitted for publication.

Anthony, E. J. (1957). The system makers: Piaget and Freud. *British Journal of Medical Psychology, 30,* 255–269.

Bell, S. M. (1970). The development of the concept of object as related to infant–mother attachment. *Child Development, 41,* 291–311.

Boccia, M. L., & Campos, J. J. (1983, April). *Maternal emotional signals and infants' reactions to strangers.* Paper presented at the meeting of the Society for Research in Child Development, Detroit, MI.

Bouffard-Bouchard, T., & Pinard, A. (1988). Sentiment d'auto-efficacité et exercice des processus d'auto-régulation chez des étudiants de niveau collégial [The feeling of self-efficiency and the practice of self-regulation processes in college students]. *Journal International de Psychologie, 23,* 409–431.

Bower, T. G. R. (1974). *Development in infancy.* San Francisco: W. H. Freeman.

Bradshaw, D. L., Goldsmith, H., & Campos, J. J. (1987). Attachment, temperament and social referencing: Interrelationships among three domains of infant affective behavior. *Infant Behavior and Development, 10,* 223–231.

Bretherton, I. (1991). Intentional communication and the development of an understanding of mind. In D. Frye & C. Moore (Eds.), *Children's theories of mind* (pp. 49–76). Hillsdale, NJ: Lawrence Erlbaum Associates.

Bruner, J. S. (1966). *Studies in cognitive growth.* New York: Wiley.

Bruner, J. S. (1975). The ontogenesis of speech acts. *Journal of Child Language, 2,* 1–19.

Bruner, J. S. (1977). Early social interaction and language acquisition. In H. R. Schaffer (Ed.), *Studies in infant–mother interaction* (pp. 271–289). London: Academic Press.

Bruner, J. S. (1981). The social context of language acquisition. *Language & Communication, 1,* 155–178.

Bruner, J. S. (1983). The acquisition of pragmatic commitments. In R. M. Golinkoff (Ed.), *The transition from prelinguistic to linguistic communication* (pp. 27–42). Hillsdale, NJ: Lawrence Erlbaum Associates.

Bruner, J. S., & Ninio, A. (1978). The achievement of antecedents of labelling. *Journal of Child Language, 5,* 1–15.

Bruner, J. S., & Sherwood, V. (1975). Peekaboo and the learning of rule structures. In J. Bruner, A. Jolly, & K. Sylva (Eds.), *Play: Its role in development and evolution* (pp. 277–287). Middlesex: Penguin.

Butterworth, G., & Light, P. (Eds.). (1982). *Social cognition studies of the development of understanding.* Brighton GB: Harvester Press.

Bzock, K. R., & League, R. (1980). *Assessing language skills in infancy* (2nd ed.). Baltimore, MD: University Park Press.

Clyman, R. B., Emde, R. N., Kempe, J. E., & Harmon, R. J. (1986). Social referencing and social looking among twelve-month-old infants. In B. Brazelton & M. Yogman (Eds.), *Affective development in infancy* (pp. 75-94). New York: Ablex.

Deleau, M. (1983). Présentation. In J. S. Bruner, *Le développement de l'enfant: Savoir faire, savoir dire* [Infant development: Knowing to act, knowing to speak] (pp. 11-35). Paris: Presses Universitaires de France.

Deleau, M. (1990). *Les origines sociales du développement mental* [The social origins of mental development]. Paris: Armand Colin.

Desrochers, S., Ricard, M., Gouin Décarie, T., & Allard, L. (in press). Developmental synchrony between social referencing and Piagetian sensorimotor causality. *Infant Behavior & Development.*

Dickstein, S., Thompson, R. A., Estes, D., Malkin, C., & Lamb, M. (1984). Social referencing and the security of attachment. *Infant Behavior and Development, 7,* 507-516.

Evans, A., & Tomasello, M. (1986). Evidence for social referencing in young chimpanzees. *Folia Primatologica, 47,* 49-54.

Feinman, S. (1983). How does baby socially refer? Two views of social referencing: A reply to Campos. *Merrill-Palmer Quarterly, 29,* 467-471.

Feinman, S., & Lewis, M. (1983). Social referencing at ten months: A second-order effect on infants' responses to strangers. *Child Development, 54,* 878-887.

Feinman, S., Roberts, D., & Morissette, L. (1986, April). *The effect of social referencing on 12-month-olds' responses to a stranger's attempts to "make friends."* Paper presented at the Fifth International Conference on Infant Studies, Los Angeles, CA.

Gouin Décarie, T. (1965). *Intelligence and affectivity in early childhood* (E. P. Brandt & L. W. Brandt, Trans.) New York: International Universities Press. (Original work published 1962)

Gouin Décarie, T. (1966). Intelligence sensori-motrice et psychologie du premier âge [Sensorimotor intelligence and infancy psychology]. In F. Bresson & M. de Montmollin (Eds.), *Psychologie et épistémologie génétiques: Thèmes piagétiens* (pp. 299-305). Paris: Dunod.

Gouin Décarie, T. (Ed.). (1974). *The infant's reaction to strangers* (J. Diamanti, Trans.) New York: International Universities Press. (Original work published 1972)

Gouin Décarie, T. (1978). Affect development and cognition in a Piagetian context. In M. Lewis & L. A. Rosenblum (Eds.), *The development of affect* (pp. 183-204). New York: Plenum.

Gouin Décarie, T. (1980). Les origines de la socialisation [The origins of socialization]. In J. -F. Saucier (Ed.), *L'enfant: Explorations récentes en psychologie du développement* (pp. 16-41). Montréal: Presses de l'Université de Montréal.

Gouin Décarie, T., & Ricard, M. (1982). La socialisation du nourrisson [Infant socialization]. *La Recherche, 13,* 1388-1396.

Goulet, J. (1974). The infant's conception of causality and his reactions to strangers. In T. Gouin Décarie (Ed.), *The infant's reaction to strangers* (pp. 57-96). New York: International Universities Press. (Original work published 1972)

Gunnar, M., & Stone, C. (1984). The effects of positive maternal affect on one-year-olds' reactions to toys. *Child Development, 55,* 1231-1236.

Hoffman-Wilde, S., & Rothbart, M. K. (1985). *A longitudinal investigation of social referencing in infancy.* Unpublished manuscript, University of Oregon, Eugene.

Hornik, R., & Gunnar, M. R. (1986). *A descriptive analysis of social referencing during infant exploration of a highly engrossing novel event.* Unpublished manuscript, University of Minnesota, Minneapolis.

Hornik, R., & Gunnar, M. R. (1988). A descriptive analysis of infant social referencing. *Child Development, 59,* 626-634.

Hornik, R., Risenhoover, N., & Gunnar, M. R. (1987). The effects of maternal positive, neutral and negative affective communications on infants' responses to new toys. *Child Development, 58,* 937-945.

Jackson, E., Campos, J. J., & Fischer, K. W. (1978). The question of décalage between object permanence and person permanence. *Developmental Psychology, 14*, 1–10.

Klinnert, M. D. (1984). The regulation of infant behavior by maternal facial expression. *Infant Behavior and Development, 7*, 447–465.

Klinnert, M. D., Campos, J. J., Sorce, J. F., Emde, R. N., & Svejda, M. (1983). Emotions as behavior regulators: Social referencing in infancy. In R. Plutchik & H. Kellerman (Eds.), *Emotions in early development: Vol. 2. The emotions* (pp. 57–86). New York: Academic Press.

Laurendeau, M., & Pinard, A. (1962). *La pensée causale* [Causal thinking]. Paris: Presses Universitaires de France.

Laurendeau, M., & Pinard, A. (1968). *Les premières notions spatiales de l'enfant* [The infant's first spatial concepts]. Neuchâtel: Delachaux et Niestlé.

Lécuyer, R. (1989). *Bébés astronomes, bébés psychologues: L'intelligence de la première année* [Baby astronomers, baby psychologists: Intelligence in the first year]. Brussels: Mardaga.

Lefebvre-Pinard, M., & Pinard, A. (1985). Taking charge of one's own cognitive activity: A moderator of competence. In E. D. Neimark, R. DeLisi, & J. L. Newman (Eds.), *Moderators of competence* (pp. 191–212). Hillsdale, NJ: Lawrence Erlbaum Associates.

Mehrabian, A., & Williams, M. (1971). Piagetian measures of cognitive development for children up to age two. *Journal of Psycholinguistic Research, 1*, 113–125.

Moore, M. K. (1974). *The genesis of object permanence*. Unpublished doctoral dissertation, Harvard University, Cambridge, MA.

Moore, M. K., Borton, R., & Darby, B. (1978). Visual tracking in young infants: Evidence for object identity or object permanence? *Journal of Experimental Child Psychology, 25*, 183–198.

Piaget, J. (1951). *Play, dreams, and imitation in childhood* (C. Gattagno & F. M. Hodgson, Trans.) New York: Norton. (Original work published 1945)

Piaget, J. (1952). *The origins of intelligence in children* (M. Cook, Trans.) New York: International Universities Press. (Original work published 1936)

Piaget, J. (1954). *The construction of reality in the child* (M. Cook, Trans.) New York: Basic Books. (Original work published 1937)

Piaget, J. (1967). *Études sociologiques* [Sociological studies]. Geneva: Droz.

Piaget, J. (1970). Piaget's theory. (G. Gellerier & J. Langer, Trans.) In K. Mussen (Ed.), *Carmichael's Child Psychology* (pp. 703–732). New York: Wiley.

Piaget, J. (1981). *Intelligence and affectivity: Their relationship during child development*. (T. A. Brown & C. E. Kaegi, Trans.) Palo Alto, CA: Annual Reviews Monographs. (Original work published 1954)

Piaget, J., & Inhelder, B. (1966). *L'image mentale chez l'enfant* [The mental image in the child]. Paris: Presses Universitaires de France.

Poulin-Dubois, D., & Schultz, T. R. (1988). The development of the understanding of human behavior: From agency to intentionality. In J. W. Astington, P. L. Harris, & D. R. Olson (Eds.), *Developing theories of mind* (pp. 109–125). Cambridge, England: Cambridge University Press.

Ratner, N., & Bruner, J. S. (1977). Games, social exchange and the acquisition of language. *Journal of Child Language, 5*, 391–401.

Reynell, J. (1977). *Reynell Developmental Language Scales* (rev. ed.). Windsor, GB: NFER-Nelson Publishing.

Ricard, M. (1983). L'identité de l'objet chez le jeune enfant [Object identity in infants] [Monographs Serial No. 9]. Geneva: *Archives de psychologie, 51*, 259–325.

Ricard, M. (1986). Le décalage dans le développement de la notion d'objet: Mobilité et immobilité de l'objet [The décalage in object concept development: Mobile versus immobile objects]. *Revue Canadienne de Psychologie, 40*, 272–281.

Ricard, M. (1989). Les conduites sociales de 17 bébés "audacieux" de 9–10 mois [Social behaviors in 17 "bold" infants aged 9–10 months]. *International Journal of Psychology, 24*, 523–538.

Ricard, M., & Gouin Décarie, T. (1983). *Object identity in infants.* University of Montreal. (ERIC Document Reproduction Service No. ED 231 527)

Ricard, M., & Gouin Décarie, T. (1989). Strategies of 9–10-month-old infants with a stranger and a novel object. *Revue Internationale de Psychologie Sociale, 2,* 97–111.

Ricard, M., & Gouin Décarie, T. (1993). Distance-maintaining in infants' reaction to an adult stranger. *Social Development, 2,* 145–164.

Rome-Flanders, T. (1989). *Mother-infant games and the development of language.* Unpublished doctoral dissertation, Université de Montréal.

Rome-Flanders, T., & Ricard, M. (1992). Infant timing of vocalizations in two mother–infant games: A longitudinal study. *First Language, 12,* 285–297.

Rubin, K., Fein, G., & Vandenberg, B. (1983). Play. In P. Mussen (Series Ed.) & E. M. Hetherington (Vol. Ed.), *Handbook of child psychology: Vol. 4. Society, personality, and social development* (4th ed., pp. 693–774). New York: Wiley.

Saint-Pierre, J. (1962). *Étude des différences entre la recherche active de la personne humaine et celle de l'objet inanimé* [A study of the differences between the infant's active search for persons and for inanimate objects]. Unpublished doctoral dissertation, Université de Montréal.

Simoneau, K., & Gouin Décarie, T. (1979). Cognition and perception in the object concept. *Canadian Journal of Psychology, 33,* 396–407.

Solomon, R., & Gouin Décarie, T. (1976). Fear of strangers: A developmental milestone or an overstudied phenomenon? *Canadian Journal of Behavioral Science, 8,* 351–361.

Sorce, J. F., Emde, R. N., Campos, J. J., & Klinnert, M. D. (1985). Maternal emotional signaling: Its effect on the visual cliff behavior of 1-year-olds. *Developmental Psychology, 21,* 195–200.

Stern, D. N. (1985). *The interpersonal world of the infant.* New York: Basic Books.

Uzgiris, I., & Hunt, J. McV. (1975). *Assessment in infancy: Ordinal scales of psychological development.* Urbana, IL: University of Illinois Press.

Wellman, H. M. (in press). Early understanding of mind: The normal case. In S. Baron-Cohen, H. Tager-Flusberg, & D. Cohen (Eds.), *Understanding other minds: Perspectives from autism.* Oxford, England: Oxford University Press.

Wishart, J. G. (1979). *A further investigation and evaluation of the identity hypothesis in the development of the object concept in infancy.* Unpublished doctoral dissertation, University of Edinburgh.

Young, G., & Gouin Décarie, T. (1977). An ethology-based catalogue of facial/vocal behavior in infancy. *Animal Behavior, 25,* 95–107.

9 Self-Recognition in Infants: Some Reflections Beyond the Mirror

Andre Vyt
University of Ghent—NFSR

Visual self-recognition in infancy is an insular field of study in which a variety of developmental researchers and theorists have become interested. Infants' reactions toward their self-image have been incorporated in the form of items in different developmental scales and have been the subject of baby biographies and studies of eminent pioneers in developmental psychology, including Preyer (1888), Baldwin (1897), Darwin (1877), and—especially among the French—Piaget (1936/1952), Wallon (1963/1981), and Zazzo (1948). Over time, it has become a standard paradigm for assessing development of self-knowledge and self-awareness in the preverbal period, as a basic component of social cognition.

This chapter examines what self-recognition studies outside Anglophone countries have had to say about self-knowledge, self-awareness, and the underlying learning processes themselves. Instead of being a unitary additional cognitive capacity that suddenly emerges in infancy, self-recognition can be seen as the result of a conglomerate of cognitive functions that undergo a developmental spurt in the 2nd year of life. Without enforcing a reductionist view, a cautiousness in making inferences from certain visual self-recognition tasks of behaviors to the field of self-awareness is to be envisaged, and more focus has to be given to sensorimotor development that underlies performance on these tasks. The conceptual step from observing behavior in front of the mirror to inferring self-recognition and self-awareness is not an entirely straightforward one.

In early studies, spontaneous social and emotional reactions in front of the mirror image were frequently included as indexes of self-recognition, forming a stagewise development of behaviors that were likely to occur in certain age periods (e.g., Amsterdam, 1972; Dixon, 1957). Typical mirror behaviors for given periods, however, are only meaningfully interpretable when compared with behaviors in other—dyadic—situations. For example, shyness or embarrassment in the 2nd year of life can also occur when confronted with another child, so the same behavior in front of a mirror could indicate an emerging social awareness of the self without necessarily indicating recognition of the self-image. Thus, mirror situations have to be complemented with conditions in which the infant is confronted with another child, or with the image of another child. Also, if a child responds differentially, we do not know if this is related to self-recognition on the basis of featural characteristics or on the basis of perceived contingency between movements of the self and of the image. In France, it is the merit of René Zazzo to have tried to master this methodological problem by experimentally controlling self–image correspondence and self–other comparisons without using modern techniques of videotape feedback or closed-circuit television. In a study with an ingenious setup, Zazzo (1977a, 1977b) used monozygotic and dizygotic twins in front of a mirror and in front of each other through a transparent screen. He could demonstrate that emotional reactions toward the mirror image were typical for the second half of the 2nd year, with the emergence of avoidance, shyness, surprise, and fascination, whereas contingency play with hands and face appeared already in the beginning of the 2nd year.

THE SEARCH FOR A DEVELOPMENTAL SEQUENCE

Renowned and widely cited investigations of self-recognition in infancy were performed by Bertenthal and Fischer (1978) and by Lewis and Brooks-Gunn (1979). Bertenthal and Fischer (1978) used the visual self-recognition paradigm to demonstrate an acquisition sequence of infants' responses to the mirror within a cognitive-developmental framework. According to their thesis, self-recognition develops through an epigenesis of abilities rooted in cognitive developments of the sensorimotor infancy period. The stages in this sequence are defined in terms of the type and complexity of coordinated actions under the infant's control. These are formalized in Fischer's model of cognitive development (Fischer, 1980), which provides an alternative and supplemented description of the Piagetian stages in the sensorimotor period. Bertenthal and Fischer derived a self-recognition task or criterion for each presumed stage, and, indeed, demonstrated a sequence in mastering the different mirror tasks. In the first stage, around and before the first birthday, children simply explore their mirror images tactually. Children a couple of months older can solve a hat task, in which they are prompted to find a hat suspended above their heads after seeing its reflection in the mirror, where the movement of the hat is contingent on their own movement. When they are a few months older–in Piaget's Stage V–children solve a toy task, in which they locate reflected objects not attached to them and whose movement is not contingent on their own movements. A more difficult task is the rouge task, in which children must discover a (surreptitiously marked) spot of rouge on their noses when viewing their mirror images. Finally, at the end of the infancy period, children communicate verbally that they recognize their mirror image as their own by naming themselves.

In contrast with Bertenthal and Fisher's findings, Zazzo (1975, 1977a, 1977b) reported that finding a spot on the nose was observed in the majority of infants at the end of their 2nd year, followed by the ability to locate spontaneously a reflected object—a flashlight—a couple of months later. Infants seemed to continue exploring the mirror space in discovering the flashing light, even when they were able to find the spot on their face. Zazzo interpreted this in terms of the existence of two distinct spatial fields, having a different degree of salience or objectivation for the child. According to this assumption, objects at a greater distance would be less eliciting than a spot on the face, because they are less relevant to the infant's immediate sensorimotor field of acting and perceiving.

The findings of Zazzo's studies provided a source of discussion around a sequential acquisition of self-recognition abilities, and especially around Bertenthal and Fischer's reported sequence of object-locating and spot-locating, which had been supported by other studies (e.g., Lewis & Brooks-Gunn, 1979). In an effort to evaluate Zazzo's assumption regarding spatial salience, Gouin Décarie, Pouliot, and Poulin-Dubois (1983) studied the effect of characteristics of objects and the effect of distance between the object and the infant on the ability to locate the object or spot. Infants in age groups ranging from 6 to 30 months were observed in mirror conditions confronted with their rouged face (*l'image altérée*), an elephant object located at two different distances behind them, and their mother at two different distances. According to this study, both turning to a close object and turning to a distant object precede mark manipulation, rejecting the assumption of Zazzo on spatial relevance, and corroborating the sequence found by Bertenthal and Fischer. In fact, the infants in Gouin Décarie et al.'s study seemed very bright: At 9 months of age, most of them were already able to locate the objects, whereas the successful performance on the spot test was reserved for the 18-month-olds.

With the experiment of Gouin Décarie et al., the debate on sequential acquisition of self—or better, the sequential mastery of mirror tasks—was seemingly closed, and the proposed sequence solidified. Still, in essence, different procedural aspects can be conceived to which infants may be sensitive and which may confound any sequential nature of results. The distance to the object, but also the attractiveness of the toy, the movement characteristics of the reflected object, any accompanying referential spatial landmarks, the prompting of the infant by the experimenter or the parent, and the amount of time within which an infant is credited with a response are all very influential contextual aspects that have not been used in standard ways across studies.

As an experimental technique, the visual self-recognition paradigm is vulnerable to procedural influences. For the rouged-face task, Zazzo (1977b), for example, demonstrated that the application of the mark on the cheek instead of on the nose and the use of a larger mirror resulted in a difference in mark-detection of not less than 7 months. Also, both the object-locating and the mark-on-the-nose tasks are not easy to set up without artificially introducing disturbing factors. For the object-locating task, for example, important factors to control are the sound that accompanies the movement of the suspended object, and the problem of crediting the infant who accidentally sees the object in his or her peripheral vision. Finally, the hat task is difficult to organize without problems. Two replications of this task have failed (Chapman, 1987; Vyt, 1988). Also, the earlier success in this task may have been a consequence of more contingent play because of the special characteristic of the hat attached to the infant. It can elicit more curiosity and more body movement, which in turn has an influence on the movement of the object and its eliciting potential.

The question then arises about to what extent sequences in self-recognition behaviors are a reflection of procedural aspects or of developments in sensorimotor skills, rather than an epigenesis in self-recognition or self-awareness. Both object-locating and mark-locating tasks have a certain amount of overlap, because they are search tasks accomplished by means of a reflected image. Both are objects in the real space, although the mark differs in that it is on the face of the child, that it is two-dimensional, usually smaller than any toy object used, and that it certainly moves contingently with the child's image. In the course of the 2nd year of life, a spot or mark on the face may acquire a special kind of salience for the child in the framework of his or her growing sensitivity to standards and their deviations, which occurs primarily toward the end of the 2nd year (Kagan, 1981). A spot or dirt on the face can be considered as something that belongs to the sphere of standards and norms, that is, what is proper and improper. Up to a certain age, the child simply does not care about the presence of a mark on his or her face. Mark-directed behavior in the mark task, which is now widely held as the most valid index of visual self-recognition (Anderson, 1984; Jézéquel & Baudonnière, 1991; Robinson, Connell, McKenzie, & Day, 1990), could reflect, to a large extent, this kind of sensitivity.

THE VALIDITY OF PRECURSORS

Notwithstanding the foregoing critical remarks, the sequence of object-locating and mark-directed behavior found by Bertenthal and Fischer (1978) was regarded as normative for the sequential nature of the development of both self-recognition and even various aspects of self (see, e.g., Harter, 1983). Also Lewis and Brooks-Gunn (1979), who conducted an impressive array of cross-sectional studies with a variety of representational modes suggested a relatively early onset of the ability to turn toward reflected persons (or objects). These authors additionally distinguished between the infant's appreciation of the self as subject or active agent—the *existential self* in Jamesian terminology—and the self as an object with recognizable features—the so-called *categorial self*.

Self-recognition on the basis of stable featural (i.e., facial) characteristics, and independent of the contingency between the bodily self and the mirror-image, become consolidated at the end of the 2nd year. The emergence of this featural or categorical self would already be prepared by a self–other differentiation in the last quarter of the 1st year of life, because from this age on, infants are able to discriminate a noncontingent video image of the self from an image of a peer. At around the same time, an awareness of the self as active agent, different from others, becomes apparent in the successful performance of object-locating tasks in contingent mirror situations and would be already implicit in contingent play as a form of action–effect sequences (Lewis & Brooks-Gunn, 1979).

Discussions will always exist regarding whether precursors must be treated as nothing more than precursors, or whether the concepts must be revised according to new findings, and thus be situated earlier in development. In this field of self-recognition, for example, H. Papoušek and M. Papoušek (1974) found that 5-month-olds discriminate a live video image of the self from a recorded image of self. Infants showed their discrimination by preferentially looking at the noncontingent, recorded display of themselves over the contingent, live display (which, however, lacked eye contact). In another study, Field (1979) found that 3-month-olds already responded differentially to a contingent mirror image of the self and a noncontingent presentation of a peer. In this case, they looked more to their own mirror image, but vocalized and smiled more to the other image.

Cautiousness is needed when inferring self-awareness and self-recognition at an early age from these studies on contingency. What can be said is that, at this age, infants preferentially discriminate between stimuli according to the most salient characteristic that meets their current mental abilities. For example, in the cited studies, at 3 months, preferential fixation was oriented toward contingent self-representation, but at 5 months toward noncontingent representation. In large part, of course, this is due to procedural differences between the two studies, which, for this reason, cannot be really compared. For example, in the study of H. Papoušek and M. Papoušek (1974), the possibility of eye contact functioned as one major potential determinant of infants' attention. Attentional skills, which undergo a major development in the first months of life and beyond, may also play a part. For example, 5-month-old infants can choose between a noncontingent and a contingent representation, but they may prefer the noncontingent one because it provides more stimulation without their having to be physically active. At that age, infants have an attention span that probably allows them to focus their attention for longer periods. Infants of 3 months, on the other hand, most likely have shorter attention spans, which may result in their being more easily attracted to the experience of contingency.

Perceptual discrimination of contingent versus noncontingent stimulation does not automatically imply an emergence of an existential self-awareness. No doubt, however, findings on contingency awareness can still support Lewis and Brooks-Gunn's (1979) assumption that the contingency between visual and proprioceptive information of self-motion serves as a basis for the development of self in the early months of life (see, also, Samuels, 1986). In addition, in the study by H. Papoušek and M. Papoušek (1974), the infants had to learn about the contingency and only gradually became more focused on the contingent (but no-eye-contact) image.

On the level of featural self-recognition, similar precursors can be observed. For example, although mark-directed behavior is only well established at the end of the 2nd year, an increase in self-directed behavior is visible among 12-month-old children confronted with their marked faces, even when it does not result in effectively locating the mark (Lewis & Brooks-Gunn, 1979). One could argue that lack of postural control and fine motor movements impedes clear measurement of what, in essence, the child could do mentally. In a similar vein, with proper modifications in measurement, it is possible to demonstrate, for example, that 3- to 4-month-old infants already possess a notion of object permanence (Baillargeon, 1987). Violation of a rule has been put forward as a good method of diagnosing infants' early levels of object concept (LeCompte & Gratch, 1972), but nobody will contend that the emerging notion at 3 months is comparable to the notion as it is measured at the end of the 1st year. From a contextual viewpoint, a notion is best circumscribed by the way it is measured at different ages, and not by any optimal condition that researchers may have sketched out in the child's mind retrospectively. This certainly is the case with the notion of self-recognition.

Francophone research in this field can be characterized as showing a certain degree of prudence toward premature use of concepts like *self, ego,* and *identity,* and toward construing a neat sequence of solid acquisition of the self in mirror tasks. Even well into the preschool years, children are highly suggestible and easily misled when it concerns adequate reactions on mirrored situations. Zazzo (1979) demonstrated this in an experiment in which mothers approached their infants (sitting in front of a mirror) from behind with a box of chocolates. Strikingly, even at 3 years of age a substantial proportion of the children went behind the mirror to search for their mothers. Of course, we are not inferring from this situation that 3-year-olds lack self-recognition skills in front of mirrors, nor that they lack any featural self-representation. It tells us, however, that, when confronted with unexpected situations, children become destabilized and revert to primitive responses even after infancy.

Zazzo (1976) did an even more convincing experiment on destabilization with preschoolers who were confronted with a series of video self-images. Here, 3-year-olds almost instantly confirmed that they saw their own image on TV, but 4- and 5-year-olds demonstrated an initial disbelief, either because of a lack of contingency or because of a left–right inversion of mirror symmetry. Once again, disbelief does not mean that the children suddenly lost their self-recognition ability, but that they had become sensitive to unexpected and new experiences that they wanted to understand fully. The scrutiny and experimental cautiousness of Zazzo on this matter (Zazzo, 1983) is, to a large degree, influenced by Jean Piaget, who contended that focusing on observation and a clinical interview method was at least as important as statistically significant figures. The second spiritual father of Zazzo was Henri Wallon, and a central concept used by Zazzo in the Wallonian framework (see Wallon, 1963/1981) is that of *appropriation,* which can be compared with the Piagetian concept of cognitive assimilation. The term appropriation of the self-image indicates an active process in which perception, cognition, and the original bodily awareness are intrinsically linked to each other. The infant must, in a way, incorporate his or her visual appearance so that it coincides with the primary experience of his or her own body. A perceptual match has to be construed mentally, and as such, it is a constructivistic process of acquisition, rather than an automatic one, and one not without obstacles (Zazzo, 1983).

In this respect, it should be noted that developmental psychology in Paris in the years after World War II stood in closer relation with psychoanalytic ideas than is the case nowadays. It is not purely a coincidence that Zazzo (1948) published his first paper about self-recognition in the same period when the French extreme psychoanalyst, Lacan (1949) published an article about the emergence of the *I*. In the latter article, the notion of a solidified self was undermined, and the alienating character of the mirror experience was stressed. The human infant does not develop a self-awareness without losing a sense of identity: By appropriating a visual image of the self as its own, the child identifies himself or herself with something that comes from outside. Also, an important factor in this process is the role of the parent. It is the parent who provides the infant—and the infant's image—with labels that set his or her identity.

UNDERLYING PROCESSES

Sometimes, a research paradigm can acquire a certain inertia in a search for consistency in results while the premises about "confounding" variables have not been adequately sorted out. A worthwhile endeavor, then, is to look at underlying processes that influence performance on different tasks of self-recognition, such as locating mirrored objects. In this venture, both experimental studies and longitudinal studies that follow children during infancy are valuable. Unfortunately, very few studies are performed longitudinally. Boulanger-Balleyguier (1964, 1967) was the first researcher who followed a large sample of subjects for an extended period. More than 10 years later, Bigelow (1981) observed infants monthly, for about 8 months during the 2nd year of life, in a series of self-recognition settings. The infants in this study showed self-recognition (by turning to a reflected object or by verbal identification of the image) in conditions in which there was a self- and image-movement correspondence before they recognized themselves in conditions where there was no such contingency. More interestingly, the movement contingency testing showed a significant increase in the session prior to self-recognition.

Contingency learning is not always clearly visible in an infant confronted with his or her own image, trying to locate mirrored objects. There is a simple reason for this: A child, seeing a mirror-reflection, can have an intuitive image (a sort of expectancy, based on experience with mirrors) of a mirror having certain characteristics, such as reflecting real space in a virtual image. In other words, infants may have learned the reflective characteristic of a mirror without a deductive process based on contingency cues with the self-image. A recent study (Robinson et al., 1990), indeed, found no evidence to indicate that infants must refer to their own image in order to locate an object. Although it may be true and hardly doubtful that children use contingency testing during their history of mirror experience, a conservative stance may consider turning to a reflected object as an index of self-recognition only for children with no experience or familiarity with mirrors. Turning behavior, in this view, is a valid measure if the child must make the inference using himself as reference point by correspondence, and is strengthened when deductive processes in the infant become visible by means of, for example, contingency testing behavior preceding the object-locating (i.e., turning) behavior.

Familiarity with Mirrors

One study that systematically controlled the degree of familiarity with mirrors in children was performed by Priel and de Schonen (1986). They compared infants between 6 and 26 months who had no previous experience with mirrors with a control group of children who had normal mirror experience, in locating mirrored objects and on rouge tests. Results of this study suggested that self-recognition in the mirror, as observed by mark-directed behavior at the end of the 2nd year, is independent of the child's familiarity with reflecting surfaces. The capacity to relate the mirror to real space (by locating an object), on the other hand, seems to be strongly dependent on previous experience with mirrors. Specifically, mark-manipulation showed a sudden increase in the oldest children in the study, and this, in both the familiar and unfamiliar subjects, while location of the object showed a slightly earlier development in the familiar group. Of the oldest non-familiar children in the study, the authors found more than one third manipulated the mark but failed to turn to the object. Here, also, an explanation can be suggested without the necessity of utilizing the concepts of self-recognition and self-awareness. Possibly, the older infants were more sensitive in detecting the spot on the nose as a deviation from norms. Also, this task requires less spatial inference capability. For locating an object behind oneself, which relies more heavily on spatial coordinative ability and mirror insight, an effect of experience with mirrors may very well be assumed, even for the oldest age group. The study of Priel and de Schonen demonstrated that object-locating and mark-locating, however similar they may be in some respects, differ from each other in underlying processes of acquisition. As the authors suggested, object-locating behavior is not necessarily linked to a capacity for self-recognition, but rather to a capacity to relate real to virtual space. Experience with mirrors may enable the child to immediately interpret the reflection of an object as an object behind him (Priel & de Schonen, 1986). For mark-directed behavior, other processes may be of more important influence, as described earlier.

Experimental Control of Learning Processes

Another way of tackling the problem of familiarity with reflecting surfaces is to try to gain experimental control over learning processes involved in a new visual self-experience. A control of learning experience was used by Vyt (1988, see also 1993) in an experimental design with 60 infants in five age groups, ranging from 15 to 28 months of age. In this study, all children lacked previous experience with television as a possible reflecting surface by closed circuit presentation, and had no experience with presentation of video-images of themselves or other familiar persons on television. The video characteristics in this study were kept as mirror-like as possible to enhance the same processes as in real mirror situations. The video-image was similar to a mirror in left–right symmetry, color-image, and real 1:1 scale of the image (upper body and face), while still maintaining the outlook of a TV so that transfer of knowledge from mirror to TV was in initial control of the training process.

Search tasks (locating an object) seem to be much more difficult when using video than when using mirrors. Some previous video studies therefore have given infants training in turning to the object or person before the actual experimental tasks took place (e.g, Lewis & Brooks-Gunn, 1979). In our own study, children were given the opportunity to learn the characteristics of simultaneous video-reproduction, helped by two possible sources of information. One group of children received training in which they saw their parent's image on TV for 1 minute. These parents had been instructed to direct the children's attention to the image and to try to explain that the TV is a mirrorlike instrument—thus verbally and visually inducing a transfer of learning without the child experiencing self–image correspondence by himself. In the other group, each child viewed himself or herself on TV sitting on a parent's lap, while the parent forced the child to perform any form of contingency play with his or her video-image (e.g., bouncing, waving, or clapping hands) and asked him or her to point out different parts of the parent's face (e.g., "where is Mommy's nose?"). In these ways children could have either an indirect learning transfer possibility (with a strong verbal component) in the first training, or a direct transfer opportunity on the basis of contingency movement testing with his or her own image, as well as on the basis of spatial structuring of the virtual image with the self as a reference cue, in the second one.

Following the training, the infants experienced video–self conditions during which a toy appeared behind and in front of the infant, but was only visible in the "reflected" video-image. Parents prompted their children to take the object, without giving any further referential suggestions. As the different locations also provided different landmark cues, it was hypothesized that differences between the behind and in front conditions would become apparent. For example, in the latter condition a wooden barrier was also visible in both real and virtual space. Finally, after the object-locating conditions, the infant saw himself or herself with a spot on his cheek, surreptitiously administered by the parent.

After this, part of the object permanence subscale (Uzgiris & Hunt, 1975) was administered, which involved solving a single invisible displacement of an object (Piaget's early Stage VI). The experimenter placed a puppet in a small plastic container and then hid the container and its contents under one of three covers in front of the infant. After leaving the toy under the cloth, the experimenter showed the empty container to the child and asked where the puppet had gone. The procedure was then repeated by hiding the toy in the same manner under the other cover; the infant was given two credits to pass each trial. Piaget claimed that infants do not possess a real capacity for representation until Stage VI of the sensorimotor period, that is, when they begin to search for objects hidden through invisible displacements (Piaget, 1936/1952). A correspondence between self-recognition performance and Stage VI object permanence performance was expected, because many skills are shared by the two kind of tasks, not least the ability to search for hidden objects by making mental inferences. Both the tasks of locating mirrored objects and the object permanence tasks for Stage VI may need a kind of deductive referential reasoning process. In the object permanence task, inferences must be made about the place of a puppet that was first hidden in a box and then left under a towel (invisible displacement); in the self-recognition search task, inferences must be made about the place of a toy with the help of referential cues (seeing himself or herself, the chair, and eventually the wooden barrier in front of the child reflected). Children who score on object-locating in the video settings should, thus, also score positively on the object-permanence Stage VI task.

One measure of interest in the study was the ability to make sustained attempts at finding the object in the right place. Intentional *self-directed search* in the object-locating tasks was, therefore, defined as turning, reaching, or grasping in the immediate spatial field around the infant, irrespective of whether the child did or did not actually find the object. It assessed the insight that the virtual object must be located in real space, with credit for mistakes in three-dimensional orientation (left–right or front–behind). Effectively locating the doll, which was viewed as a successful self-directed search, was scored only when it consisted of a direct look in the correct location of the object that was being presented and that was visible on the TV. In the spot-on-the-nose tasks, *mark-directed behavior* was defined as correctly mark-*locating* (which consisted of pointing and/or touching responses directed at the region of the mark immediately following image regard), or mark-*manipulating* (by exaggerated facial expressions of the cheeks in an effort to get rid of the mark).

Both the intentional self-directed search and mark-directed behavior increased (although not significantly) with age. In fact, very few of the infants did find the object, in the older age groups as well as in the younger groups, and only the doll in front was effectively found. Also, the children who had received the contingency training were virtually the only ones who did find the doll, and a slight training effect was noticed on self-directed search behavior. For mark-directed behavior, however, no significant difference between the two training groups was present.

The age effects found in this study did not rule out a trend of growing self-recognition behavior at the end of the 2nd year, although the task was seemingly difficult for most children. Specifically, for the inability correctly to locate the doll-behind compared to the doll-in-front condition, procedural and perceptual explanations can be readily found. For example, in the doll-in-front condition, children had an additional visual cue as reference in the form of the wooden barrier in front, which was visible both in the immediate field of vision and on the TV.

The findings regarding object permanence were quite straightforward: Infants who succeeded in the inferential object permanence task also displayed significantly more self-directed search behavior in the task of locating the object behind or in front of them. On the other hand, an association between level of object permanence and the occurrence of mark-directed behavior was absent.

These results, according to training experience and object permanence status, suggest the plausibility that mark and object conditions differ in several respects that influence a different developmental course. These findings are in concordance with the results of the earlier mentioned study of Priel and de Schonen (1986), in which no significant differences were found in mark manipulation between populations familiar or unfamiliar with mirrors. Perhaps what is most needed here, besides a certain level of cognitive development, is enough experience with normal faces without marks of rouge on and a sensitivity to what is proper and improper. Object-locating search behavior, on the other hand, seems to be linked more to the ability of objective spatial representation Piaget called *allocentrism*. It appears to be dependent on experience with the medium involved, but it is also at least as much dependent on maturational aspects.

Infants can make use of and rely on contingency cues (shown by the training effect) and visual referential cues (shown by the contextual effect of the barrier in front) to guide their search behavior. This finding strengthens the hypothesis that in order to have a transfer of mirror cognition, infants in this age range need to be represented themselves or to have a direct visual cue in real space represented in the medium to which transfer is supposed to occur. That is, infants may have difficulty in transferring knowledge of self-recognition to an apparently new (but essentially identical) situation without having sensorimotor experience with that new situation or medium. Learning still takes place via perception and experimentation, even if the infant is supposed to have a growing symbolic capacity to abstract and if this knowledge about objects is no longer restricted to the basic sensorimotor level.

CONCLUSION

Going from behavior in front of mirror situations to the development of self-recognition, self-awareness, and identity formation, is all but straightforward. Some findings underline that self-recognition, as measured by the mark task, is to be seen as the result of a conglomerate of cognitive functions solidified in late infancy, together with other aspects of growing self-awareness. The mark task and the object-locating task differ from each other in several respects that suggest different developmental courses. Findings suggest that the value of object-locating tasks in the self-recognition paradigm has to be reformulated in a certain sense. Object-locating tasks in mirror conditions may be a good paradigm for studying specific visual sensorimotor information processing, but they may not always be accepted as a valid indicator of self-recognition.

In evaluating self-recognizing competencies and in designing measures for them one must take into account the sensorimotor organization and attentional abilities of children at different ages in infancy. In fact, the mirror paradigm provides a very interesting opportunity to study cognitive and spatial skills by use of contingency and landmark cues. Implementation of experimental control of learning processes and conditions in this domain may be worth further study.

Finally, self-recognition is a complex process influenced by a number of variables, of which contingency experience by simultaneity of movement in mirror-conditions is but one. Nevertheless, it appears to be an important cue in this early self-discovery. In a constructivistic view, it is through action that children initially understand the world, and it is through their interaction with their own reflections that they understand the nature, the meaning, and the identity of these reflections. The most important milestone in self-recognition, however, remains the ability to recognize oneself independent of this contingency.

ACKNOWLEDGMENTS

My research was conducted at the Laboratory of Developmental and Personality Psychology of the University of Ghent, and became possible through financial support from the Belgian National Fund for Scientific Research, of which I held a position as senior research assistant. I wish to thank Francine Vander Linden for assistance in conducting the studies.

REFERENCES

Amsterdam, B. K. (1972). Mirror self-image reactions before age two. *Developmental Psychology, 5,* 297–305.

Anderson, J. R. (1984). Monkeys with mirrors: Some questions for primate psychology. *International Journal of Primatology, 5,* 201–212.

Baillargeon, R. (1987). Object permanence in 3½- and 4½-month-old infants. *Developmental Psychology, 23,* 655–664.

Baldwin, J. M. (1897). *Social and ethical interpretations in mental development.* New York: Macmillan.

Bertenthal, B. I., & Fischer, K. W. (1978). Development of self-recognition in the infant. *Developmental Psychology, 14,* 44–50.

Bigelow, A. E. (1981). The correspondence between self- and image-movement as a cue to self-recognition for young children. *Journal of Genetic Psychology, 139,* 11–26.

Boulanger-Balleyguier, G. (1964). Premières réactions devant le miroir [First reactions in front of the mirror]. *Enfance, 16,* 51–67.

Boulanger-Balleyguier, G. (1967). Les étapes de la reconnaissance de soi devant le miroir [Stages of self-recognition in front of the mirror]. *Enfance, 19,* 91–116.

Chapman, M. (1987). A longitudinal study of cognitive representation in symbolic play, self-recognition, and object permanence during the second year. *International Journal of Behavioral Development, 10,* 151–170.

Darwin, C. R. (1877). A biographical sketch of an infant. *Mind, 2,* 285–294.

Dixon, J. C. (1957). Development of self-recognition. *Journal of Genetic Psychology, 91,* 251–256.

Field, J. (1979). Differential behavior and cardiac responses of 3-month-old infants to a mirror and peer. *Infant Behavior and Development, 2,* 179–184.

Fischer, K. W. (1980). A theory of cognitive development: The control and construction of hierarchies of skills. *Psychological Review, 87,* 477–531.

Gouin Décarie, T., Pouliot, T., & Poulin-Dubois, D. (1983). Image spéculaire et genèse de la reconnaissance de soi: Une analyse hiérarchique [Mirror image and development of self-recognition: A hierarchical analysis]. *Enfance, 35,* 99–115.

Harter, S. (1983). Developmental perspectives on the self-system. In P. H. Mussen (Series Ed.) & E. M. Hetherington (Vol. Ed.), *Handbook of child psychology: Vol. 4. Socialization, personality, and social development* (4th ed., pp. 275–385). New York: Wiley.

Jézéquel, J.-L., & Baudonnière, P.-M. (1991). *The magic mirror: Knowledge of the reflecting properties of the mirror in 2- to 8-year-old children.* Unpublished manuscript, Ecole des Hautes Etudes, Paris.

Kagan, J. (1981). *The second year: The emergence of self-awareness.* Cambridge, MA: Harvard University Press.

Lacan, J. (1949). Le stade du miroir comme formateur de la fonction du je [The mirror stage as shaper of the I function]. *Revue Francaise de Psychanalyse, 13,* 449–455.

LeCompte, G. K., & Gratch, G. (1972). Violation of a rule as a method of diagnosing infants' levels of object concept. *Child Development, 43,* 385–396.

Lewis, M., & Brooks-Gunn, J. (1979). *Social cognition and the acquisition of self.* New York: Plenum.

Papoušek, H., & Papoušek, M. (1974). Mirror-image and self-recognition in young human infants: A new method for experimental analysis. *Developmental Psychobiology, 7,* 149–157.

Piaget, J. (1952). *The origins of intelligence in children* (M. Cook, transl.) (2nd ed.). New York: Norton. (Original work published 1936)

Preyer, W. (1988). *The mind of the child.* New York: Appleton.

Priel, B., & de Schonen, S. (1986). Self-recognition: A study of a population without mirrors. *Journal of Experimental Child Psychology, 41,* 237–250.

Robinson, J. A., Connell, S., McKenzie, B. E., & Day, R. H. (1990). Do infants use their own images to locate objects reflected in a mirror? *Child Development, 61,* 1558–1568.

Samuels, C. A. (1986). Bases for the infant's developing self-awareness. *Human Development, 29,* 36–48.

Uzgiris, I., & Hunt, J. McV. (1975). *Assessment in infancy: Ordinal scales of psychological development.* Urbana, IL: University of Illinois Press.

Vyt, A. (1988, April). *Visual self-recognition in infants.* Poster presented at the Sixth International Conference on Infant Studies, Washington, DC.

Vyt, A. (1993). Processes of visual self-recognition in infants: Experimental induction of "mirror" experience via video self-image presentation. Manuscript submitted for publication.

Wallon, H. (1981). Comment su développe chez l'enfant la notion du corps propre [How does the bodily self develop in infancy]. In P. Mounoud & A. Vinter (Ed.), *La reconnaissance de son image chez l'enfant et l'animal [The recognition of the self image in infant and animal].* (pp. 21–45). Paris: Delachaux et Niestlé. (Original work published 1963)

Zazzo, R. (1948). Images du corps et conscience de soi: Materiaux pour l'étude expérimentale de la conscience [Bodily reflections and self-awareness: Materials for the experimental study of consciousness]. *Enfance, 1,* 29–43.

Zazzo, R. (1975). Des jumeaux devant le miroir: Question de méthode [Twins in front of the mirror: A methodological question]. *Journal de Psychologie Normale et Pathologique, 72,* 389–413.

Zazzo, R. (1976). C'est moi quand-même [It is me indeed after all]. (Documentary on film). Paris: CNRS.

Zazzo, R. (1977a). Image spéculaire et conscience de soi [Mirror image and self-awareness]. In G. Oléron (Ed.), *Psychologie expérimentale et comparée: Hommage à Paul Fraisse [Experimental and comparative psychology: Homage to Paul Fraisse].* (pp. 325–338). Paris: Presses Universitaires de France.

Zazzo, R. (1977b). Image spéculaire et image anti-spéculaire [Mirror image and anti-mirror image]. *Enfance, 29,* 223–230.

Zazzo, R. (1979). Des enfants, des singes, et des chiens devant le miroir [Infants, monkeys, and dogs in front of the mirror]. *Revue de Psychologie Appliquée, 29,* 235–246.

Zazzo, R. (1983). *Où en est la psychologie de l'enfant?* [Where does infant psychology stand?]. Paris: Denoël.

10 Inducing Cognitive Strategies

Jean Claude Fraysse
Annie Desprels-Fraysse
Université de Provence

The induction of cognitive strategies in 4- to 7-year-olds is aimed at providing children with very general cognitive tools. Such inductions are a particular form of *sensu lato* learning based on the very laws of development (Piaget, 1959a). The researchers who use induction exercises refer to Piaget's theory, not so much in an attempt to test it, which seems to be the specific approach of the English-speaking community, but rather to clarify its obscure points. The availability to the French-speaking world of Piaget's rich writings has allowed Francophone research to clearly distinguish experimentally derived facts from logical formalizations. In support of this claim, note that Inhelder, Sinclair, and Bovet, in the introduction to their book, *Apprentissage et structures de la connaissance* (1974), pointed out the following open issues: (a) the transition from one developmental stage to the next, (b) the connections between different knowledge domains, (c) dynamic factors, and (d) the interdependence of those factors (*equilibration*).

Learning research began in Geneva in 1959 (Piaget, 1959a,b). Work in this field became so prolific that even the best overviews of the issue have never been comprehensive (Bideaud, 1988; Khun, 1974; Oléron & Thong, 1968; Strauss, 1972). In this chapter, we briefly summarize the common points and specificities of the main studies in Francophone research on learning, their role in the subsequent questioning of certain aspects of Piaget's theory, and their respective contributions and current research perspectives.

CHARACTERISTICS OF COGNITIVE
STRATEGY INDUCTION

Experimental Paradigms

The experimental paradigms used in learning research always consist of a pretest, one or more learning sessions applied to one or more experimental groups, and a comparison of the experimental and control groups performance on posttests, immediately following or delayed. This type of paradigm applies both to operatory learning and to the induction of logical structures.

In *operatory learning,* classical Piagetian tasks are used for the pretests, learning sessions, and posttests. These tasks include conservation, seriation, and inclusion (e.g., Bideaud, 1988; Botson & Deliège, 1975; Inhelder et al., 1974; Lasry & Laurendeau, 1969; Lefebvre & Pinard, 1972). This has been the approach used mostly by English-speaking authors, such as Beilin, Brainerd, Kuhn, Flavell, Siegel, and Smedslund, to mention a few. In *rule induction,* the tasks used in the learning sessions are different from the pretest and posttest tasks. They are designed to act on a fundamental nucleus characterized by a basic invariant. In these paradigms, original tasks called *covariations* are used. The experimenter introduces a variation and the child is supposed to respond by proposing the inverse variation in order to reestablish the initial configuration; one invariant is maintained throughout the transformations (Desprels-Fraysse & Fraysse, 1977; Orsini-Bouichou, 1975, 1982; Paour, 1980, 1991). The acquisition of an invariant at level $n + 1$ is induced from the level n invariant spontaneously used by the child. A developmental scale defining the order of invariant acquisition was proposed by Orsini-Bouichou (1975). This author showed that children in situations with virtually no constraints organize their behavior on the basis of sequential rules or regularities. These regularities are supported by general systems of rules or operators, which the author described as functions. For children in the preoperatory period (ages 3 to 7), Orsini-Bouichou found evidence of four types of operators:

1. At about age 3, children repeat (I) the same action on the same object (x). This operator is called *identifier, iterator* and is expressed by the function $y = I(x) = $ constant.

2. At approximately age 4, a newly acquired operator allows children to establish pairs of similar objects by opposing one term to another that is not that term: $y = I(x, \text{not } x)$.

3. By age 6, children maintain a correspondence relation (cr) between the two terms in a pair: $y = I(x \text{ cr } z)$.

4. Finally, at about age 7 or 8, children are capable of combining two operators and four terms, based on a notional invariant: $y = \{I(x \text{ cr } z) \text{ R } (x' \text{ cr}'$

z')}. This operator allows children to establish relations of relations, thus bringing them to proportionality by age 11 or 12.

The acquisition of these invariants is detected by means of criterial covariation and quantitative covariation tasks. *Criterial covariations* involve the maintenance of an invariant while changing object properties (in exercises like Raven's Progressive Matrices; Raven, 1938). In *quantitative covariations,* beads of two different colors are placed, one by one, in a sectioned box through a hole in the lid. The lid is slid along as the sections inside the box are filled, thus hiding the beads as they are inserted. One invariant is maintained as the experimenter and child take turns inserting the beads. For example, if the invariant is "Insert a total of five beads," then each time the experimenter takes his turn, the child must insert the complementary set of beads (two red beads/three white beads, no red beads/five white beads, etc.).

Mechanisms Responsible for Progress

The mechanisms responsible for progress, in both operatory learning and rule induction, are (a) maintenance of an invariant, (b) cognitive conflict, and (c) the subject's transition to awareness of his or her own actions.

Induction exercises are designed in such a way that an invariant can be maintained throughout the various transformations. In Desprels-Fraysse and Fraysse (1977), we triggered two successive inductions in the same group of children by using their ability to detect a difference between two objects. First, we induced the use of a transformation invariant: maintenance of the difference over a large number of objects. Once the ability to make an invariant-based collection was acquired, a more general invariant was induced: application of a rule that combines two transformations, either via quantitative covariation (maintenance of the number of five beads while varying their color: two reds and three whites, one red and four whites, etc.) or via criterial covariation (maintenance of a transformation, such as thick/not-thick while varying another criterion such as spotted/not-spotted). Paour (1980, 1981, 1991) taught children transformation permanence by having them take objects in and out of a "magic box." He then taught them transformation coordination by asking them to obtain one object from another (for example, to "transform" a little white car into a big red car by putting the object into the hole that changes its size, and then into the hole that changes its color, or vice versa).

The same principle can be found in operatory learning, even if it does not play the role of experimental variable. In an exercise designed to teach the conservation of liquids, Lefebvre and Pinard (1972) manipulated either the perceptual invariance of the levels of liquid in different vases or the invariance of the amount of liquid in similar or different vases. In a learning task bearing on inclusion, Inhelder et al. (1974) varied the number of members in the subclasses while keeping the number in the superordinate class constant. This same principle underlies the quantitative covariation tasks already mentioned, in which the child is asked to keep the total number of beads constant while the number inserted by the experimenter varies. Skourass' (1976) experiment led children to discover the invariant on which seriation is based by using material that could be ordered in three ways: by door size, window size, or house size.

Another source of progress results from *cognitive conflict*. In Piaget's theory, the dynamics of cognitive construction are based on equilibration processes defined by the functional relationships between assimilation and accommodation. In this perspective, one of the possible sources of progress lies in disequilibrium or cognitive conflict. Conflict is thus a major mechanism used in the inductions: The child responds to a disruption introduced by the experimenter, who changes one of the givens in the initial situation. In the operatory learning tasks directly derived from the Piagetian framework, the conflict invoked can be intraindividual (cognitive conflict) or interindividual (sociocognitive conflict). The notion of sociocognitive conflict has developed within the European research trend called *genetic social psychology*, a trend that is strongly marked by Vygotsky's theory (Doise & Mugny, 1981; Perret-Clermont, 1979).

In operatory learning, *la prise de conscience* (the child's transition to awareness) is a neglected mechanism. In cognitive strategy inductions, however, children are often led to focus on the course and goal of their actions. They are asked to anticipate what they are going to do and to express what they have just done. The purpose of this is to allow children to make a permanent representation (one that is independent of their actions unfolding in time). This cognitive capability, or *metacognition*, develops spontaneously in ontogenesis (Flavell, 1982, 1985; Piaget, 1974).

Although these mechanisms are the ones most commonly invoked, other authors have also stressed the importance of imitation in learning by observation (Robert, 1983) and the role of empirical discovery and reinforcement (Bideaud, 1981; Botson & Deliège, 1975).

Assessment of Acquisitions

In all types of learning tasks, progress is analyzed by comparing pretest and posttest performance across the various control and experimental groups. Control group performance is supposed to be indicative of ordinary progress during the learning period. The children in these groups either do not benefit from outside intervention or are subject to some neutral activity on the part of the experimenter, who only actually intervenes with the experimental group.

The learning setup, as used here, is ideal for studying (a) the transition from one stage to the next, (b) the relative effectiveness of the various mechanisms alone or in combination, and (c) the knowledge transferred to the posttest tasks.

Unfortunately, the results obtained have been quite disappointing. Piaget's cognitive conflict does not lead to better learning than a traditional teaching method (Bideaud, 1981; Lasry & Laurendeau, 1969) or a learning-by-observation method (Charbonneau, Robert, Bourassa, & Gladu-Bissonnette, 1976; Robert & Turcotte, 1983). In addition, the results of past experiments have not always been replicated. The learning of conservation via the cognitive conflict method can either be very effective (Lefebvre & Pinard, 1972), moderately effective (Case, 1977; Inhelder et al., 1974), or ineffective (Fortin-Thierault, 1977). The success of methods designed to trigger the learning of general rules by criterial and quantitative covariations also turns out to be highly variable, even when the same authors conduct the experiments (Flores & Orsini-Bouichou, 1979). These findings have led Francophone researchers to take several considerably different positions. Some, like many North Americans, have completely rejected Piaget's theory. A greater number have searched for the reasons behind the failures, assessing the points where discrepancies occurred and adjusting the Piagetian contribution, rather than rejecting it altogether. This latter approach has led to new learning paradigms.

QUESTIONING PIAGET'S THEORY

Difficulty in Assessing Operatory Level

A strong link between children's initial abilities and later behavioral progress can be found in pretest–learning–posttest observation solely by analyzing a whole range of behaviors, and most of all, through a detailed look at the sequence of actions performed and procedures followed (Desprels-Fraysse & Fraysse, 1977; Inhelder et al., 1974; Lefebvre & Pinard, 1974). The assessment criteria used are indeed reliable, because the same hierarchy is consistently found in similar situations, but they are not very sensitive. Behavioral indices, such as nonconservant, noninclusive, and lack of seriation, are all negative (indicating the things children are unable to do), and apply to long periods of development. Moreover, they are highly situation dependent. For example, inclusion responses can appear between the ages of 7 and 12, depending on the task (Bideaud, 1988). The same is true for other tasks (seriation, conservation, classification, etc.). In contrast, the behavioral indices used in criterial and quantitative covariation tasks give us a positive qualification (indicating what children can do) and delimit a period that is shorter, but still too long (lasting approximately 2 years). These, also, are highly dependent on the task (Desprels-Fraysse, 1980, 1983). In addition, this type of evaluation does not account for the socially significant variables linked to the status of the partner(s) (Fraysse, 1985, 1991; Monteil, 1988). Non-operatory tasks (e.g., NEMI, WISC, conflict sensitivity tasks) are no better at predicting learning performance. Nor are the many diverse tasks used to evaluate cognitive level, which, by the way, make it difficult, if not impossible, to compare different types of learning. Laurendeau-Bendavid (1985) suggested that new instruments for measuring preoperatory thought should be designed before testing the influence of the various learning mechanisms. She jokingly compared the lack of precise instruments for diagnosing thought to the inaccuracy of a scale that only states whether a person weighs more or less than 100 kg. Thus, operatory tasks provide us with good, but much too macroscopic, developmental indicators. They are designed to study development, not to assess developmental level (Vinh-Bang, 1985).

Lack of Homogeneity in the Indices Used to Assess Behavior

Another difficulty has led researchers to question the existence of general structures. This difficulty is due to the absence of homogeneity in the indices used to assess behavior on tasks from different domains. The postulated connections between domains have not been shown to exist. For example, a child who is able to conserve on the substance conservation task is not necessarily performing well on inclusion tasks, yet theoretically both of these behaviors occur at the concrete operations stage. Authors who use several operatory tasks on the pretests and posttests regularly mention how difficult, if not impossible, it is to find a homogeneous operatory stage (Rieben, de Ribaupierre, & Lautrey, 1983). Logical formalizations of general structures (INRC groupings) cannot be supported, especially because within the same domain, behavior varies considerably across situations that appear to be only minimally different (Bastien, 1987). However, it remains to be shown why postlearning transfers have been noted, and why a certain degree of homogeneity has been observed.

Diversity of the Mechanisms

Finally, the priority Piaget placed on the cognitive conflict mechanism seems exaggerated. Maintenance of an invariant across transformations appears to be more important. Reinforcement, empirical discovery, and imitation, also, certainly play a significant role. Moreover, it is worth noting that on precise analysis of actual learning procedures, multiple mechanisms are, in fact, shown to be jointly at play (Beaudichon, Verba, & Winnykamen, 1988; Gilly, 1988). In particular, this is the case when the authors' orientation is mainly a pedagogical one, where the major concern is to help intellectually deficient learners to progress (Paour, 1991).

The question that remains is whether this plurality of mechanisms overlays a fundamental invariance. In any case, the description of structures based on the teleonomy of an ending point (the logic of logicians) is not adequate, as witnessed, moreover, by Piaget and Garcia's book *Vers une logique des significations,* published in 1987.

Through its repeated testing of Piaget's hypotheses, research on learning has led us to seriously question the theory. The general "grouping" structures cannot account for the horizontal lags observed in development, although the Piagetian hierarchy for the establishment of relations still remains valid: The same hierarchy is always found, whether we observe different children at various ages or the same children at different ages in an identical situation. This appears to be the core of development, the part that is both permanent and common to all current ontogenetic theories (Case, 1985; Fisher, 1980; Halford, 1982; Mounoud, 1986; Pascual-Leone, 1987; Piaget & Inhelder, 1959; Siegler, 1981). Recent research on learning has made it possible to specify (a) the onset of the processes involved in establishing relations, (b) the mechanisms responsible for the implementation of new relations and their mode of action, and (c) the possibility of transfer from one situation to the next.

CONTRIBUTION OF THE INDUCTIONS

Genesis of Relation–Establishment Processes

Cognitive strategy induction is designed to trigger change; it can therefore be used to pinpoint changes when they occur. The different intraindividual pathways followed in situations that initiate the establishment of relations can be used as the basis for comparative analysis to determine the onset of those relations, provided the unfolding of the entire learning period is analyzed. Because it takes time, cognitive strategy induction is a relatively cumbersome method of investigation. The same children are followed for several (i.e., at least 3: pretest, learning, posttest) sessions. To our knowledge, the maximum number of sessions ever used was 20 (Desprels-Fraysse & Fraysse, 1977). In that study, children were observed for 2½ years, during which they took a pretest (3 sessions), attended 12 learning sessions, and then took two posttests (5 sessions). The evaluation of operatory tasks and training sessions was done using functional levels and sublevels, a considerable refinement over the classical assessment techniques.

This same method of analysis was applied more recently with a more specific methodology (Desprels-Fraysse & Fraysse, 1987). Four groups (4-, 5-, 6-, and 7-year-olds) were observed during four object-classification sessions. All sessions were recorded on videotape to allow behavior changes to be better observed. The classification situations chosen were ones that emphasized the establishment of relations. The initial evaluation phase consisted of free classification of a complex set of materials (three shapes, nine colors, seven sizes). The induction phase consisted of classification training sessions for individuals and homogeneous dyads, and the material was varied along several dimensions. At the beginning of each training session, each child was asked to sort the objects into several small boxes by presenting them, one by one, to the experimenter, who accepted or refused the object. The child was then asked to decide, as quickly as possible, what property was common to all of the objects in each box. In the second part of the session, the roles were reversed: The child invented a sorting rule, and the adult selected the objects in order to discover the rule. Based on the changes observed in the behavioral procedures employed, the existence of three classification stages were inferred, with fine gradations within each stage (Desprels-Fraysse, 1985b, 1987). The child first grouped objects together by establishing step-by-step links between two objects that formed a pair, and then made links among a larger and larger number of objects. Once about 10 objects had been collected in this way, an abrupt change in procedure was observed: The child actively searched for objects that possessed some common property and then made collections that united all equivalent objects (e.g., all the red objects, then all the round objects). The number of collections constructed increased very gradually; then, once again, at the point where the child could make several collections, he or she changed and began simultaneously filling up the various collections that constituted equivalency classes based on a more general dimension (the circles, the rectangles, the triangles, i.e., classification by shape). The term *cognitive threshold* is used for the abrupt procedural changes, because the amount of time required for strategy practice before procedural changes occur is highly variable across subjects.

Characterization of the Mechanisms

Induction studies have contributed to defining the exact status of invariants. Although the inductions used at first dealt successively with the different levels of invariants, such as maintenance of a relation and coordination of relations (Orsini-Bouichou, 1982), current work has led researchers to recognize that the various properties of objects play different roles in the establishment of relations, despite Piaget's hypothesis that all properties are equivalent. Accordingly, in the classification learning example just cited, practice with the two-modality dimension, weight (light/heavy), even led to a drop in performance by children who had already recognized the various shapes learned during the first session (Desprels-Fraysse, 1985a). As another example, the nesting relation (cut-out/not-cut-out, as in puzzles) found in criterial covariations is more easily recognized and abstracted than thick/not-thick variations. Inversely, relations involving a change in spatial position are much more difficult (Desprels-Fraysse, 1980). The hypothesis that the varying difficulty of properties depends on their status as "more or less identifying" is in the process of validation (Desprels-Fraysse, 1990b, 1991). This premise has led to the emergence of a new mechanism for cognitive progress based on the existence of variable-status properties. A child who begins to classify objects according to the basic colors, also continues to classify objects by shades of different colors, but not vice versa (Desprels-

Fraysse, 1990a). For example, children who make collections by searching for red, blue, yellow, and green objects can transpose this strategy onto objects in shades of blue. However, children who start with shades of blue proceed via object-by-object identification. The shades of blue are less identifying, requiring one object to be compared to another before being recognized (a blue can only be called light when compared to another object of a darker blue), whereas an object is recognized as red, blue, yellow, or green on its own. The horizontal lags in the use of relations, which are initiated by diverse object properties, would thus be a source of progress by virtue of the procedural transpositions they enable. The color coding of various properties allowed Pineau and Beaufils (1987) to trigger the learning of strict identity (by comparison of all the properties of the objects) in 7–8-year-olds.

The results of induction studies have pointed out the importance of the mainte-nance of a relation between objects. The maintenance in time and space of a relation allows for its abstraction. This principle was already implicitly incorpo-rated into the design of certain operatory learning tasks. Inhelder et al. (1974) used variations in spatial layout in a learning task involving a term-by-term mapping where tokens were placed in a row, in the shape of an L, or in a circle. In a substance conservation task, the authors used clay rolls, first placed side by side, and then gradually stuck together by twos, by fours, etc., until the entire set was united. An analogous principle was put to play in Botson and Deliège's (1975) learning-without-errors technique, although these authors did not use an operatory learning paradigm. Seriation is learned by the execution of a series of very gradual exercises that deal with spatial proximity and item layout.

Maintenance in time is promoted in most learning sessions by requesting that actions by remembered, anticipated, or verbalized. The lid sliding along the box in the quantitative covariation task (Orsini-Bouichou, 1982) forced the children to remember what they had just done. The same was true for the magic box (Paour, 1980), where the relationship between the two objects could not be established by simultaneous comparison because the initial object was already in the box when the target object came out.

The role of conflict has been demonstrated in operatory learning tasks. Induc-tion studies have since qualified its impact, however. In order for a cognitive or socio-cognitive imbalance to occur and instigate progress, a certain number of conditions must be simultaneously met. First, subjects must have fulfilled certain prerequisites. Lefebvre and Pinard (1974) used conflict sensitization exercises before presenting the conservation learning exercises. All authors have insisted on the importance of the child's initial skill level. The kind of learning proposed is directly related to this initial level. Second, the conflict must attain a certain level of intensity. When the conflict is pushed to the maximum level of tolerance, it leads to a significant amount of progress that is both stable and generalizable (Doise & Mugny, 1981).

As for sociocognitive conflict, it must appear during the interaction, and must lead to a negotiated solution void of all forms of compliance (Doise & Mugny, 1981). According to this approach, coordination within individuals stems from coordination between individuals, the latter preceding and generating the former.

The analysis of the behavior of children during induction sessions has shown that cognitive or sociocognitive conflict only appears at certain precise moments in the course of development. From the results of an experiment on 4- to 8-year-olds, Fraysse (1987) showed how children gradually take their partners into account as their cognitive level increases. Four stages were defined: (a) syntonization (meaning connection with a personal aspect of environment and involving total ignorance of the other person); (b) initial attempts to relate, characterized by the intention to communicate, as well as mimicking followed by analytic imitation; (c) confrontation between partners, with potentially different points of view, and (d) cooperation. Sociocognitive conflict can only occur during the confrontation period (Fraysse, 1988). This confrontation period depends not only on the initial cognitive level of the children, but also on task difficulty and contextual variables, such as the status of the adult-experimenter (Fraysse & Desprels-Fraysse, 1990), the representation each child builds of the task (Fraysse, 1991, 1992), and the amount of affinity between each child and his or her partner (Fraysse, 1992). Other authors studying the free activity of children between the ages of 1 and 5 years have found activity construction processes resulting from imitation, construction through cooperation, and tutoring (Verba, 1987; Verba & Isambert, 1983). The very notion of imitation can even have different acceptations (Winnykamen, 1987, 1990).

Transfer of Established Relations

The lack of behavioral homogeneity across tasks can result in an erroneous a priori analysis of postulated equivalencies. After taking children through two phases to teach them conservation and inclusion, Inhelder et al. (1974) wanted to test the equivalency (the simultaneous acquisition) of these two concepts. They found that the learning of inclusion had a greater effect on conservation behavior than vice versa. They concluded by stressing that substance conservation and flower inclusion are not equivalent indices for evaluating subjects: "In conservation, quantification is reduced to a constant equality, whereas with inclusion quantification can take at least two main values" (p. 291). The whole remains equal to itself when it is divided into two subclasses, and the whole is always greater than one of the subclasses.

In a study of ours, involving the induction of an invariant bearing on the composition of relations, children found it more difficult to abstract spatial properties than physical properties (Desprels-Fraysse & Fraysse, 1977). An experiment designed specifically to study this developmental lag compared children's behavior in the establishment of physical relations (shape, color, and size) with their ability to transpose spatial relations (Desprels-Fraysse, 1986). Although the developmental lag separating these behaviors was confirmed, the former being acquired before the latter, a high degree of concordance was found between the two. Accordingly, at about age 6, children maintain a given property (roundness, blueness, etc.) in order to put together all objects that have that property. This behavior is contemporaneous with choosing, among all the possible positions two objects can have with respect to each other, the position that is proposed and must be maintained. The equivalence of these two forms of action appears to result from the child's ability to simultaneously consider several properties of an object and to favor and maintain one of them. The study of what is ultimately transferred involves the detailed analysis of changes in the strategies used by the child (Inhelder et al., 1974).

Attempts to Model Learning

A new line of learning research emerged in the 1980s. It has grown out of the need to more accurately describe the procedures children use and the availability of new computerized modeling techniques. At first, Francophone research in this area was limited to modeling children's behavior in a given situation (for a review, see Bonnet, Hoc, & Tiberghien, 1986). Nguyen-Xuan (1987) designed a computer model of how children learn a game called *la course à vingt* (the race for 20), In this game, two players compete. Each one takes a turn by laying down either 1 or 2 tokens. The winner is the person who reaches the number 20. The learning model includes 19 production rules (actions, event memorization, knowledge acquisition, checking, etc.). The model is applicable to several situations of the same type: reaching a given number starting from 0, or inversely, starting from a given number and going down to 0 by subtracting 1 or 2. Such models are interesting because they require the thorough and minute description of the behavior being modeled. However, because they are so demanding, they remain limited to short-term acquisitions for a restricted set of situations. Moreover, even if a computer model could produce responses that were analogous to the ones produced by children (including errors), it would still remain impossible to pursue the analogy by postulating the identity of the underlying mechanisms. Such acquisition models are a way of specifying "both problem solving capabilities and learning capacity at a given age level" (Nguyen-Xuan, 1990, p. 205).

CONCLUSION

Researchers using cognitive strategy induction tasks have provided detailed descriptions of the procedures initially used and later transformed by children as they learn. The precise description of children's procedures has made it possible to design computer models of learning. In the current state of the art, each of these models describes a given developmental stage. An increase in the number of models, in addition to their improvement, should eventually enable us to better understand child development as a whole (Anderson, 1983, 1987). The contributions made by Vygotsky's theory, and by subsequent work based on it, have provided us with fine-grained descriptions of interactive behavior in dissymmetrical dyads (Bruner's formats). They can be applied to the definition of new forms of cognitive strategy induction, which should take into account children's representation of the task and of their partner, while paying strict attention to cognitive level, established with ever-increasing precision (Fraysse, 1992).

The various theoretical trends should be incorporated into future attempts to define new induction tasks aimed at gradually improving our overall understanding of cognitive development. Although current induction tasks can already be applied to the efficient correction of certain minor difficulties in school, the new perspectives provided by learning research should facilitate the design of better programs for educational action.

REFERENCES

Anderson, J. R. (1983). *The architecture of cognition*. Cambridge, MA: Harvard University Press.

Anderson, J. R. (1987). Skill acquisition: Compilation of weak-method problem solutions. *Psychological Review, 94*, 192–210.

Bastien, C. (1987). *Schèmes et stratégies dans l'activité cognitive de l'enfant* [Schemas and strategies in the cognitive activity of the child]. Paris: Presses Universitaires de France.

Beaudichon, J., Verba, M., & Winnykamen, F. (1988). Interactions sociales et acquisition des connaissances chez l'enfant: une approche pluridimensionnelle [Social interactions and knowledge acquisition of children: A pluridimensional approach]. *Revue Internationale de Psychologie Sociale, 1*, 129–141.

Bideaud, J. (1981). Les expériences d'apprentissage de l'inclusion et la théorie opératoire [Inclusion learning experiments and Piagetian theory]. *Psychologie Française, 26*, 238–258.

Bideaud, J. (1988). *Logique et bricolage chez l'enfant* [Logic and tinkering in the child]. Lille: Presses Universitaires.

Bonnet, C., Hoc, J. M., & Tiberghien, G. (Eds.). (1986). *Psychologie, intelligence artificielle et automatique* [Psychology, artificial and automatic intelligence]. Brussels: Mardaga.

Botson, C., & Deliège, M. (1975). *Le développement intellectuel de l'enfant II: Une méthode d'approche. Les apprentissages sans erreurs* [The child's intellectual development II. A method of study: Error-free apprenticeships]. Brussels: Department of National Education.

Case, R. (1977). Responsiveness to conservation training as a function of induced subjective uncertainty. M-space, and cognitive style. *Revue Canadienne des Sciences du Comportement, 9*, 12–25.

Case, R. (1985). *Intellectual development: Birth to adulthood*. New York: Academic Press.

Charbonneau, C., Robert, M., Bourassa, G., & Gladu-Bissonnette, S. (1976). Observational learning of quantity conservation and Piagetian generalization tasks. *Developmental Psychology, 12*, 211–217.

Desprels-Fraysse, A. (1980). Le schéma de covariation: Moyen d'analyse du fonctionnement opératoire [The covariation schema as a means of analyzing the operatory behaviour]. *L'Année Psychologique, 80*, 169–191.

Desprels-Fraysse, A. (1983). Une contribution expérimentale à l'étude des relations entre structures et procédures [An experimental contribution to the study of the relations between structures and procedures]. *Archives de Psychologie, 51,* 341–354.

Desprels-Fraysse, A. (1985a). Etude des décalages dans l'utilisation de relations fonctionnelles en rapport avec des propriétés d'objets physiques [A study of the lags in the use of functional relations as applied to the properties of material objects]. *Archives de Psychologie, 53,* 439–446.

Desprels-Fraysse, A. (1985b). The sequence of development of certain classification skills. *Genetic Psychology Monographs, 1,* 67–82.

Desprels-Fraysse, A. (1986). Domaine logique, domaine spatial: Étude de quelques relations chez les enfants de 4 à 8 ans [Logic and space: A study of a few relations in children aged 4 to 8]. *Archives de Psychologie, 54,* 79–94.

Desprels-Fraysse, A. (1987). Genèse des conduites de classification: discontinuité structurale et/ou continuité fonctionnelle [A genesis of classification behaviours: Structural discontinuity and/or functional continuity]. *L'Année Psychologique, 87,* 489–508.

Desprels-Fraysse, A. (1990a). Comment aider l'enfant à catégoriser? [How to help children to categorize]. *Revue Française de Pédagogie, 92,* 15–22.

Desprels-Fraysse, A. (1990b). Complementation in children: Negation of objects or negation of properties. *European Bulletin of Cognitive Psychology, 10,* 65–78.

Desprels-Fraysse, A. (1991). Children's abstraction of color properties: Is it dependent on what objects actualize the properties? *European Bulletin of Cognitive Psychology, 11,* 441–452.

Desprels-Fraysse, A., & Fraysse, J. C. (1977). *Induction des structures logiques élémentaires chez des enfants d'âge préscolaire et analyse fonctionnelle des comportements observés* [Induction of elementary logical structures in pre-school children and functional analysis of their behaviours]. Unpublished masters thesis, University of Provence, France.

Desprels-Fraysse, A., & Fraysse, J. C. (1987). Apprentissage et développement: Une approche génétique [Apprenticeship and development: A genetical approach]. *Enfance, 3,* 231–244.

Doise, W., & Mugny, G. (1981). *Le développement social de l'intelligence* [The social development of intelligence]. Paris: Inter Editions.

Fisher, K. W. (1980). A theory of cognitive development: The control and construction of hierarchies of skills. *Psychological Review, 87,* 477–531.

Flavell, J. H. (1982). On cognitive development. *Child Development, 53,* 1–9.

Flavell, J. H. (1985). Développement métacognitif [Metacognitive development]. In J. Bideaud & M. Richelle (Eds.), *Psychologie développementale* (pp. 29–42). Liège, Belgium: Mardaga.

Florès, C., & Orsini-Bouichou, F. (1979). *Induction et formation de la pensée logique chez l'enfant* [Induction and the construction of the child's logical thought]. Unpublished A.T.P. report.

Fortin-Thierault, A. (1977). *Comparaison de deux méthodes d'apprentissage par conflit cognitif* [A comparison between two methods of learning through cognitive conflicts]. Unpublished doctoral dissertation, University of Montréal, Canada.

Fraysse, J. C. (1985). Relation entre niveaux fonctionnels et prise en compte d'un partenaire dans une tâche de tri d'objets [The relation between functional levels and the taking into account of a partner in a classification task]. *Archives de Psychologie, 53,* 447–452.

Fraysse, J. C. (1987). Etude génétique de la prise en compte du partenaire dans la construction des opérations [A genetical study of the child's relation to a partner in the construction of operations]. *Bulletin de Psychologie, 40,* 915–922.

Fraysse, J. C. (1988). Nature des prérequis et types d'interactions sociales [The nature of prerequisites and types of social interactions]. *Archives de Psychologie, 56,* 5–21.

Fraysse, J. C. (1991). Effect of social insertion mode on performance and interaction in asymmetric dyads. *European Journal of Psychology of Education, 6,* 45–53.

Fraysse, J. C. (1992). *Relation entre développement cognitif et compétences interactives* [The relation between cognitive development and interactive abilities]. Unpublished doctoral dissertation, University of Provence, France.

Fraysse, J. C., & Desprels-Fraysse, A. (1990). The influence of experimenter attitude on the perfor-

146   FRAYSSE AND DESPRELS-FRAYSSE

mance of children of different cognitive ability levels. *Journal of Genetic Child Psychology, 151,* 169–179.

Gilly, M. (1988). Interactions entre pairs et constructions cognitives: Modèles explicatifs [Interactions between peers and cognitive constructions: Explanatory models]. In A. N. Perret-Clermont & M. Nicolet (Eds.), *Interagir et connaître* (pp. 19–29). Cousset (Fribourg).

Halford, G. S. (1982). *The development of thought.* Hillsdale, NJ: Lawrence Erlbaum Associates.

Inhelder, B., Sinclair, H., & Bovet, M. (1974). *Apprentissage et structures de la connaissance* [Apprenticeship and structures of knowledge]. Paris: Presses Universitaires de France.

Khun, D. (1974). Inducing development experimentally: Comments on a research paradigm. *Developmental Psychology, 10,* 590–600.

Lasry, J. C., & Laurendeau, M. (1969). Apprentissage empirique de la notion d'inclusion [Empirical apprenticeship of inclusion]. *Human Development, 3,* 141–163.

Laurendeau-Bendavid, M. (1985). L'apprentissage des structures cognitives: Perspectives d'avenir après 25 années de recherche [Learning of cognitive structures: Future prospects after 25 years of research]. *Archives de Psychologie, 53,* 495–501.

Lefebvre, M., & Pinard, A. (1972). Apprentissage de la conservation des quantités par une méthode de conflit cognitif [Learning of conservation of quantity through a method of cognitive conflict]. *Revue Canadienne des Sciences du Comportement, 4,* 1–12.

Lefebvre, M., & Pinard, A. (1974). Influence du niveau initial de sensibilité au conflit sur l'apprentissage de la conservation des quantités par une méthode de conflit cognitif [The influence of the initial level of sensitivity to conflict on the learning of conservation of quantity through a method of cognitive conflict]. *Revue Canadienne des Sciences du Comportement, 6,* 398–413.

Monteil, J. M. (1988). Comparaison sociale, stratégies individuelles et médiations socio-cognitives: Un effet de différenciations comportementales dans le champ scolaire [Social comparison, individual strategies, and socio-cognitive mediations: An effect of behavioural differentiations at school]. *European Journal of Psychology of Education, 1,* 3–19.

Mounoud, P. (1986). Similarities between developmental sequences at different age. In I. Levin (Ed.), *Stage and structure* (pp. 40–58). Norwood, NJ: Ablex.

Nguyen-Xuan, A. (1987). Apprentissage par l'action d'un domaine de connaissance et apprentissage par l'action du fonctionnement d'un dispositif de commande [Learning through action of a field of knowledge and apprenticeship through action of the functionning of a command device]. *Psychologie Française, 32,* 237–246.

Nguyen-Xuan, A. (1990). Apprentissage et développement [Apprenticeship and development]. In J. F. Richard, C. Bonnet, & R. Ghiglione (Eds.), *Traité de psychologie cognitive* (Vol. 2, pp. 196–206). Paris: Dunod.

Oléron, P., & Thong, T. (1968). L'acquisition des conservations et l'apprentissage [The acquisition of conservations and apprenticeship]. *L'Année Psychologique, 68,* 549–575.

Orsini-Bouichou, F. (1975). *Régularités dans les organisations spontanées chez l'enfant et genèse des comportements cognitifs* [Regularity in the spontaneous organizations of the child and the genesis of cognitive behaviours]. Unpublished doctoral dissertation, René Descartes University, Paris, France.

Orsini-Bouichou, F. (1982). *L'intelligence de l'enfant: Ontogenèse des invariants* [The child's intelligence: Ontogenesis of invariants]. Paris: C.N.R.S. Editions.

Paour, J. L. (1980). *Construction et fonctionnement des structures opératoires concrètes chez l'enfant débile mental: Apport des expériences d'apprentissage et induction opératoire* [The construction and functioning of concrete operatory structures in the mentally deficient child: The contribution of learning experiments and operatory induction]. Unpublished masters thesis, Université de Provence, France.

Paour, J. L. (1981). L'apprentissage des structures logiques comme instrument d'investigation du fonctionnement cognitif des arriérés mentaux [The learning of logical structures as instruments for the investigation of the cognitive functioning of the mentally deficient]. *Neuropsychiatrie de l'Enfance et de l'Adolescence, 29,* 31–38.

Paour, J. L. (1991). Un modèle cognitif et développemental du retard mental pour comprendre et intervenir [A cognitive and developmental model to understand and act on mental deficiency]. Unpublished doctoral dissertation, University of Provence, France.

Pascual-Leone, J. (1987). Organismic processes for neo-Piagetian theories: A dialectical causal account of cognitive development. *International Journal of Psychology, 22,* 531–570.

Perret-Clermont, A. N. (1979). *La construction de l'intelligence dans l'interaction sociale* [The construction of intelligence in social interaction]. Berne, Switzerland: Peter Lang.

Piaget, J. (1959a). Apprentissage et connaissance I [Apprenticeship and knowledge I]. In P. Greco & J. Piaget (Eds.), *Apprentissage et connaissance* (pp. 21–67). Paris: Presses Universitaires de France. Serial Nr. 7 of *Etudes d'épistémologie génétique.*

Piaget, J. (1959b). Apprentissage et connaissance II [Apprenticeship and knowledge II]. In M. Goustard, P. Greco, B. Matalon, & J. Piaget (Eds.), *Apprentisssage et connaissance* (pp. 159–188). Paris: Presses Universitaires de France. Serial Nr. 10 of *Etudes d'épistémologie génétique.*

Piaget, J. (1974). *La prise de conscience* [The transition to awareness]. Paris: Presses Universitaires de France.

Piaget, J., & Inhelder, B. (1959). *La genèse des structures logiques élémentaires* [The genesis of elementary logical structures]. Neuchâtel, France: Delachaux et Niestlé.

Piaget, J., & Garcia, R. (1987). *Vers une logique des significations* [Towards a logic of meaning]. Geneva: Murionde.

Pineau, A., & Beaufils, F. (1987). Acquisition de la notion "pareil, pas pareil" chez l'enfant d'âge pré-scolaire [The acquisition of the notion of "same, not the same" in pre-school children]. *L'Année Psychologique, 88,* 343–358.

Raven, J. C. (1938). *Progressive matrices: A perceptual test of intelligence, and individual form,* London: Lewis.

Rieben, L., de Ribaupierre, A., & Lautrey, J. (1983). *Le développement opératoire de l'enfant entre six et douze ans: Élaboration d'un instrument d'évaluation* [The operatory development of children aged 6 to 12: The elaboration of an instrument of evaluation]. Paris: C.N.R.S. Editions.

Robert, M. (1983). Observational learning of conservation: Its independence from social influence. *British Journal of Psychology, 74,* 1–10.

Robert, M., & Turcotte, P. (1983). Position sérielle des arguments du modèle et apprentissage de la conservation par observation [The serial position of the arguments of the model and conservation learning through observation]. *LAnnée Psychologique, 83,* 91–107.

Siegler, R. S. (1981). Developmental sequences within and between concepts. *Monographs of the Society for Research in Child Development, 46,* 1–74.

Skourass, E. (1976). Les apprentissages cognitifs chez des enfants de milieux défavorisés [Cognitive learning in socially underpriviledged children]. *Enfance,* 133–144.

Strauss, S. (1972). Inducing cognitive development and learning: A review of short-term training experiments. *Cognition, 1,* 329–357.

Verba, M. (1987). Interactions entre jeunes enfants et organisation des savoir-faire: apport des enfants plus âgés dans le groupe [Young children interaction and the organization of know-how: The contribution of the older children of the group]. In J. Cresas (Ed.), *On n'apprend pas tout seul* [You can't teach yourself]. Paris: E.S.F. Editions.

Verba, M., & Isambert, A. L. (1983). Les mécanismes de collaboration entre enfants de 2 à 4 ans [Cooperation and mechanisms between children aged 2 to 4]. In T. Musatti & Mantovani (Eds.), *Bambini al nido, gioco, communicazione, e rapporti affettivi* (pp. 35–52). Bergame: Juvenilia.

Vinh-Bang (1985). Le mesure de l'apprentissage en psychologie génétique [Measuring learning in genetical psychology]. *Archives de Psychologie, 53,* 523–526.

Winnykamen, F. (1987). *Imitation–Modélisation: Modalités sociales des acquisitions* [Imitation-Modeling: The social modalities of acquisitions]. Doctoral dissertation, Renée Descartes University, Paris.

Winnykamen, F. (1990). *Apprendre en imitant?* [Learning through imitation?]. Paris: Presses Universitaires de France.

11
Action, Interaction, and Cognitive Development: Process-Oriented Research With 5- to 8-Year-Old Children

Christiane Vandenplas-Holper
Université Catholique de Louvain-la-Neuve

According to Piaget's theory, cognitive development proceeds by *equilibration*, a continuous balancing between assimilation and accommodation (Piaget, 1975). Since the 1970s, researchers have tried to test empirically the construct of equilibration, which has only a theoretical status in Piaget's theory. Different designs have been used. Some clinically oriented studies have provided a more or less detailed description of the child's interaction with his or her physical and/or social environment. Experimental studies have systematically manipulated sociocognitive conflict. Finally, other studies have related process-oriented variables and outcome-oriented variables.

In the classic studies of Inhelder, Sinclair, and Bovet (1974), conducted with children in transition to Piaget's concrete operational stage, various procedures, used according to the objectives of the *méthode clinique*, tried to enrich the inputs of the physical environment and to activate the assimilatory schemes of the children. These procedures resulted in cognitive conflicts between subsystems developing at different levels or between the subjects' assimilatory schemes and the obstacles included in the experimental situations. They obliged the children to accommodate their judgment and to take into account certain variables they had previously neglected. The disequilibria which were thus created led to pretest–posttest progress, the magnitude of which was a function of the children's pretest level. Similar studies have been reported by Bovet and Voelin (1990) and by Inhelder et al. (1976). These studies have a clinical format: Guidelines for observation are more or less precise, and no statistical tests are computed. Although the studies that have been mentioned focus on the child's interaction with the physical world, the studies of Doise and Mugny (1981),

149

Perret-Clermont (1979) and other European sociodevelopmentally oriented researchers (Mugny, 1985; Perret-Clermont & Nicolet, 1988) have shown that sociocognitive conflict is one of the factors causing children's progress in the operational tasks inspired by Piaget. In these studies, various forms of sociocognitive conflict are experimentally created by bringing together children of different operational levels or by the experimenter's interaction with the children. These studies are outcome-oriented: Pretest–posttest changes are compared for experimental and control groups; the interaction that was manipulated by experimental conditions is not studied in detail.

The studies of Gilly and his collaborators (Dalzon, 1988; Gilly, 1989; Gilly, Fraisse, & Roux, 1988) were not based on tasks assessing general intelligence viewed in the light of Piaget's structuralist theory, but were aimed at devising procedural, rather than structural, models of problem-solving activities. These authors adopted a systemic point of view, contending that, under certain subject–task conditions, sociocognitive functioning initiates cognitive changes through three possible types of action: affecting the representation of the task, the solving procedures, and the control of the activity. Social interaction was mainly considered as cooperation, not as conflict. The authors adopted an experimental approach and implemented different types of social interaction in different groups. The process of interaction was also analyzed, but the analyses remained rather global and were not systematically related to the outcome of the intervention (Dalzon, 1988; Gilly et al. 1988). Other studies conducted within the cognitive-developmental framework have analyzed carefully the process of children's interaction in different settings. Some studies concerned moral development, within the Kohlberg tradition (Berkowitz, 1985; Damon & Killen, 1982; Oser, 1984), and others concerned cognitive development (Miller & Brownell, 1975). Berkowitz systematically analyzed social interaction with respect to sociocognitive conflict; Damon and Killen analyzed sociocognitive conflict and cooperation. In both studies, process-oriented variables derived from the interaction sessions were related to outcome-oriented measures of pre-posttest change. Like Damon and Killen (1982) and more explicitly Gilly (1989), other studies, grounded in Vygotsky's work, have focused on cooperation and tutoring as a means for enhancing cognitive development (Brown & Reeve, 1987; Winnykamen, 1990).

In the studies described in this chapter, the children were pretested individually. Three children from three different cognitive levels were then brought together to solve a problem situation jointly. They were asked to help each other to solve the task and to give justifications for what they were doing. The children were then posttested individually. The main objective of these studies was to derive indicators of sociocognitive conflict and cooperation, among others, from the observation of the process of problem solving, and to relate these indicators to the outcome of the intervention measured by pretest–posttest change. Individual task-specific action was also observed and related to pretest–posttest change.

I have elsewhere compared this approach to those of other researchers and pointed to some methodological difficulties (Beaudichon & Vandenplas-Holper, 1985). In this chapter, I first present a general outline of three studies that have been conducted according to the same paradigm. Second, the method and the process-oriented results of these studies are briefly presented. Finally, I compare this process-oriented approach with other microgenetic approaches, stressing advantages, costs, and limits.

THE GENERAL PARADIGM OF THE PROCESS-ORIENTED STUDIES

The three studies I describe in this chapter focus, respectively, on left–right role-taking, spontaneous measuring, and number conservation. The pretests and post-tests used in the three studies and the learning sessions conducted to produce pretest–posttest change, require the coordination between different pairs of dimensions: between left–right concepts on one's own body and on another person placed in a face-to-face situation in the left–right decentration study (Piaget, 1924/1967) and between perceptual and numerical cues in the number conservation study (Piaget, 1941). To master the spontaneous measuring task, the child has to realize that direct visual comparisons of the length of two elements composed of items of different dimensions are unreliable; he or she has to understand how to use a third element as a common tool for measurement (Piaget, Inhelder, & Szeminska, 1948).

The three studies were conducted according to the same paradigm. Children aged 5 to 8 years were first pretested individually. Three children drawn from three different cognitive levels were then brought together to solve a problem jointly: Of the three children, one had not mastered the concept on which the study was grounded, a second child had mastered it at an intermediate level, and a third had mastered the concept completely. It was supposed that triads composed in this way would be stimulating for all of the children, because they would create an optimal mismatch on the one hand between the child who had not mastered the concept and the child who had mastered the concept at an intermediate level and the child who had mastered it completely. The children composing these triads were generally drawn from three different classes. Finally, the children were posttested individually.

During the learning sessions, the children were asked to help each other to solve the task and to give justifications for what they were doing. The role of the experimenter was to get each child to be active and to express his or her point of view, and to point out opposing points of view. These interaction situations were supposed to bring about conflict on an intraindividual level, because the materials were designed to resist the children's strategies to solve the task. Conflict was also supposed to arise on an interindividual level, because the children, all functioning at different cognitive levels, had conflicting points of view. The spontaneous measuring and the number conservation studies also elicited cooperation between the children. In the spontaneous measuring study, cooperation was brought about among the three children, because they had to perform the task jointly and agree on the final outcome. In the number conservation study, cooperation was stimulated because the conserving child had to help the nonconserving child and the intermediate child to solve the task. Joint action was also stimulated, because the nonconserving and intermediate child had to choose and share one of three arrays of counters. The spontaneous measuring and the number conservation situations—and, to a lesser degree, the left–right decentration study—called for a two-level tutoring: The children were asked to tutor each other, and the experimenter tutored each of the three children. Cognitive and sociocognitive conflict was supposed to elicit a restructuring of the child's present cognitive structures and bring about progress from the pretest to the posttest. Cognitive change was also supposed to be mediated by cooperation and individual task-specific action.

The learning sessions were implemented 1 to 2 weeks after the pretest. In the spontaneous measuring study and in the number conservation study, two identical learning sessions were conducted. They differed only by minor details concerning the materials. In the left–right decentration study, three tasks were used. Each task was presented first in two different sessions. Learning sessions were then conducted with a 1- to 2-week interval. The posttest was presented about a week after the last learning session.

In two of the studies, the pretest–posttest change of the children who participated in the learning sessions was compared with the pretest–posttest change of the children of a control group who did not participate in learning sessions. The results of this outcome-oriented part of the studies are only briefly presented in this chapter, whose main focus is on the process-oriented approach I have adopted.

Most studies used to assess the role of social interaction on change in cognitive development have used either various conservation tasks or variations of the three mountains task to measure spatial role-taking (Doise & Mugny, 1981). To my knowledge, no previous study on social interaction and cognitive development has used a spontaneous measuring situation, and only one study (Dalzon, 1988) has used a left–right role-taking task, but in a way different from ours. The pretest and posttest in my left–right role-taking study used the tasks devised by Galifret-Granjon (1958/1969), and her device for scoring was adopted, as well. The pretest and posttest in the spontaneous measuring task consisted of a semi-structured clinical interview that was especially devised for my study. It was based on a systematization of the clinical descriptions provided by Piaget et al. (1948). The pretest and posttest of the number conservation study used a semi-structured clinical interview adapted from Inhelder et al. (1974).

Although the three learning sessions were based on the concept of cognitive conflict, the sessions were conducted in a different way in the left–right de-centration study on the one hand, and in the spontaneous measuring and number conservation studies on the other. In the left–right decentration study, a pre-established set of trials was presented by the experimenter, and the children took turns acting as players and referees. In the spontaneous measuring and number conservation studies, the experimenter proposed an open-ended problem-solving situation and only stimulated the children's task-specific action and interaction.

The two or three learning sessions of each triad were videotaped. In the left–right decentration study, the movements the children used when performing the tasks were coded by systematic observation and the arguments they used to explain their point of view were coded from the tapes of their verbal utterances. In the spontaneous measuring and number conservation studies, the videorecord-ings were submitted to a more detailed microgenetic analysis combining system-atic observation of nonverbal action and content analysis of children's verbal statements. The videorecordings were divided into temporal units of 15 seconds. For each child, the units of analysis were combined in both summed and sequen-tial ways, producing several process-oriented variables referring to the children's overall activity in the sessions; their intraindividual specific task-related actions; and their interindividual activity, which related to cooperation in the spontaneous measuring study and to sociocognitive conflict and cooperation in the number conservation study.

The three studies provide detailed descriptions of the process of individual and interindividual activity and relate it to the children's pretest level and to pretest–posttest change.

OVERVIEW OF THE THREE STUDIES

The Left–Right Decentration Study

Only children who had mastered left–right relations on their own body were selected to participate in the study. In order to compose groups of children of three different developmental levels, three decentration levels were defined ac-cording to the scores obtained in a face-to-face task, which assesses the child's mastery of left–right relations on a person seated in front of him or her, and the schematic figures task, which focuses on the reproduction of movements from schematic figures.

The experimental group was made up of 32 triads. Three situations—ball game, jumping jack game, and figurines game—were based on the cognitive conflict that arises between the children due to the noncoordination of different perspectives. In each situation, two children, seated one in front of the other, performed tasks that require the mastery of left–right relationships on their own body and on another person seated in a face-to-face position. A third child, seated in a lateral position, served as the referee. He or she evaluated if the two "players" performed the task correctly, and the latter were invited to present their respective points of view as to whether the referee correctly evaluated the players' mistakes. The children took turns, and each performed the role of player and referee. Children in a control group did not participate in the learning sessions.

The learning sessions were analyzed separately with respect to the number of answers that were initially correct. Certain children spontaneously displayed different kinds of movements that were interpreted as facilitators of the task. These movements and the arguments children used to justify their actions were also analyzed. For example, certain children give the impression that they lift their hands before answering; others cross them on the table; others lift one hand as if to serve as a marker. Certain children turn their heads to the left or the right, but do not move their shoulders. Body rotations refer to movements in which children turn their shoulders about 90° or turn completely in order to be oriented in the same direction as the person on whom they have to designate, or referee the designation, of left or right. Certain children displace themselves to the other side of the table in order to be able to justify their answer.

The children use various arguments to justify their answers and to give explanations to each other. The arguments "Me in different positions" and "Other, face-to-face" refer directly to decentration. By the argument "Me in different positions," the child explains that a real or virtual displacement of his body is related to the relativity of left–right relations: "When I return myself, it is my left hand and I belief that at the opposite side, it is also his left hand, but if I put myself in his position, I always put myself in his position, then I say, 'It is the right hand'." By the argument "Other, face-to-face," the child refers to another child who is in a face-to-face position and for whom the left–right relations are reversed, relative to his or her position: "Because his right hand, it is not the same as for me. His right hand, it is on the other side, because we are on other sides. We are on the other side; then it is the other hand." By the argument, "Marker on own body," the child refers to an action or a distinctive feature of his or her body that facilitated his or her left–right discrimination: "One has to hold his pencil in the right hand," or "I have a scratch here that never goes away, so I remember that it is my left hand, the one with the scratch." Several miscellaneous arguments were also used.

Comparisons between pretest and posttest scores for the experimental and the control groups showed that, with one exception, the children of the experimental group had higher positive change scores than those of the control group for each of the three decentration levels, for the face-to-face task, and for the schematic figures task (Vandenplas-Holper, 1985). Correct answers increased significantly, as compared with those on the pretest, for each of the tasks. Also, the movements the children displayed spontaneously in the sessions and the arguments by which they justified their actions and gave explanations to each other increased with the children's pretest level. Different combinations of the process variables were correlated with the pretest–posttest change concerning the decentration scores, but no significant correlations emerged (Vandenplas-Holper, 1987b).

The Spontaneous Measuring Study

As a pretest, the children were individually given a semiclinical assessment of spontaneous measuring, based on Piaget et al. (1948). They were shown a model tower made of wooden cubes and parallelipipeds and placed on a table in front of them. The experimenter asked the child to build, on the floor, a tower of the same height as the model tower. The child was given more building blocks than he or she needed, and the dimension of the blocks, which were also cubes and parallelipipeds, were different from those of the model tower. The child was also given several wooden sticks of varying lengths shorter than, longer than, or identical to the model tower. In a semiclinical way, the experimenter gave countersuggestions and asked justifications of the child's actions and utterances. If the child did not spontaneously use the sticks, the experimenter asked him or her to use a stick that was longer than or of equal length to the model tower. The data gathered in the pretest and posttest were analyzed in both a simplified and an expanded way. The simplified way considered only the child's accurate use of one or several sticks and classified the children according to four mastery levels. The expanded way was based on items referring to the totality of the child's actions and classified each child according to Piaget et al.'s (1948) Substages Ia, Ib, IIa, IIb, IIIa, and IIIb (Vandenplas-Holper, 1986).

Six mixed cognitive-developmental level triads participated in the learning sessions. The children were selected on the basis of the simplified assessment. Each triad was made up of a Level 1 child, who had no mastery (NM) of spontaneous measuring; a Level 2 child, who had intermediate mastery (IM) of spontaneous measuring; and a Level 4 child who had complete mastery (CM) of spontaneous measuring. A control group of 24 children was given only the pretest and posttest, but did not participate in the learning sessions.

In the learning sessions, the situation was basically identical to the one used during the pretests and posttests. The dimensions of the material used and the way in which it was arranged, however, was different. Whereas the children had to build a "tower" in the pretest and posttest, they were asked in the learning sessions to line the blocks up horizontally on a table, in such a way as to make a "wall" or "train." In order to avoid simple visual transposition, the children were asked to put the wall together at a right angle to the model wall. The children had at their disposal strips of paper of different lengths.

Two independent raters rated the children's activity or cooperation during the learning sessions on a 7-point scale. Activity was defined as the children's participation in the required building task (putting blocks side by side, putting blocks in between those that had already been placed), the children's participation in measuring (counting blocks, comparing the model blocks and the "wall" while building it), and their task-related utterances. Cooperation was defined as mutual aid in building or measuring that was spontaneous or that was encouraged by the experimenter (e.g., holding the end of the strip of paper used by the child as a measuring unit, stretching the strip of paper tightly, putting a finger on the paper as a marker), and as utterances addressed to another child in connection with the task. Cooperation was rated for each of the possible dyads: NM–IM, IM–CM, and NM–CM.

Two observers who had not participated in the ratings coded each child's actions and interactions into the following categories:

1. Non-goal-oriented manipulation (moving or touching the blocks or the strips of paper).
2. Construction (lining up, inserting, or removing blocks).
3. Referencing the model (looking at the model).
4. Measurement, including (a) choice and comparison of blocks, (b) counting and reference to number, and (c) use of a unit of measurement (using the body or part of it as a measuring tool; bringing the model close to the construction; putting together a third set of blocks as a measuring tool; or putting a strip of paper next to the construction being made).
5. Task-related utterances oriented either toward the experimenter or toward peers.

For every 15-second interval, each observer coded the actions observed. The identity of the social partner was also coded when one of the building or measuring actions was performed with one or two social partners and for peer-oriented utterances. Interactive activity was defined as the number of task-related peer-oriented utterances made by each child, added to the number of joint construction and measuring actions performed during the same interval. Utterances were divided into "descending" utterances, when a child of a higher level talked to one of a lower level (e.g, IM to NM), and "ascending" utterances, when a child of a lower level talked to one of a higher level (e.g., IM to CM). The experimenter's interventions during the learning sessions, addressed either to the group or to individual children, were also counted.

For the activity variable, each child was rated on a 7-point scale. For the cooperation variable, each child was characterized by the sum of ratings given to him or her for each of the two dyads in which he or she was involved. The data gathered from systematic observation were combined into several indicators referring to the child's overall individual activity. The mean number of actions per interval considered all the actions that had been observed. The index of activity was based on actions referring to categories 2, 3, 4, and 5; that is, non-goal-oriented actions were not considered. The inactivity index was based on the number of intervals during which the child displayed none of the actions of the categories 1–5. Several other indicators operationalized the child's differential activity for non-goal-oriented actions, construction, reference to the model tower, measuring, and verbal utterances.

If pretest–posttest change was considered according to the simplified assessment, it appeared that 6 children in the experimental group progressed between pretest and posttest, and 6 did not; although 6 children in the control group progressed, 18 did not. This difference, however, failed to reach significance. If pretest–posttest change was considered according to the expanded assessment, it appeared that 8 children in the experimental group progressed between the pretest and the posttest, and 4 did not, whereas 8 children of the control group progressed, and 16 did not. This difference was significant (Vandenplas-Holper, Pierret, & Chapeaux, 1986).

Comparisons of children at the different pretest levels showed that the assessment of activity increased significantly with pretest level. For overall indices of activity derived from systematic observation, only the index of inactivity tended to be significant. Interactive activity tended to vary with the pretest level. The comparisons between the 6 children who progressed between the pretest and the posttest and the 6 children who did not progress (according to the simplified assessment) showed that, for variables derived from the ratings, the differences for activity and cooperation were slightly significant, with the children who progressed being more active and engaged in cooperation than the children who did not progress. As far as the overall indices of individual activity, assessed from systematic observation, are concerned, the children who progressed had a significantly higher mean number of actions per interval and a significantly higher index of activity. On the whole, the differential indices of activity were higher for the children who progressed. Finally, the children who progressed tended to be more engaged in interactive activity.

A detailed analysis of interaction in the data gathered by systematic observation showed that the proportion of joint building and measuring actions performed in dyads was .88 and in triads only .12. IM and CM children interacted most frequently, NM and IM interacted less frequently, and NM and CM showed the least joint activity. Of task-related, peer-oriented utterances, 90% occurred in a descending direction and only 10% in an ascending direction. Descending utterances were directed from IM to NM children 18 times, from CM to IM children 10 times and from CM to NM children 7 times.

Kendall's Tau correlations for rankable scores computed for the 18 children in the experimental group showed that activity and cooperation ratings were significantly correlated with each of the three overall indices of activity and with interactive activity (Vandenplas-Holper, Ghysselinckx, & Chapeaux, 1985).

The Number Conservation Study

After a pretest consisting of two semistructured number conservation tasks, the children participated in two sessions in which they had to jointly resolve a number conservation problem. The tasks proposed to them were identical in the two sessions. Three arrays of counters, each a different color and consisting of two lines, were displayed on a table. Array 1 contained 6 counters for each of the lines, arranged in a one-to-one correspondence; Array 2 also contained 6 counters in each line, but one line was longer than the other; Array 3 contained 6 counters in one line and 5 in the other line, but the lines were of the same length. That is, the two lines of Array 1 had the same number and the same density; the lines of Array 2 had the same number, but their density was different; and the two lines of Array 3 had both an unequal number and different densities. The colors of the different arrays and their positions on the table were randomly varied across triads and sessions.

The experimenter asked the nonconserving child (N) and the intermediate child (I) to choose one of the arrays: Each child would have one of the two lines, and the children should choose the array so that each would have an equal number of counters. The experimenter also asked the conserving child (C) to help his or her peers to solve the task. When the children chose Array 1, the experimenter told them that she had promised this array to other children and asked them to choose between Arrays 2 and 3. The function of Array 1 was only to focus the children's attention on the one-to-one correspondence. The role of the experimenter consisted in stimulating social interaction between the children and eliciting task-related activity.

With respect to the prediction of outcome from the process variables, cognitive conflict and cooperation were considered as the main variables related to the pretest–posttest change. However, because cognitive conflict and cooperation occur rather infrequently, and also because Piaget's theory considers activity as essential to cognitive development, two overall activity variables, one concerning the child and one concerning the experimenter, were also designed. In the spontaneous measuring study, these variables were significantly correlated with pretest–posttest change.

The two sessions of each group were videotaped and submitted to microgenetic analysis combining systematic observation of nonverbal action and content analysis of children's verbal statements. A coding frame was elaborated, and applied to 17 groups. Its main features is in being multidimensional with regard to the type of action observed and to the type of process variables derived. Verbal and nonverbal actions were considered in their individual and interindividual features. Some of the variables considered action in an overall way; other microgenetic variables were designed from complex considerations of simultaneous and sequential temporal relationships.

The analysis focused on the three children and the experimenter. The main categories of the coding frame applied to the three arrays and, particularly, to Arrays 2 and 3, in their initial disposition and in subsequent dispositions resulting from the children's modifications by non-goal-oriented actions and the establishment of one-to-one correspondence.

The nature of the task solicits decisions concerning choices ("We can take the blue ones") or rejections ("We cannot take the yellow ones"). Processes leading to decisions are expressed in terms of equivalence or nonequivalence ("They are not the same"), task-oriented procedures, other-oriented procedures, and surprise. Task-oriented procedures refer to spatial and numerical features of the arrays. They are very complex and concern the present disposition of the arrays (e.g., "They have been laid in the same way") as well as real and virtual modifications that could be made on the initial disposition of the arrays. Real modifications are, for instance, made by non-goal-oriented action or by the far more elaborated procedure of establishing one-to-one correspondence. Virtual modifications consist of the child mentioning that the spatial disposition of the arrays could be changed ("You can put them closer") or that their numerosity could be changed ("You can add one"). Other-oriented procedures concern agreement or disagreement by the specific linguistic markers of *yes* and *no,* as in *N:* "We can take the yellow ones." *C:* "No, we can't take them." Children also use tutoring actions, either by giving directions to another child concerning what to do to solve the task ("Take the red ones"; "You can count") or by using nonverbal actions, such as coming closer to another child in order to interact with him or her. Some children expressed surprise, which can be considered as overt expressions of intraindividual conflict, using such interjections as "Ah!" or "Oh!"

The verbal statements of the experimenter are diverse. Her questions refer to decisions, and to equivalence and nonequivalence ("What are you going to take?" "Are the orange ones the same?"). She focuses the children's attention ("Wait!"; "Come closer!") or invites manipulation ("You can move the pawns"). The experimenter also stresses interindividual conflict ("You say you can take the blues ones, and he says you can't") or intraindividual conflict ("Just a moment ago, you said you take the red ones and now you say you can't").

According to the multidimensional feature of the content analysis frame, the data collected in this way were combined into several categories of variables referring to overall activity, intraindividual differentiated activity, and interindividual activity. The density of the child's overall activity is obtained by summing all of the verbal and nonverbal actions performed by each child and expressing these actions proportionally to 1 minute. The density of the experimenter's overall activity is obtained in the same way. Intraindividual differentiated activity is measured by three composite variables, two of which refer to more or less complex task-oriented procedures. Intraindividual conflict is measured by the sum of occurrences of spontaneous intraindividual conflict, the number of occurrences where the experimenter stresses an intraindividual conflict, and the number of expressions of surprise. Interindividual activity is measured by interindividual conflict and cooperation. Interindividual conflict is measured by the number of times a child initiates an interindividual conflict, the number of times a child is acted on by another child in a conflictual episode, and the number of times the experimenter stresses an interindividual conflict. Cooperation is measured by the tutoring actions initiated by the child, the tutoring actions in which the child is acted on, and joint action defined by the fact that two or three children act simultaneously on the same array.

Results from a preliminary analysis of 17 groups are now available. They show that most of the indicators of the children's action and interaction in the two sessions varied moderately as a function of the children's pretest level. Very significant differences were found for cooperation: Intermediate children were far more engaged in cooperation than both nonconserving and conserving children. Differences were also significant for interindividual conflict: Nonconserving and intermediate children were more often engaged in interindividual conflict than conserving children. Intercorrelations between the process variables and the outcome variable, defined as pretest to posttest change, were also computed. Because the magnitude of a potential pretest–posttest change was expected to be different for the children of the three pretest levels, separate analyses were conducted. Correlations were expected to be significant, particularly for nonconserving and intermediate children.

Overall activity of children and of the experimenter, one of the variables referring to intraindividual differentiated activity, interindividual conflict, and cooperation were correlated with the outcome variable. The correlations varied, however, as a function of the children's pretest levels. For the intermediate children, the correlation between interindividual conflict and pretest–posttest change was the most significant. Surprisingly, the negative correlation between cooperation and pretest–posttest change tended to be significant for the nonconserving children. Furthermore, a qualitative analysis of children's action and interaction showed interesting features concerning tutoring actions (Vandenplas-Holper, 1992). If the ascending and descending directions of tutoring actions are defined in the same way as in the spontaneous measuring study, intermediate children, who were the only ones who could engage in both ascending and descending actions, were engaged 14 times in descending actions, and not a single ascending tutoring action was observed. Comparing the tutoring actions between N and I, I children initiated a descending action toward N 14 times, and N children initiated an ascending tutoring action toward other N children 6 times (Vandenplas-Holper, 1992).

PROCESSES, STAGES, AND STRUCTURES

These three studies have shown that most of the process-oriented variables increase significantly with the children's pretest level. This trend was most apparent in the left–right decentration study and least apparent in the number conservation study, in which the C children were given a different status than the N and I children by the experimenter.

In the left–right decentration study, no relation between the process-oriented variables and outcome was found. In the spontaneous measuring and number conservation studies, overall variables, variables concerning more differentiated activity, and variables concerning interindividual activity were related to outcome, as measured by pretest–posttest change. These results confirm Piaget's theory, which considers activity to be crucial to cognitive development. It is true, however, that the activity considered here is only observable action. Mixed findings have been found with regard to cooperation. In the spontaneous measuring study, cooperation assessed from the ratings and interactive activity assessed from systematic observation were related to pretest–posttest change. In the number conservation study, cooperation tended, surprisingly, to be negatively correlated with pretest–posttest change for nonconserving children. Cooperation was certainly present in the experimenter's mind in inviting the children to pursue a common goal, but it might not have been present in the children's minds. The supposedly observed cooperation might, thus, have been only parallel action, which impeded the intraindividual processing of the situation. Because the children's view of the situation has not been assessed, this interpretation can not be confirmed, of course.

Some interesting, more clinically oriented patterns emerged. In the spontaneous measuring study, task-related, peer-oriented utterances and tutoring actions more often took a descending than an ascending direction. Similar results were found in the number conservation study. It seems that the children have good insight into their respective cognitive abilities and choose their social partner in a way that the interaction is directed from the more competent to the less competent child. It is true that children may infer their competence from their age, which is, itself, mediated by their stature: The older children are taller than the younger ones, and height is an important cue children use to infer competence (Graziano, 1978). Many triads, indeed, were composed of children of different grades: for instance, the last year of kindergarten and the first and second years of primary school. This arrangement, however, did not exist in all triads and in some of them, all three children were from the same grade.

The fact that process-oriented variables were not related to outcome in the left–right decentration study, was contrary to my hypotheses. Furthermore, the fact that the numbers of movements of the head and body and of displacements increased with pretest levels seemed astonishing. According to Piaget's theory, which considers overt action to be interiorized into covert thought, it would be expected that body rotations would be performed more frequently by nondecentered children than by decentered children. It may, indeed, be supposed that when asked to discriminate lateral parts on another person, young children compensate overtly for the differences in orientation between themselves and the other person, and that older children execute this more covertly or only virtually. This consideration led to a more complex study of the development of left–right decentration in relation to body rotations and the level of children's explanations referring to left–right relations. In this study, it was found that body rotations and the level of children's explanations increased significantly with age and were significantly correlated with performance in decentration tasks (Ghysselinckx-Janssens & Vandenplas-Holper, 1991). These data corroborate those of the left–right decentration intervention study (Vandenplas-Holper, 1987b) and require a revision of Piaget's concept of interiorization. Experiments in the domain of nonverbal behavior conducted with adults have shown that gestural and motoric activity increases when the speaker encounters difficulties in encoding. The decentration tasks used in the Vandenplas-Holper (1987b) and the Ghysselinckx-Janssens and Vandenplas-Holper (1991) studies are definitely of great complexity, which the child might be expected to cope with by using his or her body rotations.

The Ghysselinckx-Janssens and Vandenplas-Holper (1991) study questions one of the key concepts of Piaget's theory. Studies of other researchers have also proposed alternative views of spontaneous measuring (e.g., Bryant, 1982) or conservation (e.g., Rieben & de Ribeaupierre, 1990). Taking into account these alternative views questions the Piagetian concept of cognitive stages and structures.

Piaget's stages are qualitatively different ways of conceptualizing reality as organized into structured wholes. Studies based on pretest–posttest changes endeavor to use more detailed scales of measurement than the traditional Piagetian substages, which classify 5- to 8-year-old children as preoperational, intermediate, or operational. In the three studies I have described, I do not deny the use of the initial Piagetian conceptualization concerning left–right role-taking and the interest of clinical assessments in a study that is purely descriptive or exploratory. In the left–right role-taking and the number conservation study, I have, nevertheless, tried to use measures of a more quantitative nature. This option is shared by numerous other researchers studying social and moral development in the cognitive-developmental framework (Vandenplas-Holper, 1987b).

In the spontaneous measuring study, I have stuck more closely to the Piagetian descriptions concerning the development of spontaneous measurement, but I have tried to provide more detailed descriptions of the children's activity than Piaget et al. (1948) did in their original study. In this study, the simplified and the expanded assessment devices did not lead to the same results. In the left–right role-taking and in the number conservation studies, I made an effort to keep the cutting points used to classify the children according to the three levels of cognitive development coherent with the conceptualization initially proposed by Piaget. The very precise nature of the cutting points, however, was established only after inspection of the data provided by the pretest. The pretest and posttest measures I used, thus, were of a qualitative–quantitative nature and were adapted to the pragmatic requirements of the research paradigm I adopted.

The considerations about Piagetian substages led to more general considerations about structures and procedures. According to Inhelder and Piaget (1979), structures tie together transformations in order to establish relationships in atemporal structured wholes. The only aim of describing structures is a very general one: that of understanding the nature of cognition. Procedures also use transformations, but they use them in order to attain particular and specific goals. Thus, they are mainly temporal processes, consisting of goal-oriented sequences of goals and means to reach the goals. These considerations are still shared by Genevan researchers. According to Bovet and Voelin (1990), recent studies of cognitive development have shifted away from the consideration of successive forms of organization of cognition to the study of intelligence while it is functioning. Within the paradigm used by these and other Genevan researchers (e.g., Inhelder et al., 1976), the subject's activity in its temporal dimension has to be considered with its forms of organization and the structures in which it results. Structures and functioning are closely complementary and cannot be dissociated. According to the Genevan researchers (Bovet & Voelin, 1990; Inhelder et al., 1974), learning interventions like those implemented by Inhelder et al. (1974) are, in some respect, short longitudinal studies that enlarge the processes that are hardly noticed in other, more punctual studies. This microgenetic approach is often considered as a means of understanding the developmental processes that are at work in the macrogenesis. Microgenetic approaches have been used in other conceptual frameworks besides Piaget's theory, particularly by researchers relying on Vygotsky's work or on the information-processing framework. They have proved especially helpful for investigating the interaction through which teachers and learners, or learners working together, acquire new competencies (Catan, 1986; Siegler & Crowley, 1991).

The three studies described in this chapter are part of a broader research project on social development, parts of which were briefly presented in Vandenplas-Holper (1987a). They use a microgenetic approach similar to the one used in the Genevan studies. The approach, however, has elaborated much more precise observational tools for the description of the problem-solving process than the studies of the Genevan researchers. During more than 10 years, we have tried to establish progressively more fine-grained instruments for observation and content analysis.

Such a microgenetic approach is extremely strenuous. It requires innumerable revisions of the coding frames, and coders have to be involved in long training before they can engage in the formal phase of coding. Furthermore, the data derived from the analysis of the process of problem solving have some important limitations. Subject-to-subject variability is very important; this was particularly true for our left–right decentration study. Because the microgenetic analysis is very time consuming, the samples are sometimes small. Consequently, the use of statistical tests is limited. The results of our spontaneous measuring study, particularly, must be considered with caution, because we have established a great number of variables that are based on a very limited sample. Because the microgenetic approach we have used is very fine-grained, it focuses on some conceptually important variables that occur very infrequently. Implications for intercoder reliability are important: A few discrepancies in the coding of infrequently occurring observational categories considerably lower the reliability coefficients and require absolutely precise coding instructions. Requirements of statistical tests may lead us to aggregate infrequently occurring variables. As mentioned by Siegler and Crowley (1991), this aggregated depiction of change poses challenges of its own.

REFERENCES

Beaudichon, J., & Vandenplas-Holper, Ch. (1985). Analyse des interactions et de leurs effets dans la communication référentielle et la maîtrise des notions [Analysis of interactions and of their outcome in referential communication and the mastery of concepts]. In G. Mugny (Ed.), *Psychologie sociale du développement cognitif* (pp. 125–149). Berne, Switzerland: Peter Lang.

Berkowitz, M. W. (1985). The role of discussion in moral education. In M. W. Berkowitz & F. Oser (Eds.), *Moral education: Theory and application* (pp. 197–218). Hillsdale, NJ: Lawrence Erlbaum Associates.

Bovet, M., & Voelin, D. (1990). Examen et apprentissages opératoires: Faut-il choisir entre approches structurale et fonctionnelle? [Assessment and operational learning: Do we have to choose between a structural and a functional approach?]. *Archives de Psychologie, 58,* 107–212.

Brown, A. L., & Reeve, R. A. (1987). Bandwidths of competence: The role of supportive contexts in learning and development. In L. S. Liben (Ed.), *Development and learning: Conflict or congruence?* (pp. 173–223). Hillsdale, NJ: Lawrence Erlbaum Associates.

Bryant, P. E. (1982). The role of conflict and of agreement between intellectual strategies in children's ideas about measurement. *British Journal of Psychology, 73,* 243–251.

Catan, L. (1986). The dynamic display of process: Historical development and contemporary uses of the microgenetic method. *Human Development, 29,* 252–263.

Dalzon, C. (1988). Conflit cognitif et construction de la notion de droite/gauche [Cognitive conflict and the construction of the notion of right and left]. In A. N. Perret-Clermont & M. Nicolet (Eds.), *Interagir et connaître: Enjeux et régulations sociales dans le développement cognitif* (pp. 55–71). Fribourg, Switzerland: Delval.

Damon, W., & Killen, M. (1982). Peer interaction and the process of change in children's moral reasoning. *Merrill–Palmer Quarterly, 28,* 347–367.

Doise, W., & Mugny, G. (1981). *Le développement social de l'intelligence* [The social development of intelligence]. Paris: Interéditions.

Galifret-Granjon, N. (1969). Batterie Piaget-Head [The Piaget-Head battery]. In R. Zazzo (Ed.), *Manuel pour l'examen psychologique de l'enfant* [Handbook of the psychological assessment of the child]. (3rd ed., pp. 49–56). Neuchâtel: Delachaux et Niestlé. (Original work published 1958)

Ghysselinckx-Janssens, A., & Vandenplas-Holper, Ch. (1991). The development of left–right decentration in 4- to 7-year-old children. *European Journal of Psychology of Education, 6,* 303–324.

Gilly, M. (1989). The psychological mechanisms of cognitive constructions: Experimental research and teaching perspectives. *International Journal of Educational Research, 13,* 605–621.

Gilly, M., Fraisse, J., & Roux, J. P. (1988). Résolution de problèmes en dyades et progrès cognitifs chez des enfants de 11 à 13 ans: Dynamiques interactives et mécanismes socio-cognitifs [Problem-solving in dyads and cognitive progress for 11- to 13-year-old children]. In A. N. Perret-Clermont & M. Nicolet (Eds.), *Interagir et connaître: Enjeux et régulations sociales dans le développement cognitif* (pp. 73–92). Cousset, Fribourg: Delval.

Graziano, W. G. (1978). Standards of fair play in same-age and mixed-age groups of children. *Developmental Psychology, 14,* 524–530.

Inhelder, B., Ackermann-Vallado, E., Blanchet, A., Karmiloff-Smith, A., Kilcher-Hagedorn, H., Montangero, J., & Robert, M. (1976). Des structures cognitives aux procédures de découverte [From cognitive structures to procedures of discovery]. *Archives de Psychologie, 44*, 57–72.

Inhelder, B., & Piaget, J. (1979). Procédures et structures [Procedures and structures]. *Archives de Psychologie, 47*, 165–175.

Inhelder, B., Sinclair, H., & Bovet, M. (1974). *Apprentissage et structures de la connaissance* [Learning and structures of knowledge]. Paris: P.U.F.

Miller, S. A. (1973). Contradiction, surprise, and cognitive change: The effects of disconfirmation of belief on conservers and nonconservers. *Journal of Experimental Child Psychology, 15*, 47–62.

Miller, S. A., & Brownell, C. A. (1975). Peers, persuasion, and Piaget: Dyadic interaction between conservers and nonconservers. *Child Development, 46*, 992–997.

Mugny, G. (Ed.). (1985). *Psychologie sociale du développement cognitif* [Social psychology of cognitive development]. Berne, Switzerland: Peter Lang.

Oser, F. (1984). Cognitive stages of interaction in moral discourse. In W. M. Kurtines & J. L. Gewirtz (Eds.), *Morality, moral behavior, and moral development* (pp. 159–174). New York: Wiley.

Perret-Clermont, A. N. (1979). *La construction de l'intelligence dans l'interaction sociale* [The construction of intelligence in social interaction]. Berne, Switzerland: Peter Lang.

Perret-Clermont, A. N., & Nicolet, M. (Eds.). (1988). *Interagir et connaître: Enjeux et régulations sociales dans le développement cognitif* [Interaction and knowledge: Issues and social regulations in cognitive development]. Cousset, Fribourg: Delval.

Piaget, J. (1967). *Le jugement et le raisonnement chez l'enfant: Etudes sur la logique de l'enfant* [Judgment and reasoning in the child: Studies of the children's logic]. Neuchâtel: Delachaux et Niestlé. (Original work published 1924)

Piaget, J. (1941). *La genèse du nombre chez l'enfant* [The development of the concept of number in the child]. Neuchâtel: Delachaux et Niestlé.

Piaget, J. (1975). *L'équilibration des structures cognitives* [The equilibration of cognitive structures]. Paris: P.U.F.

Piaget, J., Inhelder, B., & Szeminska, A. (1948). *La géométrie spontanée chez l'enfant* [Spontaneous geometry in the child]. Paris: P.U.F.

Rieben, L., & de Ribaupierre, A. (1990). Structural invariants and individual modes of processing: On the necessity of a minimally structuralist approach of development for education. *Archives de Psychologie, 58*, 29–53.

Siegler, R. S., & Crowley, K. (1991). The microgenetic method: A direct means for studying cognitive development. *American Psychologist, 46*, 606–620.

Vandenplas-Holper, Ch. (1985). L'apprentissage en groupe de la décentration relative aux notions de gauche et de droite: Evaluation de l'efficacité des séances d'apprentissage [Group learning of left-right role-taking: Assessment of the outcome of learning sessions]. *Revue de Psychologie Appliquée, 35*, 79–103.

Vandenplas-Holper, Ch. (1986). L'évaluation de la maîtrise de la mesure spontanée par des enfants de 5 à 8 ans à partir d'un instrument clinique semi-structure [The assessment of the mastery of spontaneous measuring by 5- to 8-year-old children from a clinical semi-structured device]. *Education et Recherche, 2*, 79–104.

Vandenplas-Holper, Ch. (1987a). *Education et développement social de l'enfant* [Education and the child's social development]. Paris: P.U.F.

Vandenplas-Holper, Ch. (1987b). Interactions sociales et décentration spatiale: Analyse des arguments et des comportements non-verbaux produits dans le cadre d'interactions sociales relatives à la décentration spatiale [Social interactions and spatial role-taking: Analysis of arguments and non-verbal behavior referring to social interaction]. *Les Sciences de l'Education, 5*, 25–63.

Vandenplas-Holper, Ch. (1982, July). *Cooperation and socio-cognitive conflict in socio-cognitive problem solving situations: A process-oriented research.* Paper presented at the 25th International Congress of Psychology, Brussels, Belgium.

Vandenplas-Holper, Ch., Ghysselinckx, A., & Chapeaux, R. (1985). Action and interaction in the learning of spontaneous measuring. *International Review of Applied Psychology, 34,* 105–125.

Vandenplas-Holper, Ch., Pierret, M., & Chapeaux, R. (1986). L'apprentissage de la mesure spontanée dans les groupes verticaux restreints [The learning of spontaneous measurement in small vertical groups]. *Enfance, 1,* 24–41.

Winnykamen, F. (1990). *Apprendre en imitant?* [Learning by imitation?]. Paris: P.U.F.

12 The Roots of Intellectual Development

Peter Bryant
University of Oxford

The four chapters in this section are about what children learn from other people and how they learn it. This is a particularly appropriate question to pose in a book that attempts to bridge the gap between Francophone developmental psychologists and others in the field. In the past, Francophone psychologists and their colleagues in other countries used to think quite differently from each other about these issues. The Francophone approach, dominated by Piaget, stressed the idea that children learn for themselves on the basis of their informal experiences in the environment. Although some of these experiences certainly involve interactions with other people, nothing in their intellectual development is the result of direct instruction from other people. Children construct their own intellectual development; it is not constructed for them.

In stark contrast, Anglo-Saxon developmental psychologists, guided initially by the behaviorist tradition and more recently by a growing interest in the ideas of Vygotsky (1986; see also van de Veer & Valsiner, 1991), have always concentrated on the possibility that children's intellectual development can be helped and even shaped by those around them, particularly by their parents and teachers. The behaviorist basis for this view is now gone, because it is generally acknowledged that theories based on the stimulus–response (S–R) connection cannot produce a convincing explanation for either language acquisition, in particular, or cognitive development, in general. The Vygotskian notion of the *zone of proximal development* (what the child does with an adult's help today, he will be able to do on his own tomorrow) and of the transmission of cultural tools across generations, however, is still very influential.

How do the two sides, if sides they are, stand today? The divide between them on this central issue—whether the child learns for himself or herself or learns from others—is much narrower now, and may well be about to disappear. Both sides are now interested in developmental acquisitions that children plainly do construct for themselves, and Francophone psychologists have actually led the way in discovering other aspects of development in which social interactions probably play an important part.

Areas of development that children almost certainly construct for themselves are mentioned in two of these four chapters. Vyt reports an excellent study in which children had to search their environment with help from information on a video screen. One group had the principles of video filming explained to them by an adult, whereas the other was allowed some prior active experience with a video setup. Those in the latter group subsequently used information from the video monitor more successfully than the others. Here, the children definitely had to work things out for themselves. These results fit well with other work, which is well reviewed by Vyt, on the importance of contingent experiences, and it also can be connected to the work of Kermoian and Campos (1988), who showed that children who are given extra active locomotor experience (in the form of time in baby walkers) may actually go through the stages of object permanence more quickly as a result. Contingent experience in space may give young children more than just spatial knowledge.

Ricard, Gouin Décarie, Desrochers, and Rome-Flanders deal with another aspect of development, where the causal question is a great deal more controversial. The debate on the roots of language acquisition has gone this way and that, but Ricard et al.'s failure to find any correlational data for Bruner's hypothesis (or erstwhile hypothesis) makes it more likely that parents and others play a small role in the child's acquisition of language, apart from providing the necessary linguistic environment.

Thus, spatial knowledge and language may be developmental acquisitions that children construct for themselves without the help of others, but what about logic? Piaget's claim was that children also manage logical development largely by themselves, but the (distinctly Francophone) line of research, which was started by Perret-Clermont (1980) and by Doise and Mugny (1984) on the effects of social interactions on logical development, suggests otherwise. The importance of the work of these two researchers can hardly be overstated. It produced some striking data but, even more importantly, it showed us that it was possible for someone to entertain the idea that social interaction and communication were an important spur to intellectual development and still to remain within the Piagetian framework.

One of the ways in which these researchers remained Piagetian was in maintaining his idea of conflict. When Doise and Mugny (1984) showed that children begin to solve the perspective problem after having argued among themselves about it, and when Perret-Clermont (1980) found the same thing with conservation problems, both used the idea of conflict—in this case, social conflict—to explain their remarkable results. There were clearly two reasons for their doing so. One was that the children plainly did at first disagree, and so, there was some conflict, but the other was probably more important: It was that the notion of conflict lies at the heart of Piaget's analysis of the reasons for developmental change, and although these researchers were prepared to think of the process of developmental change as more social than Piaget had, they still agreed with him that conflict was the engine of these changes.

Yet, it need not have been so. There was nothing, for example, in Perret-Clermont's (1980) data to demonstrate that it was the conflict per se that led to the striking improvement that she found in children's conservation performance. An alternative was that the children who improved were easily persuaded, usually by the more able children in the group, to change their views.

There are certainly very great problems with the idea of conflict, as the chapters by Fraysse and Desprels-Fraysse and by Vandenplas-Holper point out. One of these is, as Fraysse and Desprels-Fraysse show, that it has not always been possible to demonstrate empirically that conflict improves children's performance in various logical tasks. Another problem is a conceptual one: Conflict on its own can never provide all the information needed for a new development to take place (Bryant, 1986). Conflict, whether intraindividual, as in Piaget's formulation, or interindividual, as in Doise and Mugny's and Perret-Clermont's experiments, and also in those reported by Vandenplas-Holper here, is simply a signal that one or more views is wrong because there are two incompatible views about the same thing. All this tells us is that either one or both of these views is incorrect: It does not tell us what the right view is. The Hegelian thesis–antithesis–synthesis process, on which Piaget based so much, is still plagued with magical obscurity.

I mentioned an exception, and it is quite an interesting one. All that a child needs in order to understand how to reach a correct solution in perspective problems is the knowledge that people in different positions have different views of the same scene. That knowledge, as Doise and Mugny (1984) pointed out, can be acquired quite quickly by two children, each of whom begins by arguing, incorrectly, that their own egocentric representation is the right one, but it is worth knowing that this interindividual conflict is not the only kind that works. Emler and Valliant (1982) compared the effects of this sort of conflict with those of intraindividual conflicts (the same child representing the same scene from two different points of view at different times) and found this to be as effective as the Doise and Mugny technique.

What is to be done about the idea of conflict? As far as I can see, we are offered two different solutions in this book. One, given by Fraysse and Desprels-Fraysse, is to look for different causal mechanisms. The other, which is to be found in the chapter by Vandenplas-Holper, is to analyse in detail exactly what goes on when conflict is supposed to take place.

The notion of rule induction described by Fraysse and Desprels-Fraysse is an intriguing one, and it is exciting to see that it works so well. The methods that they adopt for this rule induction, which they rightly contrast with conflict, seem to me to be both delicate and didactic. These methods remind me of Vygotsky much more than of Piaget. When a child is being asked to guess an adult's sorting rule, and is then asked to make up one of his own for the adult to guess, we are very close to the zone of proximal development. I think that there is a connection to be made between this work and the research of those who are trying to provide an empirical basis for the Vygotskian ideas, such as Wertsch (1985), Cole (1985) and Brown and Ferrara (1985).

The most important aspect of the studies that Vandenplas-Holper describes is the analysis in minute detail of what children do in a learning phase that involves three children: in this case, one who cannot do the task in question, another who definitely can, and a third who is at an intermediate level. Vandenplas-Holper notes that there is evidence of conflict here, but also of considerable cooperation among the children. There are also signs that the ability of the children to communicate information changes quite radically during the experiment: That, in my view, is what may lie behind the fact that their communicative movements actually increased as time went on.

Together, these four chapters clearly show that research on the social and the asocial roots of developmental change is making a great deal of progress. We owe much of this progress to the Francophone approach to developmental psychology. It is good to see that this tradition is still a lively and flexible one.

REFERENCES

Brown, A. L., & Ferrara, R. A. (1985). Diagnosing zones of proximal development. In J. V. Wertsch (Ed.), *Culture, communication and cognition* (pp. 273–305). Cambridge, England: Cambridge University Press.
Bryant, P. E. (1986). Theories about the causes of cognitive development. In P.L.C. van Geert (Ed.), *Theory building in developmental psychology* (pp. 167–188). Amsterdam: North-Holland.
Cole, M. (1985). The zone of proximal development: Where culture and cognition create each other. In J. V. Wertsch (Ed.), *Culture, communication and cognition* (pp. 146–161). Cambridge, England: Cambridge University Press.
Doise, W., & Mugny, G. (1984). *The social development of the intellect.* Oxford: Pergamon.
Emler, N., & Valliant, G. (1982). Social interaction and cognitive conflict in the development of spatial coordination skills. *British Journal of Psychology, 73,* 295–303.
Kermoian, R., & Campos, J. J. (1988). Locomotor experience: A facilitator of cognitive development. *Child Development, 59,* 908–917.
Perret-Clermont, A. N. (1980). *Social interaction and cognitive development in children.* London: Academic Press.
van de Veer, R., & Valsiner, J. (1991). *Vygotsky: A quest for synthesis.* Oxford: Blackwell.
Vygotsky, L. (1986). *Thought and language.* Cambridge, MA: M.I.T. Press.
Wertsch, J. V. (Ed.). (1985). *Culture, communication and cognition.* Cambridge, England: Cambridge University Press.

13

Francophone Perspectives on Cognition and Social Cognition in Preschool-Age Children

Marc H. Bornstein
National Institute of Child Health and Human Development

Among developmental researchers from different French-speaking countries—in Montréal in Canada, in Belgium, or in Aix-en-Provence in France—Jean Piaget has exercised continuing influence. Piaget was one of the few theoreticians in cognitive development who not only focused on understanding the properties and transitions that characterize stages of mental development after infancy and before adolescence, but contributed to that understanding in a major way. This period—encompassing as it does schooling of the most basic and formative sort—is critical to the mental growth of the child. Normally, greater emphasis is placed on curricula and associated institutional issues, and less emphasis is given to the cognitive characteristics of the child who is learning. As a consequence, an area of considerable importance in the study of mental development, broadly conceived, is the nature of school-age cognition. These chapters on cognitive development by Ricard, Gouin Décarie, Desrochers, and Rome-Flanders, by Vyt, by Fraysse and Desprels-Fraysse, and by Vandenplas-Holper demonstrate that the application of continuing attention and vigor to the study of this important age period by developmental researchers in the Francophone tradition has yielded valuable insights into what children themselves bring to their cognitive development.

In their chapter on cognition and social-cognitive development, Ricard, Gouin Décarie, and their colleagues recount a series of imaginative experimental studies aimed at updating some key Piagetian insights. Their efforts explore person–object décalage, the development of social referencing in relation to the child's achievement of causality (Piaget's Stage V), and relations between language competence and game play. Basically, the research from this Montréal laboratory examines in different ways the important implications of a broader view of Piaget's cognitive theorizing. Their approach leads consistently into social-cognitive domains of thinking. In the end, the inferences from these diverse but progressive lines of research are modern and provocative in moving us through a view of children's construction of social reality (faithful to Piaget) toward a modernist approach to how children acquire a theory of mind.

Vyt's chapter on the development of self-recognition underscores the importance of the child's self-awareness—including its antecedents, components, and consequences—for cognitive growth. Self-recognition has been discussed under many guises (perception, awareness, and consciousness) and, as is made clear in this chapter, the social cognition of self-recognition implies multiple perceptual and mental processes. Through a close analysis of the literature and contributions of his own, Vyt ably decomposes this otherwise fascinating but elusive phenomenon, revisiting the several experimental paradigms that have been developed to address the issue and highlighting the strengths, weaknesses, and deductions that may be drawn from each. Piaget is a generative figure in this literature too, for his initial observations on self-consciousness (along with those of Wallon, Zazzo, and others), for the stages of development he defined (the child's achieving the capacity for representation and acquiring object permanence articulate with the advent of self-recognition), and for defining cognitive capabilities that might underpin self-recognition (cause and effect). Children's recognition of self spills over into questions of who they conceive themselves to be, and in this very central way research and thinking regarding self-recognition again point up the ineluctable interpenetration of cognitive and social spheres of development. As Vyt concludes—echoing Piaget—perception, experimentation, and action are critical to children's understanding the world and to their reflections of themselves in it.

Interest in the use of cognitive strategies in preschool children has enabled Fraysse and Desprels-Fraysse to focus on territory Piaget visited when taking up cognitive growth in the school-aged child. Their work systematically explores the origins, mechanisms, timing, and consequences of cognitive strategy induction. As they persuasively argue, induction is a process that is critical for learning, and it is crucial for understanding cognition per se. In this work as well, children's increasing understanding and self-understanding—*la prise de conscience*—play leading roles.

In focusing on higher-level cognitive processes in children, Vandenplas-Holper picks up on another Piagetian élan: The author wishes to operationalize disequilibration as a motive for social cognitive development and explore it as a basis for the development of problem solving. Three tasks have been experimentally harnessed in this research effort—role-taking, measurement, and conservation—and the converging operations brought to bear have contributed to the positive nature of the findings. A key result of this line of investigation has been to expose the significant contribution of the child's insights into his or her own cognitive level as defining and motivating mental development.

Vandenplas-Holper's emphasis on process (*contra* status) constitutes an additional commendable feature of this research focus. Thus, the author has been able to mesh structure with function in defining developmental processes.

The authors of these four chapters work in different locales on different topics but share many common perspectives. The subject matter—stages, transitions, and sources of progress or motives for development—is either special to or was introduced by Piaget. However, their work has evolved not to "test" Piaget, but rather, in the words of one group, to "clarify" Piaget. This clarification takes place through detailed designs and experimental operationalizations of phenomena once observed, noted, and explored by Piaget and those who immediately followed him in the Genevan school. Each effort is marked by multiple tasks and converging operations. We are reminded by these studies that, in many respects, Piagetian assertions still merit attention (e.g., that activity is crucial to cognitive development), but these essays are also revisionist, revealing a particularly modernist stance in their open-mindedness and in their opening of Piagetian theoretical constructs to evolving reconceptualization. On an experimental level, microgenetic approaches supplant the *méthode clinique* at the same time that theory of mind perspectives supplement *disequilibration*. Taking heart, the reader finds some clarity in connecting cognitive developmental theorizing across nearly a century.

The four essays in this section also betray the elusiveness of pinning down cognitive developmental phenomena in experimentation. To his credit, Piaget captured some truisms of mental life, truths that cognitive developmentalists themselves often observe, but that apparently do not readily or easily submit to experimental analysis.

Finally, the work recounted in these chapters is pervaded—more by what is left unsaid than by explicit statement—by latent educational implications. The actual "stuff" of research concerns learning through cognitive induction, the achievement of self-understanding, cooperative learning, and theory of mind, but, even if underdeveloped, there are manifestly rich veins of cognition to mine in the mind of the school-aged child. In the context of the contemporary crisis of schooling youth, with its flailings centered around institutions and curricula, the work reported here suggests that an alternative focus on the mind of the child and the processes of learning might prove rewarding. Until now, the French language has, in the words of one of the contributors, constituted a "barrier" to understanding for people outside French-speaking countries and an impediment, perhaps, to embracing Piaget. These chapters tell us that the questions to which Piaget addressed himself and the issues to which he drew our attention may yet speak to a wider scientific and educational audience.

III VERBAL AND COMMUNICATIVE DEVELOPMENT

14 The Development of Communication: Wallon's Framework and Influence

Jacqueline Nadel
Ecole des Hautes Etudes-CNRS

In the 1940s, when Piaget's influence was approaching its zenith in France and the other Francophone European countries, Wallon (1970, 1973c) proposed a model of early communication and social development, as well as hypotheses about their role in cognitive development. He also put forward an overview of ways to study ontogenesis, in which he stressed the value of taking emerging and disappearing abilities and features of development into account simultaneously.

Prerequisite and precursors were of essential concern to Piagetians, whereas Wallon emphasized the importance of transitory adaptations to understanding epigenesis. Transitory adaptations are interesting in that they highlight the heterotypic aspect of developmental adaptation, as well as the basic, rather than the vestigial, function of momentary adaptive means. In other words, the study of transitory adaptations helps us to recognize that distinct behaviors may fulfill the same adaptive function at different developmental periods, and that similar behaviors may have different meanings according to the individual's developmental level.

This option opened up a functionalist perspective in development that profoundly challenged the Piagetian system. It gained only a few followers in the realm of cognitive studies, but it provided a useful framework for educational and clinical practitioners, and for researchers in the area of early communication, although only a few of its hypotheses have been tested (Nadel, 1980b, 1984). Furthermore, it could account for why the cognitive model of socialization derived from Piaget's view of moral development (1932) had had so few European Francophone advocates, despite its having been so popular in Anglophone countries since the 1970s.

This chapter focuses on an analysis of Wallon's influence on European Francophone concepts, methods, and data in the realm of nonverbal and prelinguistic communication. I delineate what has been tested, and what remains to be proved of what is still original and testable. Throughout, an important point must be kept in mind: We can rely on contemporary creativity and clarification when analyzing historical originality, and the present is a generous analyzer of the past, possibly too generous in attributing paternity and filiation to current models and findings.

THE SOCIABLE INFANT

According to Wallon, the human infant is fundamentally sociable: *genetically* sociable, as he said. Social exchanges exist from birth on, changing in nature and content in the course of ontogenesis. By *social exchange,* Wallon meant any contingency between one person's actions and another's, indicating an influence of the one on the other. *Sociability* is the basic capacity for social exchanges that allows primary adaptation to the human environment.

In his opinion, there was no empirical reason to adhere to a model of social development that describes the initial state of the infant as *egocentrism,* according to Piaget's contemporary claim. On this point, Wallon (1947/1973b) wrote a famous criticism, which may seem trivial now, but was very thought-provoking at the time:

> Even if Piaget's thesis seems to be well balanced, it does not seem to fit observational data. It does not describe the real relationships of infants with their milieu, which are not of simple succession, which are not the by-product of pure reasoning or intellectual intuition, but that intertwined their life and their environmental climate. . . . Maybe, as Piaget has held against me, it is exaggerated to say that newborns are social beings. Nevertheless, because they depend on the human climate for all that they urgently need, this factual situation has immediate consequences that orient their psychological development. For weeks they need assistance not only to be fed, but to be cleaned, to be moved, to be rocked, to be changed from painful postures. . . . (pp. 306–307, my translation)

The result is that the first utilitarian relationships are not with the physical environment but with the human milieu, and the means for these relationships are expressive behaviors. This is why, even if they are not consciously members of society, young infants are primarily and totally socially oriented. Expressive behaviors, insofar as they support emotions, are agents of affective fusion. Via emotions, infants belong to their milieu before they belong to themselves. In a complete *affective symbiosis,* totally immersed in the social world, young infants are, at first, almost too receptive, too sensitive to their social atmosphere. Therefore, social development must not be described as increasing social influence, but as decreasing sensitivity and accommodation to the immediate social environment. That is why Wallon never used the notion of *socialization* but referred to *sociability:* The process described points out qualitative, not quantitative, changes.

In the early 1940s, this was a very personal position, resulting from an original conception of socio-constructivism. This socio-constructivism implies a cascade view of different social environments from family to culture: Bronfenbrenner's (1977) ecological model of development actually represents, at best, a similar interest. Further, Wallon's definition of *milieu* is important in appreciating the originality of his model of social development (Nadel, 1979). In a period when French psychologists were still strongly influenced by Auguste Comte, who conceived the milieu as the physical world (gravity, motion, temperature, air, etc.), specifically " the total set of external circumstances necessary for each organism to exist" (1907, p. 153), Wallon was Darwinian and saw the living milieu as the primary and main environment for humans. He defined the milieu as "the total set of physical, human, or ideological circumstances which are simultaneously encountered" (1973a, p. 296). This definition includes a metarepresentational inner world—composed of motives, emotional representations, logical predictions, and causal inferences—that can be sometimes contrasted and sometimes combined with concrete events and that deeply influences the interactions with the physical world and the social world. Evident today in the realms of social cognition and theory of mind, at that time this view was only shared by Russian thinkers, such as Vygotsky (1978).

Wallon's original position stood at the intersection of a Darwinian definition of interdependence as the main interaction, a cascade view of different levels of milieu— including individual as well as cultural representations—and the notion of a social constructivism, viewed as an evolving self–other system (Zazzo, 1975). Indeed, his unique contribution is the meshing of a developmental description of prelinguistic exchanges and a theoretical view of the progressive individuation of the self. Stern (1985) has recently structured a theory of the self that presents similarities, but his view appears to be more precise and enriched by current findings on infant social development. What clearly distinguishes the two contributions is that Stern pointed out different types of self (physical, subjective, verbal), whereas Wallon distinguished evolving systems of self–other states of differentiation.

SELF–OTHER DIFFERENTIATION

The process of differentiation hypothesized by Wallon (1973c) may be outlined in the following way. Wallon's theory describes three fundamental levels of the self–other system, each associated with a predominant mode of social exchange:

1. *Undifferentiated syncretism,* which culminates at around 6 months in the emotional stage.

2. *Differentiated syncretism,* when the self and the other are consistently cohering.

3. *Personalism,* which opens up the period of a clear differentiation of the motives, roles, and social positions of self and other in the course of interindividual exchanges.

I examine only here the first two systems, because the third one implies verbal exchanges.

Undifferentiated Syncretism and Expressivity

The idea that social life begins in an undifferentiated way was shared by most contemporary authors, psychoanalysts (of course), and Piaget. According to Piaget's view, the process of differentiation implies a shift from egocentrism to social perspective-taking ability and objectivization of the self. Wallon's idea appears to have close ties to Mead's (1934), certainly because of their common reference to Baldwin (1895). This idea is that the process is more likely one of learning to distinguish what is mine and what is yours, that is, learning to attribute to others feeling and mental states through complementary roles, simultaneously gaining from initial self–other confusion both self-awareness and awareness of others. Perspective-taking, according to Wallon, is an advanced level of social behavior, not the definition of being social. Developing one's own perspective, far from being at the beginning of differentiation, is what still has to be achieved.

As I have indicated, Wallon argued for the empirical evidence of sociability in young babies. Influenced by Darwin (1872), he detected the first indices of sociability in innate universals, namely, in emotional expressions, but his model of emotional prelanguage differed from Darwin's on two points. First, unlike Darwin who focused on facial expressions, Wallon attributed the main expressive role to bodily postures, which he believed denoted the nature and intensity of involvement in events. Secondly, Wallon emphasized the core, not the vestigial, function of emotion, and its psychogenetic role in prelinguistic communication and construction of mental states. The differences between Darwin's and Wallon's conceptions were explained by Wallon (1938) in the following terms:

Those, like Darwin himself, who searched for the origin of emotion in primitive reactions toward the milieu that are now obsolete, have essentially seen expression itself. They have not understood the autonomous nature of this expressive capacity. They have not seen that it differs from actions whose immediate aim is located in the external world. It is primarily an autogenous modeling of the organism proceeding from tonic motricity. Emotions are the mental realizations of this autogenous bodily modeling, from which impressions of consciousness are first drawn. (pp. 824–825, my translation)

Thus, there was something in Wallon's model of emotional prelanguage that was not in Darwin's: Emotion permits the organization of a primary mode of communication and the first step toward building awareness of mental states out of an innate capacity of bodily modeling.

According to Wallon, the semantic attribution of emotional meaning to bodily expressions was a direct and innate capacity of matching via a mimetic mechanism (Wallon, 1934/1973c). In Wallon's view, bodily mimetism has two main vehicles: facial expressions and postures. As postural mimetism is included in what we now call *gestural imitation,* it can easily be conceived that immediate imitation and emotional contagiousness were seen by Wallon as two faces of the same phenomenon of matching. Cases of immediate imitation are described as mimetic behaviors in Wallon's work. It is likely that Wallon would have treated neonatal imitation as a case of bodily mimetism, not so different from Field, Woodson, Greenberg, and Cohen (1982), who used facial expressions of emotion, not facial movements (like tongue protrusion or mouth opening), when they studied neonatal imitation. Thus, a modern equivalent of the idea of an innate capacity of sharing emotional experiences via mimetism is the idea of an innate capacity for matching, mediated by an amodal (or transmodal) representational system, processing equivalences between an act seen and an act done (Meltzoff & Moore, 1977).

Note, however, that the infant–caregiver system of *affective symbiosis* resulting from emotional sharing does not, according to Wallon, take place before the age of 3 months. More recently and independently, Trevarthen (1977) described a very similar mode of infant–mother exchanges in terms of *primary intersubjectivity,* but dated the appearance of this system at around 3 weeks of age. Wallon clearly was influenced by contemporary beliefs concerning the larval state of the newborn. For the same reasons, he denied the possibility of neonatal imitation, although his student, Zazzo, reported evidence of this phenomenon already in 1945. In the scientific environment of Piaget and Wallon, who were both hostile to his findings, Zazzo refrained from publishing his data for 12 years (Zazzo, 1957), and his work was not taken up again until Maratos's work (1973) with Pierre Mounoud in Geneva.

In summary, from 3 to around 8 months, babies were described by Wallon as tied to the social climate in an undivided way. During this period, they were said to predominantly use body expressivity, modifying behavior and affective state as a whole. Being global, emotional expressivity is well adapted to provoking a "*unanimous raptus*" (Wallon, 1968, p. 126) creating an undifferentiated self–other system of exchange.

Several researchers in France and in Switzerland have been involved in testing the existence of this primary form of social exchange. De Ajuriaguerra (1970) described *l'aimantation du regard,* a piercing, fascinated eye-to-eye contact so captivating for young babies that they may stop sucking. Postural adjustments between mother and infant were considered by de Ajuriaguerra as the most obvious behavioral sign of primary bodily expressiveness in the Wallonian framework: He proposed calling these mutual adjustments *the tonic dialogue*.

Observational data from mother–neonate pairs led Stambak (1963) to classify different tonical types in infants, whereas Lézine, Robin, and Cortial (1975) proposed a categorization of mothers' bodily postures during the first feeding experiences. Robin (1978), in the framework of Lézine and de Ajuriaguerra's previous analyses, showed that kinaesthetic and tactile stimulations from the mother influenced the visual behavior of the newborn toward her. Further, Robin (1980) studied mothers' ways of holding and their role in primary interactions. She compared fullterm babies with ones that were preterm, and added a 3-months follow-up of some of them. Mothers' ways of holding appeared to be mostly consistent throughout the first 3 months, with changes linked to significant circumstances. For instance, difficult feeding led to more contracted postures. Infant's increasing gazes at the mother induced more face-to-face postures. Tonical releasing in the newborn was linked to maternal fondling. In mothers of preterm babies, searching distal interactions (eye-to-eye contact, face-to-face orientation, motherese) was more frequent than touching the baby. Robin's data, mostly descriptive, put the emphasis on the maternal postural adjustments and responses to infant tonic reactivity, rather than on tonic dialogue.

Widmer-Robert-Tissot, (1981), working with Pierre Mounoud in Geneva, contributed more clearly to this question, by studying postural sequencing rather than static postures, and mother–stranger differentiation on the basis of postural indices. She observed infants, aged 9 to 52 weeks, who were held by the mothers and by a female experimenter. Each infant was silently taken out of his or her infant seat in the dark and held for 40 seconds (a) against the right shoulder, (b) against the left shoulder, and (c) face-to-face on the lap. At all ages, infants were more relaxed and in fusion with the mother, and more agitated and more resistant to being picked up (with increasing motor control, holding head and trunk at a distance) with the female experimenter. These findings were seen as evidence of early processing of proprioceptive information given by the partner, and of regulative responses by controlling distance. It was concluded that the notion of symbiosis could be used to describe both postural fusion, as well as this sort of temporary distance that permits reorganization of the mother–infant postural system. Note that symbiosis does not mean passivity, as the infant appears to be able to anticipate maternal posture and to resist the stranger's manipulations as if confronted with postural misunderstanding.

Widmer-Robert-Tissot's study provides an interesting set of quasi-experimental data documenting the existence of a tonic dialogue. Nevertheless, further studies are needed, which could take into account interactional synchrony (Condon & Sander, 1974; Stern, 1977; Trevarthen, 1977) as a basis for studying earlier postural interactions.

Differentiated Syncretism and Transitive Exchanges

At the end of the 1st year, cohesion of the self and of the other begin to be established simultaneously. Wallon claimed that, at this time, the child begins to become aware of changes in roles according to the situation. A recent study by Tremblay-Leveau (1992) tests this Wallonian hypothesis. To explore self-awareness of social position in 10- to 24-month-olds, an experimental design simulated a common situation of family life: a toddler being excluded from an ongoing dyadic interaction between a familiar adult and another child. When the witness-toddler succeeds in initiating an interaction with one or both partners, he ceases to be in the witness role.

The communicative behavior of toddlers was compared in two different positions, that is, their being excluded from the ongoing dyadic interaction or their being included in it. The results showed a significant position effect, even at 10 months. When excluded, the toddlers took far more initiatives toward the other child than when they were included; they also responded to nearly all initiatives coming from the included child. These results suggest an early awareness of social position in the group (Tremblay-Leveau & Nadel, in press). This is corroborated by another finding concerning the outcomes of this tacit struggle between the two children to interact with the adult. If the included child opened the dyad toward the excluded child, he generally managed to take a new initiative toward the adult and confirmed his previous interactive position, whereas the excluded child could confirm his first overture in less than half of his or her many initiatives.

Leveau's findings documented the capacities of infants to monitor their social behavior according to a rudimentary knowledge of their position in a communicative structure, but it is an all-or-none situation, and evidence of a quantitative kind. If we start analyzing how children behave according to the contextual content, and whether or not they are able to maintain a different role from a partner, we discover that the roles are not so clear-cut, even for older toddlers.

Wallon's model suggests that, in the course of the 2nd and 3rd year, children are still splintered among their roles, which vary according to situations, and they lack a coherent perception of themselves and others. During this phase of *interchangeable personalities* (Wallon, 1934/1973c), they try out different roles by playing several characters in succession, and they may lose their fragile sense of individuality as situations change.

One of the fundamental acquisitions of the 2nd year, in Wallon's view, is the awareness of the bipolarity of roles in every dyadic situation. The simplest are the situations in which one partner is active and the other is passive: These are typical of complementary activities, with numerous everyday examples, such as mother acting and baby acted on. Dubon, Josse, and Lézine's (1981) observations show that alternating the contrasted role in a peer dyad is a very frequent structure of social interaction around 18 months of age.

The sharing of emotions remains an important part of toddlers' communicative means, although now the sharing implies an external topic Wallon (1973b). Marcos and Verba (1991) tested the importance of sharing emotion in referential communication about objects, persons, or events with an adult and with a peer. Their results demonstrated that, although conventionalized behaviors are used more frequently with adults, emotional expressions are markedly higher in toddler-peers.

By 2 years of age, children are mastering much more sophisticated distinctions, but, because they cannot combine the perception of different poles with self–other differentiation, their reactions are *transitive,* manifesting a direct transition from the state of subject to the state of object and vice versa. Children waver between a confusion of pole in a situation and a confusion of partners. Either they espouse the motives of others, which they then attribute to themselves (*sympathy,* according to Wallon), or they attribute their own motives to other people. Similarly, they may, in turn, feel the effects of their own role and the effect of the other's role, in a given situation. They are, indeed, still very sensitive to the emotions expressed around them, but these are no longer purely and simply endured. They are now torn between the other's emotion and their experience of the situation in which they feel such emotion not to be appropriate. They now need an objective motive of sharing.

An analysis of Wallon's view led me to propose (Nadel, 1980a) the following hypothesis: Synchronous imitation could be the main vehicle for transitivism, because it permits direct symmetrical exchanges with the partner and leads the toddler to sense *the same thing at the same time,* a way of experiencing identity. In this case, everyone has his or her own motive, but it has the same appearance. This should allow children to sustain durable reciprocal attention and interest toward one another, and to develop long-lasting interactions on the basis of positive emotional sharing. Thus synchronous imitation should be the main basis of sustained interactions in 2- to 3-year-old peers.

To test this hypothesis, Nadel and Baudonnière (1980, 1982) filmed triads of 30-month-old familiar peers meeting without an adult in an experimental setting. The experimental design consisted of three identical sets of 10 attractive objects each, so that each child could choose an object either for its intrinsic attractiveness or because a partner chose it. Some of the objects, such as umbrellas and cow-boys hats, allowed bodily modeling. The results showed that imitative exchanges were the dominant social behaviors in each triad. There was no prevalence for some children to be imitated or to be imitators: The more children imitated, the more they themselves were imitated. This shows that each child used imitation as an active means of communication. The same results have been replicated with an adult present (Mertan, 1990; Mertan, Nadel, & Leveau, 1993). In another study (Nadel, 1986), the same 30-month-old peers were observed in dyads in two experimental settings: one with two identical sets of 10 objects, enabling synchronous imitations to develop; the other with a single set of 20 different objects. Social behaviors were found to be far more numerous in the double-object setting, thus indicating the important role of imitation in toddler communication. The striking differences between the number of smiles and laughs in the double-object setting compared to the single-object setting (5 times more) support the Wallonian hypothesis of a strong link between emotion sharing and imitation.

Comparisons with 4-year-old peer dyads observed in the same two conditions showed that the use of imitation decreases, and the double-object setting no longer facilitates social exchanges at this age (Nadel & Fontaine, 1989). Thus, synchronized imitation can be seen as a transitory means of communication, as Wallon proposed. Further analyses of this transitory means led Baudonnière (1988) to show the difficult access to synchronous imitation at age 2. Overlapping reproductions of acts performed by a peer were not found earlier than 18 months (Baudonnière & Michel, 1988). More recently, Asendorpf and Baudonnière (1993) showed a concomitance between mirror-self-recognition and capacity of synchronous imitation.

Having documented the powerful communicative function of imitation during the transitory period of transitivism, we decided to evaluate its psychogenetic role. This led to study autistic children, who exhibit severe impairments in communication and are said to be unable to imitate gestures. Our hypothesis (Nadel & Pezé, 1993) was that, if imitation is a necessary ingredient for the achievement of self–other differentiation and for formatting primary communication, autistic high imitators would communicate more easily than low imitators, and mute autistic children able to imitate would predominantly use the imitative format.

Two comparisons led to a test of the hypothesis that synchronized gestural and verbal imitation might be a necessary step in the development of prelinguistic communication. Autistic high imitators (Uzgiris and Hunt, 1975, Imitation Scale: Level 5) were compared to autistic low imitators (Uzgiris and Hunt, 1975, Imitation Scale: Level 2 or 3) regarding their communicative repertory. The communicative repertory was recorded during dyadic sessions of free play with a nonautistic familiar agemate in the experimental design with two identical sets of 10 objects each. The results indicated that autistic low imitators differed significantly from autistic high imitators in social interest and performance. They showed few and brief social involvements, and promoted low social interest from their nonautistic agemates. Autistic high imitators were also compared to 30-month-olds meeting with either an unacquainted or a familiar peer during a dyadic session in the same experimental conditions. The autistic high imitators were able to perform active social productions, comparable to 30-month-old unacquainted peers. This result suggests that they did not differ in mature social behavior from the nonfamiliar toddler dyads, and that their behavior appeared developmentally delayed, rather than deviant. As a point of discussion, this might indicate that it is the acquisition of imitative behaviors that initiates development of social interactions with peers, and that, once begun, autistic children stop looking so deviant, starting down a route more typically seen in normal development.

Although replication is needed, these first results are congruent with Rogers and Pennington's (1991) recent model of autism. These authors suggested that a triad of early social capacities involving imitation, emotion sharing, and a theory of mind is specifically deficient in autism. They proposed a developmental model of autism, inspired by Stern (1985), in which an impairment in the formation and coordination of specific self–other representations due to lack of amodal representation abilities accounts for primary deficits in imitations of body movements, thus influencing emotion sharing, which influences formation of a theory of mind. This confirms that testing a Wallonian hypothesis may still contribute to a current international debate.

THE BASIC ROLE OF GESTURE IN EXPRESSION AND EVOCATION

A last point that calls for comment is Wallon's view of the process by which symbolic thought and communication take place. This is an important question, because it still implies postural activity. In Wallon's view, postural activity is not only aimed at expressing what somebody senses here and now; it is also the first means of distinguishing the perceived and the represented. In other words, body modeling enables the individual not only to express but also to evoke (Wallon, 1942/1978). It is the first step toward fiction, the first locus where temporal and spatial responses may be delayed. This first type of evocation implies differed imitation that is imitation starting in the perceptual absence of the model. On this point Piaget (1962) said he and Wallon were in agreement, and their works were complementary (Gratiot–Alphandèry, 1964). I have suggested elsewhere (Nadel, 1984) that Piaget interpreted Wallon's theory in a tangential manner.

According to Piaget, Wallon emphasized the link between differed imitation and figurative capacities, whereas Piaget himself was more involved in charting the process from the sensorimotor to the operative stage. Piaget recognized that figurative representation is not "in the schemes" and that this is the original contribution Wallon brought to the topic. For Piaget, figurative representation simply interfaces the sensorimotor and operative level, and he considered *sensoritonic* to be a synonym for *sensorimotor*. Wallon distinguished two functions in the postural system: one to stabilize and accompany kinetics (sensorimotor feedback), and the other is to model plastically and maintain postural forms (sensoritonic feedback). This second function is an autonomous one, permitting anticipation, as well as evocation, in social situations. It is different from the kinetic one, which develops in the present physical environment; static activities lead to simulacrum and fictive gestures, such as in mime, the finest figurative ability. Bodily evocation has enormous creative power, because it affords infinite combinations of real or fictive connections and expresses roughly the main distinction between perceiving and making the percept exist. Only one French study, by Galifret-Granjon (1981), studied postural evocation and differed imitation in this light. Children, aged 1 to 12, were asked to mime gestural actions and bodily attitudes, such as reading the newspaper, cutting a big piece of cloth, locking a door, and lighting a candle with a match. The results showed that the evocation of living beings begins between 17 to 20 months, preceding elaborate evocations of situations and incorporation of undetermined objects, which are not possible until the age of 5 years.

CONCLUSION

Since the 1960s, Wallon's framework has had a profound influence on French-language approaches to early communicative development. I argue here that his dual concept of the psychogenetic function of bodily modeling—covering both the expressive and the evocative—is the seminal feature of this developmental model.

A reexamination of the famous controversial debates between Piaget and Wallon concerning socialization and figurative symbolic development, as well as the empirical data derived from Wallon's framework, argue in favor of more future studies on figurative evocation. On this point and several others, it may be stimulating to read Wallon again.

REFERENCES

Asendorpf, J., & Baudonnière, P. M. (1993). Self-awareness and other-awareness: Mirror self-recognition and synchronic imitation among unfamiliar peers. *Developmental Psychology, 29*, 88–95.

Baldwin, J. M. (1895). *Mental development in the child and the race*. NY: Macmillan.

Baudonnière, P. M. (1988). *Evolution des compétences à communiquer chez l'enfant de 2 à 4 ans* [The evolution of communicative skills in children age 2 to 4]. Paris: Presses Universitaires de France.

Baudonnière, P. M., & Michel, J. (1988). L'imitation entre enfants au cours de la 2° année [Imitation between children during the 2nd year of life]. *Psychologie Française, 33*, 29–35.

Bronfenbrenner, U. (1977). Toward an experimental ecology of human development. *American Psychologist, 32*, 513–531.

Comte, A. (1907). *Cours de philosophie positive.* III.40e leçon. [Lessons of positive philosophy]. Paris: Schleicher frères (Original work, 1838).

Condon, W. S., & Sander, L. W. (1974). Synchrony demonstrated between movements of the neonate and adult speech. *Child Development, 45*, 456–462.

Darwin, C. (1872). *The expression of emotions in man and animals*. London: John Murray.

de Ajuriaguerra, J. (1970). *Manuel de psychiatrie de l'enfant* [Manual of child psychiatry]. Paris: Masson.

Dubon, C., Josse, D., & Lézine, I. (1981). Evolution des échanges entre jeunes enfants [Evolution of exchanges between children during the two first years of life]. *Neuropsychiatrie de l'enfance et de l'adolescence, 19,* 273–295.

Field, T. M., Woodson, R., Greenberg, R., & Cohen, D. (1982). Discrimination and imitation of facial expressions by neonates. *Science, 218,* 179–181.

Galifret-Granjon, N. (1981). *Naissance et évolution de la représentation* [Beginning and evolution of representation]. Paris: Presses Universitaires de France.

Gratiot–Alphandèry, H. (1964). L'imitation [Imitation]. *Vers l'Education Nouvelle,* nhors-série, 47–51.

Lézine, I., Robin, M., & Cortial, C. (1975). Observations sur le couple mère-enfant au cours des premières expériences alimentaires [Observations of mother-infant dyad during the first feeding experiences]. *Psychiatrie de l'Enfant, 18,* 75–147.

Maratos, O. (1973, April). *The origin and development of imitation in the first six months of life.* Paper presented at the Annual Meeting of the British Psychological Society. Liverpool, England.

Marcos, H., & Verba, M. (1991). Partager un thème dans la seconde année: Aspects émotionnels et conventionnels [Sharing a theme during the 2nd year of life: Emotional and conventional aspects]. *Enfance, 45,* 25–38.

Mead, M. (1934). *Mind, self and society.* Chicago: University of Chicago Press.

Meltzoff, A. N., & Moore, M. K. (1977). Newborn infants imitate adult facial gestures. *Child Development, 54,* 702–709.

Mertan, B. (1990). *L'effet de la présence de l'adulte sur la communication entre jeunes enfants* [The effect of the presence of an adult on communication between young children]. Unpublished doctoral dissertation, Université Paris V.

Mertan, B., Nadel, J., & Leveau, H. (1993). The effect of adult presence on communicative behaviour among toddlers. In J. Nadel & L. Camaioni (Eds.), *New perspectives in early communicative development.* London: Routledge.

Nadel, J. (1979). La conception wallonienne du milieu [The milieu according to Wallon]. *Enfance, 5,* "Centenaire d'H. Wallon," 363–372.

Nadel, J. (1980a). The functional role of imitation in personality development: Wallon's contribution. *French Language Psychology, 1,* 169–177.

Nadel, N. (1980b). *Wallon aujourd'hui* [Wallon nowadays]. Paris: Scarabée.

Nadel, J. (1984). *La fonction sociale de l'imitation directe: Tome I: Les bases du fonctionalisme de Wallon* [Social function of imitation. Vol 1: Bases of Wallon's functionalism]. Unpublished doctoral dissertation, Université Paris X-Nanterre.

Nadel, J. (1986). *Imitation et communication entre jeunes enfants* [Imitation and communication between young infants]. Paris: Presses Universitaires de France.

Nadel, J., & Baudonnière, P. M. (1980). L'imitation comme mode d'échange prépondérant entre pairs au début de la troisième année [Imitation as a prevailing modality of exchange between 2-year-old peers]. *Enfance, 1–2,* 77–90.

Nadel, J., & Baudonnière, P. M. (1982). The social function of reciprocal imitation in 2-year-old peers. *International Journal of Behavioral Development, 5,* 95–109.

Nadel, J., & Fontaine, A. M. (1989). Communicating by imitation. In B. Schneider, G. Attili, J. Nadel, & R. Weisberg (Eds.), *Social competence in developmental perspective* (pp. 131–144). Dordrecht, Netherlands: Kluwer.

Nadel, J., & Pezé, A. (1993). What makes immediate imitation communicative in toddlers and autistic children? In J. Nadel & L. Camaioni (Eds.), *New perspectives in early communicative development.* London: Routledge.

Piaget, J. (1932). *The moral judgment of the child.* New York: Harcourt.

Piaget, J. (1962). Le rôle de l'imitation dans la formation de la représentation [The role of imitation in the formation of representation]. *L'Evolution Psychiatrique, 27,* 141–150.

Robin, M. (1978). Rôle des conduites maternelles sur la réactivité visuelle du nouveau-né à terme et prématuré [Role of maternal behavior on the visual reactivity of the full-term and premature newborn]. *La Psychiatrie de l'Enfant, 21,* 133–167.

Robin, M. (1980). *Les premiers contacts corporels: Etude des postures maternelles et des contacts tactiles dans les jours qui suivent la naissance* [The first bodily contacts: A study of mothers' postures and tactile contacts in the first days after birth]. Unpublished doctoral dissertation, Universite Paris V.

Rogers, S., & Pennington, B. (1991). A theoretical approach to the deficits in infantile autism. *Development and psychopathology, 3,* 137–162.

Stambak, M. (1963). *Tonus et psycho-motricité dans la première enfance* [Tonus and psycho-motricity in infancy]. Neuchâtel, Paris: Delachaux & Niestlé.

Stern, D. (1977). *Mère et enfant, les premières relations* [Mother and infant: The first relatings]. Brussels: Mardaga.

Stern, D. (1985). *The interpersonal world of the infant.* New York: Basic Books.

Tremblay-Leveau, H. (1992). Evolution de la communication en triade pendant la deuxième année [Evolution of triadic communication during the second year]. *Enfance, 4,* 349–361.

Tremblay-Leveau, H., & Nadel, J. (in press). Young children's communicative skills in triads. *International Journal of Behavioral Development.*

Trevarthen, C. (1977). Descriptive analyses of infant communicative behaviour. In H. R. Schaffer (Ed.), *Studies of infant–mother interaction* (pp. 227–270). London: Academic Press.

Uzgiris, I., & Hunt, J. (1975). *Assessment in infancy.* Urbana: University of Illinois Press.

Vygotsky, L. S. (1978). *Mind in society: The development of higher psychological processes.* Cambridge, MA: Harvard University Press.

Wallon, H. (1938). *La vie mentale* [The mental life]. Paris: Larousse.

Wallon, H. (1968). *L'évolution psychologique de l'infant* [The psychological evolution of the infant]. (2nd ed.). Paris: A. Colin. (Original work published 1941).

Wallon, H. (1970). *De l'acte à la pensée* [From act to thought]. (2nd ed.). Paris: Flammarion. (Original work published 1942).

Wallon, H. (1973a). Les milieux, les groupes et la psychogenèse de l'enfant [Milieus, groups, and psychogenesis of the child]. *Cahiers Internationaux de Sociologie. Enfance,* 227–296. (Original work published 1954).

Wallon, H. (1973b). L'étude psychologique et sociologique de l'enfant [Psychological and sociological study of the child]. *Cahiers Internationaux de Sociologie. Enfance,* 297–308. (Original work published 1947).

Wallon, H. (1973c). *Les origines du caractère chez l'enfant* [The origins of the infant's character]. (3rd ed.). Paris: Presses Universitaires de France. (Original work published 1934).

Widmer-Robert-Tissot, C. (1981). *Les modes de communication du bébé: Postures, mouvements et vocalises* [The infant's modes of communication: Postures, movements and vocalizations]. Neuchâtel-Paris, France: Delachaux & Niestlé.

Zazzo, R. (1957). Le problème de l'imitation chez le nouveau-né [The problem of neonate imitation]. *Enfance, 10,* 135–142.

Zazzo, R. (1975). *Psychologie et marxisme* [Psychology and marxism]. Paris: Denoël/Gonthier.

15 Speech Development: Contributions of Cross-Linguistic Studies

Bénédicte de Boysson-Bardies
Pierre A. Hallé
C.N.R.S.—Paris V

Psycholinguists interested in speech development need to address the question of when infants begin to extract regularities from the language to be learned. Two possible landmarks have been successively proposed. The first one, which has always been strongly emphasized, is the appearance of phonological rules in infants' vocal productions. The second one—proposed more recently—is the appearance of language-specific influences in the phonetic and intonational patterns of productions. Since the early 1980s, our program of research was devoted to the latter aspect; it was largely based on the rationale of crosslinguistic comparisons of prespeech (and early speech) productions between French infants and infants from other linguistic environments.

Since the 1940s, theories of speech development have made the common assumptions of biological determinism in speech in the human species and of universal and systematic patterns of development. From this common commitment, different options have arisen. Emphasis was placed on the universal characteristics of the patterns of development, either in terms of the mastery of distinctive features or in terms of the evolution of constraints on articulatory capacities. Under either of these options, babbling was to bear no relation to the infants' acquisition of the ambient language. A third option emphasizes the selective role of interaction with the language and predicts an early shaping of infants' vocal productions by ambient languages.

In the structuralist model (Jakobson, 1941), linguistics—more precisely phonology—was supposed to provide the child speech researcher with carefully defined concepts and units of analysis for investigating speech development. The guideline for universal speech development was to be found in the notion of *distinctive features*. The child was said to use universal principles for distinguishing classes of sounds by distinctive features to guide his or her speech development. Throughout the course of phonological development, infants divide and redivide classes of features as new contrasts enter the system in an orderly fashion. In this view, babbling productions, which involve no constrastive use of distinctive features, would not be related to the acquisition of a phonological system.

The empirical data presented to substantiate these claims were not truly convincing. The claim that babbling bears no relation to the child's later productions was not supported by data analysis (Oller, Wieman, Doyle, & Ross, 1976; Vihman, Macken, R. Miller, Simmons & J. Miller, 1985), and neither was the alleged universality of patterns of phonological development (Ingram, 1979; Macken & Ferguson, 1983; Stoel-Gammon & Cooper, 1984; Vihman, Ferguson, & Elbert, 1986).

The second approach emphasized the physical constraints on prespeech capacities and their relevance for first word patterns (Kent & Murray, 1982; Locke, 1983). All of the biological movements possess a number of characteristic structural regularities (Viviani, 1990). Thus, the first gestures of babbling involve alternation between an open and a closed vocal tract, produced primarily by mandibular oscillations. The production of a syllable results from the passive movement of the tongue, riding on an active mandible, in one closing–opening oscillation (Holmgren, Lindblom, Aurelius, Jalling, & Zetterstrom, 1986; Mac-Neilage & Davis, 1990). These oscillations give the "frame" for the combination of consonant–vowel (CV) co-occurrences. Thus, the motor configuration of the canonical syllables of babbling is reduced mainly to closing–opening cycles of the mandible, in other words, requiring little speech-specific motor control. Pure physiology then provides the regularities that support the notion of commonalities of babbling sounds across languages (Kent, 1992; Locke, 1983). The causal explanation of prespeech patterns—and even of early speech patterns—rests mainly on a physical level, anatomical changes being an important contributory factor to the development, if not a sufficient one (Kent & Hodge, 1990, Locke, 1983). This approach drastically reduces the infants' possibility of escaping from constrained patterns and predicts "universality" of babbling patterns. The interinfant variability already mentioned by Ferguson and Farwell (1975) and by Vihman et al. (1986) is explained by individual preferences for some of the consonantal sounds or CV patterns delimited by the constrained set of CV co-occurrences (Studdert-Kennedy, 1986).

On one hand, the commonalities of babbling across languages might also be due to the fact that most languages share a core set of basic segments (Lindblom & Maddieson, 1988): Infants would acquire the basic sounds—or basic articulations—of this core set earlier in their development or more systematically than they would the more elaborated or complex segments. On the other hand, our first studies showed that babbling productions exhibit variations that should be interpreted as a selective modeling by ambient language (de Boysson-Bardies, Sagart, & Bacri, 1981; de Boysson-Bardies, Sagart, & Durand, 1984).

A CROSS-LANGUAGE APPROACH TO SPEECH
DEVELOPMENT: THE INTERACTION HYPOTHESIS

The evolution of the phonetic shaping of prelinguistic productions by ambient languages would provide information about infants' capacities for building internal representations. Evidences for this shaping have been found. We, therefore, support a third approach: the *Interaction hypothesis* (de Boysson-Bardies, Hallé, Sagart, & Durand, 1989). This approach focuses on the role of early interaction between experience and biological equipment in the evolution of phonetic organization for production. It tends to lighten the role of peripheral physical constraints on prespeech capacities, and to emphasize "biological" capacities for selection from input. The infant's brain constantly produces internal variations, or hypotheses, to test the outside world (Changeux, 1983; Gottlieb, 1976). Such mechanisms underlie processes of developmental and experiential selection of inputs. The evolution of internal states can be seen as a by-product of this selective quest.

We claim that motor performance can be molded by selection from the structured linguistic inputs furnished by the ambient language. The evolution of variegated babbling and prespeech productions should be interpreted at a higher level than the physical. This claim entails the assertion that systematic comparisons of the course of evolution of prespeech and first-speech productions of infants from different linguistic backgrounds should be used to yield insights on this point.

Experiments on perception have recently provided evidence of early developmental reorganization of initial perceptual sensitivities (Best, MacRoberts, & Sithole, 1988; Jusczyk, 1989, in press; Werker & Lalonde, 1988). This reorganization appears at around 6 months of age for vowels (Kuhl, 1990, 1991) and at 10–12 months for consonants (Werker & Pegg, 1992; Werker & Tees, 1984).

From the end of the 1970s, we were attracted by the idea of early processes of selection for both theoretical and empirical reasons. First, we were interested in the strong emphasis that some French biologists—among others—placed on biological diversity, the necessary flexibility, processes of active synaptic selection, and the role of interaction with the external world (Changeux, 1983; Changeux & Dehaene, 1989; Jacob, 1970, 1982). Second, in our first work on prespeech productions in French infants, we found some discrepancies between our data and "general" data, and also with the conclusions drawn from English infants' productions. The conclusions that were drawn from the cross-linguistic literature were not convincing. Indeed, the ways of collecting the data were not homogeneous, the phonetic transcriptions lacked cross-linguistic control, and neither the ages nor the number of subjects allowed relevant comparisons (Locke, 1983). For these reasons, we started conducting systematic cross-linguistic studies of babbling productions.

The term *babbling* denotes a specific form of vocal production that appears between the ages of 6 and 8 months for the majority of normally developing

infants (Kent & Murray, 1982; Oller, 1980; Stark, 1980). Infants begin to babble
when they utter sounds that exhibit acoustic timing constraints whose characteristics are close to those of syllables in mature speech. The *syllable* is a unit that
integrates movements into a pattern that adult listeners can segment into vowel
and consonant components. Its production has a special developmental significance (Oller, 1980). The characteristics of the babbling of 9–10-month-old infants include non-reduplicated and CV or CVC (consonant–vowel–consonant)
sequences. Babbling productions are found even long after the first words have
appeared.

The three first studies we conducted on the characteristics of babbling productions could provide only indirect evidence for the interaction hypothesis. First, a
phonetic investigation of the late babbling of a French infant (between 18 and 20
months) showed that this infant—although producing no more than 15 words—
had already selected his consonantal repertoire from the sounds of French. The
frequency distribution of his consonants were closer to the French distribution
than to the English or Thai distributions, which were taken as points of comparison. In addition, the infant had modeled his production on some of the regularities of French intonational patterns (de Boysson-Bardies et al., 1981). However, this study had the limited impact of a case study and mainly revealed that
the productions of an infant of 18 months, even when not identified as words by
adults, could be found to reflect the phonetic and intonational characteristics of
the ambient language.

It was then necessary to test whether the first evidence of specific language
tendencies could be found much earlier in the babbling period. In a second study,
we used listening tests. French-speaking adults served as judges, comparing
samples of babbling from French, Arabic, and Cantonese infants, and indicated
which samples derived from the French infants. The languages were chosen to
maximize the number of differing dimensions: phonation type, laryngeal and
supralaryngeal settings, mode of onset and release of syllables, prosody, tone
system, phonetic repertoire, and syllabic structure. Correct identification of
French babbling was found to be well above chance level. The results supported
the proposition that vocalizations of 8- and 10-month-old infants provide cues to
guide the judges' choices. The judges, however, could not specify what cues had
induced their choices. We supposed the cues to be prosodic, rather than segmental (de Boysson-Bardies et al., 1984).

The third study specifically investigated the acoustic consequences of supralaryngeal settings. Different settings of the vocal tract are required in different
languages. Acquiring such settings could be a prerequisite to learning the settings
that underlie the segmental inventory of a language. Long Term Spectra (LTS)
give an indication of the main tendencies of supralaryngeal settings in terms of
spectral characteristics. Accordingly, cross-language comparisons of LTS computed from the productions of 10-month-old infants were run. Three language
environments were used: France, Algeria, and Hong Kong. In each language

environment, 6 infants and 20 monolingual adults contributed to the data. LTS were computed for each "speaker." In each of the language groups, despite the fact that the infants produced only babbling, their LTS patterns were strikingly similar to those of the adults in their group (de Boysson-Bardies, Sagart, Hallé, & Durand, 1986).

These studies supported the proposition that interaction with the environment may shape the vocal productions of 10-month-old infants, but they gave only global indications. It was still not possible to specify which cues were involved in the first experiment and what the bases of the similarities of LTS patterns were in the second. In the latter case it was hypothesized that vocalic settings might largely account for the specificity of LTS patterns. We were particularly interested in checking whether ambient language could have influenced the characteristics of vowel-like productions and other segments in the babbling.

At this point, we decided to conduct systematic cross-language comparative investigations of babbling and early speech. This implied the close examination of vowels, consonants, and syllabic patterns, as well as an examination of the intonational and durational patterns that are necessary constituents of language processing and production.

To support the interaction hypothesis, it was necessary (a) to investigate whether systematic differences could be found in the distribution of vowels, consonants, and syllabic patterns in the utterances of infants from different linguistic communities, and their intonational and durational patterns; and (b) to determine whether the intercommunity differences reflected the structured linguistic input from adult speech in each community.

VOCALIC AND CONSONANT PRODUCTION

Vocalic Production: Evidence for Early Influence of Ambient Language

The first systematic study was designed to investigate the vocalic productions of 10-month-old infants from France, England, Algeria, and Hong-Kong. We took care to record infants in the country of origin and insure the infants were raised in monolingual households. It has been shown that infants' vocalic space seems to develop in a continuous and consistent way over the 1st year of life (Buhr, 1980; Lieberman, 1980). The study of vowels in babbling should be particularly relevant to the hypothesis concerning the early effects of the linguistic environment.

We chose to analyze the vowels produced by 10-month-old infants belonging to four language communities with clear differences in their vocalic repertoire: English has more front vowels, French has more rounded vowels, Cantonese has more back vowels, and Arabic has only three vowels, whose phonetic realizations are largely central.

Five infants in each country participated in the experiment. The vowels were extracted from 20-minute recordings. About 50 vowels per infant were selected, reflecting the distribution of the vowels from the different classes in the infant's production, and picked up in the order they appeared in his or her babbling. An acoustic investigation was conducted to examine the first two formants (F_1 and F_2). Significant differences were found between language groups. Intergroup differences were found to be larger than intragroup differences. In order to estimate the relevance of the differences between groups, we compared the infant data with adult data drawn from the existing literature on each language. Comparison of the main tendencies of infants' vowels with the adult vocalic space was undertaken by comparing mean formant frequencies and F_2/F_1 ratios by language communities for infant and adult data. The same trends were found for adult speech and for babbling: that is, English and French have more diffuse vowels than Cantonese and Arabic (here Algerian Arabic). This is shown by the pattern of variation of mean F_2/F_1 ratios across languages, shown in Table 15.1. Parallel patterns were found for adult speech and for babbling.

This research showed that a functional organization of articulatory principles, in this case the organization of the vocalic system, has already begun in babbling. The speech sounds of the surrounding language provide material for building an internal representation that infants may use to try out articulatory patterns and configurations of the vocal tract (de Boysson-Bardies et al., 1989). Support for this proposition can be found in Kuhl (1990, 1991), who showed that the typicality of a vowel affects perception and that the prototype of a category in the ambient language serves as a referent for infants as young as 6 months of age.

In a recent study, Hallé (1991) compared phonetic transcriptions of vowels in the disyllabic productions of 16-month-old French and Japanese infants. Their vocalic repertoires were found to be clearly different: Japanese infants produce more high vowels (/u/ or /i/) and fewer mid-front or central vowels (/e/ and schwas) than French infants in their babbling, as well as in their first words. These trends are also found in adult speech, where the frequency of /i/ and /u/ is higher in Japanese than in French, whereas mid-front vowels are less frequent in Japanese than in French.

TABLE 15.1
F2/F1 Ratios of Infant and Adult Vowels
by Language Community

	Language Community			
Population	English	French	Algerian	Cantonese
Infants	3.00	2.80	2.40	2.24
Adults	3.68	3.28	3.03	2.71

Consonant Production: Evidence for Infants' Selection From Ambient Language

It is often assumed that vowels are easier to produce than consonants, and it could be argued that, given the acoustic and articulatory characteristics of vowels, a matching process between vocalic production and the inputs of the environment can arise much earlier than for consonants, but an overwhelming majority of speech acquisition studies have focused on consonants. Cross-cultural comparisons have been drawn from diary studies, but in no case was consistency in collection and analysis assured. The similarity of consonantal repertoires across linguistic communities during the babbling stage has usually been emphasized. Even first words have been supposed not to require language-specific capacities (Locke, 1983).

The Stanford group, including C. Ferguson and M. Vihman (Ferguson & Farwell, 1975; Vihman, Ferguson, & Elbert, 1986), had first shown that considerable variability could be found in the sound patterns of infants from the same linguistic community. They also had first shown continuity between the sound patterns of prespeech and first words for each infant. Thus, we decided to jointly investigate, with a group of Swedish researchers, the consonantal production of English, French, Japanese, and Swedish infants during the period of transition from babbling to first words.

A cross-linguistic study was designed to follow, longitudinally, 20 infants (5 French, 5 English, 5 Japanese, and 5 Swedish). Infants were audio- and video-recorded twice a month from the age of 9 months until they each produced at least 25 identifiable word types in a recording session. (Having 25 words in a session corresponds to a cumulative lexicon of about 50 words.) The number of spontaneous word types identified in a session was used to select sessions to be analyzed. Phonetic transcription was conducted for one 0-word session, two 4-word sessions, two 15-word sessions, and one 25-word session. Transcriptions were prepared by a native transcriber using the International Phonetic Alphabet, and reliability across groups was checked and found to be adequate. Counts of consonants and of utterance types according to length in syllables were made for each subject at the six critical sessions. Intergroup comparisons were planned to test the hypothesis that linguistic background influences the distribution of consonants according to place and manner of articulation in infant productions, reflecting the main trends found in the target words from the relevant language. For place of articulation, consonants were classified into three categories: labials, dentals, and velars. For manner, four categories were taken into account: stops, fricatives, nasals, and liquids. The results demonstrate that infant consonant production presents commonalities, such as a high percentage of stops, labials, and dentals. However, the consonantal repertoire in either babbling or infant words fit so closely to the distribution of consonants in target words in each group that it was possible to argue that the infants had selected their

TABLE 15.2
Overall Distribution of Phonemes, by Place and Manner:
Percentage (*SD*)

Phonemes	French	English	Japanese	Swedish
		Place		
Labials	53.8	45.9	29.6	20.3
	(14.4)	(13.5)	(8.6)	(1.81)
Dentals	36.7	33.9	46.3	54.0
	(15.0)	(16.3)	(3.5)	(8.55)
Velars	9.5	20.2	24.0	25.8
	(8.1)	(10.3)	(9.9)	(8.99)
	French	English	Japanese	Swedish
		Manner		
Stops	56.9	68.3	61.2	72.7
	(9.9)	(9.1)	(2.4)	(10.5)
Fricatives	11.7	9.9	11.0	7.7
	(5.0)	(4.1)	(2.9)	(3.3)
Nasals	22.3	15.4	22.0	12.0
	(5.9)	(11.3)	(5.6)	(4.6)
Liquids	9.2	6.4	5.8	7.5
	(9.1)	(6.0)	(4.6)	(6.1)

repertoire from the words belonging to the relevant pragmatic environment. There was an overall significant difference in the distribution of consonants according to place and manner categories in babbling and infant words (Table 15.2). Distribution for place and manner of articulation was very similar in babbling and in infant words. However, there were fewer differences in consonantal distribution between language groups for infant words than for babbling. The repertoire of infant words was more "basic," including, for example, more labials and stops than did the babbling repertoire. This reveals the existence of motoric consequences arising from a constrained motor program to produce a word. A limited-resource assumption may account for a return to more basic adjustments when the infant tries to approximate a complex target (Kent, 1992).

    The cross-linguistic investigation of final consonants confirms infants' universal tendency to produce open syllables in final position, but also shows that the structural characteristics of the ambient language influences both the frequency and the type of final consonants in babbling and first words. Infants produce few final consonants, but these consonants are selected from the classes of word-final consonants found in their ambient language. This tendency is clearer in first words (25-word sessions) than in babbling (de Boysson-Bardies & Durand, 1991).

SYLLABIC STRUCTURE AND PROSODIC ORGANIZATION

Syllabic Structure: Evidence for Early Organization

The next step was the cross-linguistic investigation of syllabic structure. The motoric approach to babbling implies strong constraints on the structure of CV association. Co-occurrence constraints predict the association of labials with central vowels, of dentals with front vowel, and of velars with back vowels (Kent & Murray, 1982). In a case study of an English infant, Davis and MacNeilage (1990) found that the predicted "pure frame" patterns account for the syllabic structure of the infant's reduplicated babbling, whereas frame modulations account for the patterns of variegated babbling. It is important, however, to check the validity of co-occurrence constraints through cross-linguistic comparisons.

In a preliminary study comparing French and Japanese infants aged 16–18 months, Hallé (1991) showed that in each language group, preferred CV associations were similar in babbling and in words, and largely reflected those found in adult speech rather than universal associations predicted by "mechanical" constraints.

We are currently investigating the evolution of CV associations at the period of transition from babbling to early words. Analyses have been run on CV patterns in the disyllabic productions (babbling and first words) of five French infants from 10 months to 16–17 months. Babbling and word syllabic patterns were analyzed separately, as were first syllable patterns versus second syllable patterns. The purpose was to determine (a) whether co-occurrence constraints can account for the syllabic patterns of babbling as well as those of first words in French infants, (b) whether there is a more pronounced degree of mechanical co-occurrence constraint in babbling than in words, and (c) whether the syllabic structure of the target words can influence the syllabic patterns of infant productions.

For 12-month-old infants, who mainly babble, a sizable degree of affinity is found only for labials with low-central vowels (mainly [a]). The velar–back association is not favored. This supports the results of Vihman (1992), who found only a slight tendency toward a labial–central association in the analysis of the productions of infants from four different linguistic groups aged 12–13 months. In our data, we found a tendency for dentals to associate with back vowels. It may already reflect the frequency of the French words used in baby talk that terminate in a mid-back vowel often associated with a dental (as in *gâteau, allo, dodo,* etc.). Similarly, Vihman found velars to associate with back vowels only in the productions of Japanese infants, a tendency corresponding to the frequent association of back vowels with dorsal consonants in Japanese words used with children. Both studies show that the babbling productions of 12-month-old infants are not restricted to patterns presumably easier to articulate.

Some influence of the target language can be seen in the syllabic patterns of babbling.

In some instances, predicted patterns of coarticulation are found slightly more often in the vocalizations of infants aged 15–16 months. This is mainly due to the contribution of the first syllable of disyllables in either babbling or words.

To summarize, these analyses suggest the possibility of two developmental stages. One is centered around 11–13 months, when infants are still mainly producing variegated babbling; the other around 15–16 months, when the child produces about 15 words in a session.

The productions of the first stage are far from entirely limited by mechanical constraints (as they may be in canonical babbling). Furthermore, because the child is, presumably, not yet attempting target words, he or she is free from the constraint of lexical representations or motor plans necessary for producing a given word. Thus, the first stage can be seen as an experimental stage of relative freedom in which certain regularities do reflect selection of the preferred associations that characterize target words in the ambient language. Such an experimental mode of production could characterize the babbling stage at the end of the 1st year.

With the first words, the picture changes, and we find evidence for the effect of motor-planning constraints. Likewise, the distribution of consonants was found to be more "basic" in first words than in babbling (de Boysson-Bardies & Vihman, 1991). Although reduplication and assimilation patterns are frequent in the first words, separate analysis of the first and the second syllable in infants' words reveals some differences in CV combination. The first syllables of words tend to display more basic patterns than the second syllables. The second syllables are more varied, and they tend to display CV associations that are more specific to the ambient language. This may be related to the fact that in French, the utterance-final syllable is accented. A specific property of serial organization emerges in the first words with a tendency to produce first syllables that are more neutral or that assimilate to the second. The attempts to produce individual words from a program may require that infants reduce the articulatory demand of the first syllable to meet the demands of the second. This can be accomplished by "choosing" target words with a labial–central pattern as the first syllable.

Prosodic Organization

In the second half of the 1st year, infants can control the production of various intonational patterns. Shortly thereafter, they are observed to make use of pitch variations for different communicative intents (Menn, 1976). Diary studies of children acquiring a tone language suggest that the beginning of tone production roughly coincides with the period of the first words (Clumeck, 1977; Tuaycharoen, 1977). As for timing, lengthening of syllable-final vowels seems to appear in the first half of the 2nd year (Konopczynski, 1986; Oller & Smith, 1977).

A cross-linguistic comparison of French and Japanese infants was undertaken to determine the influence of the ambient language on the intonation and timing of infants' vocal productions (Hallé, de Boysson-Bardies, & Vihman, 1991). For French adults, final lengthening on the last syllable of a prosodic group or of a single word is well established, but there is no final lengthening in standard Japanese. In French, the most typical intonation is the continuation intonation rising contour. In Japanese, the continuation intonation (also frequent in Japanese) is normally falling or flat.

The disyllabic items produced by four French and four Japanese children, aged 16–18 months, were analyzed. All four French infants' vocalizations showed a substantial increment of duration on the last syllable, whereas only one Japanese child produced final lengthening. All of the Japanese infants produced a majority of falling contours, whereas all of the French infants produced a majority of rising contours (Fig. 15.1).

The differences found were not due to differences in segmental organization of production in the two language groups. Thus, French and Japanese infants at 16–18 months clearly differ with respect to fundamental frequency contours and rime durations and closely reflect the specific trends of Japanese and French adult speech.

(a) French

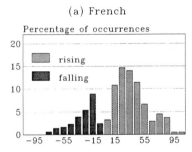

(b) Japanese

FIG. 15.1. Histograms showing the distribution of the FO excursion parameter in (a) French and (b) Japanese infants' disyllabic vocalizations. The figures given for interval centers are FO excursion values expressed in percentages.

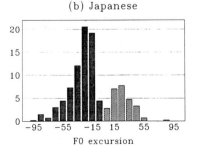

PROPOSALS FOR STEPS IN THE DEVELOPMENT
FROM BABBLING TO THE FIRST 50 WORDS

We do not know how the first linguistic representations are coded, nor do we know how they are related to the motor plan or to the temporal patterns of movements (Kent, 1992). Diverging proposals for motor–perceptual interactions may originate from the common requirement that capacities for language be biologically implemented. The adjustment of these early capacities to adaptive speech processing implies the integration and computation of perceptual data and their matching in motor planning. The evolution of speech capacities can be accounted for by successive levels of organization, each of them implying new properties and new combinational capacities in relation to the emerging function. The lower levels generate a diversity of transitory forms. The higher levels either eliminate or stabilize these forms according to the linguistic domain in which the infants practice. Analyses of cross-linguistic productions may help us to understand the transition from the first structured productions (the first syllabic productions) to the phonetically language-specific productions that precede the phonologically mastered productions.

We propose three developmental steps from canonical babbling to the prephonemic stage. First, *canonical babbling productions* (6–8 months) have not yet been shown to be language specific. An explanation in terms of output of ballistic movements or in terms of nascent motor control may be relevant (Kent, 1992; MacNeilage & Davis, 1990). *Prespeech productions* at the end of the first year (9–12 months) imply a higher level of causal explanation. Infant productions at this age evidence an "organization," due to a functional interaction between the perception and the motor performance. The phonetic repertoire and the syllabic structure of infant utterances reveal specific regularities in the selection of articulatory gestures. This selection is not only dependent on the infant's preferences, but also clearly reveals adjustments to characteristics of the linguistic input. At this level, infant productions could be organized or issued by articulatory representations of a language-specific and freely organized repertoire of consonants and vowels or of syllabic patterns.

First speech productions imply the functional interaction between a perceptual representation of serially ordered sounds—a word pattern—involving a specific articulatory representation and a related motor plan. The obligatory sequencing of syllables required by multisyllabic word production is seen to interact with performance. Infants turn to simplified patterns, and some of the simplification processes will become regular and characteristic of the next level: the phonological level.

The end of the first year (9–12 months) is an important landmark in speech acquisition: Both the "general" perceptual capacities and the "general" patterns of articulation become language-specific. At this age, both perception and production begin to be governed by the fact that the infant has discovered sound–

meaning relations (MacKain, 1982). In a recent experiment, we have shown that 11-month-old French children exhibit a preference for familiar words, as opposed to rare words, of their language even in the absence of pragmatic or prosodic contextual cues (Hallé & de Boysson-Bardies, in press). At the same age, productive performances reveal indirect or direct effects of the emergence of sound–meaning relations and of word "recognition." Development of vocal tract control cannot explain the evolution of the phonetic repertoire and of the syllabic patterns of prespeech. It is necessary to refer to a representational level to account for the selective organization of babbling in infants from different linguistic backgrounds.

The evolution of phonetic organization at the end of the 1st year led us back again to the question of building internal representations. We are now interested in understanding the organization of the first lexical level of representation that underlies the recognition of words and its relation to the articulatory planning of the first words.

CONCLUSION

The common assumption that early speech development mainly exhibits universal tendencies is seriously challenged by a growing body of cross-language studies. Although some theories based on the data yielded by single-language studies have concluded that speech development patterns are universal (due to universal constraints of maturation, and to universal principles, such as ease of articulation and sufficient contrast), comparisons conducted in our laboratory between French infants and infants from different language backgrounds have disclosed language specificity in various aspects of infants' vocalizations: prosody, vocalic space, and phonetic counts bearing on phone-types and co-occurrences of phone-types.

To summarize, the aim of our work has been to trace the role of specific experience: We have found evidence for interaction between experience and biological equipment at the end of the 1st year. Our findings support the notion that infants actively select sounds, arrangements of sounds, and (probably) words, from the language they are exposed to. One "big issue" is addressed there: the old nature–nurture question. We suggest that the cross-language approach may be helpful in shedding some new light on this matter.

REFERENCES

Best, C. T., McRoberts, G. W., & Sithole, M. (1988). Examination of perceptual reorganization for nonnative speech contrast: Zulu click discrimination by English-speaking adults and infants. *Journal of Experimental Child Psychology: Human Perception and Performance, 14,* 345–360.
de Boysson-Bardies, B., & Durand, C. (1991). Tendances générales et influence de la langue

maternelle: Les consonnes terminales dans le babillage et les premiers mots [General tendencies and effect of linguistic environment: Final consonants in babbling and first words]. *L'Année Psychologique, 91*, 139–157.

de Boysson-Bardies, B., Hallé, P., Sagart, L., & Durand, C. (1989). A cross-linguistic investigation of vowel formants in babbling. *Journal of Child Language, 16*, 1–17.

de Boysson-Bardies, B., Sagart, L., & Bacri, N. (1981). Phonetic analysis of late babbling: A case study of a French child. *Journal of Child Language, 8*, 511–524.

de Boysson-Bardies, B., Sagart, L., & Durand, C. (1984). Discernible differences in the babbling of infants according to target language. *Journal of Child Language, 11*, 1–15.

de Boysson-Bardies, B., Sagart, L., Hallé, P., & Durand, C. (1986). Acoustic investigation of cross-linguistic variability in babbling. In B. Lindblom & R. Zetterstrom (Eds.), *Precursors of early speech* (pp. 113–166). New York: Stockton Press.

de Boysson-Bardies, B., & Vihman, M. M. (1991). Adaptation to language: Evidence from babbling and early words in four languages. *Language, 67*, 297–319.

Buhr, R. D. (1980). The emergence of vowels in an infant. *Journal of Speech and Hearing Research, 23*, 62–94.

Changeux, J. P. (1983). *L'Homme neuronal* [Neuronal man: The biology of mind]. Paris: Fayard.

Changeux, J. P., & Dehaene, S. (1989). Neuronal models of cognitive functions. *Cognition, 33*, 63–109.

Clumeck, H. (1977). *Studies in the acquisition of mandarin phonology.* Unpublished doctoral dissertation, University of California, Berkeley.

Davis, B., & MacNeilage, P. F. (1990). Acquisition of correct vowel production: A quantitative case study. *Journal of Speech and Hearing Research, 33*, 16–27.

Ferguson, C. A., & Farwell, C. B. (1975). Words and sounds in early language acquisition. *Language, 51*, 419–439.

Gottlieb, G. (1976). The roles of experience in the development of behavior and the nervous system. In G. Gottlieb (Ed.), *Development of neuronal and behavioral specificity* (pp. 1–35). New York: Academic Press.

Hallé, P. (1991). Japanese and French infants' vocalizations at the onset of first words: A comparison of phonetic and prosodic cues in disyllabic productions. *Annual Bulletin of the Research Institute of Logopedics and Phoniatrics* (University of Tokyo), *25*, 195–220.

Hallé, P., & de Boysson-Bardies, B. (in press). Emergence of an early receptive lexicon: Infants' recognition of words. *Infant Behavior and Development.*

Hallé, P., de Boysson-Bardies, B., & Vihman, M. M. (1991). Beginnings of prosodic organization: Intonation and duration patterns of disyllables produced by Japanese and French infants. *Language & Speech, 34*, 299–318.

Holmgren, K., Lindblom, B., Aurelius, G., Jalling, B., & Zetterstrom, R. (1986). On the phonetics of infant vocalizations. In B. Lindblom & R. Zetterstrom (Eds.), *Precursors of early speech* (pp. 51–63). Basingstoke, England: Macmillan.

Ingram, D. (1979). Cross-linguistic evidence on the extent and limit of individual variation in phonological development. *Proceedings of the 9th International Congress of Phonetic Sciences* (pp. 253–268). Copenhagen, Denmark: University of Copenhagen.

Jacob, F. (1970). *La logique du vivant* [The logic of life]. Paris: Gallimard.

Jacob, F. (1982). *Le jeu des possibles* [The possible and the actual]. Paris: Fayard.

Jakobson, R. (1968). *Child language, aphasia and phonological universals* (A. Keiler, Trans.). The Hague: Mouton. (Original work published 1941)

Jusczyk, P. (1989, April). *Perception of cues to clausal units in native and non-native languages.* Paper presented at the meeting of the Society for Research in Child Development, Kansas City, MO.

Jusczyk, P. (in press). Infant speech perception and the development of the mental lexicon. In H. C. Nusbaum & J. C. Goodman (Eds.), *The transition from speech sounds to spoken words: The development of speech perception.* Cambridge, MA: MIT Press.

Kent, R. D. (1992). The biology of phonological development. In C. A. Ferguson, L. Menn, & C. Stoel-Gammon (Eds.), *Phonological development: Models, research and implications* (pp. 65–87). Timonium, MA: York Press.

Kent, R. D., & Hodge, K. (1990). The biogenesis of speech. Continuity and process in early speech and language development. In J. F. Miller (Ed.), *Progress in research on child language disorders*. Austin, TX: Pro-Ed.

Kent, R. D., & Murray, A. D. (1982). Acoustic features of infant vocalic utterances at 3, 6 and 9 months. *Journal of the Acoustic Society of America, 72*, 353–365.

Konopczynski, G. (1986). Etude expérimentale de quelques structures prosodiques employées par les enfants français entre 7 et 22 mois [Experimental study of some prosodic structures produced by French infants from 7 to 22 months of age]. *Travaux de l'Institut de Phonétique de Strasbourg, 7*, 171–206.

Kuhl, P. K. (1990). Towards a new theory of the development of speech perception. In H. Fujisaki (Ed.), *Proceedings of the International Conference on Spoken Language Processing* (pp. 745–748). Tokyo: The Acoustical Society of Japan.

Kuhl, P. K. (1991). Human adults and human infants show a "perceptual magnet effect" for the prototypes of speech categories, monkeys do not. *Perception and Psychophysics, 50*, 93–107.

Lieberman, P. (1980). On the development of vowel production in young children. In G. H. Yeni-Komshian, J. F. Kavanagh, & C. A. Ferguson (Eds.), *Child phonology: Production. Vol. 1.* (pp. 113–142). New York: Academic Press.

Lindblom, B., & Maddieson, F. (1988). Phonetic universals in consonant systems. In L. M. Hyman & C. N. Li (Eds.), *Language and mind* (pp. 62–78). New York: Routledge.

Locke, J. L. (1983). *Phonological acquisition and change.* New York: Academic Press.

MacKain, K. (1982). Assessing the role of experience in infants' speech discrimination. *Journal of Child Language, 9*, 527–542.

Macken, M. A., & Ferguson, C. A. (1983). Cognitive aspects of phonological development: Model, evidence, and issues. In K. E. Nelson (Ed.), *Children's language* (Vol. 4, pp. 256–282). Hillsdale, NJ: Lawrence Erlbaum Associates.

MacNeilage, P. F., & Davis, B. L. (1990). Acquisition of speech production: Frames, then content. In M. Jeannerod (Ed.), *Attention and performance: Vol. 8. Motor representation and control* (pp. 453–476). Hillsdale, NJ: Lawrence Erlbaum Associates.

Menn, L. (1976). *Pattern, control and contrast in beginning speech: A case study in the development of word form and function.* Unpublished doctoral dissertation, University of Illinois at Urbana-Champaign.

Oller, D. K. (1980). The emergence of the sounds of speech in infancy. In G. H. Yeni-Komshian, J. F. Kavanagh & C. A. Ferguson (Eds.), *Child phonology: Production. Vol. 1.* (pp. 93–112). New York: Academic Press.

Oller, D. K., & Smith, B. L. (1977). The effect of final-syllable position on vowel duration in infant babbling. *Journal of the Acoustical Society of America, 62*, 994–997.

Oller, D. K., Wieman, L. A., Doyle, W. J., & Ross, C. (1976). Infant babbling and speech. *Journal of Child Language, 3*, 1–11.

Stark, R. E. (1980). Stages of speech development in the first year of life. In G. H. Yeni-Komshian, J. F. Kavanagh, & C. A. Ferguson (Eds.), *Child phonology: Production. Vol. 1.* (pp. 73–92). New York: Academic Press.

Stoel-Gammon, C., & Cooper, J. A. (1984). Patterns of early lexical and phonological Development. *Journal of Child Language, 11*, 247–271.

Studdert-Kennedy, M. (1986). Sources of variability in early speech development. In J. S. Perkell & D. H. Klatt (Eds.), *Invariance and variability in speech processes* (pp. 58–76). Hillsdale, NJ: Lawrence Erlbaum Associates.

Tuaycharoen, P. (1977). *The phonetic and phonological development of a Thai baby: Early communicative interaction to speech.* Unpublished doctoral dissertation, University of London.

Vihman, M. M. (1992). Early syllables and the construction of phonology. In C. A. Ferguson, L. Menn, & C. Stoel-Gammon (Eds.), *Phonological development: Models, research, and implications* (pp. 393–422). Timonium, MA: York Press.

Vihman, M. M., Ferguson, C. A., & Elbert, M. (1986). Phonological development from babbling to speech: Common tendencies and individual differences. *Applied Psycholinguistics, 7,* 3–40.

Vihman, M. M., Macken, M. A., Miller, R., Simmons, H., & Miller, J. (1985). From babbling to speech: A reassessment of the continuity issue. *Language, 61,* 395–443.

Viviani, P. (1990). Motor perceptual interactions. The evolution of an idea. In M. Piatelli-Palmerini (Ed.), *Cognitive science in Europe: Issues and trends* (pp. 11–39). Boulder, CO: The Golem Press (Monograph Series No. 1).

Werker, J. F., & Pegg, J. E. (1992). Infant speech perception and phonological acquisition. In C. A. Ferguson, L. Menn, & C. Stoel-Gammon (Eds.), *Phonological development: Models, research, and implications.* Timonium, MA: York Press.

Werker, J. F., & Lalonde, C. E. (1988). Cross-language speech perception: Initial capabilities and developmental change. *Developmental Psychology, 24,* 1–12.

Werker, J. F., & Tees, R. C. (1984). Cross-language speech perception: Evidence for perceptual reorganization during the first year of life. *Infant Behavior and Development, 27,* 49–63.

16 Infant Categorization and Early Object-Word Meaning

Diane Poulin-Dubois
Susan A. Graham
Concordia University

Although most researchers would agree that language acquisition is the product of mental processes, few would attempt to explain language learning by relying exclusively on nonverbal cognition. As Johnston (1985) pointed out, "The challenge instead is to identify the specific points, if any, at which developments in nonverbal cognition help determine the course of language acquisition" (p. 962). Despite the fact that there is no existing Piagetian model of language acquisition, Piaget's view of language development has been highly influential. According to Piaget, language plays a major part in the child's representation of the world and is a manifestation of the *semiotic function,* the ability to process information on a representational level, as opposed to an action level (Piaget, 1962). Among the other cognitive abilities emerging with the advent of the semiotic function are deferred imitation, mental imagery, symbolic function, and drawing. Piaget argued that the capacity to learn words and the capacity to learn rules to put those words together into sentences build on the cognitive achievements of the sensorimotor period. In other words, cognition is a prerequisite for language. Elaboration of the constructivist view of language learning that was held by Piaget can be found in Piatelli-Palmarini, 1980.

Since the 1980s, a large number of studies have attempted to test the Piagetian hypothesis on the relation between linguistic and cognitive development in the 2nd year of life. Most of these studies have used general measures of cognitive and linguistic development, such as the achievement of a sensorimotor stage and mean length of utterance (MLU) or vocabulary size. These studies have yielded very few significant links between language and cognition (for a review, see Bates & Snyder, 1987). However, recent studies have demonstrated correspondences between specific cognitive achievements (e.g., object permanence) and particular aspects of language (e.g., relational words; Gopnik & Meltzoff, 1986; Lifter & Bloom, 1989; McCune-Nicolich, 1981; Smolak & Levine, 1984; Tomasello & Farrar, 1984).

In this chapter, we review the evidence for a relationship between the acquisition of object words and the development of categorization abilities. As Locke (1988) suggested, the cognitive approach to language is particularly appropriate for the inference of early lexical representations. We first review the literature on early lexical development, including cross-linguistic studies and studies on atypical populations. We then discuss recent research on the development of lexical categories in the 2nd year of life. The third part of the chapter then examines the evidence for any relationship between the emergence and achievement of categorization abilities and the acquisition of lexical terms, including the naming explosion.

EARLY LEXICAL DEVELOPMENT

Although the ability to communicate with others emerges during the last quarter of the 1st year, the communicative signals used during that period are not considered linguistic in the traditional sense (see Bates, Benigni, Bretherton, Camaioni, & Volterra, 1979; Golinkoff, 1983). Conventional words, that is, words that are phonetically similar to their adult forms, appear at the beginning of the 2nd year within many languages, including French (Reich, 1985). In her longitudinal study, Nelson (1973) reported a lexicon of 10 words at a mean age of 15 months, with a range of 13–19 months. These milestones have been replicated in other studies with English- and French-speaking samples (Benedict, 1979; Grégoire, 1937; McCune-Nicolich, 1981). For the majority of children, first words are typically acquired slowly, over the course of several months, followed by a faster pace of acquisition between the ages of 17 and 22 months, a phenomenon called the *vocabulary spurt* (Benedict, 1979; Bloom, 1973; Dromi, 1987; Goldfield & Reznick, 1990).

There is a great deal of consistency in the types of words reported in the emerging lexicons of young children. Labels for concrete objects constitute the largest class of words in children's early vocabulary (Benedict, 1979; Nelson, 1973). Most of these nouns refer to familiar items of food, clothing, animals, vehicles, toys, and people. This predominance of nominals in the early vocabulary has been replicated cross-linguistically. In a study of children learning different languages, the percentage of nominals ranged from 50% for a Kaluli-speaking child to 85% for an English-speaking child (Gentner, 1982). Similarly, Orlansky and Bonvillian (1988) found that nominals constituted the largest grammatical category at the 50-sign stage of the 13 deaf subjects they studied longitudinally. Object words also predominate in the vocabulary of blind children (Dunlea, 1989), although the majority of blind children's general nominals do not overlap with those produced by sighted children. For example, the early lexicon of blind children includes labels for objects that produce auditory effects (Bigelow, 1987).

Rosch, Mervis, Gray, Johnson, and Boyes-Braem (1976) have distinguished three levels of lexical or semantic categories: the superordinate, basic, and subordinate levels. Objects at the basic level (e.g., *dogs*) share many features with each other, including similarity in shape and common attributes, such as object parts, but share few features with other contrasting categories at the same level (e.g., *birds*). Basic-level categories are considered psychologically fundamental, as there is maximal similarity within members of the category but minimal similarity with members of other categories. In contrast, categories at the superordinate level (e.g., *"animals"*) are more general and include objects that are relatively diverse. Thus, it is more difficult to perceive similarities among category members. At the subordinate level, categories are more specific (e.g., *"collies"*), and within each category objects are quite similar.

Most of the early object words refer to basic-level categories, as opposed to superordinate or subordinate level (Anglin, 1977; Rescorla, 1980). The primacy of this level for adults has been demonstrated using perceptual, behavioral, and linguistic measures (Rosch, 1978). Although the lexical items in the early vocabulary correspond to adults' most salient categorization level, the basic level, children's use of these words does not always correspond to the conventional use. One of the most striking characteristics of early word use is the tendency of young children to overextend words, applying them to objects outside the normal range of application (Bramaud du Boucheron, 1981; Clark, 1973). Up to 33% of the early vocabulary has been found to be overextended (Rescorla, 1980). Studies of overextension errors have indicated that labels are overextended in reference to objects that are in the same superordinate-level category as the correct referent (e.g., *dog* for other animals) as opposed to analogical or spatiotemporal associations (Dromi, 1987; Huttenlocher & Smiley, 1987). Furthermore, overextensions are most likely to be based on a perceptual similarity to the objects with the appropriate referent (Rescorla, 1980).

A longitudinal study of early lexical development recently completed in our laboratory reported similar findings (Poulin-Dubois, Graham, & Sippola, 1993). Sixteen children, nine English-speaking and seven French-speaking, between the ages of 12 and 24 months, participated in the study. Measures of each child's vocabulary development were obtained from a diary checklist of 600 words that was filled out by the parents during the course of the study. Parents were asked to record the date a word first appeared in the child's vocabulary, the context of its use, and any variation of the word. In addition, language samples were collected during monthly 20-minute free-play sessions. To be included in the vocabulary, a word had to be phonologically similar to the adult form. The word also had to be uttered spontaneously and not simply be an imitation of an adult's utterance. Finally, it had to occur at least twice in different contexts if collected in the free-play sessions or once if it was from a diary.

The evaluation of the monthly rate of vocabulary growth revealed a developmental pattern similar to that reported in previous studies. The average vocabulary size was one word at the beginning of the study and 229 words at the end. The mean age of acquisition of a lexicon of 50 words was 19 months, for both the English-speaking and the French-speaking subjects. All of the children in the study demonstrated a period of accelerated lexical growth. This vocabulary spurt, defined as the 1-month period in which total vocabulary increased by 15 or more words, was first observed at the average age of 19 months. Ten of the 16 children showed this increase between Sessions 6 and 9, whereas 3 children had an early spurt (Session 3 or 4), and 3 children had a late spurt (Sessions 11–13).

In contrast to the vocabulary spurt, which considers all categories of words, the *naming explosion* involves a change in a particular semantic category, namely, words that refer to classes of objects (Gopnik & Meltzoff, 1987). This more specific milestone is thought to reflect the understanding that all things can and should be categorized. All but 1 of our subjects demonstrated a naming explosion, defined as the session with an increase of at least 15 names. This naming explosion first occurred at the mean age of 20 months, and varied across children from 14 to 24 months.

The proportion of words in each of the different categories of words described by Nelson (1973) was also examined in the early lexicon (50 words). These proportions were also very similar across the two linguistic groups, with a predominance of nominals ($M = 69\%$). Object words accounted for an average of 42% of the first 50 words, with a range between 19% and 66%. Furthermore, among the first 50 nominals produced, the majority were basic-level terms ($M = 77\%$).

In conclusion, research conducted on the development of the lexicon of children learning different languages in different modalities indicates a predominance of nominals in the early lexicon, the dominance of basic-level terms, a naming explosion during the second part of the 2nd year, and word meanings that sometimes diverge from the conventional use.

THE DEVELOPMENT OF CATEGORIZATION ABILITIES

Research on the development of categorization abilities in infancy has flourished since the early 1980s. There is now a great deal of evidence that infants are capable of responding categorically to perceptually similar stimuli, such as faces and geometric forms, between the ages of 3 and 7 months (e.g., Cohen & Strauss, 1979; Lécuyer, 1991; Quinn, 1987).

In the French categorization literature, there has always been a strong interest in the developmental emergence of categorization abilities. The majority of this research, however, has focused almost exclusively on the development of class inclusion in children (e.g., Desprels-Fraysse, 1987; Houdé, 1989). Bideaud and

Houdé (1989) recently summarized the different approaches to categorization, stressing the ecological determinism of natural categories, as opposed to the construction of logical categories as studied within the Piagetian tradition (see also Scholnick, 1983). The few studies that have examined categorization in infancy have investigated the sensorimotor precursors of logical categorization within the context of Piagetian theory (e.g., Sinclair, Stambak, Lézine, Rayna, & Verba, 1982).

Although much is known about infants' categorization of artificial stimuli, our understanding of how infants categorize natural items is less well developed. In this section we focus on the development of natural categories, such as familiar items of food, clothing, animals, and vehicles. As already discussed, these categories are associated with children's early words, and therefore may be prerequisites or correlates of early object-word meanings.

Taxonomy of Categories

Various types of "infant" categories have been proposed, incorporating differing degrees of variation among exemplars (Bornstein, 1984). For example, Reznick (1989) has defined three levels of categories based on within-category and between-category differences. The level of a particular category is determined by the degree of similarity among categorical exemplars and the discriminability of the category members from members of other categories.

One aspect of categories that has influenced research in both infant and adult categorization is the hierarchical structure that most natural lexical categories appear to possess (Cordier, 1986; Cordier & Dubois, 1981). In light of the fundamental nature of basic-level categories, it has been argued that the earliest types of categories formed are basic-level categories, whereas superordinate-level categories are considered to be formed after, and out of, previously acquired basic-level categories. This pattern of emergence has been found with preschoolers. For example, in a study of children aged 2½ to 5½ years, Mervis and Crisafi (1982) found that the ability to categorize artificial objects at different hierarchical levels emerged in the following order: basic, superordinate, and subordinate. Similarly, Rosch et al. (1976) found that 3-year-old children were able to pick two objects from the same basic-level category with a high degree of accuracy when the third object was from a different superordinate-level category (e.g., two cats paired with a car). Children's responses, however, were at chance-level when they were required to pick two superordinate-level category members that were from differing basic-level categories (e.g., a car and a motorcycle paired with a cat).

Results such as those of Rosch et al. (1976) suggest that basic-level categorization develops before superordinate-level categorization. However, as Merriman (1986) pointed out, stronger evidence for the claim that basic-level categories are psychologically fundamental would have been provided if high basic-level matching performance was found when the odd item was from a contrastive basic-level category, rather than from a superordinate-level category (e.g., two cats paired with a dog). Blewitt (1983) conducted such a study, using a triad sorting task similar to that of Rosch et al. (1976), and found that 3-year-old children matched 60% of the superordinate-level objects correctly and 68% of the basic-level objects correctly when the out-of-category item was from a contrastive basic-level category (e.g., two dogs paired with a bear). Thus, although basic-level categories may emerge earlier than superordinate-level categories, the difference is not great. Recently, researchers have begun to investigate whether this pattern also holds for infants.

The Developmental Emergence of Basic- and Superordinate-level Categories

Studies have demonstrated that by 9 months of age, infants can form basic-level categories of the type associated with early object words (Roberts, 1988; Roberts & Horowitz, 1986). Studies that have investigated the ability of infants to form superordinate-level categories, however, have yielded mixed results regarding the age of acquisition of these categories. Golinkoff and Halperin (1983), using a case study approach, measured an 8-month-old infant's unique emotional responses to animal stimuli (e.g., *teddy bear, frog*) versus other stimuli (e.g., *fur coat, doll*). Their results suggested that the infant had a limited version of the superordinate-level category of animals organized around a prototypical animal. Similarly, using a habituation–dishabituation procedure, Ross (1980) found that 12- to 24-month-old infants were sensitive to categories whose members are perceptually similar (e.g., *"men"*) and to superordinate-level categories in which members vary considerably in perceptual features (e.g., *"food," "furniture"*). In contrast, Roberts and Cuff (1989) reported that 9-, 12-, and 15-month-old infants did not appear to form a superordinate-level category of "animal," when habituated to perceptually similar prototypical exemplars of the animal category (i.e., a *horse,* a *dog,* and a *lion*). However, when 15-month-olds were habituated to a larger number of animal exemplars (i.e., a *dog,* a *cat,* a *horse,* a *lion,* a *tiger,* and a *cow*) in a subsequent experiment, they generalized habituation to the within-category test stimuli (a *bird*), but discriminated the out-of-category stimulus (a *car*), a pattern of responding that is consistent with categorization. Interestingly, the finding that infants generalized habituation to a *bird* indicates that the category formed extended to more peripheral two-legged animals. Thus, the results of this study suggest that by 15 months of age, infants can form a superordinate-level category for animal. It is not clear if this ability is present in younger infants, because Roberts and Cuff did not include younger children in the last experiment.

Although much has been hypothesized about the emergence of different levels of categories, few studies have systematically examined the developmental status of basic- versus superordinate-level categories within the same experiment. In the few studies that do exist, a sensitivity to superordinate-level categories has been demonstrated in 22-month-olds (Daehler, Lonardo, & Bukatko, 1979). In one of the first studies to compare directly the acquisition of basic- and superordinate-level categories in infants, Mandler and Bauer (1988) had 12- and 20-month-olds perform object manipulation tasks with items from a number of different categories. They found performance to be best on the basic-level categories at both ages, but even at 12 months of age, some children were responsive to superordinate-level categories. By 20 months of age, approximately half the children showed such sensitivity. The results of a subsequent experiment indicated that 16- and 20-month-olds differentiated basic-level categories only when the categorical contrasts were taken from different superordinate-level classes (e.g., dogs vs. cars). When categories were drawn from the same superordinate-level class (e.g., dogs vs. horses), they did not categorize above chance levels. This suggests that infants were making use of both within-class similarities and between-class differences to regulate their responses.

In a later study, Bauer, McDonough, and Mandler (1988) found that children of 18, 24, and 30 months could form basic-level categories when there was a high degree of between-category difference. However, when there was a low to moderate degree of between category difference (e.g., dogs and horses or cars and trucks), basic-level categorization performance was significantly lower.

In our laboratory, we have investigated the developmental emergence of different levels of categories using cross-sectional and longitudinal designs (Poulin-Dubois, et al., 1993; Poulin-Dubois & Sissons, 1992a). In the cross-sectional study, an object manipulation task was administered to 18- and 21-month-old English-speaking toddlers to assess their categorization of items at the superordinate (e.g., animals, furniture, and vehicles), basic (e.g., cars, trucks, dogs, horses, chairs, and tables) and subordinate levels (e.g., poodles, collies, sedans, sports cars, kitchen chairs, and rocking chairs). For each categorization trial, the number of moves the infant made—that is, the number of times he or she touched an item—and the mean run length (MRL) were measured. MRL refers to the number of objects belonging to the same category that the child touches in sequence. MRLs were compared to chance-level responding to determine if the sequential touching was above chance levels, which would indicate that the infants were selecting items based on their category membership.

Only the 21-month-olds categorized superordinate- and basic-level items at above-chance levels. It is possible, however, that the failure of the 18-month-olds to categorize at the basic level was due to the stimuli used in the experiment. Our basic-level items were drawn from the same superordinate-level class (e.g., dogs vs. horses, chairs vs. tables, cars vs. trucks), and the infants were not able to draw on between-category differences to make their judgments. Thus, consistent with previous research in which a large selection of categories was tested, the results of this study indicate that superordinate-level categorization appears around the age of 21 months. Given that infants are neither producing nor being exposed to superordinate labels at this age, this finding suggests that the ability to form categories may precede the labeling of these categories.

Between-groups designs may not be the most sensitive measure of developmental phenomena such as the emergence of categorization. Thus, as part of the larger longitudinal study described earlier, we examined the order of acquisition of superordinate-, basic-, and subordinate-level categories in Francophone and Anglophone children (Poulin-Dubois, et al., 1993). We administered an object manipulation task, identical to that used in the cross-sectional study, to 16 infants at 13, 16, 19, 22, and 25 months of age, with three trials each at the basic, superordinate, and subordinate levels.

The infants in our study were able to categorize on a superordinate basis at above-chance levels, distinguishing animals, vehicles, and furniture, by the average age of 16 months. Infants began to categorize at above-chance levels on the basic task, on average, at the age of 19 months. However, they were not able to categorize subordinate-level items at above-chance levels, even by 25 months of age. Comparing each infant's MRL for each level and each session to the chance-level criterion, we found that 8 infants reached criterion on superordinate-level tasks before basic tasks, 3 infants reached criterion for both levels at the same session, and 4 infants categorized basic-level items earlier than superordinate-level items. In general, superordinate-level categorization appears to emerge earlier than either basic- or subordinate-level categorization. The longitudinal design used provides a stringent test of the order of emergence of these categories. Once again, these findings confirm the hypothesis that it is not so much the level of abstraction that matters, but the contrast across the categories and the perceptual similarity among the category exemplars.

We further examined the effects of age and category level on the infants' categorization abilities and found that mean superordinate-level MRL was significantly higher than mean subordinate-level MRL, but not higher than mean basic-level MRL. The number of moves an infant made, that is, the number of times he or she touched an item, did not differ across the three levels of categories. Thus, the categorization we observed is not attributable to the number of times items of a specific category were touched.

This development of superordinate-level categories before basic-level categories is likely due to the level of contrast used in our basic-level tasks. As stated earlier, all the basic-level items were drawn from the same superordinate-level class (e.g., dogs vs. horses, chairs vs. tables, cars vs. trucks) and children were not able to draw on between-category differences to make their judgments. Thus, the results of this study and those of Mandler and her colleagues (Bauer et al., 1988; Mandler & Bauer, 1988) suggest that infants' early categories may not be as "basic" as the term is usually understood. Basic-level categories may be the first to emerge only under specific conditions, such as high within-category consistency and high between-class contrast.

The role of similarity among stimuli in determining categorical judgments is well established. Fenson, Cameron, and Kennedy (1988) reported that the relative difficulty of identifying a basic- or superordinate-level match to a standard was determined by perceptual similarity rather than by the conceptual relation between the items. Hence, when the basic-level categories to be distinguished are, for example, birds and horses, and the within-category similarity and between-category differences are high, 9-month-old infants are able to form the category (Roberts, 1988). However, when there is a high degree of both within- and between-class similarity (e.g., dogs and horses), it is not until 18 months of age that infants begin to distinguish basic-level categories (Poulin-Dubois, et al., 1993).

It has been argued that the differential ease in forming categories at various levels of abstraction can be explained in terms of category differentiation. The degree of differentiation generally predicts a basic-to-superordinate order of emergence (Mervis & Crisafi, 1982). Given the absence of exposure to the corresponding labels in the study of basic- and superordinate-level categorization in infancy, a major role for perceptual-cognitive factors has been suggested in the development of categorization abilities (Roberts & Cuff, 1989). These perceptual-cognitive factors include, for example, the complexity and familiarity of the stimulus (Bornstein, 1981). The influence of perceptual-cognitive factors is particularly clear in studies using the habituation–dishabituation paradigm, where performance is directly related to the type of stimuli presented (Reznick, 1990; Reznick & Kagan, 1983). Later in development, adult labeling practices may influence the order in which the labels for different levels of category abstraction are acquired (Goldfield, 1987; Lucariello & Nelson, 1986).

THE RELATION BETWEEN OBJECT-WORD MEANING AND CATEGORIZATION

Although many studies have been conducted on early lexical development and on the formation of semantic categories, studies that have attempted to document the interrelationship of these two domains are scarce. A comparison of the data reported in the first two sections of this chapter suggests both some convergences and some discrepancies between the development of categorization abilities and the nature and meaning of the first lexical items. For instance, although basic-level terms predominate in the early lexicon, the emergence of categories at that level lags behind.

The data on the evolution of the meaning of words, however, seem to correspond fairly well with the development of categorization skills. Indeed, the low performance on sorting tasks measuring semantic categorization at any of the three levels of abstraction described earlier coincides with a period in lexical development when children attribute an overrestrictive meaning to new words, making underextension errors (Barrett, 1986). The emergence of basic-level categorization between the ages of 16 and 20 months seems to correspond, chronologically, to a period of faster rate of vocabulary development. Moreover, the presence of superordinate-level categories in the second part of the 2nd year of life is in agreement with the restriction of overextended labels to members of the same superordinate-level categories (Poulin-Dubois & Laurendeau-Bendavid, 1984; Rescorla, 1980).

Despite a general correspondence in time between object-word meaning and categorization, the appropriate testing of the hypothesis of a relationship between these abilities requires that the same children be tested in these two areas. Recent research has shed some light on this issue. Bloom, Lifter, and Broughton (1985) observed that the vocabulary spurt occurred subsequent to a shift from separating play activities to a balance between separating and constructing play activities in three children. The vocabulary spurt was also subsequent to, or coextensive with, the ability to make constructions incorporating the specific properties of objects. More recently, Gopnik and Meltzoff (1987) reported strong relations between categorization abilities and the naming explosion in 12 children. These relations were expressed in a short temporal gap between these two developments and a large correlation between the age of the naming explosion and the age of onset of the highest level of categorization.

The data on the development of categorization and language collected in the context of our longitudinal study of 16 children from French- and English-speaking families were also analyzed to test the hypothesis of a temporal relationship between the two abilities. Unlike the previous studies, our assessment of categorization skills focused on categories that are linguistically relevant, such as "dogs," "cars," and "birds." The age of onset of the naming explosion, defined as the first 1-month period with at least 15 new names, was found to be related to the emergence of categorization, defined as the age corresponding to the first session with a MRL higher than chance. One child did not achieve a naming explosion and thus, was not included in the analyses. For most subjects, the categorization performance at the session of the naming explosion or the session preceding it was greater than the performance at all the preceding sessions combined for the basic level. This pattern held for both linguistic groups: 6 English-speaking children and 5 French-speaking children exhibited greater basic-level categorization at the naming explosion as compared to earlier sessions; 4 children did not follow this pattern. This pattern contrasted with the categorization performance at the time of the naming explosion as compared to the following sessions, where a trend indicating a decrease in performance was observed for each level of categorization. In sum, the naming explosion coincided with, or was preceded by, a peak in categorization abilities.

The percentage of object words in the vocabulary at the end of this study, which varied from 30% to 53%, was also compared with the emergence of semantic categories at each level of abstraction. There was a relationship between this linguistic measure and the age of passing each of the categorization tasks. In other words, children with a high proportion of object words were more precocious in the development of categorization skills relevant for early lexical development.

In conclusion, the research comparing conceptual development and different aspects of early lexical development, such as the naming explosion and the proportion of object words in the early vocabulary, indicates that achievements in these two domains are related. Our own research suggests that the child has to achieve a certain level in his or her categorization abilities, specifically those relevant to labeling basic- and superordinate-level categories, before understanding what naming is all about. We have seen that the naming explosion, which is mainly an increase in basic-level labels, is associated with changes in basic- and superordinate-level categorization. Furthermore, cognitive correlates of a referential style were found, which suggest that children who concentrate on learning nouns are those who are the best categorizers. We now consider new research looking at the cognitive strategies used for learning the meaning of object words.

Object-Word Meaning and Abstraction of Object Parts

Different models or hypotheses have been proposed over the years to account for differences in word meanings between children and adults (e.g., Barrett, 1982, 1986; Clark, 1973; Mervis, 1984, 1987). All of these hypotheses about object-word meaning share the basic postulate that learning the conventional meanings of words requires the ability to abstract the features of objects. Recent research on adults' semantic categories has indicated that object parts (e.g., wings of a bird), particularly those with distinct functions, may be very important for differentiating basic-level categories (Tversky & Hemenway, 1984). As a result, it has been suggested that partonomic knowledge might be an important factor in the dominance of basic-level terms in the early lexicon (Mervis & Greco, 1984). Research with preschoolers has demonstrated the facilitative effect of shared parts in the formation of taxonomic categories (Tversky, 1989). Unfortunately, until recently there was no evidence for the role of abstraction of object parts as a categorization process in the formation of early object-word meaning. We recently completed two studies in our laboratory that provide strong evidence for such a link.

In a first study, we were interested in determining whether young infants in the early stages of lexical development use knowledge about object parts to determine the extension of familiar words (Poulin-Dubois & Sissons, 1992b). Three groups of children ($N = 78$), aged 12, 15 and 18 months, participated in the experiment. The preferential looking paradigm was used to test the extension of nine familiar words (Golinkoff, Hirsh-Pasek, Cauley, & Gordon, 1987). There were three different types of pairs presented to test the meaning of each word: (a) a target exemplar versus a target exemplar (e.g., two identical dogs), (b) a target exemplar versus a non-exemplar (e.g., a dog vs. a chair), or (c) two trials of a complete exemplar paired with an incomplete exemplar (e.g., a dog vs. a dog with no tail). Each infant's percentage looking time to each stimulus was obtained by summing looking times to the left and to the right screens. As hypothesized, children fixated longer on a picture when it was the referent of a target word compared to when it was not the referent of a target word. Analyses of the part-removed trials revealed that the 18-month-old infants looked significantly longer at the incomplete referent than at the complete referent, whereas 12- and 15-month-olds showed no preference (see Fig. 16.1). Moreover, looking time at the incomplete referent was greater than looking time at the complete referent for the words reported to be known (according to a parental checklist), but not for unknown words.

Thus, the findings from this first experiment suggest that infants can respond to the absence of important object parts by the age of 18 months. Furthermore, the reaction to the incomplete referents was related to knowledge about the meaning of the words, because this reaction was only observed with highly familiar words. Although infants associated object parts with object-word meanings, it remains to be clarified whether this ability really represents a word learning strategy. It is possible that the ability to abstract parts corresponds to a later step in the acquisition of object words. A second study attempted to disambiguate this issue by using a word learning paradigm.

This second study was designed to assess directly the instrumental role played by object parts in the acquisition of object labels (Poulin-Dubois, Graham, & Riddle, 1993). Novel object words referring to categories characterized by the presence or absence of salient parts were taught to young children in the early stages of lexical development. It was hypothesized that the presence of salient parts would have a facilitative effect on word learning because of the increased likelihood that the contrastive features would be identified. Moreover, it was

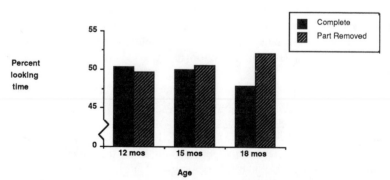

FIG. 16.1. Percent looking time at the complete and part-removed referents as a function of age.

predicted that children with a referential style, that is, with a higher proportion of nominals in their vocabulary, would benefit most from the manipulation.

Twenty-two English-speaking children participated, ranging in age from 16 to 25 months at the beginning of the study. Three words whose referents possessed at least one salient part were selected: *peacock, camel,* and *forklift.* Three other categories were matched with the experimental words in terms of number of syllables and frequency of occurrence in the English language: *pigeon, hamster,* and *jeepster. Jeepster* is a British variation of the word *jeep.* It was used for methodological purposes. Each child was taught the words over four learning sessions, which took place approximately 1 week apart. During each session, photographs of three exemplars for each of the six categories were presented, for a total of 18 presentation trials per session. Each category exemplar was labeled on its presentation (e.g., "See the peacock," "Look at the peacock"). On completion of each training session, each child was administered a multiple-choice receptive language test, in which each of the six labels was requested twice. For each trial, an exemplar of the target category was contrasted with the second member of the pair and with two additional categories of the same superordinate-level category (e.g., pigeon, peacock, ostrich, and seagull). The first picture pointed to or touched by the child was coded as the response.

Across the four comprehension tests, each word was requested eight times (2 trials × 4 sessions); therefore, children's possible scores ranged from 0 to 8 for each word. The percentage of correct choices across all comprehension tests was used as a measure of word learning. As Fig. 16.2 indicates, the hypothesis that salient parts have a facilitative effect on word learning was confirmed for two of the three pairs of words.

The relation between the learning of salient versus nonsalient categories and vocabulary, as assessed by the parental checklist, was also examined. Only

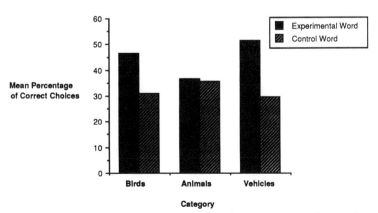

FIG. 16.2.   Mean percent of correct choices for objects with salient and nonsalient parts.

children having a vocabulary of at least 10 words were included in this analysis ($N = 16$). As expected, children with a high proportion of nouns in their vocabulary learned the salient words more easily than the nonsalient words. In conclusion, these findings strongly suggest that the acquisition of object words involves the abstraction of the features that allow the differentiation of the new categories from categories in the same semantic field.

CONCLUSION

Language acquisition is a complex process that cannot be explained by mere reduction to cognitive underpinnings. Since the cognition hypothesis was proposed in the late 1960s, an impressive amount of research has been carried out in order to clarify the relationship between these two domains of human knowledge (see Cromer, 1991, for a recent review). Research focusing on specific cognitive and verbal achievements within the Piagetian framework has demonstrated the primacy of cognition, at least in the early stages of cognitive development. However, there is also some evidence that language development and the related cognitive developments could occur in either order, as different manifestations of the same underlying capacity (Bates et al., 1979; Gopnik & Meltzoff, 1986; Tomasello & Farrar, 1984). Because of the difficulty in demonstrating links between general verbal and cognitive measures, recent research has focused on fine grained cognitive achievements and their expression in language, as well as cognitive abilities outside the Piagetian framework.

The research presented in this chapter clearly suggests that the development of categorization skills constrains the acquisition of the meaning of object words during the 2nd year of life. For instance, the occurrence of the naming explosion follows a major shift in the structure of object categorization, that is, the ability to group objects in classes (Gopnik & Meltzoff, 1986; Poulin-Dubois, et al., 1993). Moreover, individual differences in the proportion of object words in the lexicon are clearly related to individual differences in categorization skills, including the ability to abstract object parts (Poulin-Dubois & Sissons, 1992b). These findings should not be interpreted as indicating that the linguistic input has no role to play in the early stages of lexical development (Goldfield, 1987; Huttenlocher, Haight, Bryk, Seltzer, & Lyons, 1991). For instance, it seems that the amount of parental speech and the parental linguistic style play some role in determining the size of the vocabulary and the type of words (e.g., basic-level terms) that will be dominant in the child's early vocabulary. After all, children must pay attention to the way in which a word is used by others in order to learn its correct extension. However, the linguistic input received by a child appears to have little importance in the evolution of semantic categories (Mervis, 1987).

Among the researchers who acknowledge that many words map onto prior established nonlinguistic categories, many also agree that linguistic input may facilitate nonlinguistic categorization. In fact, it is well established that providing labels, even nonsense labels, helps preschool children detect a category not previously noticed (Markman & Hutchinson, 1984; Waxman, 1990). Teaching a novel name for a novel object is also used by children this age as a cue to search for the category of objects to which the name refers (Kuczaj, Borys, & Jones, 1989). However, this facilitative effect has been difficult to demonstrate in children who have not been through the naming explosion (Bauer & Mandler, 1989; Roberts & Jacob, 1991).

In conclusion, it should be noted that certain associations or correlations between linguistic and cognitive skills observed in normally developing children are not definitive for resolving the language–cognition debate. Cases of dissociation between conceptual and linguistic abilities clearly suggest that at least some aspects of language are independent of nonverbal cognition (Curtiss, 1982; Furth, 1966). Despite these caveats, there is strong support for the hypothesis that, in the early stages of language development, children are motivated to talk about what they know and that their learning is guided by general hypotheses about the structure of the world.

ACKNOWLEDGMENTS

The research reported in this chapter was supported by Natural Sciences and Engineering Research Council of Canada and Social Sciences and Humanities Research Council grants to the first author. We thank Bonnie Klein, Véronique Lacroix, Ingrid Oestling, Wendy Seifert, Lorrie Sippola, and Beth Sissons for their assistance.

REFERENCES

Anglin, J. M. (1977). *Word, object, and conceptual development*. New York: Norton.
Barrett, M. D. (1982). Distinguishing between prototypes: The early acquisition of the meaning of object names. In S. A. Kuczaj (Ed.), *Language development* (Vol. 1, pp. 313–334). Hillsdale, NJ: Lawrence Erlbaum Associates.
Barrett, M. D. (1986). Early semantic representations and early word usage. In S. A. Kuczaj & M. D. Barrett (Eds.), *The development of word meaning* (pp. 39–67). New York: Springer.
Bates, E., Benigni, L., Bretherton, I., Camaioni, L., & Volterra, V. (1979). *The emergence of symbols: Cognition and communication*. New York: Academic Press.
Bates, E., & Snyder, L. (1987). The cognitive hypothesis in language development. In I. C. Uzgiris & J. M. Hunt (Eds.), *Infant performance and experience: New findings with ordinal scales* (pp. 168–204). Chicago, IL: University of Illinois Press.
Bauer, P.J., & Mandler, J.M. (1989). Taxonomies and Triads: Conceptual organization in one- to two-year-olds. *Cognitive Psychology, 21,* 156–184.
Bauer, P., McDonough, L., & Mandler, J. (1988, April). *The role of contrast in basic- and superordinate-level categorization of natural objects*. Poster presented at the International Conference on Infant Studies, Washington, DC.

Benedict, H. (1979). Early lexical development: Comprehension and production. *Journal of Child Language, 6,* 183–200.

Bideaud, J., & Houdé, O. (1989). Le développement des catégorisations: "Capture" logique ou "capture" écologique des propriétés des objets? [The development of categorization: Logical or ecological abstraction of object properties]. *L'Année Psychologique, 89,* 87–123.

Bigelow, A. (1987). Early words of blind children. *Journal of Child Language, 14,* 47–56.

Blewitt, P. (1983, April). *What determines order of acquisition of object categories?* Paper presented at the biennial meeting of the Society for Research in Child Development, Detroit, MI.

Bloom, L. (1973). *One word at a time: The use of single-word utterances before syntax.* The Hague: Mouton.

Bloom, L., Lifter, K., & Broughton, J. (1985). The convergence of early cognition and language in the second year of life: Problems in conceptualization and measurement. In M. Barrett (Ed.), *Children's single word speech* (pp. 149–180). New York: Wiley.

Bornstein, M. H. (1981). Psychological studies of color perception in human infants: Habituation, discrimination and categorization, recognition, and conceptualization. In L. P. Lipsitt (Ed.), *Advances in infancy research* (Vol. 1, pp. 1–40). Norwood, NJ: Ablex.

Bornstein, M. H. (1984). A descriptive taxonomy of psychological categories used by infants. In C. Sophian (Ed.), *Origins of cognitive skills* (pp. 313–338). Hillsdale, NJ: Lawrence Erlbaum Associates.

Bramaud du Boucheron, G. (1981). *La mémoire sémantique de l'enfant* [Semantic memory in children]. Paris: Presses Universitaires de France.

Clark, E. V. (1973). What's in a word? On the child's acquisition of semantics in his first language. In T. E. Moore (Ed.), *Cognitive development and the acquisition of language* (pp. 65–110). New York: Academic Press.

Cohen, L. B., & Strauss, M. S. (1979). Concept acquisition in the human infant. *Child Development, 50,* 419–424.

Cordier, F. (1986). La catégorisation naturelle: Niveau de base et typicalité [Natural categorization: Basic level and typicality structure]. *Revue Française de Pédagogie, 77,* 61–70.

Cordier, F., & Dubois, D. (1981). Typicalité et représentation cognitive [Typicality and cognitive representation]. *Cahiers de Psychologie Cognitive, 1,* 299–333.

Cromer, R. I. (1991). *Language and thought in normal and handicapped children.* Oxford: Basil Blackwell.

Curtiss, S. (1982). Developmental dissociations of language and cognition. In L. K. Obler & L. Menn (Eds.), *Exceptional language and linguistics* (pp. 285–312). Boston, MA: Academic Press.

Daehler, M. W., Lonardo, R., & Bukatko, D. (1979). Matching and equivalence judgments in very young children. *Child Development, 50,* 170–179.

Desprels-Fraysse, A. (1987). Genèse des conduites de classification: Discontinuité structurelle et/ou continuité fonctionnelle? [Origins of classification: Structural discontinuity and/or functional continuity]. *L'Année psychologique, 87,* 489–508.

Dromi, E. (1987). *Early lexical development.* New York: Cambridge University Press.

Dunlea, A. (1989). *Vision and the emergence of meaning: Blind and sighted children's early language.* New York: Cambridge University Press.

Fenson, L., Cameron, M. S., & Kennedy, M. (1988). Role of perceptual and conceptual similarity in category matching at age two years. *Child Development, 59,* 897–907.

Furth, H. G. (1966). *Thinking without language: Psychological implications of deafness.* New York: The Free Press.

Gentner, D. (1982). Why nouns are learned before verbs: Linguistic relativity versus natural partitioning. In S. Kuczaj (Ed.), *Language development: Language, culture, and cognition* (pp. 301–334). Hillsdale, NJ: Lawrence Erlbaum Associates.

Goldfield, B. A. (1987). The contributions of child and caregiver to referential and expressive language. *Applied Psycholinguistics, 8,* 267–280.

Goldfield, B. A., & Reznick, J. S. (1990). Early lexical acquisition: Rate, content, and the vocabulary spurt. *Journal of Child Language, 17,* 171–183.

Golinkoff, R. M. (1983). *The transition from prelinguistic to linguistic communication.* Hillsdale, NJ: Lawrence Erlbaum Associates.

Golinkoff, R. M., & Halperin, M. S. (1983). The concept of animal: One infant's view. *Infant Behavior and Development, 6,* 229–233.

Golinkoff, R. M., Hirsh-Pasek, K., Cauley, K. M., & Gordon, L. (1987). The eyes have it: Lexical and syntactic comprehension in a new paradigm. *Journal of Child Language, 14,* 23–45.

Gopnik, A., & Meltzoff, A. N. (1986). Relations between semantic and cognitive development in the first word stage: The specificity hypothesis. *Child Development, 57,* 1040–1053.

Gopnik, A., & Meltzoff, A. N. (1987). Early semantic developments and their relationship to object permanence, means–ends understanding, and categorization. In K. E. Nelson & A. van Kleeck (Eds.), *Children's language* (Vol. 6, pp. 191–121). Hillsdale, NJ: Lawrence Erlbaum Associates.

Grégoire, A. (1937). *L'apprentissage du langage: Vol. 1. les deux premières années* [Language acquisition: Vol. 1. The first two years]. Paris: Droz.

Houdé, O. (1989). Logical categorization and schemas: A study of their relationships in 6- to 11-year-olds. *European Bulletin of Cognitive Psychology, 9,* 401–429.

Huttenlocher, J., Haight, W., Bryk, A., Seltzer, M., & Lyons, T. (1991). Early vocabulary growth: Relation to language input and gender. *Developmental Psychology, 27,* 236–248.

Huttenlocher, J., & Smiley, P. (1987). Early word meanings: The case of object names. *Cognitive Psychology, 19,* 63–89.

Johnston, J. R. (1985). Cognitive prerequisites: The evidence from children learning English. In D. I. Slobin (Ed.), *The crosslinguistic study of language acquisition* (Vol. 2, pp. 961–1004). Hillsdale, NJ: Lawrence Erlbaum Associates.

Kuczaj, S. A., II, Borys, R. H., & Jones, M. (1989). On the interaction of language and thought: Some thoughts and developmental data. In A. Gellatly, D. Rogers, & J. A. Sloboda (Eds.), *Cognition and social worlds* (pp. 168–189). Oxford: Clarendon.

Lécuyer, R. (1991). La catégorisation de formes géométriques continues chez des enfants de cinq mois [Categorization of geometric forms in five month old infants]. *Archives de Psychologie, 59,* 143–155.

Lifter, K., & Bloom, L. B. (1989). Object knowledge and emergence of language. *Infant Behavior and Development, 12,* 395–423.

Locke, J. (1988). The sound shape of early lexical representations. In J. Locke & D. Smith (Eds.), *The emergent lexicon* (pp. 3–22). New York: Academic Press.

Lucariello, J., & Nelson, K. (1986). Context effects of lexical specificity in maternal and child discourse. *Journal of Child Language, 13,* 507–522.

Mandler, J. M., & Bauer, P. J. (1988). The cradle of categorization: Is the basic level basic? *Cognitive Development, 3,* 247–264.

Markman, E. M., & Hutchinson, J. E. (1984). Children's sensitivity to constraints on meaning: Taxonomic vs. thematic relations. *Cognitive Psychology, 16,* 1–27.

McCune-Nicolich, L. (1981). The cognitive bases of relational words in the single-word period. *Journal of Child Language, 8,* 15–34.

Merriman, W. E. (1986). How children learn the reference of concrete nouns: A critique of current hypotheses. In S. A. Kuczaj & M. F. Barrett (Eds.), *The development of word meaning* (pp. 1–38). New York: Springer-Verlag.

Mervis, C. B. (1984). Early lexical development: The contributions of mother and child. In B. Sophian (Ed.), *Origins of cognitive skills* (pp. 339–370). Hillsdale, NJ: Lawrence Erlbaum Associates.

Mervis, C. B. (1987). Child-basic object categories and early lexical development. In U. Neisser

(Ed.), *Concepts and conceptual development: Ecological and intellectual factors in categorization* (pp. 201–233). New York: Cambridge University Press.

Mervis, C. B., & Crisafi, M. A. (1982). Tigers are kitty-cats: Object labeling by mothers for their thirteen-month-olds. *Child Development, 52,* 267–273.

Mervis, C. B., & Greco, C. (1984). Parts and early conceptual development: Comment on Tversky and Hemenway. *Journal of Experimental Psychology: General, 113,* 194–197.

Nelson, K. (1973). Structure and strategy in learning to talk. *Monographs of the Society for Research in Child Development, 38* (1–2, serial No. 149).

Orlansky, M. D., & Bonvillian, J. D. (1988). Early sign language acquisition. In M. D. Smith & J. L. Locke (Eds.), *The emergent lexicon* (pp. 263–292). New York: Academic Press.

Piatelli-Palmarini, M. (1980). *Language and learning: The debate between Jean Piaget and Noam Chomsky.* London: Routledge & Kegan Paul.

Piaget, J. (1962). *Play, dreams, and imitation in childhood.* New York: Basic Books.

Poulin-Dubois, D., Graham, S. A., & Riddle, A. (1993). *Object parts and the acquisition of novel object words by young children.* Manuscript submitted for publication.

Poulin-Dubois, D., & Laurendeau-Bendavid, M. (1984, July). *Overextension of object words in production and comprehension.* Paper presented at the Third International Conference for the Study of Child Language, Austin, TX.

Poulin-Dubois, D., Graham, S., & Sippola, L. (1993). Parental labelling, categorization, and early lexical development. Manuscript submitted for publication.

Poulin-Dubois, D., & Sissons, M. E. (1992a). *The development of object categories during the second year.* Unpublished manuscript.

Poulin-Dubois, D., & Sissons, M. E. (1992b). *Parts and infants' early semantic categories.* Unpublished manuscript.

Quinn, P. C. (1987). The categorical representation of visual pattern information by young infants. *Cognition, 27,* 145–179.

Reich, P. A. (1985). *Language development.* Englewood Cliffs, NJ: Prentice-Hall.

Rescorla, L. A. (1980). Overextension in early language development. *Journal of Child Language, 7,* 321–335.

Reznick, J. S. (1989). Research on infant categorization. *Seminars in Perinatology, 13,* 458–466.

Reznick, J. S. (1990). Visual preferences as a test of infant word comprehension. *Applied Psycholinguistics, 11,* 145–166.

Reznick, J. S., & Kagan, J. (1983). Dishabituation and category detection in infancy. In L. P. Lipsitt & C. K. Rovee-Collier (Eds.), *Advances in infancy research* (Vol. 2, pp. 79–111). Norwood, NJ: Ablex.

Roberts, K. (1988). Retrieval of a basic-level category in prelinguistic infants. *Developmental Psychology, 24,* 21–27.

Roberts, K., & Cuff, M. D. (1989). Categorization studies of 9- to 15-month-old infants: Evidence for superordinate categorization. *Infant Behavior and Development, 12,* 265–288.

Roberts, K., & Horowitz, F. D. (1986). Basic-level categorization in seven- and nine-month-old infants. *Journal of Child Language, 13,* 191–208.

Roberts, K., & Jacob, M. (1991). Linguistic vs. attentional influences on nonlinguistic categorization in 15-month-old infants. *Cognitive Development, 6,* 355–375.

Rosch, E. (1978). Principles of categorization. In E. Rosch & B. Lloyd (Eds.), *Cognition and categorization* (pp. 27–48). Hillsdale, NJ: Lawrence Erlbaum Associates.

Rosch, E., Mervis, C. B., Gray, W. D., Johnson, D. M., & Boyes-Braem, P. (1976). Basic objects in natural categories. *Cognitive Psychology, 8,* 382–439.

Ross, G. S. (1980). Categorization in 1- to 2-year-olds. *Developmental Psychology, 16,* 391–396.

Scholnick, E. K. (1983). *New trends in conceptual representation: Challenges to Piaget's theory?* Hillsdale, NJ: Lawrence Erlbaum Associates.

Sinclair, H., Stambak, M., Lézine, I., Rayna, S., & Verba, M. (1982). *Les bébés et les choses* [Babies and things]. Paris: Presses Universitaires de France.

Smolak, L., & Levine, M. P. (1984). The effects of differential criteria on the assessment of cognitive–linguistic relationships. *Child Development, 55,* 973–980.

Tomasello, M., & Farrar, M. (1984). Cognitive bases of lexical development: Object permanence and relational words. *Journal of Child Language, 11,* 477–493.

Tversky, B. (1989). Parts, partonomies, and taxonomies. *Developmental Psychology, 25,* 983–995.

Tversky, B., & Hemenway, K. (1984). Objects, parts, and categories. *Journal of Experimental Psychology, 113,* 169–193.

Waxman, S. R. (1990). Linguistic biases and the establishment of conceptual hierarchies: Evidence from preschool children. *Cognitive Development, 5,* 123–150.

17 Development of Meta-Abilities and Regulatory Mechanisms in the Use of Linguistic Structures by Children

Jean Emile Gombert
Université de Bourgogne

The neologism *metalinguistic* has only been in use for a short time. Between 1950 and 1960, linguists employed it to refer to anything related to *metalanguage*, the language whose lexicon is composed of all the words comprising linguistic terminology (such as *syntax, semantics, phoneme, lexeme*, etc., but also more common terms, like *word, sentence, letter*, etc.).

In its linguistic sense, then, *metalinguistics* pertains to linguistic activity that focuses on language. In a functional perspective, which views language in operation as it is used by real speakers, this metalinguistic level of language—where the language's signifiers become the signified—is given considerable importance and is granted a new status in the subject's activity of language. Thus, as Benveniste (1974) stated, the metalinguistic faculty is the "ability we have to distance ourselves from it, contemplate it, while still using it in our reasoning and our observations" (my translation). Nevertheless, from his viewpoint metalinguistics is restrictively dependent upon the capability of language to refer to itself (Bonnet & Tamine-Gardes, 1984). This meaning of the term is very different from the one currently used in psycholinguistics.

Following Flavell (particularly 1976, 1978, 1981), many psychologists began to consider metalinguistic activities as an integral part of metacognition. The field of *metacognition* encompasses all knowledge that either takes as an object, or regulates, any aspect of any cognitive task, or, as Flavell (1981) concisely put it, "cognition about cognition" (p. 37). In this perspective, metacognition includes introspective knowledge about cognitive states and their operations, as well as the ability of individuals to intentionally control and plan their own thinking processes.

From a metacognition specialist's point of view, metalinguistic activity does

227

not correspond, as it does for linguists, to language about language, but to cognition about language, and it is a full-fledged member of the set of metacognitive activities. Nevertheless, the cognitive products on which metalinguistic reflection partially operates (the linguistic objects) have certain specific features that give this subdomain of metacognition some highly original characteristics: Linguistic objects are symbolic objects, but they are still easily perceived, and they are probably the ones most frequently (quantitatively speaking) manipulated by children. Therefore, they may be of primary importance to the general development of thought and, in particular, to metacognitive development.

Thus, from the perspective of metacognition, the psycholinguistic meaning of the term *metalinguistic* differs from the meaning accepted by linguists who use this notion. From a linguistic point of view, *metalinguistic* refers to anything that relates to metalanguage. In other words, linguists pinpoint "the metalinguistic" by identifying linguistic markers in verbal productions that reflect self-referential processes (the use of language to refer to itself). Psychologists, on the other hand, look into subjects' behavior (verbal or otherwise) to find elements that permit them to infer the cognitive processes that underlie the conscious monitoring of language objects (*reflection on* or *intentional control over*), either as objects *per se* or in terms of their utilization by the locutors.

This precision of terminology is not superfluous. Indeed, something that is metalinguistic for some is not necessarily metalinguistic for others. This means, for example, that the ability to formulate a polite request (in other words, the ability to formulate indirect requests in a suitable way, see Bernicot, 1991)—if, indeed, the subject voluntarily adapts to the situation—will be considered by psychologists as a metalinguistic ability. However, if this adaptation does not translate into self-referencing surface marks, then linguists will not call it metalinguistic. At the very most, functional linguists will stress the metacommunicative nature of this skill (*metacommunication* being understood to refer to the nonverbal or not-specifically-verbal aspects of the communication). In contrast, the comments young children make about their own language, which linguists would unambiguously classify as metalinguistic productions (Bonnet & Tamine-Gardes, 1984), would not necessarily be viewed by psychologists as a manifestation of metalinguistic competence. For this to be the case, it would have to be established that the production, in fact, fell under the jurisdiction of a conscious and reflection-based cognitive activity.

It is necessary, at this point in our discussion, to bring up a contradiction, which is of appearance only, that could lead to futile controversy. The linguists's chosen object of study is language. In the linguistic perspective, it is the metalinguistic utterance that constitutes an object of study for the discipline, and non-linguistic factors that may affect the production are considered to be only secondary. Yet some of those factors are, in fact, the focus of attention of psychologists, for whom a linguistic production cannot be legitimately qualified unless the acting psychological factors are taken into account (particularly the cognitive ones). Psychologists speak of metalinguistic awareness, abilities, behavior, and attitudes, and the corresponding productions will not be the same as the ones defined by linguists, who only construe them as sets of traces.

METALINGUISTIC BEHAVIOR VERSUS EPILINGUISTIC BEHAVIOR

It is generally agreed by the psycholinguists of metacognition that, like all other metacognitive activities, metalinguistic activities can only be granted the "meta-activity" status if they are consciously performed by the subject, and that, by virtue of this, their emergence presupposes the ability to reflect and to engage in intentional self-monitoring.

The fact that, generally, this ability has not yet emerged in young children (for a review, see Gombert, 1990) does not imply that their cognitive activities are not controlled. This issue was dealt with in 1983 by Karmiloff-Smith who explored "a model which situates meta-processes as an essential component of acquisition, which continuously function at all levels of development, and do not merely occur as a late epiphenomen" (pp. 35–36). In fact, Karmiloff-Smith used the term *metaprocess* in a broader sense, which led her to distinguish among all metaprocesses between "unconscious metaprocesses" and other metaprocesses (which appear later on) that are available to conscious access and verbal statement (Karmiloff-Smith, 1986, 1987). This distinction, made within the vast range of processes encompassing all those "which operate on the internal representations themselves" (Karmiloff-Smith, 1983, p. 36), whether conscious or not, can also be found in Kolinsky's (1986) work on metalinguistic activities. Kolinsky distinguished between early episodic metalinguistic behavior and later metalinguistic behavior, which can be obtainable through outside prompting.

The distinction comes up again in the work by Levelt, Sinclair, and Jarvella (1978), who qualified as "metalinguistic" not only certain phenomena they themselves considered to be at the border of awareness (e.g., spontaneous self-repairs and reformulations performed by the young child), but also other phenomena that are clearly the result of very explicit reflection on language (e.g., reference to a grammatical rule that has been violated in an incorrect production). Acceptance of a definition this broad has led a certain number of authors to the conclusion that early metalinguistic activities do indeed exist, sometimes emerging as early as age 2 (for a detailed review of this issue, see Gombert, 1990).

In fact, it seems that *metalinguistic* is used to refer to dissimilar phenomena whose apparent similarity is a result of an observation bias. In 1984, Gilliéron wrote, "All knowledge is necessarily 'meta' from the observer's point of view. It does not deal with that which is real, but with the intelligibility of that which is real" (p. 232, my translation). Therefore, it suffices to confound the observer's and the subject's points of view to consider all cognitive behavior as the product of metacognitive control. A relevant psychological description cannot be made from an abstract point of view; it requires the psychologist or theorist to decentralize his or her approach in order to determine the meaning of behaviors in the cognitive context of the subjects who are their authors.

In accordance with previous researchers (for reviews, see Bredart & Rondal, 1982; Gombert, 1990), I think the distinction should be made between the skills manifested in spontaneous behavior (e.g., the child's ability to automatically adapt discourse to the listener's age, cf. Gombert, 1987) and the abilities based on systematically represented and intentionally applied knowledge (e.g., voluntary adapting narratives to different audiences, cf. Beaudichon, Sirgurdsson & Trelles, 1978; Brami-Mouling, 1977). I contend that it is more than a difference in degree that separates these two sets of behavior, but rather a qualitative difference between the cognitive activities themselves. Only the observer's adult-centeredness can, via a deforming assimilation process, prevent recognition of the specificity of the so-called "early metalinguistic" behaviors. To attain clarity in our linguistic terminology, then, the same expression must not be used to refer to the different cases I have just described.

In 1968, the French linguist Antoine Culioli wrote, "Language is an activity that itself supposes a perpetual epilinguistic activity (defined as an 'unconscious metalinguistic activity'), and a relation between a model (competence, or appropriation of the acquired mastery of a system of rules bearing on units) and its realization (performance), for which we have a phonic or graphic trace, the text" (p. 108).

The concept *epilinguistic* has never spread beyond the boundaries of the French-speaking world. Nevertheless, it has been used by several French-speaking linguists and psycholinguists (Berthoud, 1982; Besse, 1980; Boutet, Gauthier, & Saint-Pierre, 1983; Caron, 1983; Christinat-Tièche, 1982), and seems to be perfectly suitable to refer to the class of phenomena being described here, that is, the set of unconscious metalinguistic activities. The use of this permits us to posit that a reflective, intentional character is inherent in strictly metalinguistic activity.

For Culioli, such epilinguistic activities are involved in all language behavior, and thus represent the implicit self-reference automatically present in any linguistic production. This is a linguist's conception, and is, therefore, based on an understanding of *metalinguistic* as "pertaining to metalanguage." The semantic shifting of this term in the usage of psycholinguists, who are more interested in linguistic behavior than in traces (Gombert, 1990), should, thus, be found again in the psycholinguistic definition of *epilinguistic*. I shall, therefore, restrict the term *epilinguistic* to behavior that, although isomorphic to metalinguistic behavior, is not the result of the subject's conscious monitoring of his or her own linguistic processing.

It should be clear that I am in no way defending the absurd idea that linguistic behaviors that are nonmeta are not controlled. Linguistic organizations stored in long-term memory (organizations that are the product of the subject's experience within the confines of innate preprogramming constraints) control linguistic manipulations, both in comprehension and in production. However, only metalinguistic control is intentionally driven by the subjects themselves.

As for other behaviors, we must take into account the fact that cognitive control is not always apparent in the behavior itself. In most cases, researchers infer it from the degree of processing complexity assumed to be required by the observed response. This suggests that a distinction should be made between types of linguistic behaviors even within the set of all nonmetalinguistic behaviors. The point that distinguishes epilinguistic behaviors from other non-metalinguistic behaviors is that the cognitive control is explicitly marked in the behavior itself (e.g., as is the case in repair activities). This likens these behaviors to metalinguistic ones, so we should attempt to differentiate them.

If we call *epiprocesses* those unconscious metaprocesses that govern epilinguistic behavior, it could easily be agreed that they are at work in all linguistic behavior whose control level lies beyond the initial, purely associative responses that often constitutes the child's first deictic utterances, vocal games, greetings, or ritual usages (see, e.g., Nelson, 1973, 1974). However, epilinguistic behavior is the only kind of behavior in which the action of epiprocesses is manifested in the behavior itself.

From a developmental point of view, a twofold question arises concerning, on the one hand, the emergence of epiprocesses, and on the other, the question of how metalinguistic abilities are acquired.

PHASES OF METALINGUISTIC DEVELOPMENT IN CHILDREN

Using Karmiloff-Smith's (1986) model for support, I postulate that metalinguistic development is comprised of four successive phases. Each of the aspects of language (aspects whose exact scope I am currently unable to specify) is affected by metalinguistic development in a manner that is initially independent of (and not necessarily contemporaneous with) the other aspects. Finally, only the first two phases are virtually mandatory for all aspects; the occurrence of the third and fourth are strongly dependent on nonsystematic contextual factors. The first phase corresponds to the acquisition of the first linguistic skill, the second to the acquisition of epilinguistic control, and third to the acquisition of metalinguistic awareness, and the fourth to the automation of metaprocesses.

Phase 1: Acquisition of the First Linguistic Skills

In all respects, this first phase is identical to the one described in Karmiloff-Smith's (1986) model. Basic linguistic skills are acquired via the model presented by adults in conjunction with negative and positive feedback that results in the rejection of incorrect productions and the reinforcement of correct ones. This leads to storage in memory of a multiplicity of unifunctional pairs for which a correspondence is established between a given linguistic form and each of the pragmatic contexts in which it has continuously been positively reinforced. At the end of this phase, the child's usage of that particular linguistic form is close to that of adults (although simplified to suit the characteristics of the adult models presented to the children; see the notion of *format,* Bruner, 1983). This is one of the first processes of linguistic behavior automation.

To be more precise, it is obvious that the assertion that each individual linguistic form is associated with its context of occurrence is metaphorical. What the child actually stores in memory is a sound pattern that most likely encompasses a set of linguistic forms and meanings that frequently coexist in short segments of the speech stream.

The behavioral stability gained in the first phase is then brought into question, due to an increase in the size and complexity of the adult models and the length of the child's own productions. This causes the reorganization process, which is characteristic of the second phase. Indeed, the mere increase in the length of speech stream segments the child takes into account has two consequences. First, new functions for the forms that were previously associated with certain contexts may appear (namely, discursive functions; e.g., anaphoric reference becomes one of the new functions of definite articles—as in "there were a dog and a cat; *the* cat . . ."—that previously served only as deictic prefixes—as in "look at *the* cat"). Second, because the new and old functions generally interact with each other, the number of form–function pairs in one-to-one correspondence, or more precisely, the number of sound-pattern–context pairs, increases so cextensively that it jeopardizes the simple practicability of the initial associative means of operation.

In this respect, the behavioral success and recurring positive feedback that follow mark the end of the first phase, but, in my mind, do not suffice to trigger the second. It is the subsequent reappearance of negative feedback that, in this particular case, will be determining. (Such negative feedback may be implicit, and consists of simple difficulty or failure to communicate.)

I share Karmiloff-Smith's point of view (and would like to stress its importance) concerning the inadequacy of an explanation of macrogenetic development as the simple result of children's attempts to overcome failure in their successive modes of functioning. I believe that success plays a crucial role during the transition between the first and second phases, but that role is not to trigger moving on to a higher level of functioning, but to consolidate the current level. A consolidation of this sort is a prerequisite to the appearance of a destabilization process (which presupposes prior stability). It is this process that will determine the increasing reorganization of knowledge.

In this perspective, errors that reappear in places where previous linguistic behavior was always correct are not just the consequence of the transition to a higher level of cognitive functioning (it is in this way that several authors explain U-curves frequently observed in the evolution of linguistic and other performances in children), but the partial cause of that transition. Such errors are made because, contrary to what an overly local analysis seems to suggest, the child is required to resolve increasingly complex communication problems as the model taken increasingly requires the interaction of different linguistic forms.

Phase 2: Acquisition of Epilinguistic Control

The second phase corresponds to the organization in long-term memory of the implicit knowledge accumulated during the first phase. It involves the substitution of multifunctional forms for the initial multitude of form–function pairs. My description of this phase differs from Karmiloff-Smith's on several points.

First, I believe the driving force of development is not only the innate inclination to control the internal organization of the knowledge acquired during Phase 1, but also, owing to that organization, the need to interrelate that knowledge with other newly discovered knowledge about those same forms, or about other forms frequently associated with those currently being organized. This new knowledge is being acquired under the effects of (a) the enrichment of available adult models and (b) the increase in the speech segment size taken into account (or in the precision with which the segments are analyzed by the child).

Second, I contend that the extralinguistic context of children's linguistic processing plays a very important role during this second phase. The general process in operation during this phase is the internal articulation of implicit knowledge, which leads to a functional (i.e., unreflected) awareness of a system. Nevertheless, the building of usage rules for the linguistic form in question is determined by, and of significant interest to, the real and thus contextualized use of those forms.

For example, the early epilinguistic detection of agrammatical statements may be affected by two factors. First, the child may be alarmed by the dissonance of the utterance. This dissonance is not absolute, but relative, because it depends on the context of the utterance. The control process responsible for the detection is, in part, dependent on the contexts previously encountered by the child and, in particular, on the contexts with which the current situation is functionally assimilated. The second potential factor has to do with the child's possible inability to understand the ill-formed utterance. In effect, this is equivalent to the inability to locate a linguistic structure in memory that, in a context similar to the current context, activates a representation.

Another example would be epilinguistic, or more precisely episyntactic, cross- and self-repairs, which are subordinate to the wording (or rewording) of the child's perceived (or desired) meaning. In other words, the young child who perceives a poorly constructed utterance, yet nonetheless comprehends it, may correct it by simply verbalizing the perceived meaning (Gombert & Boudinet, 1988). This process leads to a verbal production that is appropriate to the current context without the child ever paying the slightest attention to syntax. It is similar in nature to the process whereby young children automatically adapt their productions to the characteristics of the utterance context (such as the characteristics of the addressee; Gombert, 1987).

These two examples show how epilinguistic behavior is the output of the control exerted by the linguistic organizations the context activates in long-term memory.

Thus, during this phase, the child progressively acquires the ability to refer implicitly to a prototypical context by constructing a system of usage rules for the linguistic form currently implicated. This context, which corresponds to the common denominator of the most frequent and salient contexts in which that form usually occurred, may serve as a reference whenever the current context is unfamiliar (in particular, in formal experimentation situations). The elaboration of a stable pragmatic standard for each linguistic form is the main feature of this second phase of development. This stable state marks the end of the second phase, and provides subjects with a top–down component in the control they exert on their own linguistic processing. However, the establishment of this epilinguistic skill will not necessarily be in evidence in linguistic productions. That would only be the case in epilinguistic productions, where the control is manifested in the production itself.

Awareness of the system of rules set up in this manner—that is, the step up toward metalinguistic control—is not automatic. It can only be attained following a metacognitive effort that manifests itself only when necessary. Because epilinguistic control has become stable and efficient at handling daily verbal exchanges, new external prompting is necessary for awareness to set in.

Functional mastery is characteristic of the end of the second phase. During this phase, the epilinguistic behavior, through which language activities involving the linguistic aspects currently being organized are controlled, reflects the application of rules that become increasingly general in scope and gradually come to constitute systems.

Phase 3: Acquisition of Metalinguistic Awareness

Unlike what happens at the end of the first phase, the changeover to this functioning level does not stem from the obvious inadequacy of a previous state of stability, but from the need to intentionally control the stability acquired by the end of the second phase. This explains the optional character of access to this third level of functioning, which does not always occur. As suggested in many studies (in particular, those conducted by researchers at the Free University of Brussels, which revealed the low performance level of illiterate adults on metalinguistic tasks; Gombert, 1990; Morais, Alegria, & Content, 1987), only those aspects of language that *must* be mastered in order to accomplish the required linguistic tasks will be mastered in a "meta" fashion (that is, consciously).

Morais, Cary, Alegria, and Bertelson (1979) asked two groups of adults either to add a certain phoneme to the beginning of words, or to remove the initial phoneme. The subjects from one group were illiterate; the other group was comprised of subjects who were from the same social background, but had gained literacy either as adolescents or as adults. Although the first group attained only a 19% success level, 72% of the second group performed successfully. This result indicates that the metaphonological ability involved in phonemic analysis is a consequence of learning to read.

In fact, mastery of reading and writing requires conscious knowledge and intentional control of many aspects of language. In our society, then, it plays the role of triggering the acquisition of metalinguistic awareness. However, according to results obtained following formal metalinguistic training in the oral medium, other factors can play this role prior to the onset of learning to read and write (Gombert, 1990). In that case, early metalinguistic awareness seems to facilitate the acquisition of abilities that, if necessary, stimulate this awareness in turn.

This facilitation is probably linked to the lightening of the work load during learning. Children who are already capable of the necessary conscious analysis of language can devote their attention to learning the rules of written language.

An absolute prerequisite of metalinguistic awareness is epilinguistic control. An activity can only be consciously mastered when it has already been mastered at the functional level. A probable consequence of the fact that the acquisition of metalinguistic competence is not mandatory (i.e., is not determined by maturational—or exogenous, but systematic—factors, but instead by external situations, which may or may not rise) is that certain aspects of language never reach this level of control.

To give an example, it is probable that for many individuals, most formal modifications that are designed to adjust a production to suit its addressee (Beaudichon, 1982; Brami-Mouling, 1977; Gombert, 1987; Lafontaine, 1983), or that adapt one to the processing of indirect requests (Bernicot & Legros, 1987a, 1987b) are never the objects of metalinguistic awareness (i.e., they are not the object of intentional decision), and thus remain at the epilinguistic level.

Because conscious monitoring is a cognitively expensive operation, everything cannot be consciously mastered at the same time. The complexity of the systems to be acquired, their frequency in the language, and their usefulness to new, yet unresolved problems are at the origin of the horizontal *décalages* found in the time of appearance of the corresponding metalinguistic skills. In other words, the various metalinguistic developments are noncontemporaneous.

Phase 4: Automation of Metaprocesses

It is evident that meta-level functioning incurs very high cognitive costs, and it is known that we do not always consciously monitor our linguistic processing. For the most part, this is due to the automation of metaprocesses, that is, the processes responsible for the conscious self-monitoring subjects exert on the execution of their own linguistic problem solving.

In a more general discussion of metacognition, the same point of view was defended by Borkowski, Carr, and Pressley (1987), who considered automation as the final state in the repeated use of metacognitive strategies. Similarly, Sternberg (1986) contended that when experts are confronted with familiar tasks, the role of the executive system is restricted to determining which automatic processes need to be activated. What, in fact, ends up being automated are the metalinguistic functions that have been frequently and efficiently repeated.

Contrary to what was suggested by Karmiloff-Smith (1986, 1987) in regard to related encapsulated modules, I think that automatic metaprocesses are usually accessible by the conscience (this differentiates them from epiprocesses, which are also automatic, but inaccessible). At the very least, without having to resort to postulating potential access to a module's content, it is conceivable that returning to a metamode of functioning enables the subject to rediscover the resolution mode as it stood before being automated and modularized. This return to a meta mode of functioning will only occur (with varying degrees of difficulty) when the activity in progress encounters an obstacle as it unfolds, or when the subject decides to pay particular attention to the task to be accomplished or to a given aspect of that task.

Thus, there are two types of automatic processes that should not be confused with each other: the epiprocesses and the automated processes. In both cases, the cognitive work is done unconsciously, but unlike epiprocesses, automated processes can always be replaced by metaprocesses if an obstacle hinders the automatic progression of the linguistic processing.

CONCLUSION

Within the metalinguistic development, I have made a distinction between first linguistic skills typical of a first phase, epilinguistic abilities that appear during a second phase under the influence of an organization of the implicit knowledge accumulated during the first phase, and metalinguistic capabilities (of intentional character), which do not emerge until a third phase.

In a post-Piagetian perspective, I contend that there exists a vertical *décalage* between early epilinguistic skills and later metalinguistic capabilities. Similar linguistic behaviors that belong to the former or to the later, are determined in a totally different manner. That which is functional at epilinguistic level becomes reflective at the metalinguistic level.

For instance, the apparent isomorphism between the 4-year-old's adaptation of his or her discourse to the listener's age and the adult's way of telling a story to children in a noninteractive context conceals cognitive processes of different levels. Unlike the adult's intentional discursive adaptions, the linguistic manifestations of the fact that the child has taken on a social role in no way imply or require reflection on the language and its usage (Gombert, 1987).

Thus, the first three phases of metalinguistic development seem to correspond to different structural levels. Does this mean that my use of the term *phase* rather than *stage,* and my affirmation that control of the different microaspects of language develops independently for each aspect are but a question of style and a concession to a functionalist mode? Of course not.

From a strictly structural point of view *à la Piaget,* it is possible to consider first linguistic skills as presymbolic actions; manifestations of epilinguistic competence as the fruit of intuitive, pre-operatory control; and metalinguistic behavior as the application of operations to the manipulation of the language's rules. Nonetheless, this structural framework can only define the lower bounds, and in no way imposes simultaneity nor interdependence on the development of specific metalinguistic abilities.

During development, neither confrontation with the linguistic environment nor the linguistic knowledge base is homogeneous. The acquisition of strategies will consequently depend on what linguistic aspect is involved, and processing abilities will vary as a function of the knowledge base for that aspect. There are learning factors of primary importance here, ones that are the determinants of numerous horizontal *décalages.* At different levels of metalinguistic development, the familiarity, complexity, and abstraction level of tasks—or, in Piaget's terms, perceptual and intuitive obstacles—lead to substantial discrepancies in the age at which the first manifestations of epilinguistic and, later, metalinguistic behaviors are found.

What has just been described as *décalages* in stages can thus be described in terms of systems of parallel, but noncontemporaneous, phases. Moreover, the detailed chain I have described is, indeed, composed of a sequence of events, and is not simply the linguistic dimension of the successive stages of operatory development. Thus, although it fits quite naturally into Piaget's structural framework, my approach is resolutely a functionalist one.

REFERENCES

Beaudichon, J. (1982). *La communication sociale chez l'enfant* [The social communication of the child]. Paris: Presses Universitaires de France.

Beaudichon, J., Sirgurdsson, T., & Trelles, C. (1978). Etude chez l'enfant de l'adaptation verbale à l'interlocuteur lors de la communication [Study of the child's verbal adaptation to her addressee]. *Psychologie Française, 23,* 213–220.

Benveniste, E. (1974). *Problèmes de linguistique générale* [Questions of general linguistics]. (Vol. 2). Paris: Gallimard.

Bernicot, J. (1991). French children's conception of requesting: The development of metapragmatic knowledge. *International Journal of Behavioral Development, 14,* 285–304.

Bernicot, J., & Legros, S. (1987a). La compréhension des demandes par les enfants de 3 à 8 ans: Les demandes directes et les demandes indirectes non conventionnelles [How 3- to 8-year-old children understand requests: Direct and non-conventional indirect requests]. *Cahiers de Psychologie Cognitive, 7,* 267–283.

Bernicot, J., & Legros, S. (1987b). Direct and indirect directives: What do young children understand? *Journal of Experimental Child Psychology, 43,* 346–358.

Berthoud, A.-C. (1982). Sur la relative fiabilité du discours métalinguistique des apprenants [About the reliability of the learners' metalinguistic speech]. *Encrages, 8–9,* 139–142.

Besse, H. (1980). Métalangage et apprentissage d'une langue étrangère [Metalanguage and learning a foreign language]. *Langue Française, 47,* 115–118.

Bonnet, C., & Tamine-Gardes, J. (1984). *Quand l'enfant parle du langage* [When the child speaks about language]. Brussels: Mardaga.

Borkowski, J. G., Carr, M., & Pressley, M. (1987). "Spontaneous" strategy use: Perspectives from metacognitive theory. *Intelligence, 11,* 61–75.

Boutet, J., Gauthier, F., & Saint-Pierre, M. (1983). Savoir dire sur la phrase [Knowing how to speak about sentences.] *Archives de Psychologie, 51,* 205–228.

Brami-Mouling, M.-A. (1977). Notes sur l'adaption de l'expression verbale de l'enfant en fonction de l'âge de son interlocuteur [Remarks about the child's verbal adaption to her addressee's age]. *Archives de Psychologie, 45,* 225–234.

Bredart, S., & Rondal, J. A. (1982). *L'analyse du langage chez l'enfant: Les activités métalinguistiques* [The language analysis by the child: Metalinguistic activities]. Brussels: Mardaga.

Bruner, J. (1983). *Le développement de l'enfant: Savoir faire, savoir dire* [Child development: Knowing how to do, knowing how to tell]. Paris: Presses Universitaires de France.

Caron, J. (1983). *Les régulations des discours* [Speech regulations]. Paris: Presses Universitaires de France.

Christinat-Tièche, C. (1982). Segmentation d'enoncés et construction d'une histoire par de jeunes enfants: Une approche de l'analyse des segments constitutifs du récit [Text segmentation and construction of a story by young children: An analytic approach to the segments compounding narratives]. *Archives de Psychologie, 50,* 251–260.

Culioli, A. (1968). La formalisation en linguistique [Formalization in linguistics]. *Cahiers pour l'Analyse, 9,* 106–117.

Flavell, J. H. (1976). Metacognitive aspects of problem solving. In B. Resnick (Ed.), *The nature of intelligence* (pp. 127–146). Hillsdale, NJ: Lawrence Erlbaum Associates.

Flavell, J. H. (1978). Metacognitive development. In J. M. Scandura & C. J. Brainerd (Eds.), *Structural/process models of complex human behaviour* (pp. 61–92). Alphen aan den Rijn, Netherlands: Sijthoff & Noordhoff.

Flavell, J. H. (1981). Cognitive monitoring. In W. P. Dickson (Ed.), *Children's oral communication skills* (pp. 35–60). New York: Academic Press.

Gilliéron, C. (1984). Réflexions préliminaires à une étude de la négation [Reflections prior to a study of the negation]. *Archives de Psychologie, 52,* 231–253.

Gombert, J. E. (1987). Are young children's speech adaptions conscious or automatic? A short theoretical note. *International Journal of Psychology, 22,* 375–382.

Gombert, J. E. (1990). *Le développement métalinguistique* [Metalinguistic development]. Paris: Presses Universitaires de France; New York: Harvester-Wheatsheaf; and Chicago: University of Chicago Press.

Gombert, J. E. (1991). Les activités métalinguistiques comme objet d'étude de la psycholinguistique cognitive [Metalinguistic activities as an object of study for cognitive psycholinguistics]. In

J. Beaudichon & E. Cauzinille (Eds.), *Les processus de contrôle dans la résolution de tâches complexes: Développement et acquisition* [Control processes in the solution of intricate tasks: Development and acquisition]. *Bulletin de Psychologie, 44,* 92–99.

Gombert, J. E., & Boudinet, S. (1988, January). *Le contrôle de la grammaticalité de phrases par l'enfant de 4–5 ans* [Monitoring of sentences' "grammaticality" by 4- to 5-year-old children]. Paper presented at the annual conference of the experimental psychology section of the Société Française de Psychologie, Dijon, France.

Karmiloff-Smith, A. (1983). A note on the concept of "metaprocedural processes" in linguistic and non-linguistic development. *Archives de Psychologie, 51,* 35–40.

Karmiloff-Smith, A. (1986). From meta-processes to conscious access: Evidence from metalinguistic and repair data. *Cognition, 23,* 95–147.

Karmiloff-Smith, A. (1987). Function and process in comparing language and cognition. In M. Hickmann (Ed.), *Social and functional approaches to language and thought* (pp. 185–202). New York: Academic Press.

Kolinsky, R. (1986). L'émergence des habiletés métalinguistiques [Emergence of metalinguistic skills]. *Cahiers de Psychologie Cognitive, 6,* 379–404.

Lafontaine, D. (1983). L'adaptation des enfants à leur interlocuteur lors de la communication [Children's adaptation to their listeners during communication]. *L'Année Psychologique, 83,* 199–224.

Levelt, W.J.M., Sinclair, A., & Jarvella, R. J. (1978). Causes and functions of linguistic awareness in language acquisition: Some introductory remarks. In A. Sinclair, R. J. Jarvella, & W.J.M. Levelt (Eds.), *The child's conception of language* (pp. 1–14). Berlin: Springer-Verlag

Morais, J., Alegria, J., & Content, A. (1987). The relationship between segmental and alphabetic literacy: An interactive view. *Cahiers de Psychologie Cognitive, 5,* 415–438.

Morais, J., Cary, L., Alegria, J., & Bertelson, P. (1979). Does awareness of speech as a sequence of phonemes arise spontaneously? *Cognition, 7,* 323–331.

Nelson, K. (1973). Structure and strategy in learning to talk. *Monographs of the Society for Research in Child Development, 38* (Serial No. 149).

Nelson, K. (1974). Concept, world and sentence: Interrelations in acquisition and development. *Psychological Review, 81,* 267–285.

Sternberg, R. J. (1986). The trikie theory of untouched giftedness. In R. J. Sternberg & J. E. Davidson (Eds.), *Conceptions of giftedness* (pp. 223–245). Cambridge, England: Cambridge University Press.

18 Language and Thought in Children: A Look Behind Curtains

Hanuš Papoušek
Mechthild Papoušek
Research and Consulting Unit for Early Development and Parenting, Institute for Social Paediatrics, University of Munich

The idea of facilitating English-speaking psychologists' access to French traditions in developmental research is coming in an interesting political context: As the most visible curtain separating scientists—the Iron Curtain between East and West—is disappearing, the less obvious ones, such as the nationalistic prejudices, are becoming more visible. One can imagine an American reader finding that French psychologists have someone at the level of Piaget or Vygotsky, whose name is not very difficult to pronounce, but who is very difficult to find in American referencing systems. At the time that it is becoming more important to push the right buttons than to talk to other people, the reader checks the main manuals of child psychology, the handbooks of infancy research, or the reviews of human development; or activates his or her personal computer to look for the name of Henri Wallon in available referencing systems, but in vain. It is difficult to say whether a similar experience happened to the American editor of the present volume and motivated him to look for another editorial assignment. However, he certainly has the reputation of a polyhistoric psychologist, who passionately visits allied disciplines of psychology, lifts curtains among disciplines and cultures, and may lead the reader to unexpected areas of arts, engineering, biology, anthropology, or history.

Thirty years ago—a negligible span of time, but with respect to scientific progress a historical epoch—in the 1960s, American developmental psychologists were among the first scientific communities to overcome the Iron Curtain and organize a wide international exchange of information. Several outstanding conferences helped to disengage them from a behavioristic dominance and opened the area of thought and language in children to the concepts of Piaget and Vygotsky. Scientists from the Eastern bloc participated, but French scientists did not. Henri Wallon remained almost unknown, and was certainly underrepresented in English reviews of developmental psychology.

Political competition between France and the United States might indicate the presence of a political curtain, but Bornstein would hardly lead the reader to areas so distant to scientific thinking. The fact that all three editors are engaged in research on early development suggests that they expect major contributions from lifting other than political curtains, namely, the curtains between scientific disciplines and between "schools" within individual disciplines. It was specifically infancy research that made it evident that interdisciplinary cooperation can overcome obstacles, find access to difficult areas, develop necessary methodologies, and open ways for scientific verification of concepts that had been based on mere speculations. Infancy researchers were fast in overcoming dichotomic views, rejecting dogmatized theories, and replacing them with concepts open to both criticism and creative improvements. Innovative approaches soon forced revisions onto traditional interpretations of developmental processes and attracted so many new co-workers in the 1960s and 1970s that psychology experienced a real infancy boom. Together with the fast progress in research technologies, the present level of verified knowledge makes it much more important to confront former interpretations with this present knowledge than to stress differences among authorities in opinions formulated prior to present verifications. This obviously corresponds to the intention of the present editors as expressed in the subtitle of this volume.

In a major proportion of her chapter, Nadel follows the editors' intention while reviewing interesting and valuable studies of her colleague followers of Wallon. In that part, she also helps the reader to visualize the empirical experience that motivated Wallon's theoretical deductions. However, considering the lack of background information on Wallon available to English-speaking readers, it would be equally valuable to help the reader to visualize Wallon's personality and the historical roots of his concepts. The indicated parallelism with Vygotsky in the early 1940s is somewhat confusing, if we realize that Vygotsky died in 1934 and the first English translation of his *Thought and Language* appeared in 1962. Vygotsky did not mention Wallon's work, although he did comment, at least on the earlier French publications by Piaget. The introductory confrontation of Wallon with Piaget includes only abbreviated, general, and thus too abstract indications of differences that might have partly resulted from different empirical evidence and partly from apodictic interpretations. Explaining these aspects would be useful.

It remains difficult to understand why Wallon's theory, in contrast to Piaget's, received so little attention in English-speaking countries. Both were Francophone Europeans, and the risk of nationalistic prejudices was equal. In Piaget's case, of course, we should not forget Bärbel Inhelder's enormous merit in making Piagetian ideas understandable to American developmental psychologists, infancy researchers in particular. Speaking fluent English, she participated at both the Conference on Thought in the Young Child (in Dedham, MA, in 1960) and the Conference on European Research in Cognitive Development (in Voksenäsen, Oslo, Norway, in 1962), which represented turning points in international and interdisciplinary orientation in developmental research. In a charming way, she patiently kept helping American colleagues to interpret and understand terms or formulations of a Francophone theoretician for whom rich eloquent variations may sometimes mean more than easily understandable definitions. Single-step translations seldom suffice in French–English communication; it frequently requires dual translations, first from one language to the other, then from the vocabulary of one school of thinking to that of the other.

Nadel's chapter is interestingly contrasted by the chapter of de Boysson-Bardies and Hallé. Although the latter chapter richly profits from cross-cultural linguistic comparisons, it simultaneously documents how any cultural specificity of French researchers may disappear due to a cosmopolitan identification with a professional community. Linguistic predispositions may facilitate this adjustment, which allows a smooth intradisciplinary—and electronic—communication. However, the mimicry of a professional jargon concealing nationality may also function as yet another curtain to be lifted, if the reader does not want to miss the interdisciplinary significance of the chapter and is a linguistic outsider. One's self-confidence may rapidly decrease, because the authors do not lose time and space with auxiliary explanations for developmentalists with insufficient polyhistoric background, yet a little pain pays off: Cross-cultural phonological comparisons have accumulated important evidence on the effects of linguistic environment on preverbal stages of speech acquisition.

As de Boysson-Bardies and Hallé put it, the growing body of cross-linguistic findings challenge the common assumption that early speech development mainly exhibits universal tendencies. Although the authors do not elaborate on it, that seeming controversy may need a comment, because it appears in other developmental issues as well. For instance, studies on parental contributions to infant communicative development also show that these contributions are based on universal tendencies, yet simultaneously show interindividual variations that help identify each caregiver. Universal tendencies do not eliminate individuality: Human production of vocal sounds is based on universal predispositions, but voice-prints safely differentiate individuals (more or less). The theory of highly dynamic systems offers interesting interpretations in this direction; however, there are still more curtains to be lifted on the way toward the application of this theory.

19 Francophone Views on Verbal and Communicative Development: A Non-Francophone Commentary

Paul van Geert
University of Groningen

The style, methodology, general frameworks, and inspiration of scientific re-search are more directly determined by culture, and especially by the culture of scientific education, than by language. There are numerous historical examples to illustrate this general point. Of course, language often coincides with culture, and then the two aspects are indistinguishable. In the case of Francophone psychology, however, there are at least two major cultures involved, the French-speaking culture of Western Europe, involving France and parts of Switzerland and Belgium, and that of Northern American French-speaking Canada. So we might expect to see differences in research coming from these two cultural spheres, and the differences found might be even more outspoken if we also had contributions from French-speaking African nations. However, it is important to keep in mind that language often channels cultural exchange, in focusing the speakers of a language into the culture of the language's dominant nation. In this sense, France has always played an important role in the whole of the French-speaking culture.

The modern scientific world, however, has drastically changed, thanks to the availability of fast communication channels, enabling the establishment of inten-sively used international networks of information exchange. Important as this factor undoubtedly is, it does not wipe out the effects of a scientific tradition that grew in a time when science was more nation- and culture-bound than it is today. Although the works of major French-speaking developmental psychologists have been translated into English and many other languages, the effect of such transla-tions is often different from that of the original works. The time that translations became widely available differs markedly from the time the original works appeared in French, corresponding with major differences in the local and temporal scientific frameworks in which such works exerted their primary influence. Piaget's work is a case in point. His major works became widely available to English-speaking readers at a time when the scientific frameworks that originally inspired and shaped Piaget's work had undergone drastic historical changes. Moreover, the translated works were read and studied against a completely different background of tradition and history. In the United States, for instance, Piaget offered a welcome alternative to the behaviorist background, which was clearly on its return in the early 1960s, when Flavell's book on Piaget's theory appeared.

There are more differences to be noted, however. Although major authors, such as Piaget, have been translated—and more importantly, have been translated successfully, as far as their spreading of ideas is concerned—some scholars who held major positions in the French-speaking scientific community have been less lucky. Wallon is a good example. There is no doubt that his ideas could form a source of inspiration for contemporary developmental research, but his influence does not really reach much further than France.

There is a final important difference that is particularly related to the topics of the present four chapters, namely, verbal and communicative development. In view of the dominance of English-speaking scholars in the available literature, most of the investigations reported in internationally easily accessible journals are carried out with English-speaking children. So, from a comparative view, studies of French-speaking children could cast a different light on claims of universality or specificity of the findings at issue.

The papers in this section on verbal and communicative development are of two kinds: theoretical reflection and empirical reports. For some reason or other, which I cannot really explain, I identify a strong reliance on theoretical and especially conceptual specificity much more with a French than with an English/American approach to developmental science. This emphasis on theoretical and conceptual frameworks is comparable to the *baguette:* You can find this form of bread everywhere nowadays, but it remains typically French. The paper on Wallon is a good example of how the work of a scholar who is world famous in France can still be both very inspiring and also very relevant to new ideas and approaches. The empirical papers are a good example of work inspired by international lines of information exchange that are no longer hampered by national, linguistic, or cultural boundaries.

BODY, EMOTION, AND COMMUNICATION: WALLON'S CONTRIBUTION

As a "licentiate"-student in Ghent, Belgium, I came across Wallon's books in the departmental library, and found many things relating directly to the topic I was interested in at that time: consciousness and its development. Therefore, Wallon's work is not unfamiliar to me, as it probably is to most English or American readers. Nadel has done a good job in concisely explaining some major points of Wallon's theory on the development of communication. It is interesting to see how different these major points are in comparison to the current cognitive approach to communication. The latter emphasizes formal rule structures (more precisely, formal rules as descriptions of the infant's behavior and activity), the cognitive-rational as the core domain, and the necessity and importance of internal representations. It is also basically solipsistic, in that it conceives of the child as an information system, processing inputs and producing outputs. Nadel explains that, in Wallon's view, the child was basically social and sociable, to the extent that there is not even a real distinction between others and the self at the beginning, and that the self basically merges into a social rather than an indiscriminate syncretic system. Wallon's emphasis lay on emotions, not on cognitions. Emotions were seen as basic ways of understanding, representing, and differentiating the world. Finally, it was not the internal representations that were important, but the bodily expressions that should be studied as the roots and essence of communication.

Modern research on infant communication and cognitive development shows that Wallon's position provides a better way of understanding what really happens than does the straightforward cognitive way. Nadel cites a number of examples of research based on a Wallonian framework, thus showing that Wallon is still inspiring a number of Francophone developmental researchers. I would like to add that there is much of a (probably unintended) Wallonian flavor in work by scholars who were not directly inspired by Wallon. A good example is Alan Fogel's work carried out at the University of Utah, Salt Lake City (Fogel, 1991; Fogel & Thelen, 1987). Fogel views the development of communication as the result of a complicated, fine-tuned system of dynamic interactions between infant and direct caretaker (usually the mother). He sees no underlying or overarching rule systems at work: The structures of communication are made "on the spot" and are based on the dynamics of the bodily interaction. The infant is basically sociable, in that his or her activities make communicative sense only in the direct physical and bodily interaction with the mother. It appears that Fogel's notion of a dynamic process of communication development is much more closely related to Wallon's "transitory adaptations" than it is to the Piagetian notion of precursors, prerequisites and structures.

Wallon's emphasis on emotions as important shaping aspects of development was shared by the North American developmentalist, Kurt Fischer, himself nevertheless in the tradition of structuralist theories (Fischer, Shaver, & Carnochan, 1990). Fischer's work is another example of how a researcher can come to ideas that converge on Wallon's by starting from a different framework.

In summary, Nadel's chapter supports the belief that a wider spread of Wallon's ideas and their becoming more directly available outside the Francophone research community would be to the benefit of scholars who seek a way out of the dominant framework based on structuralist and purely cognitivist views of how human communication and knowledge develop.

META AND EPI IN THE CHILD'S REGULATION
OF LANGUAGE USE

From my room on a little hilltop, I overlook Stanford University, so in a sense I occupy a meta-viewpoint over the place where Flavell has done so much research showing how important the meta-aspect was in cognitive development. Although mine is a very physical overview, Gombert's overview presents a conceptual analysis of the concept of "meta" as it appears in the literature on metalinguistic awareness and metacognition. Almost everybody who uses this concept of "meta," especially in the framework of language development, does so in a rather uncritical way. This, at least, is Gombert's message, and he gives a number of good reasons for us to support it.

Gombert follows two lines of attack. First, he makes a relevant conceptual distinction between epilinguistic and metalinguistic operations. The definition of *epilinguistic*, however, relies heavily on the predicate *unconscious*, and therefore on consciousness as a distinctive criterion. As far as I understand the distinction clearly, I would be inclined to call *epilinguistic* those aspects or episodes where language rules actually operate on language rules. The choice of a pragmatic style or code dependent on the audience, or self-repairs in the case of sentences found ungrammatical are examples of such rules operating on rules. One could, of course, claim that under this general definition all linguistic activity is epilinguistic, which actually boils down to saying that there is no distinction between these two, and hence, no reason to use different words. I shall not go into this potential discussion, but confine myself to the criterion that Gombert uses, namely conscious versus unconscious monitoring. The problem with that criterion is that, although it appeals to our common-sense understanding of what the distinction might be, it is actually very difficult to deal with in a scientific and methodological context (van Geert, 1983). The only clues we have for telling the difference are either the subject's introspective reports or the observable properties of the associated activities. Both are quite unreliable, as far as objectively determining the distinction between consciously and unconsciously entertained processes is concerned, so it might be worthwhile to look for a sharper criterion (which Gombert has possibly explained elsewhere).

The second line of attack against a unitary notion of metalinguistic activity consists in presenting a four-phase theory of the development of such activity. The first and second phases culminate in the acquisition of a truly epilinguistic language. The third and fourth cover the development of metalinguistic awareness and its automatization. Automatized metalinguistic activity has become unconscious again, but it basically differs from epilinguistic activity in that it can be made conscious if need be.

The phase model has various attractive properties. First, it is a combination of necessary and contiguous states. The necessary states, Phases 1 and 2, follow automatically from the way in which language is acquired by human beings. The contiguous states, Phases 3 and 4, depend on the availability of explicit schooling in metalinguistic skills. Second, by coming back to the unconscious monitoring on a higher level, this model shares the cyclical feature with classical theories, such as Werner's, in which one observes a cyclicity of differentiation and integration processes. Most of our developmental models are aiming at a steady state, a "point-attractor," but there is an intuitive attractiveness in the idea that many forms of development are cyclical, or more precisely, spiroidal, in the sense that there is a combination of increase (e.g., higher levels of abstractness, more conscious monitoring) and cyclicity (e.g., equilibrium–disequilibrium, differentiation–integration).

It is a pity that this chapter could not give more empirical data to support the phase model, except for the data on the phonological skills in illiterate people. Moreover, the emphasis on reinforcement as a mechanism that shapes the development during the first phase at least, seems somewhat outdated. Reinforcement certainly plays a role, but it is not the reinforcement itself that governs development, but the structure in which this reinforcement, in addition to many other forms of learning, is embedded.

BABBLING IN FRENCH

The chapter by de Boysson-Bardies and Hallé is a good illustration of how a general problem can profit from being investigated in different cultural and, in this case, language contexts. Put differently, it demonstrates the widely accepted importance of comparative research.

The basic question is whether early speech development is determined by genetic or by environmental features. Genetic features are universal and can be of two kinds. They are either of a structuralist nature, and then boil down to the effect of universal structural constraints on language production, or they are of a physicalist nature, in which case they emphasize the shaping role of the physical articulatory apparatus. The genetic theory would predict common patterns in early speech, which then gradually diverge on the basis of language-specific input. The environmental theory would predict that from its earliest beginnings, infants' speech productions show the clear mark of the ambient language. Against these possibilities, the authors put their interaction hypothesis, which claims that there is an early interaction between biological equipment (structural or physical) and environment. The mechanism that regulates this interaction is the infant's biologically determined, hence universal, capacity to distinctively select specific input from the environment. Interesting as this hypothesis is, it still leaves a number of possibilities open.

For instance, is the biological mechanism such that it first detects the major underlying speech features of any language, features that strongly depend on universal structural and physical properties of the human speech apparatus? If this is so, then the interaction hypothesis comes up with the same starting point as the genetic hypothesis would, namely, a common starting point for all infants. It may differ, though, in its prediction as to how long this common period would last in infants. If the mechanism does not pick up the universal ground features first, but is sensitive to language-specific speech patterns, then how specific to the language are these patterns? for instance, are they specific to the language family, the language, or the dialect? If the first is the case, then infants from different language communities belonging to the same families would show similar starting points, differing from infants from other families. If infants pick up really specific features, then their earliest productions differ from infants from different dialect groups, for instance. So, without specifying the nature of the selective mechanism, the interaction hypothesis remains rather unspecific as to what to expect in the earliest stages of speech production. The authors have chosen for a presentation of the available empirical evidence without going into details as to what exactly their theory would predict, and why it would do so.

Meanwhile, however, they present a number of detailed and interesting data on infant speech in various languages. Most of the data were gathered from infants who were either in or beyond the second step in speech development, namely, the prespeech production stage. At this prespeech production level, and the more so on the level of first speech productions, there is a very clear influence of the ambient language on the infant's speech. The canonical babbling stage, however, seems to form the major testing point for the interaction hypothesis. The authors report that, as yet, no language-specific influences have been found. Productions at this stage will no doubt be strongly determined by biological constraints. However, the interaction hypothesis would predict that even these highly universal productions must be colored to some extent by the language-specific properties that the infant must have been able to pick up.

COGNITION AND LANGUAGE IN MONTRÉAL

The chapter by Poulin-Dubois and Graham is a good example of research that does not in an obvious way relate to a specific cultural and linguistic background. It is probably not accidental that this chapter was written by two North American researchers. On the other hand, one should not exaggerate the importance of such a coincidence found in a sample of only four chapters.

The authors try to cast the old question of how cognition and language relate in a new mold. Instead of focusing on a general relationship—like "cognition shapes language" or "cognition is greatly enhanced by the symbolic powers of language"—they come up with a much more dynamic and context-dependent view. Cognition and language are undoubtedly related in a variety of ways. In the transitory stage between preverbal intelligence and the use of language, cognition most surely contributes a lot to language development, but its contribution differs among language domains. It will probably be very strong in meaning acquisition and in the building up of the lexicon, and less so in the acquisition of syntax.

There is strong evidence for the assertion that the acquisition of early word meaning relate quite strongly to a major cognitive capacity, namely, *categorization*, the spontaneous and unreflected uses of classes and distinctions, but how does the relation work out?

Poulin-Dubois and Graham present the reader with a number of empirical investigations that clearly show that the relation is far from simple. For instance, previous researchers have started from a logical conceptualization of cognitive difficulty and developmental precedence, thus placing the acquisition of basic-level categories clearly ahead of superordinate-level categories. The authors show that the real sequence of cognitive difficulty depends strongly on the context and the concrete nature of the categories involved. This point of view relates clearly to the ecological approach (in the Gibsonian sense), in that an activity (categorization) is not determined by the complexity of its internal representation, but by the way in which it dovetails with a specific environment. Another important finding is that the pathways to lexical meaning are far from universal or uniform. There exist marked individual differences among children. This is the kind of finding that is often concealed in research reports. The prevailing method treats children as instances of a single kind, studying groups of such allegedly uniform beings as a way to filter out the effects of noise and error on the observations made, but cognitive development, even in such young infants, probably works in a rather different way. The environment affords a variety of different ways of approaching a similar problem, such as the acquisition of the meaning of a lexical item in a specific context. It sometimes depends on purely accidental variations whether children take one aspect as a starting point or another. Once a starting point has been chosen among a variety of almost similar alternatives, however, it tends to shape very explicitly the routes toward the common endpoint, namely, the acquisition of a word's meaning.

Individual differences are also seen in the timing of the naming explosion versus the emergence of categorization abilities. Again, a more traditional way of thinking would imply hypothesizing either a cognition-to-language dependency or a language-to-cognition approach. Cognition and categorization always appear earlier than language, so for quite some time the relationship is asymmetric (cognition preceding and therefore codetermining language). But this temporal delay could well be reconciled with the hypothesis that word meaning acquisition and categorization are mutually supportively related. In my own work, I have studied the potential long-term behavior of such mutually coupled variables (van Geert, 1991). Slight differences in the parameters determining the growth of these variables and the way they mutually reinforce can produce major, unexpected changes in the way these variables relate over time. Thus, a consistently later growth spurt in one as compared to the growth spurt in the other is no sufficient evidence for the hypothesis that it must be the earliest emerging variable that determines the later one. Likewise, small differences in underlying parameters can cause major individual differences.

The authors rightly conclude that their research demonstrates that word meaning is constrained by the development of categorization skills, but their work also illustrates that this constraint works out in ways that differ among contexts and individuals, and that there is a subtle interplay between task- and context-requirements and the trajectories of acquisition and development.

ACKNOWLEDGMENTS

This paper was written when I was a Fellow at the Center for Advanced Studies in the Behavioral Sciences, Stanford, California, 1992–1993.

REFERENCES

Fischer, K. W., Shaver, P., & Carnochan, A. (1990). How emotions develop and how they organize development. *Cognition & Emotion, 4*, 81–127.
Fogel, A. (1991, July). *Movement and communication in human infancy.* Paper presented at the ISSBD Conference, Minneapolis, MN.
Fogel, A., & Thelen, E. (1987). Development of early expressive and communicative action: Reinterpreting the evidence from a dynamic systems perspective. *Developmental Psychology, 23,* 747–761.
van Geert, P. (1983). *The development of perception, cognition and language: A theoretical approach.* London: Routledge & Kegan Paul.
van Geert, P. (1991). A dynamic systems model of cognitive and language growth. *Psychological Review, 98,* 3–53.

IV INTERACTION AND DEVELOPMENT

20 Parent–Infant Interactions and Early Cognitive Development

Marie-Germaine Pêcheux
Florence Labrell
Université René Descartes Paris V-CNRS

Empirical research on parent–infant interaction is surprisingly infrequent in France, at least in nonclinical populations. Before presenting some of our own investigations, and in order to locate them in the present state of art, we put forward some general reasons that may explain this lack of emphasis. Two types of reasons may be identified: theoretical reasons and institutional ones. More-over, how independent they are should be analyzed.

A FRENCH THEORETICAL PERSPECTIVE: HENRI WALLON

French psychology of the young child developed quite early in France, initiated by Henri Wallon (1879–1962). From his first writings, he considered man to be essentially social (Wallon, 1934). Long before Trevarthen (1977), he posited that the life of a human infant "opens in social interactions" (Wallon, 1938/1982, p. 203). Sociability is basic to the infant's adaptation to its state of helplessness at birth; it is not dependent on external contingencies, but genetically programmed. Therefore, infant development must be described as the development of its interactions with its social environment, first of all, with its mother. Wallon's *Origins of Character* (1934) was published simultaneously with Gesell and Thompson's *Embryology of Behavior* (1934), but the theoretical views were quite different, Wallon being a transactionalist long before the word was created. That French developmental psychology is now considered as essentially struc-turalist, due to the world-renowned work of Piaget, is the result of the neglect—

or the foreclosure?—of an active school of thought (Birns, 1973; Netchine-Grynberg, 1991).

How are mother–infant interactions pictured in this theoretical perspective? For Wallon their fundamental core consists of emotions, in both mother and infant. Infant emotional behaviors have primarily an expressive function. They indicate first internal sensations, which are interpreted and regulated by the caregivers. Emotional behaviors maintain early communication and, through their effects on the adult, support the development of self-awareness. Between infant and parent, emotions produce an immediate communication, and Wallon described an "emotional stage," which comes to a peak at around 6 months of age. Furthermore, the roots of emotions are found in variations of muscle tone. States of tone tension are first solved in biological emotional bursts, which the parent–infant interaction converts into tools for the infant to act in his social environment. Such a process implies that the mother detects her infant's tone states, responds to them, and possibly alters them. Consequently, in this conception of early development, research on mother–infant interactions should be more focused on proximal contacts than on distal stimulations.

However, Wallon, as a philosopher, a pediatrician, and a psychologist, did not turn to experimental validations. Only later, his followers, with Irène Lézine as the leader, substantiated his intuitions on systematic observations of large samples of mother–infant dyads. Such empirical work confirmed Wallon's theoretical analyses and extensively demonstrated their relevance. Normative mean trends were less investigated than interindividual differences, and their development through interactions. For instance, Lézine, Robin, and Cortial (1975) studied how maternal postural interventions are involved in the regulation of temporal aspects of sucking in newborns, and Robin (1978) compared eye-to-eye exchanges of premature newborns with their mothers to those of dyads in which the infant was born at term. Through a microanalytic approach, she further stressed the large individual variability of dyadic interactions during the first days of life and, more precisely, in the mothers' tactile activity (Robin, 1980). In older infants, Lézine, Dubon, Josse, and Léonard (1976), using longitudinal observations on a sample of 25 dyads, showed how the variability in styles of motor activity, related to state and variations of muscle tone, is associated with the style of parents' attitudes toward the child and with the individual characteristics of each member of the dyad. De Ajuriaguerra (1962) further elaborated the role of emotions as the primary mode of communication, and of muscle tone as the origin of emotions. He introduced the notion of *dialogue tonique* (dialogue through variations in muscle tone), which stresses psychomotricity as having the meaning and function of some sort of language. Even when incorporating elements from the Anglo-Saxon literature, Widmer-Robert-Tissot (1981) explicitly turned to concepts elaborated by Wallon and de Ajuriaguerra in studying infants' postures, movements, and vocalizations as modes of communications with their mothers or strangers.

INFANCY AND FRENCH INSTITUTIONS

Wallon played a key role in French developmental psychology not only as a scientist, but as a citizen and a militant. His name appeared explicitly in the title of the project for the French public school system after World War II (the Langevin–Wallon plan). From then on, professionals working in public institutions concerning infancy referred to his theoretical positions, and researchers working in his laboratory got involved in these institutions and in the problems that needed to be solved.

French governments have long been concerned with infancy and toddlerhood, in connection with demographic problems. As early as 1874, the Roussel Law organized the control of paid nurses, a common caregiving system in the 19th century in France for about 35% of infants born in towns. This law created districts with appointed officers. *L'Ecole Maternelle* (the maternal school), which cares for children between 2 and 6 years of age, stems from the *salles d'asile* (shelters) created in 1828. It "constitutes the transition between family and school, as it preserves the loving and indulgent kindness of the family while it initiates one to school work and regularity" (Norvez, 1990, p. 19, our translation). The National Committee for Childhood was created in 1902. In 1913, a law concerning women's rest after birth and allowances to large families corroborated the moral and financial responsibility of the state in the solution of problems about infancy. *L'Ecole de Puériculture* (nursing school) was founded in the dark days of 1917. World War I caused the end of paid nursing out of home, and the number of daycare centers increased tremendously, although the 1929 depression slowed the expansion of women's working. Finally, a State Act of 1945 created the institution of *Protection Maternelle et Infantile* (PMI), which, among other responsibilities, is in charge of providing caregiving out of homes. Since that time, this powerful institution has developed with only minor changes.

Although the physical health of young children was the first concern of the PMI, it very rapidly became interested in psychological development. At the same time, it became crucial to demonstrate that daycare centers were not harmful for infants. For these two reasons, the intervention of researchers was requested; moreover, researchers in France are civil servants, and have to meet the state concerns. Consequently, followers of Wallon got directly involved in the development of daycare centers. The journal *Enfance,* founded by Wallon in 1948, was largely open to research in infancy. A special issue (Davidson, 1968) showed the role of researchers in psychology in daycare institutions (e.g., David & Appell, 1966). In such circumstances, research is tightly linked to institutional life. A number of papers written by Irène Lézine, a prominent CNRS researcher, conveyed this point of view, and demonstrated how daycare centers could be beneficial to the infant's social and cognitive development (Brunet & Lézine, 1951; Lézine, 1955, 1964, 1985; Lézine & Stambak, 1959).

The concern with daycare meant that the study of parent–infant interaction was not a priority goal. Moreover, the substantial entrance of women into the workforce made empirical research in this domain problematic. In 1962, 39% of mothers of a child younger than 2 years worked full time out of the home; this reached 75% in 1982, and it is still higher in big cities, compared to small towns and the country. Not only working mothers have problems finding time to participate in research. Basically, it is a stressful situation for all mothers, as it forces them to face painful questioning. (The *Zeitgeist* is contradictory on the aspect of professional status for mothers, praising simultaneously mothering and out-of-home working.) This ideological ambivalence makes mothers feel guilty in some sense, whether they work or not, and to experience any observation of their relationship with their infant with suspicion. In the 1980s, this attitude was standard. When one of us started empirical research in homes, any data collection implied long preliminary contacts, with comforting and supportive talks. By comparison, fathers participated easily, always proud to display their unexpected competencies in childrearing. Basic to the mothers' stress is the fear that their infant, because of them, will not be "normal."

THE CLINICAL APPROACH

Research in mother–infant interaction actually developed in France, but in a clinical perspective. However, in an orthodox psychoanalytical tradition, which is very deep-rooted in France, in spite (or maybe because) of quarrels between various tendencies, empirical observations of mother–infant dyads are not mandatory. Thus Kreisler and Cramer (1981) and Lebovici (1983) inclined toward the study of fantasmatic interactions. Behavioral interactions are only clues to maternal and infant's internal life, to their object relations and reciprocal investments. Maternal fantasmatic (i.e., internal) life may be reached through her verbalizations, and what they mean, but how may the fantasmatic life of the infant be reached, if not through observed behaviors, and how may the pertinence of an interpretation be assessed? For instance, Lebovici and Mazet (1989) calling on Winnicott (1971), interpret the infant looking at the mother as follows: "What an infant expects when he looks at his mother is to see his mother's eyes looking at him. Through his looking the mother is affirmed as mother" (p. 220, our translation). However, Lebovici and Mazet did not provide criteria to support this interpretation. The first affirmation may be true, but the infant may as well just make sure that his mother is not far from him—in which case the looking behavior is different. The second affirmation, in turn, allows two interpretations: Is it the child, or the mother herself, who acknowledges the mother as mother? Here, too, interactional behaviors that can be observed may guide the interpretation. In a fascinating book, too subtle to be summarized in a few words, Piñol-Douriez (1984), studying proto-representations in infants, argued that direct observation and metapsychological reconstruction supplement each other.

Clinical research, focused on dysfunctions, was oriented to a more systematic methodology only recently, under the influence of ethology (Cosnier, 1983). The experimental approach—considering parent–infant interactions in a laboratory, through microanalyses—was unacceptable to clinicians, but the ethological approach—considering behaviors in their usual context, without any intervention of an experimenter—was perceived as associating an ecological validity with some scientific precision. After research was performed on normal newborns and their mothers (Montagner 1974, 1978, 1988; Montagner et al., 1989; Schaal, 1986), the method was used on clinical dyads (Maury, Visier, & Montagner, 1989). However, at present only fined-grained monographs are published, in which data are not referred to normal behaviors; and coding systems, though they help to standardize data about mother–infant interaction, do not produce objective evaluations. A significant exception is found in Switzerland, where the Group for Family Study in Lausanne explicitly compares parent–infant interactions in clinical and nonclinical families, using infants as young as 3 months (Corboz, Forni, & Fivaz, 1989), in an approach that combines experimental and clinical research.

NEW TRENDS IN FRENCH RESEARCH ON MOTHER– INFANT INTERACTION

Even researchers on normal infant development first may have studied handicapped children. For instance, before turning to the study of communication between adults and young children, Deleau was involved in research on deaf children; he then came to a penetrating theoretical analysis of the role of language in interactive routines (Deleau, 1980), and of the development of symbolic activity (Deleau, 1988, 1990). In 1982, Deleau was a founding member of the *Groupe Francophone du Développement Psychologique de l'Enfant Jeune* (GROFRED), which associates clinicians and experimentalists working on infancy.

Since the early 1980s, a number of French researchers have developed empirical work on parent–infant interaction. Marcos, for example, has investigated the transition from nonverbal to verbal communication, showing how infants use pitch variations in early communication (Marcos, 1987), and how early fixed routines develop into flexible strategies in preverbal expressions of request (Bernicot & Marcos, 1990). Rabain-Jamin has questioned the universality of interaction processes, like responsiveness, found in Western infant research. Studying African immigrant samples, she has shown how the role attributed by the mothers to objects, and the content expressed in their language, are highly culture-dependent (Rabain-Jamin, in press). In a Vygotskian perspective, Moro and Rodriguez (1989) have extended the notion of semiotic mediation to objects and practices involved in mother–infant interactions as early as 9 months of age.

We now briefly present some data from our own work, as examples of the historical tendency of French research to focus on specificities and individual differences, rather than on means, which risk being interpreted as norms. The first example presents tentatives of assessing the effects of various types of maternal interventions on infant's attention; the second concerns the role of fathers in toddlers' cognitive development.

THE IMPACT OF MATERNAL FOCUSING BEHAVIOR ON INFANT ATTENTION

In order to go beyond the assumption of a global effect of social environment on infants' cognitive development, specific effects of parental educational practices may be demonstrated (Bornstein, 1989a). It has been shown, on various samples of 5-month-old infants (Bornstein, Azuma, Tamis-LeMonda, & Ogino, 1990; Bornstein & Tamis-LeMonda, 1990; Bornstein, Tamis-LeMonda, Pêcheux, & Rahn, 1991; Findji, Pêcheux, & Ruel, 1993; Pêcheux, Findji, & Ruel, 1992), that the total duration during which mothers mobilize their child's attention on objects is correlated with the total duration during which the infants actually concentrate their attention on objects. Moreover, the duration of maternal behavior at 5 months is correlated with the infant's behavior at 8 months. Thus, it may be considered that as long as the infant is not able to self-monitor his or her attention, the mother may scaffold this growing ability. Maternal mobilizing, however, lasts about 10% of 1 hour of observation, whereas infant focusing lasts 34% of the total time at 5 months, and 48% at 8 months. In order to provide additional support for the role of mother in the infant's attentional behavior, we studied the sequential organization of both behaviors and looked for the timing that enables maternal interventions to be efficient.

We analyzed occurrences of mothers' target behavior to investigate, first, what the infant's ongoing activity is when the mother starts mobilizing his or her attention, and second, whether the maternal intervention has an effect on the infant's activity.

Concerning the first point, three situations may be individualized: The child's attention was not focused on any target when the mother started focusing attention, or the child was already attending to the object the mother is using, or the child was attending to another object. In the first case, the mother actually mobilizes a floating attention; in the second, she helps the child to maintain his or her attention; in the third, she interferes in an ongoing activity to redirect it. At 5 and 8 months, maternal focusing of her infant's attention on objects happens mostly when the child's attention is not focused. However, nearly half of the occurrences take place when the child is already busy. Moreover, large differences among mothers are observed: Some help more than they mobilize; some do the opposite. As a mean, interfering is as frequent as helping, but at 8 months, the distribution varies with the locomotor abilities of the infant. Although the frequency of helping is the same in the two groups, for locomotor infants mobilizing occurrences are less frequent and interfering increases: Here, interfering obviously means redirecting the infant's attention away from a forbidden object. Such data show that the didactic component of maternal interventions needs to be qualified: One may wonder whether interfering brings information to the infant, and further elaboration on the length of mobilizing occurrences must test how supportive they are. In any case, maternal focusing must be evaluated in relation to the infant's ongoing activity.

How efficient can maternal focusing be? Immediate effects are the most obvious, when the infant focuses his or her attention on the object the mother is currently using, or using a few seconds after. In a second category, the child may attend to the object after a delay, in which case it is the infant who decides to focus his or her attention on an object that the mother has put at his or her disposal. Last, the maternal behavior may have no effect at all. We find that, on average, one third of focusing occurrences are efficient immediately after being performed. For another third, the infant gets interested in the object referred to by the mother after a delay of at least several minutes. Can such occurrences be termed efficient, even though, in this case, it is the infant who has mobilized his or her attention? Once again, large differences between dyads are observed.

These two sets of data show how global the index of total length of maternal attention focusing is, and how the same value may correspond to several strategies. A given duration may correspond to the repeated presentation of the same object, or to brief presentations of various objects. Mothers who score the highest at efficiency do not have the longest total duration of intervention; mothers who are more helpful and who elaborate several times on the same object may have more effect on their child's acquisition of attentional self-control. Further elaborations are now being performed, that consider the child's activities corresponding to various types of mothers. Results presented here are given as an example of a tentative effort to reach the complexity of the mother–infant interaction.

FATHERS' PLAY WITH TODDLERS: CREATION, RECREATION, AND TEASING

In the samples we have observed, both parents work full time, and fathers are significantly involved in infant caregiving. As a consequence, father–infant interaction should be studied as well as mother–infant interaction. If the maternal model is taken as a norm, however, fathers will be evaluated as "more" or "less" than mothers, and paternal specificities will not be able to be demonstrated. For instance, a common procedure in studying mother–infant interaction, which was adopted for studying father–infant interaction as well, is play with familiar objects having a canonical use: a tea set, a telephone, and a toaster (Belsky,

Goode, & Most, 1980; Power, 1985; Power & Parke, 1983). Such objects constrain what may be done, because some uses and combinations are very salient. We may consider such settings to enhance only a few types of play; thus, no wonder paternal play resembles maternal play, including demonstrations and symbolic play: What else can be done with such objects? If we want evidence of paternal specificities, then we have to observe parents in a situation that fosters a wider range of behaviors. We hypothesized that fathers initiate nonconventional play more than mothers, and thus broaden their children's experience. This hypothesis is congruent with that of Pepler and Ross (1981), who argued that divergent play, implying several types of object manipulation, has positive effects on problem-solving abilities, enhancing a more creative and flexible cognitive processing.

Consequently, we introduced a set of objects with nonconventional uses, such as plain plastic containers fitting together, colored square sponges, plastic dishes (the kind used under house plants), sticks, rugs, styrofoam chips, and a teddy bear. These objects may be used in various ways: For instance, the sponges' texture may be tactually explored, or the sponges may be piled up, or one of them may be used to bathe the bear. Twenty 16-month-old infants were video-recorded while playing with their mother or their father. Play episodes initiated by the parents were coded into three categories. First, in focalizations, the parent attracts the infant's attention toward an object. Second, conventional play involves canonical aspects of objects and actions. Two types were distinguished: Functional play, including appropriate manipulations of a single type of object (piling up, fitting, filling, etc.); and relational play, mobilizing schemes that are commonly used (pouring from one container into another, feeding the bear). Finally, nonconventional play involved noncanonical aspects of objects and actions. In this, we distinguished creative play, relating objects in an unexpected way (e.g., filling the bear's sweater with chips), from recreational play, in which objects mediate social interactions and physical play (e.g., by throwing objects toward the other).

As expected, fathers initiated more nonconventional play than mothers, for creations as well as for recreation: Only fathers used chips as snow, and sticks as fencing foils. Thus, if the situation makes it possible for parents to display routines as well as new types of play, fathers choose the last strategy more often than mothers do. It may be argued that such nonconventional play has an important role in cognitive and social development. Creative play broadens the range of possible uses of an object, and adds to the maternal teaching of canonical use; canonical rules are questioned, which may be a second level of pretend play. In such actions, "meanings represented in play become increasingly detached from particular and immediately present situations, persons and objects" (Fein, 1979, p. 2). In recreational play, physical interactions reveal social interactions: Fathers tend to have more recreational play with boys, who learn through them their assigned sex role (Jacklin, DiPietro, & Maccoby, 1984). Therefore, it seems important to study nonconventional play—more typical of fathers—as well as conventional play.

Another paternal-specific behavior, which appears mostly during nonconventional play, is teasing (Labrell, 1992). We observed it fairly often in our sample, and mothers report it as a typical paternal behavior—of which they disapprove! It is not mentioned in the literature, however. This may be a consequence of the small number of studies on fathers, of the inescapable reference to mothers (and mothers do not tease), and, moreover, of an omission of any behavior that may be viewed as negative. We argue that teasing may have a structuring role in the infant's social and cognitive development, just as was shown for maternal responsiveness (Ainsworth, Bell, & Stayton, 1974; Bornstein, 1989b; Pêcheux, 1990).

Teasing may be defined as an interactive process between the infant and the parent, during which the child has to cope with a destabilizing stimulation that contradicts the rules previously fixed by the parent. Three types of teasing may be described: obstruction, innovation, and struggling. *Obstructions* consist in attempts to impede, bar, or stop the infant's ongoing activity. For example, the father surreptitiously blocks the opening of the container that the child is trying to fill with chips. *Innovations* refer to parental behaviors provoking surprise or bewilderment in the context of creative play. For example, after pretending the chips were snow, the father suddenly uses a sponge as a snowflake, which the child looks at with wide open eyes and mouth. *Struggling* also happens during physical games, when the object becomes a weapon or a challenge: The father throws sponges on his son, who seems to force himself to laugh, and comments "You are a tough guy, you!"

Teasing is not mere emotional destabilization. Novelty underlies teasing behaviors which, as well as destabilization, imply cognitive accommodative mechanisms. When the parent blocks the infant's ongoing activity, the infant has to elaborate solutions to by-pass the obstacle. Likewise, in the case of teasing innovations, the child has to cope with new rules for using objects, as in nonconventional play. Last, in struggling teasing, the parent pretends to set up a confrontation in a usually cooperative context. Novelty is basic to cognitive development, as intelligence is "the ability to deal with novel kinds of task and situational demands, and the ability to automatize the processing of information" (Sternberg, 1985, p. 68).

Moreover, unpredictability, which is typical of teasing, is considered by Deleau (1985) as an essential aspect of interactive routines: Unpredictability introduces playfulness and stimulates the infant's vigilance. Such an interpretation of teasing implies not a lesser, but a greater degree of control by the parent. Teasing may be a structuring stimulation, even if it is not "one step ahead" (Heckhausen, 1987): In a Vygotskian perspective, the parent requires of the child a performance that is one level up from what the child is able to perform alone.

Thus, we argue that taking into account the specificities of paternal contributions—namely nonconventionality and teasing—leads to a broadening, if not a basic change, in the factors that are invoked in explaining development.

CONCLUSION

To summarize, we argue that French empirical research on parent–infant interaction is well in progress, with its own specificities. Problems raised by the extension of daycare centers in France had to be solved first, and mothers needed to adjust between work and caregiving. Wallon's seminal insights are now operationalized, and French research has inherited his predilection for differences, Cartesian doubt, however is still at work in the French way of thinking, and parents, institutions, and even researchers are skeptical about the possibility of capturing objectively the essence of parent–infant interaction. The process of demonstration is now on the way.

REFERENCES

Ainsworth, M.D.S., Bell, S. M., & Stayton, D. J. (1974). Infant–mother attachment and social development: "Socialization" as a product of reciprocal responsiveness to signals. In M.P.M. Richards (Ed.), *The integration of a child into a social world* (pp. 99–125). London: Cambridge University Press.

Belsky, J., Goode, M. K., & Most, R. K. (1980). Maternal stimulation and infant exploratory competence: Cross-sectional, correlational and experimental analyses. *Child Development, 51,* 1163–1178.

Bernicot, J., & Marcos, H. (1990). Le développement des formes prélinguistiques de la demande: Adaptation à la situation sociale [The development of prelinguistic forms of request: How infants adapt to social contexts]. *Canadian Journal of Behavioral Science, 22,* 236–253.

Birns, B. (1972–1973). Piaget, J., and Wallon, H.: Two giants of unequal visibility. *International Journal of Mental Health, 1,* 24–28.

Bornstein, M. H. (1989a). Between caretakers and their young: Two modes of interaction and their consequences for cognitive growth. In M. H. Bornstein & J. S. Bruner (Eds.), *Interaction in human development* (pp. 197–214). Hillsdale, NJ: Lawrence Erlbaum Associates.

Bornstein, M. H. (Ed.). (1989b). *Maternal responsiveness: Characteristics and consequences.* San Francisco: Jossey-Bass.

Bornstein, M. H., Azuma, H., Tamis-LeMonda, C. S., & Ogino, M. (1990). Mother and infant activity and interaction in Japan and in the United States: A comparative micro-analysis of naturalistic exchanges. *International Journal of Behavioral Development, 13,* 267–287.

Bornstein, M. H., & Tamis-LeMonda, C. S. (1990). Activities and interactions of mothers and their first-born infants in the first six months of life: Covariation, stability, continuity, correspondence and prediction. *Child Development, 61,* 1206–1217.

Bornstein, M. H., Tamis-LeMonda, C. S., Pêcheux, M.-G., & Rahn, C. W. (1991). Mother and infant activity and interaction in France and in the United States: A comparative study. *International Journal of Behavioral Development, 14,* 21–43.

Brunet, O., & Lézine, I. (1951). Le développement psychologique de la première enfance [Psychological development in infancy]. Paris: Presses Universitaires de France.

Corboz, A., Forni, P., & Fivaz, E. (1989). Le jeu à trois entre père, mère et bébé: méthode d'analyse des interactions visuelles triadiques [Triadic play between father, mother, and infant: A method to analyze triadic visual interactions]. *Neuropsychiatrie de l'Enfance, 37*, 23–33.

Cosnier, J. (1983). Observation directe des interactions précoces, ou les bases de l'épigénèse interactionnelle [Direct observation of early interaction: The bases of interactional epigenesis]. *Psychiatrie de l'Enfant, 27*, 107–126.

David, M., & Appell, G. (1966). Etude de 5 patterns d'interaction entre mère et enfant à l'âge d'un an [Five patterns of mother–infant interaction at age 1]. *Psychiatrie de l'Enfant, 9*, 445–531.

Davidson, F. (Ed.). (1967). Infant psychology in the Department of Infant and Mother Protection [Special issue]. *Enfance, 3–4.*

de Ajuriaguerra, J. (1962). Le corps comme relation [The body as relationship]. *Revue Suisse de Psychologie, 21*, 137–157.

Deleau, M. (1980). Faire pour dire, dire pour faire: échanges précoces et débuts de la communication [Acting for talking, talking for acting: Early interactions and the beginning of communication]. In A.N.P.E.D.A., *L'enfant sourd avant 3 ans: Enjeu et embûches de l'éducation précoce.* Paris: CTNERHI.

Deleau, M. (1985). De l'interaction à la communication non verbale [From interaction to nonverbal communication]. In G. Noizet, D. Belanger, & F. Bresson (Eds.), *La communication* (pp. 243–270). Paris: Presses Universitaires de France.

Deleau, M. (1988). Interaction, imitation et communication non verbale du nourrisson [Interaction, imitation, and non-verbal communication in infancy]. *Psychologie Francaise, 33*, 37–44.

Deleau, M. (1990). *Les origines sociales du développement mental: Communication et symboles dans la première enfance* [Social origins of mental development: Communication and symbols in infancy]. Paris: Armand Colin.

Fein, G. G. (1979). Echoes from the nursery: Piaget, Vygotsky and the relationship between language and play. In E. Winner & H. Gardner (Eds.), *Fact, fiction, and fantasy in childhood* (pp. 1–14). San Francisco: Jossey-Bass.

Findji, F., Pêcheux, M.-G., & Ruel, J. (1993). Dyadic activities and attention in the infant: A developmental study. *European Journal of Psychology of Education, 8*, 23–33.

Gesell, A., & Thompson, H. (1934). *Infant behavior: Its genesis and growth.* New York: McGraw-Hill.

Jacklin, C. N., DiPietro, J. A., & Maccoby, E. E. (1984). Sex-typing behavior and sex-typing pressure in child–parent interaction. *Archives of Sexual Behavior, 13*, 413–425.

Heckhausen, J. (1987). Balancing for weaknesses and challenging developmental potential: A longitudinal study of mother–infant dyads in apprenticeship interactions. *Developmental Psychology, 23*, 762–770.

Kreisler, L., & Cramer, B. (1981). La psychiatrie du nourrisson [Infant psychiatry]. *Psychiatrie de l'Enfant, 24*, 223–263.

Labrell, F. (1994). A typical interaction behavior between fathers and toddlers: Teasing. *Early Development and Parenting, 3.*

Lebovici, S. (1983). *Les interactions parents–nourrisson et le psychanalyste: Les interactions précoces* [Parent–infant interaction and the psychoanalyst: Early interactions]. Paris: Le Centurion.

Lebovici, S., & Mazet, P. (1989). A propos de l'évaluation des interactions fantasmatiques [About the evaluation of fantasmatic interactions]. In S. Lebovici, P. Mazet, & J. P. Visier (Eds.), *L'évaluation des interactions précoces entre le bébé et ses partenaires* [Evaluating early interaction between infants and their partners]. (pp. 217–236). Paris: Eshel.

Lézine, I. (1955). Etude récente sur le développement de l'enfant en France: Attitudes des parents et comportements des enfants [Recent findings on child development in France: Parental attitudes and children's behavior]. *Mental health and child development.* London: Routledge & Kegan Paul.

Lézine, I. (1964). *Psychopédagogie du premier âge* [Infant psychopedagogy]. Paris: Presses Universitaires de France.

Lézine, I. (1985). Recherches sur la prime enfance en France [French research on infancy]. In R. Zazzo (Ed.), *La première année de la vie* [The first year of life]. (pp. 139–150). Paris: Presses Universitaires de France.

Lézine, I., Dubon, C., Josse, D., & Léonard, M. (1976). Etude des modes de communication entre le jeune enfant et l'adulte [A study of communicative modes between adults and young children]. *Enfance, 1–4*, 5–60.

Lézine, I., Robin, M., & Cortial, C. (1975). Observations sur le couple mère-enfant au cours des premières expériences alimentaires [Observations of mother–infant dyads during the first feeding episodes]. *Psychiatrie de l'Enfant, 18*, 75–147.

Lézine, I., & Stambak, M. (1959). Quelques problèmes d'adaptation du jeune enfant en fonction du type moteur et du régime éducatif [Infants' adaptive problems in relation to motor types and educational circumstances]. *Enfance, 2*, 95–115.

Marcos, H. (1987). Communicative functions of pitch range and pitch direction in infants. *Journal of Child Language, 14*, 255–268.

Maury, M., Visier, J.-P., & Montagner, H. (1989). Intérêt d'une approche intégrée psychiatrique et éthologique des interactions entre le bébé et sa mère et leurs dysfonctionnements [Advantages of an ethological and integrated psychiatric approach of mother–infant interactions and their troubles]. In S. Lebovici, P. Mazet, & J. P. Visier (Eds.), *L'évaluation des interactions précoces entre le bébé et ses partenaires* (pp. 71–98). Paris: Eshel.

Montagner, H. (1974). Communication non-verbale et discrimination olfactive chez le jeune enfant: Approche éthologique [Non-verbal communication and olfactory discrimination in young children: An ethological approach]. In E. Morin & M. Piatelli-Palmarini (Eds.), *L'unité de l'homme* (pp. 246–270). Paris: Seuil.

Montagner, H. (1978). *L'enfant et la communication* [Communication and the child]. Paris: Stock.

Montagner, H. (1988). *L'attachement, les débuts de la tendresse* [Attachment: The beginning of love]. Paris: Odile Jacob.

Montagner, H., Millot, J.-L., Fillâtre, J.-C., Cimaresco, A.-S., Bonnin, F., Rochefort, A., & Taillard, C. (1989). Approche expérimentale du système d'interaction entre le nouveau né et sa mère [An experimental approach of the interactional system between mother and infant]. In S. Lebovici, P. Mazet, & J. P. Visier (Eds.), *L'évaluation des interactions précoces entre le bébé et ses partenaires* (pp. 43–70). Paris: Eshel.

Moro, C., & Rodriguez, C. (1989). L'interaction triadique bébé-objet-adulte durant la première année de la vie de l'enfant [Triadic interaction between adult, infant, and object in the first year of life]. *Enfance*, 75–82.

Netchine-Grynberg, G. (1991). The theories of Wallon: From act to thought. *Human Development, 34*, 363–379.

Norvez, A. (1990). *De la naissance à l'école: santé, modes de garde et préscolarité dans la France contemporaine* [From birth to school: Health, caretaking, and preschool in contemporary France]. Paris: Presses Universitaires de France.

Pêcheux, M.-G. (1990). L'ajustement maternel: Un concept utile et flou [Maternal responsiveness: A useful but elusive concept]. *Année psychologique, 90*, 567–583.

Pêcheux, M.-G., Findji, F., & Ruel, J. (1992). Maternal scaffolding of attention between 5 and 8 months. *European Journal of Psychology of Education, 7*, 209–218.

Pepler, D. J., & Ross, H. S. (1981). The effects of play on convergent and divergent problem solving. *Child Development, 52*, 1202–1210.

Piñol-Douriez, M. (1984). *Bébé agi–bébé actif: l'Emergence du symbole dans l'économie interactionnelle* [Acted infant, active infant: The emergence of symbols in the organization of interactions]. Paris: Presses Universitaires de France.

Power, T. G. (1985). Mother– and father–infant play: A developmental analysis. *Child Development, 56*, 1514–1524.

Power, T. G., & Parke, R. D. (1983). Patterns of mother and father play with their 8-month-old infants: A multiple analysis approach. *Infant Behavior and Development, 6,* 453–459.

Rabain-Jamin, J. (1989). Culture and early social interactions: The example of mother–infant object play in African and native French families. *European Journal of Psychology of Education, 4,* 295–305.

Rabain-Jamin, J. (in press). Language and socialization in the child in African families living in France. In P. M. Greenfield & R. R. Cocking (Eds.), *Continuities and discontinuities in the cognitive socialization of minority children.* Hillsdale, NJ: Lawrence Erlbaum Associates.

Robin, M. (1978). Rôle des conduites maternelles sur la réactivité visuelle du nouveau-né à terme et prématuré [The role of maternal behavior on the visual reactivity of term and pre-term newborns]. *Psychiatrie de l'Enfant, 21,* 133–169.

Robin, M. (1980). Interaction process analysis of mothers with their newborn infants. *Early Child Development and Care, 6* 93–108.

Robin M. (1986). Les comportements tactiles de la mère à la maternité [Maternal tactual behavior at birth]. *Neuropsychiatrie de l'Enfance, 34,* 421–430.

Schaal, B. (1986). Presumed olfactory exchanges between mother and neonates in humans. In J. Lecamus & J. Cosnier (Eds.), *Ethology and psychology* (pp. 101–110). Toulouse, France: Privat.

Sternberg, R. J. (1985). *Beyond IQ: A triarchic theory of human intelligence.* Cambridge, England: Cambridge University Press.

Trevarthen, C. (1977). Descriptive analyses of infant communicative behaviour. In H. R. Schaffer (Ed.), *Studies in mother–infant interaction* (pp. 227–270). London: Academic Press.

Wallon, H. (1934). *Les origines du caractère chez l'enfant* [The origins of character]. Paris: Presses Universitaires de France.

Wallon, H. (1938/1982). La vie mentale [Mental life]. In *Encyclopédie Française* (Vol. 8). Paris: Larousse. Second edition, Paris: Editions Sociales.

Widmer-Robert-Tissot, C. (1981). *Les modes de communication du bébé: Postures, mouvements et vocalises* [Communicative modes in infancy: Postures, movements, and vocalizations]. Neuchâtel: Delachaux et Niestlé.

Winnicott, D. (1971). Le miroir de la mère et de la famille dans le développement de l'enfant.In D. Winnicott (Ed.), *Jeux et réalité* [Play and reality] (pp. 153–162). Paris: Gallimard.

21

From Dyadic To Triadic Relational Prototypes

Blaise Pierrehumbert
Elisabeth Fivaz-Depeursinge
Université de Lausanne

There is now a palpable transition process in the psychology of social interactions, from the study of dyadic toward the study of triadic patterns of relationships. Whatever the focus may be—observed or represented interactions—and whatever the domain—clinical or developmental psychology—the same transition is operating.

Of course, dyadic and triadic relationships are to be understood in a metaphoric sense, because isolating dyads or triads—as much as isolating monads or any kind of *n*-ads—is, in fact, illusory. As Winnicott (1958) put it, "There is no such thing as a baby" (p. 99): One should not expect to be able to study an infant as an individual, as an observation unit; rather, what we may observe is a "nursing couple," an "environment–individual set-up." At this point, one might ask whether any couple is not, in fact, a triad rather than a dyad, because it is not clear that we can exclude the observer from the dyad. Furthermore, it is no longer clear that we can exclude from a triad or from a polyad any person who, although not physically present, nevertheless counts, as a missing person, a desired or ignored person, ancestors, or a child to come.

We are obviously dealing here with models rather than with persons present in a setting. In fact, we could hypothesize that there are at least three levels in the models describing the relations between the individual and the environment: monadic, dyadic, and triadic kinds of models. In the monadic model of influence, the individual and his or her environment are interdependent, each one influencing the other. The social learning theory (Bandura, 1971) describes how the child learns by observing and imitating others, or by modeling on others; aggressive behavior, for instance, would increase if the child were exposed to others' aggression. In the dyadic model of interactions, one would suppose that the environment—which influences the individual—is precisely created, altered by the individual; this clearly involves the true notion of interaction. The caregiver influencing the infant is the one who has been influenced by the infant. The individual in such a model is an active participant in its own growth, corresponding to what Sameroff and Chandler (1975) called the transactional model of development.

Emde (1991) noted that the broad popular developmental theories have been oriented around primary caregiving relationships, and only recently has the clinical and the scientific literature widened our interests to, for example, fathering (see Parke, 1990) or to the marital relationships. These triadic kind of models should not be limited to the relationships with secondary caregivers, but should also extend to the consideration that, as Emde (1991) put it, relationships have an effect on other relationships. Dickstein and Parke (1988), for instance, showed how marital satisfaction can predict child–parent relationships.

If it was just the number of people in the spotlight that was at stake, we could go on the same incremental inventory toward *n*-ads, referring to the increasing complexity of interactions. However, our point of view is that there is some kind of theoretical discontinuity between the models describing influence, interaction, or transaction on the one hand, and what we refer to as *triadic models,* on the other. A true triadic model does not deal just with *n*-adic interactions, as if the triad were made of an addition of monads and dyads; rather, it would consider the triad as a unit in itself, with its own rules, especially concerning the relation between the global system and its subsystems. Our conviction is that there is currently a move in the scientists' and the therapists' popular models, toward triadic ones, and that there might be several possible rationales to such a move.

THE DEVELOPMENTAL SCOPE OF TRIADS

First, we should consider that the theoretical and clinical transition from dyadic to triadic relationships could reflect a developmental transition. According to psychoanalysis and to the broad developmental theories of the early and mid-20th century, such as Winnicott's, Piaget's, or Bowlby's, triadic relationships would represent a developmental achievement as compared to dyadic relationships, which are supposed to be more primitive. Winnicott (1957) suggested that, during the first stages of a child's development, an adequate mother will express love by organizing, in a significant and nonchaotic manner, her child's needs and feelings and the world around him or her through her basic care. Through "the day-to-day enrichment of the infant–mother relationship," the child becomes "a whole human being among whole human beings" (pp. 6–7), caught up in triangular relationships, with their share of love and hate. In the psychoanalytic tradition, dyadic relationships involving partial love-objects represent a necessary step for later triadic, oedipal relationships with whole human beings.

In turn, the oedipal triangulation will help the child to express his or her separate identity.

According to Piaget's constructivist theory, the ways in which children come to differentiate between the self and others run parallel to those processes involved in nonsocial cognition. Recognition that objects have a permanence and an existence of their own, differentiation of the self from the non-self, and decentration from an egocentric point of view are all processes involved in the construction of both the inanimate universe and the social universe. These processes condition the understanding of the viewpoints, emotions, thoughts, and intentions of the self and of others.

As a biologically oriented epistemologist, Piaget argued that there is a deep continuity between the individual's mental operations and social coordinations: "From a logical point of view [individual thought and interindividual regulation] are still dependent on the conditions of all general coordination of action and so have the same biological origins." (Piaget, 1976, p. 55). In short, mental coordinations would enable the child to develop full social interactions based on reciprocity and then ensure balanced dyadic relationships. Piaget underlined that individual cognitive operations and interindividual operations (cooperation, *stricto sensu*) are one and the same thing. Although he did not address the issue, we could further extend Piaget's constructivist perspective to make assumptions concerning triadic relationships: In a typical triangular setting, a social partner interacting with another might be taking into account all other possible interactions (i.e., between himself or herself and a second partner, as well as between the two partners themselves). From such a perspective, balanced triangular relationships would require much more complex coordinations than dyadic relationships necessitate, as, for instance, representing and anticipating possible—and not only of immediate—interactions and coordinating these interactions in a system surely more elaborate than that entailed in Piagetian mental reciprocity.

It appears, then, that triadic relationships would suppose elaborate internal representations of the self and of others, which is consistent with Bowlby's (1969) notion of working models of the attachment figures and of the self. That notion suggests, in a developmental perspective, how dyadic relations prefigure the development of later broader networks. The construction of a secure, stable, and predictable internal working model of the principal figure of attachment would enable the child to explore the social world and, later, to expand his or her social network.

However, not everybody is in agreement on a developmental perspective that supposes triadic relationships to occur relatively late. They might, in fact, appear much earlier. Melanie Klein (1975), for example, located the beginning of the oedipal conflict much sooner (i.e., in the second part of the 1st year) than was traditionally supposed. An opinion that is widespread among French psychoanalysts is that, on conception of the child, the third person—the father—is present, at least in the mother's fantasmatic interaction with her child to be born.

The father's presence is materialized, as Thys (1989) put it, in the placenta itself, which genetically contains the father's mark, making an early material and symbolic barrier between the child and the mother.

In sum, although there might be precocious triadic relationships, a classical interpretation considers the transition from dyadic to triadic interactions to reflect the developmental progression from early to later patterns of relationships. It appears especially relevant when we consider the growing interest in the life-span perspective, which requires multiple levels of analysis: individual as well as dyadic or triadic developmental pathways (Parke, 1988). Nevertheless, the broadening of the focus is probably not the only explanation for such a move. Additional causes could be envisaged, such as methodological, epistemological, cultural, or even psychological.

The transition of the focus from dyadic to triadic relationships might be interpreted as a methodological move from the study of simple social subsystems to the study of complex subsystems (Parke, Power, & Gottman, 1979). Just consider the hypothesis that some kind of triadic relationships, even if primitively organized, may exist in early developmental stages, and that triadic relationships are intrinsic to any social system. Subsequently, isolating dyads would correspond to an easy, however artificial and perhaps obsolete, procedure to cut through a complex structure in order to study smaller parts of it. Just as, from a methodological point of view, large units of observation cannot be reduced to merely the addition of more elementary units, the study of polyads becomes unavoidable (Minuchin, 1985). Moreover, we will not be able to avoid the study of larger units indefinitely, because simpler units—such as dyadic relationships —only exist in reference to a third party: a situation, a person, or an object. It may be hoped that this will lead us into a less "Victorian" era in psychological methodology.

If any relationship is potentially triadic, do these theoretical and methodological considerations satisfactorily explain why the history of psychology needed such a long time to envisage triadic interactions? The "eternal triangle," as Emde (1991) called it, actually represents an omnipresent theme throughout the ages, in literature or even in religion. Nevertheless, even if omnipresent, the theme has also constantly been avoided, as if our oedipally oriented culture preferred the intimacy of the dyad. In fact, psychological, cultural, and epistemological explanations of the move toward the triad also deserve to be mentioned briefly.

If we consider the hypothesis that the triad is intrinsic to all relations, we could suppose that this development, instead of moving from dyads to triads, proceeds through a differentiation of the triad into its dyadic and monadic components. Then, it might be that our traditional cultural models, highlighting the dyad, reflect only the most differentiated patterns—that is, dyadic patterns—which are probably more easily accessible to consciousness and to the thinking processes. The transition from the dyad to the triad would then reflect a psychological move of the consciousness toward more primitive aspects of the interaction processes.

Another point to make is that day-to-day life presses for an epistemological and cultural move. There is a deep evolution in the social, familial, and therapeutic interactional styles, and, whereas the dyadic model fits the values of the traditional society and culture, the triadic model perhaps better reflects present Western child-rearing routines, which are no longer limited to maternal care (Minuchin, 1985). Also, certain models, such as the systemic approach to families and social networks, broaden the understanding and treatment of symptoms, considering the individual and his or her environment as an interactional system. In fact, we suggest that the psychology of dyadic relationships is established on a traditional model of exclusive maternal care, in a context of parental affective specialization, associated with the allocation of work and social roles. If this metaphorical model is the prototype of the developmental theories, such as psychoanalysis and the theory of attachment, it probably is no longer adapted to multiple caregiving, shared among several people, inside and outside of the family, and favoring multiple attachment patterns. Similarly, the traditional clinical relationship, essentially dyadic, is now challenged by new prototypes of the therapeutic relationship.

Are these theoretical, methodological, psychological, cultural, and epistemological moves exclusive or complementary? Two research teams in Lausanne, each with its own theoretical and methodological background, share a similar interest in the issue and in the exploration of the functioning and dysfunctioning of the triadic pattern of social interactions. The next two sections of this chapter present these two perspectives, with empirical illustrations and considerations of the theoretical and clinical stakes associated with the transition toward triadic prototypes of relationships.

THE FAMILY: AN ADDITION OF DYADS OR A TRIAD?

Our observations of early parent–infant interaction in high-risk families (e.g., postpartum breakdown) in which both mother and infant are frequently hospitalized together, take place in a therapeutic consultation setting in the *Center for Family Studies,* which includes the semistandardized observation of the family's interactions and thus provides data for microanalysis. The clinical families (with an identified patient) come to this consultation with their therapist, whereas the nonclinical ones (without an identified patient) come on a voluntary basis. After the observation, they receive expert feedback in exchange for their collaboration in research. A detailed description of this important aspect is provided elsewhere (Fivaz-Depeursinge, 1991). The advantages of the combination of clinical and research considerations are manifold; in particular, the reciprocal relationship between the subjects and the professionals satisfies deontological concerns, while the clinical nature of the situation ensures the ecological validity of the data with regard to therapeutic concerns.

We refer to the systemic model of framing interactions (see E. Fivaz, R. Fivaz, & L. Kaufmann, 1982), which specifies the conditions favorable to the coevolution of a system in which one of the parties (here, the parents) has the function of framing the development of another (the child) in order to promote autonomization. In this context, autonomy should not be considered as opposed to dependency, but as a balance of control (between the child and his or her parents) that is constantly being readjusted to the growing capacities of the child (Wertheim, 1975). The family coevolutive system is considered both as a whole (triadic composite unit) and as a hierarchy between the parents and the child, because neither perspective taken separately is sufficient to account for the composite group's cooperation or for its capacity to promote autonomization. Two parameters characterize the properties of the framing interaction. They are the empirical notions of predictability and adjustment, which are frequently used in connection with parent–infant interaction. To speak of framing implies that the respective contributions of the two parties are carried out in an asymmetrical relation in which the framing system is more predictable and more adjusted than the one that is framed. From this interaction emerges a new systemic property, which we call the *alliance,* which is qualitatively new, irreducible to the sum of its components, and confers its identity on the composite system.

Microanalysis is primarily an exploratory method that applies to sets of single cases. It starts with the within-subject comparison, but it may proceed to between-subjects designs in reference to external variables. The data are selected from a sequence that is clinically significant and is transcribed as exhaustively as possible, in slow motion (in our studies, at half-second intervals). The analysis begins with the visual inspection of graphical data that preserve the temporal sequence; it proceeds with the computation of representative indexes of central tendencies and, if possible, with sequential analysis, in order to create taxonomies of interactions. Assuming that the most salient interactional contexts in parent–infant interactions are formed by nonverbal interactions, we have started with the microanalysis of these modalities and formulated the observed interactive patterns in terms of engagement versus disengagement.

Dyadic Subsystems in the Family

A first extensive study involved the microanalysis of holding and gaze interactions in 16 families (8 of which were in clinical consultation). The families were matched on educational level of both parents, and on gender and age of the infants. The infants were aged 5–13 weeks and were observed successively in interaction with their mother, their father, and a stranger. The detailed account of the notation (BTNS; Frey, Hirsbrunner, Florin, Daw, & Crawford, 1981), measures, and pattern analysis for holding and gaze interactions, as well as the results, are reported extensively by Fivaz-Depeursinge (1987, 1991). The study resulted in a typology of dyadic engagement in play dialogue. Dyads adopted one of the following three types, covering success to failure in mutual engagement: consensual, conflictual, or paradoxical engagement. In the *consensual* mode (typical for nonclinical parental dyads), the partners agree on the goal of their exchange and their behavior converges toward reciprocal engagement. In the *conflictual* mode (typical for stranger–infant dyads), the partners show some readiness to interact, but their goals diverge: one of them (the adult) offers to engage in dialogue, while the other one (the infant) refuses dialogue (at gaze level); in the *paradoxical* mode (typical of many clinical parental dyads), signals are mixed in such a way as to obscure the goal of interaction: incitements to engagement are mixed with signals that prevent it. With respect to the systemic property that emerges from interactions, it is the consensual and the conflictual modes of engagement that create the alliance (partial in the conflictual mode), whereas the paradoxical mode engenders a misalliance.

Empirically, the adoption of one of these types was demonstrated to depend, in the first place, on the adult's holding an offer and, in the second place, on the infant's gaze counter-offer (itself linked to the familiarity of the adult). In other words, there was a hierarchical relationship between the adult holding and the infant gaze. When results were compared between dyads as a function of the independent variables, in particular, clinical versus nonclinical status, some of them were puzzling. First, whether the parent did or did not have a psychiatric record did not entirely predict a dyadic engagement. Although most (but not all) clinical mothers engaged in paradoxical interactions with their children (a few of them engaged in consensual interaction), two thirds of the fathers in clinical families engaged in paradoxical interactions—and none of the fathers had a psychiatric record. In addition, a few non-clinical parents engaged conflictually or paradoxically. These differences obviously were not attributable to the child, because the children in the paradoxical parental dyads were able to engage in a more appropriate way with the stranger (either consensually or conflictually, depending, in part, on their age). In fact, in two thirds of the families, parental dyads (infant with father and infant with mother) were both either consensual or paradoxical, and the kind of engagement with both parents predicted the engagement with the stranger (conflictual or consensual). Thus, we hypothesized the presence of some kind of organization at a higher degree than dyadic organization. As a support for a triadic kind of family organization, there are empirical considerations suggesting that the interaction of the parental dyads might be different when they are observed separately versus within a triadic setting (Pedersen, 1980), because the parents would then have to combine their behaviors in order to frame their infant together. Would one of them compensate for the influence of the other, or would they reinforce each other? In other terms, what would be the triadic outcome of the separate dyadic alliances and misalliances? A review of the literature pointed to the importance of this issue, but the methods to date have not focused on the triad as a whole, but rather on its dyadic components (Parke, 1990).

The Family as a Triadic System

Our approach to this admittedly complex problem was, on the one hand, to narrow down to directly observable interactions and, on the other hand, to deliberately neglect the differences between parental roles. Thus, we considered the interaction in terms of collaboration between two functionally interchangeable parents. Theoretically (see Corboz et al., 1989) we differentiate two positions for the parents in relation to the child:

1. *The third party—parent–infant dyad* position. The third party (one of the parents) frames the dyad formed by the other parent and the child; the third party maintains throughout the exchange a position that is sufficiently external to ensure a primary focus on the interaction itself, rather than on the individual behavior of either party (predictability parameter). In the meantime, he or she also remains ready to adjust his or her behavior to the temporary states of the dyad (adjustment parameter).
2. The *parental couple–child* position. The parental dyad frames the child, and both parents interact directly with the child. They coordinate their behavior and adjust to the child's orientations toward either of them. Clearly, it is only progressively that the infant becomes able to focus his or her attention on the interaction between his or her partners and to participate as a partner in his or her own right. In this regard, the position in which both parents interact directly with the infant is pre-eminently triadic.

A situation of observation was set up (Corboz, Forni, & E. Fivaz, 1989) that enacts these positions among the partners. In practice, the trio is seated in a triangular formation and the parents are instructed to play with their child in three successive phases: One of them plays with the baby and the other one is simply present (Phase 1); the parental roles are reversed (Phase 2); and finally, they play together with the baby (Phase 3). The data of 30 clinical and non-clinical families have been microanalyzed, and a longitudinal study is in progress.

As in the dyads' study, the microanalysis of body and gaze interactions evidenced the presence of some hierarchical organization between these two modalities (asymmetry of the temporal sequences). In addition, however, the partners and the dyads themselves were engaged in hierarchical framing systems, such as a partner or a dyad with an asymmetrical framing relation (predictable and adjusted) with another partner or dyad. Likewise, the triadic engagement can be described in terms of consensual, conflictual, and paradoxical modes (Corboz-

Warnery, 1991; Gertsch Bettens, Corboz-Warnery, Favez, & Fivaz-Depeursinge, in press). An isomorphism between dyadic and triadic functioning does not prevent moving beyond the additive model of dyads, however. The addition of the components does not equate the triadic product due to the moment-to-moment spatiotemporal coordination of the components. Because the format of this chapter excludes a detailed demonstration, we use two examples chosen from current analyses to illustrate this argument.

First, the body and gaze modalities in this situation are hierarchically ordered, as in the study of dyads. Consequently, criteria of body proxemics as necessary conditions for the triadic gaze engagement have been defined, but they are much more complex than those that preside over the realization of dyadic engagement. For instance, it is not sufficient to consider separately the body address of each of the parents in relation to the child. It is also necessary to consider the relative alignments of the parents' bodies: their alignment to each other as well as their equidistance in relation to the child are found to be necessary (but not sufficient) conditions for the triadic gaze engagement. Therefore, the separate consideration of either parent with the child and of the parental dyad is not sufficient to account for the triadic coordination. The same argument holds when one considers the quasi-dyadic phases of the observation setting (Phases 1 and 2) versus the preeminently triadic one (Phase 3). The success or failure of the dyadic engagement during the quasi-dyadic phases has been found not to predict the success or failure of the triadic engagement during Phase 3. However, the predictive power is much higher when the quality of engagement of the third party during these apparently quasi-dyadic phases is also taken into account. Again, it is the three-some's composite coordination that is pertinent here. In other words, the triadic alliance emerges out of the combination of all contributions considered together, as opposed to their addition. To summarize, it is worthwhile to take up the challenge of studying the complexity of the triad, provided that appropriate means exist. The systemic theory, in combination with an appropriate clinical setting and the microanalytic method, prove to be useful in approaching such a complex domain.

MULTIPLE CAREGIVING AND THE TRIADIC PROTOTYPE

Fathering, as a spreading practice, has tended to become a recognized value in most of our modern industrialized societies. The growing interest for within-family triangular patterns of relationships might not be independent of such an evolution. However, triangular patterns of child care also extend outside of the family. The constantly increasing rate of women being employed outside the home, in most cases associated with too-short parental leaves, as well as the growing number of single-parent families, induce multiple caregiving, which also implies triangular patterns of relationships in early childhood involving parental and nonparental caregivers. That evolution has given rise to an accentuation of the ambivalence between two cultural and spontaneous models of infant care: the dyadic model, with exclusive parental care (not differentiating between fathering and mothering), and the triadic model (in the metaphorical sense), which acknowledges multiple and nonparental caregiving.

Such ambivalence may be expressed by the parents or by other caregivers and can also be identified in social policies concerning early childhood. It can also be reflected in ideological polarizations; for instance, it is usual now in Western countries, for people of the working class to favor parental care, whereas people with higher social status favor early group care in day-care centers (Broberg & Hwang, 1991). Ambivalence between these two models also imprints the style, training, and attitudes of nonparental caregivers: Whereas the first model would advocate caregiving as substitute mothering, the second would favor professionally oriented caregiving promoting children's education and socialization, and would be seen as complementary to parental care. When faced with an increasing demand, public authorities often hesitate between the two choices reflecting these two models: whether to extend parental leave or to increase the provision of child-care services.

The balance between these two models, then, has a strong impact on the daily life of most parents and young children of Western countries, because it deeply inspires not only private decisions concerning child care, but social policy choices, as well. These choices and their corresponding models certainly concede too much to ideological beliefs, and efforts have recently been made around the industrialized world to provide some scientific evidence in the field. With that perspective, a team at the Lausanne Child Psychiatry Department undertook a longitudinal project on the implications of nonparental care in the early development of the child.

The Longitudinal Child-Care Study

The study was based on naturalistic observation of 50 children (from birth to 5 years of age) with varying experience of care. It has provided some indications of the difficult attainment of a balanced pattern of triangulation, for the children, as well as for the caregivers. From 6 to 24 months of age, the children (two thirds of whom had some experience of nonparental care) were observed every 3 months with the mother and the nonparental caregiver, at the beginning and at the end of the day, and every 6 months they were observed in a strange situation-like setting, involving a brief separation, a reunion with the mother, and contact with a stranger. Ainsworth, Blehar, Waters, and Wall's (1978) interactive scales were used for the codings. The data illustrated the precarious transition between dyadic and triadic prototypes of relationships (Pierrehumbert, Bettschart, Frascarolo, Plancherel, & Melhuish, 1991; Pierrehumbert & Robert-Tissot, 1988).

First, we wanted to know whether children who experienced nonparental day care presented exclusive or multiple attachment patterns. We found (Pierrehumbert et al., 1991) that the intensity of positive social contacts with the mother remained higher than those directed toward the nonparental caregiver throughout the first 2 years of life. We also found that the intensity of positive behaviors with the nonparental caregiver were rated as closer to those directed toward a total stranger rather than to those directed toward the mother, at least in the 2nd year of life. This suggests that young children—given the specific conditions of our sample—who experience multiple caregiving, are far from establishing multiple (triadic) attachment relationships in the 2nd year. If children do not establish true triadic relationships during the 2nd year, we can ask whether the relations with the primary and with the secondary caregivers are related in some way. We could expect that a good relation with the principal caregiver would help the child to develop positive relations with the nonparental caregiver. In the 2nd year of life, when both the mother and the nonparental caregiver were present in the setting, the positive behaviors directed toward these two partners were not correlated. Therefore, in their 2nd year, children seem to treat their principal and secondary caregivers in an exclusive way: There are neither competitive nor matched behaviors to the child's two partners. In their 1st year, however, children tended to show a triadic-undifferentiated pattern (at 6 months, the correlation between the behaviors directed toward the child's two partners was high: .62). Then, the development seems to go toward a differentiation of the relationships (the correlation dropped to .00 at 24 months).

It is interesting to find such a dramatic decrease in the correlation of the behaviors directed toward the primary and the secondary caregivers, at the time when—according to Bowlby (1969)—an exclusive attachment with a primary caregiver is being formed. There is a differentiation of the relationships that is not without analogies with reference to the particularization of the attachment patterns with the father and with the mother in the 2nd year. There is a certain amount of empirical evidence that the quality of attachment with the caregivers can be reduced neither to the individual temperament nor to a particular trait of the child. Rather, investigators like Belsky and Rovine (1987) found no correlation, at 12 months of age, in the attachment relationships with the mother and the father: An infant can be insecure with the mother and secure with the father. Goossens and van IJzendoorn (1990) have also shown the absence of correlations between attachments to the parents and to nonparental caregivers. It could be that the nonparental—but familiar—caregiver, instead of representing a substitute figure might represent a complementary, or even a compensatory figure.

If there is a differentiation of the relationships with distinct caregivers during the 2nd year, a further question is to know how the relationships with nonfamiliar people evolve. We can ask, especially, whether the relationship with the primary caregiver represents a positive condition for the establishment of good relationships with other people. The attachment theory predicts that a positive relationship with the principal caregiver would help the child to become more open toward other people. Again, we found, in the first 2 years of life, a developmental decrease of the correlation between the social behaviors directed toward the mother and the strangers when they were observed in the same setting. Of course, this is not inconsistent with the attachment theory, because a positive and secure relationship with the principal caregiver does not imply that the child would be more open with strangers in the 2nd year—quite on the contrary. According to Ainsworth et al. (1978), in the strange situation, securely attached children may not be as friendly with the strangers as some insecure-avoidants. Only later, at preschool age or even later, children who have experienced a positive relationship with the principal caregiver may prove to be more open to others.

This was confirmed by another study (Pierrehumbert, Iannotti, Cummings, & Zahn-Waxler, 1989), in which a secure relationship with the mother in the 2nd year predicted higher social responsiveness with peers, up to 3 years later. The same study suggested that children with a secure relationship were more likely to behave in a triadic manner than other children. They showed more positive behaviors toward the mother as well as toward their playmate in the same free-play session, whereas the general trend was to a negative correlation between the social behaviors directed toward the mother and toward the playmate. If a secure relationship with the primary caregiver, giving shape to an internal model of a predictable and undisrupted caregiving relationship, represents an important con-tributing factor for later social development, we then wondered whether the experience of multiple caregiving in the first 2 years would represent an aversive factor—because it involves disruptions in parental care—or, on the contrary, a positive factor regarding later socialization, in providing stimulating social expe-riences. Comparative data (Pierrehumbert, 1992) between children with different experiences of nonparental care showed that those with a collective kind of secondary care (day-care center) initiated in the 1st year, showed more dependent behaviors with the mother in the 2nd year when facing slightly stressful experi-ences (i.e., the strange situation). They were more anxious on separation, looked more than other children to be comforted on reunion, and were more apprehen-sive with strangers.

If children who experience a collective form of nonparental care early in their development appear to be more dependent on the mother and more wary of other people in their 2nd year, we can wonder whether this pattern persists later in their development. When we observed children at the beginning of school age (about 5), those who experienced multiple caregiving in their first 2 years presented, in fact, a reversed tendency (Grimm, 1992). They appeared socially more open than other children to extended social relationships, especially with their peers.

Quality of Dyadic Relationship With Primary Caregiver and Peer-Group Experience as Predictors of Later Triadic Relationships

As a whole, these data appear to be consistent with the model of a developmental transition from dyadic toward triadic relationships. We found evidence of a strong dyadic relationship with the primary caregiver during the 2nd year. This dyadic relationship does not appear to be hampered when children have secondary, nonparental caregivers, and it might even be reinforced. Later, through the preschool years, children become progressively more open to other people. Relationships with peers, to some extent, might be prepared through the child's experience with his or her primary caregivers (mother and father, indistinctively) as providers of emotional security. A strong attachment in the first 2 years, consistent with Bowlby's theory, would be beneficial for later socialization— and, therefore, autonomization. The early experience of the peer group in collective day-care settings does not seem to restrain either relational security or later social development. However, during the first 2 years, children do not seem to be able to establish true patterns of triadic relationships with their different caregivers. This question is critical, because modern education, family, and economical constraints expect children to be placed at earlier and earlier ages in extended social settings and experience what psychologists from Nordic countries have called a pattern of *dual socialization*. If these authors, such as Langsted (1992), explicitly refer to a dual, and not triadic socialization process, is that because the child is unable to enter into real triadic relationships with his or her principal and secondary caregivers, at least in the first two years of life? What makes him or her unable to do it?

The Triadic Negotiation in Early Childhood

We conducted observations in triadic settings involving the infant, a familiar caregiver, and a parent, when arriving and when leaving the day-care setting. These episodes represent the prototypical situation of multiple caregiving. We, therefore, expected these settings to reveal the typical problems that the child has to face. We highlight several negotiation patterns of the triadic situation (Pierre-humbert & Robert-Tissot, 1988). The child often showed signs of a conflictual mode of control of the situation, especially at the level of proxemic interactions. This resulted in distorted transactions between the three partners. The child often seemed to avoid being confronted with both adults simultaneously; nevertheless he or she was able to enter into separate successive relationships. A typical strategy for the child in the triadic setting is *relational exclusion:* The child seems to provoke the parent by reversing the usual pattern of relationship, appearing to show a preference for the caregiver; the parent then fails to enter the dyadic relation between the child and the caregiver. Another strategy for the child is the *relational splitting:* The parent functions as a secure base, encouraging the contact with the secondary caregiver, but the child fails to activate what Bowlby called an *exploratory behavioral system,* vanishing and evacuating himself or herself from the relationship with the caregiver. A third example of strategies used is *relational withdrawal:* The child withdraws from the relationships and adopts a passive behavior, being picked up by the parent or the caregiver, showing no reaction and not asking for comfort from either adult. Not only children, but also adults, can experience trouble in finding their specific place in that kind of triangular network. As Mellier (1991) observed, there is frequently a competing pattern of relationships between parents and caregivers. One reason could be that both the parents and the caregivers stick to a maternal model of caregiving. From that point of view, one should avoid perceiving professional caregivers—and they should avoid perceiving themselves—as substitute mothers.

CONCLUSION

We report the presence of a tangible transition in the field of psychology toward the study of triadic patterns of interactions. We have questioned whether this could simply reflect a change in the focus regarding development, or whether this was significant of a methodological, or even of an epistemological move, associated with psychological and cultural factors. We have brought forward some data from the Lausanne Child Care Study, empirically supporting the model of a developmental transition from dyadic toward triadic relationships during the preschool years. These data were consistent with the classical notion of a developmental move from simple, dyadic-like relationships to later, more open and triadic-like relationships. This might be an indication that mastering triadic rules supposes an emotional and relational maturity that can be achieved through the experience of satisfactory dyadic relationships. The notion that the interest for triadic models reflects, in some way, a developmental move is here strengthened.

However, the contribution of the Lausanne Center for Family Studies is the description of how dyadic relationships in the family are constructed within a triadic context. It appears that the child reacts to some aspects of the dyadic relationship between the parents. For instance, if the parental dyad is conflictual, the child may not be able to establish differentiated dyadic relationships with each of the parents. In order for the triad to provide a favorable context within which the child can build dyadic relationships, the parental dyad should consti-tute, in some way, a framing context for the child; hence, parents should interact inside the family setting in a triadic instead of in a dyadic way. From this point of view, the triad does exist at the beginning of the construction of social relation-ships, with its own specific functioning rules that cannot be reduced to an addition of dyadic rules.

Then, if the triad already shapes early relationships, there is undoubtly some resistance to entering triadic patterns of interaction. Not only young children in their first 2 years may feel more comfortable with dyadic relationships; adults themselves may seek refuge in such patterns. However, it is not impossible that, under pressure of living conditions and of changing cultural values, there will be some kind of *psychological* changes. Such an evolution would involve the care-givers' (parental and nonparental) *internal working models,* or representations of the self and others in relationships. Perhaps we are already in the process of a deep psychological move toward triadic representational models of relationship. Representations surely influence adults' attitudes in triadic situations, such as the multiple caregiving setting, and hence the children's ability to cope successfully in such settings. Our hypothesis, then, is that both parental and nonparental caregivers' internal triadic representations could be essential in ensuring a relational continuity for the child, helping him or her in building stable and reliable internal models of the self and of others.

ACKNOWLEDGMENTS

Studies reported in this chapter were conducted at the *Centre d'Etude de la Famille and at the Service Universitaire de Psychiatrie de l'Enfant et de l'Adolescent*, and were supported by the Swiss National Science Foundation: Grants #1.634-0.77, 3.903-0.80, 3.903-0.82, 3.890-0.85, 3.923-0.87, 32-028.749, and 3.984-0.84, in collaboration with A. Corboz-Warnery, C. Gertsch Bettens, W. Bettschart, and C. Robert-Tissot.

REFERENCES

Ainsworth, M. D., Blehar, M. C., Waters, E., & Wall, S. (1978). *Patterns of attachment: A psychological study of the strange situation.* Hillsdale, NJ: Lawrence Erlbaum Associates.
Bandura, A. (1971). *Psychological modeling, conflicting theories.* Chicago: Atherton.
Belsky, J., & Rovine, M. J. (1987). Temperament and attachment security in the strange situation: An empirical rapprochement. *Child Development, 58,* 787–795.
Bowlby, J. (1969). *Attachment and loss: Vol. 1. Attachment.* New York: Basic Books.
Broberg, A., & Hwang, C. P. (1991). Day care for young children in Sweden. In E. C. Melhuish & P. Moss (Eds.), *Day care for young children* (pp. 75–101). London: Routledge.
Corboz, A., Forni, P., & Fivaz, E. (1989). Le jeu à trois entre père, mère et bébé: Une méthode d'analyse des interactions visuelles triadiques [The Lausanne Triadic Play between father, mother and baby: A method of analysis of Triadic Gaze Interactions]. *Neuropsychiatrie de l'Enfance, 37,* 23–33.
Corboz-Warnery, A. (1991). Encadrement et stratégies parentales dans le jeu à trois entre père, mère et bébé [Framing and parental strategies in the Lausanne Triadic Play between father, mother and baby]. *Cahiers critiques de thérapie familiale et de pratiques de réseaux, 13,* 141–156.
Dickstein, S., & Parke, R. D. (1988). Social referencing in infancy: A glance at fathers and marriage. *Child Development, 59,* 506–511.
Emde, R. N. (1991). The wonder of our complex enterprise: Steps enabled by attachment and the effects of relationships on relationships. *Infant Mental Health Journal, 12,* 164–173.
Fivaz, E., Fivaz, R., & Kaufmann, L. (1982). Encadrement du développement, le point de vue systémique: Fonction pédagogique, parentale, thérapeutique [Framing of development, a systems perspective: Pedagogic, parental and therapeutic functions]. *Cahiers Critiques de Thérapie Familiale et de Pratiques de Réseaux, 4,* 63–74.
Fivaz-Depeursinge, E. (1987). *Alliances et mésalliances dans le dialogue entre adulte et bébé: La communication précoce dans la famille* [Alliances and misalliances in the dialogue between adult and baby: Early communication in the family]. Neuchâtel: Delachaux et Niestlé.

Fivaz-Depeursinge, E. (1991). Documenting a time-bound, circular view of hierarchies: A micro-analysis of parent–infant dyadic interaction. *Family Process, 30,* 101–120.

Frey, S., Hirsbrunner, H. P., Florin, A. M., Daw, W., & Crawford, R. (1981). A unified approach to the investigation of nonverbal and verbal behavior in communication research. In S. Moscovici & W. Doise (Eds.), *Current issues in European social psychology* (pp. 143–199). Cambridge: Cambridge University Press.

Gertsch Bettens, C., Corboz-Warnery, A., Favez, N., & Fivaz-Depeursinge, E. (1992). Les débuts de la communication à trois [The beginnings of Triadic communication: Gaze Triadic interactions between father, mother and baby]. *Enfance, 46,* 4, 323–348.

Goossens, F. A., & van IJzendoorn, M. H. (1990). Quality of infants' attachment to professional caregivers: Relation to infant–parent attachment and day-care characteristics. *Child Development, 61,* 832–837.

Grimm, S. (1992). *Attachement, modes de garde et développement social au début de l'âge pré-scolaire* [Attachment, context of care, and social development in early school years]. Unpublished manuscript, Université de Lausanne, Lausanne, Switzerland.

Klein, M. (1975). *La psychanalyse des enfants* [The psycho-analysis of children]. Paris: Presses Universitaires de France.

Langsted, O. (1992). Famille, politique sociale et accueil des enfants au Danemark [Family, social policy, and child care in Denmark]. In B. Pierrehumbert (Ed.), *L'accueil du jeune enfant: Politiques et recherches dans les différents pays* [Child care in the early years: Social policy and research in several countries]. (pp. 71–81). Paris: E.S.F.

Mellier, D. (1991). A la crèche, la place des trois partenaires, parents, enfants, professionnels [Three partners at the day care center: Parent, child, and caregiver]. *Dialogue: Recherches Cliniques et Sociologiques sur le Couple et la Famille, 112,* 49–57.

Minuchin, P. (1985). Families and individual development: Provocations from the field of family therapy. *Child Development, 56,* 289–302.

Parke, R. D. (1988). Families in life-span perspective: A multilevel developmental approach. In E. M. Hetherington, R. M. Lerner, & M. Perlmutter (Eds.), *Child development in life-span perspective* (pp. 159–190). Hillsdale, NJ: Lawrence Erlbaum Associates.

Parke, R. D. (1990). In search of fathers: A narrative of an empirical journey. In I. E. Sigel & G. H. Brody (Eds.), *Methods of family research: Biographies of research projects, Vol. I. Normal families* (pp. 154–187). Hillsdale, NJ: Lawrence Erlbaum Associates.

Parke, R. D., Power, T. G., & Gottman, J. M. (1979). Conceptualizing and quantifying influence patterns in the family triad. In M. E. Lamb, S. J. Suomi, & G. R. Stephenson (Eds.), *The study of social interactions: Methodological issues* (pp. 231–252). Madison: University of Wisconsin.

Pedersen, F. A. (1980). *The father–infant relationship: Observational studies in the family setting.* New York: Praeger.

Piaget, J. (1976). Biology and cognition. In B. Inhelder, H. H. Chipman, & C. Zwingmann (Eds.), *Piaget and his school* (pp. 45–62). New York: Springer-Verlag.

Pierrehumbert, B. (1992). Une étude longitudinale dans le contexte de la suisse francophone [A longitudinal study in the context of French-speaking Switzerland]. In B. Pierrehumbert (Ed.), *L'accueil du jeune enfant, politiques et recherches dans les différents pays* [Child care in the early years: Social policy and research in several countries]. (pp. 238–252). Paris: E.S.F.

Pierrehumbert, B., & Robert-Tissot, C. (1988). Etude longitudinale d'un groupe de bébés lors d'expériences quotidiennes de séparation et de réunions [A longitudinal study on separation and reunion episodes in early childhood]. *Enfance, 41,* 55–71.

Pierrehumbert, B., Iannotti, R. J., Cummings, E. M., & Zahn-Waxler, C. (1989). Social function-ing with mother and peers at 2 and 5 years: The influence of attachment. *International Journal of Behavioral Development, 12,* 85–100.

Pierrehumbert, B., Bettschart, W., Frascarolo, F., Plancherel, B., & Melhuish, E. C. (1991). A longitudinal study of infants' social-emotional development and the implications of extra-parental care. *Journal of Infant and Reproductive Psychology, 9,* 91–103.

Sameroff, A. J., & Chandler, M. J. (1975). Reproductive risk and the continuum of caretaking casualty. In F. Horowitz (Ed.), *Review of child development research* (Vol. 4, pp. 187–244). Chicago: University of Chicago Press.

Thys, B. (1989). Le placenta humain: Médiateur, protecteur, premier objet perdu? [The human placenta: Mediator, protector, first lost object?] In A. Bouchart, D. Rapoport, & B. Thys (Eds.), *Délivrances ou le placenta dévoilé* [Unveiled after-birth]. (pp. 107–140). Paris: Stock.

Wertheim, E. (1975). Person–environment interaction: The epigenesis of autonomy and competence: I. Theoretical considerations (normal development). *British Journal of Medical Psychology, 48,* 1–8.

Winnicott, D. W. (1957). *The child and the outside world.* London: Tavistock.

Winnicott, D. W. (1958). *Through paediatrics to psycho-analysis: Collected papers.* London: Tavistock.

22

Day Care and Social Competence in Preschoolers: Continuity and Discontinuity Among Family, Teachers, and Peer Contributions

Marc A. Provost
Université du Québec à Trois-Rivières

The increasing number of children attending child care during their preschool years has prompted developmental psychologists to study closely the effects of such arrangements on children's development. Concerns about the effects of day care spring from a generalization of Bowlby's (1969) theory of maternal deprivation that was originally proposed to define and explain the effects of more permanent separation. It was argued that the daily separation from the mother will render the child's attachment bonds to his or her mother insecure. Furthermore, it was feared that the intellectual stimulation that the child receives when he or she had to share the attention of one adult with peers would be diluted compared with the stimulation obtained at home with the mother. The voluminous research literature has been well reviewed by Belsky and Steinberg (1978), Clarke-Stewart and Fein (1983), and Provost (1980).

Francophone research literature on this topic has followed many pathways, some similar to the mainstream on socioaffective and intellectual development, some taking new points of view. This chapter deals with these aspects of research on effects of day care on child development in the Francophone world, mainly France and Quebec, with an emphasis on discontinuity and continuity between environments in which children live.

This chapter is divided into four parts. The first part deals with what can be grouped into more traditional research on motor, intellectual, and social development. In the second part, I look at the theme of discontinuity between day care and home and between day care and kindergarten. The third part provides an overview of research dealing with the continuity between children's relationships with their teachers and their mothers. This theme is reviewed using the framework of attachment theory. In the fourth section, I have selected the issue of

continuity between preschoolers' relationships with day-care peers and with siblings. These four parts are designed to give the reader new and promising
avenues in the study of children in day-care settings and are by no means an
attempt to make an exhaustive review of the literature.

THE EFFECTS OF DAY-CARE EXPERIENCE
ON CHILDREN'S DEVELOPMENT

This first topic is consistent with Anglo-Saxon research on the effects of nonparental care. The main issue here is whether daily care outside the child's own
home is good or bad for his or her development.

One of the first attempts to deal with the day-care topic in France came from
Irène Lézine, who used the developmental assessment scale she developed together with Brunet (Brunet & Lézine, 1951). She used this scale to compare the
development of day-care and home-care children. Her findings (Lézine, 1951)
suggested that day-care children were somewhat delayed in their play with toys,
their verbal development, and their toilet training. However, these results were
drawn from day-care centers that were not well organized in terms of caretakers'
knowledge of children's development. For example, Lézine and Spionek (1958)
felt compelled to recommend that teachers talk more to the children to facilitate
language development, as they observed that caretakers tended to talk to each
other instead of talking to the children.

Most of the so-called "first wave" of research (Belsky, 1984) showed few
inevitable deleterious consequences of day-care rearing. In fact, the type of
situation described by Lézine and her co-workers is now a thing of the past.
Teachers are nowadays much better trained, and day-care programs offer all sorts
of stimulations to children. Nevertheless, the debate about the possible adverse
effects of non-exclusively parental care has led researchers to new questions
addressing the issue of what type of rearing conditions are best for the development of preschoolers. This led to research to examine the possible effects of the
quality of day care, the social context, or the specific types of day care. Some
examples of these questions are found in the French literature.

Mermilliod and Rossignol (1974) analyzed medical reports of Parisian children to find which mode of care (home, nursery, family day care, or home with a
professional caregiver) seems best suited for child development. They concluded
that none of them was better than another, in itself, but that the socioeconomic
status of the family was the main predictive variable. According to these authors,
the care of mothers from the upper and middle classes was better care than any
other type of care, but in the lowest socioeconomic groups, the use of a day-care
center appeared to foster development. Although these results relied mostly on
medical data, with only partial assessment of psychological development, this
was consistent with Belsky and Steinberg's (1978) conclusions from their ex-

haustive review of the literature that children from poor socioeconomic conditions can benefit from out-of-home care.

Probably the best effort to compare different modes of care in France came from Balleyguier (1979, 1988, 1991), who included in her research design comparisons among age groups. Three groups of children were formed on the basis of a minimum of a 6-month in their present setting: a first group included children at a day-care center, a second group consisted of children who experienced family day care, and a third group contained children who lived exclusively at home with their mothers. Children of three ages were investigated: 9 months, 24 months, and 41–48 months.

Procedures included a structured interview with the mother or the caregiver and observations in the home setting. Measures included temperament, social relationships, negative reactions, childrearing environment, and the Baby's Day test devised by Balleyguier (1979), which measures some affective components of the child's personality.

A principal components analysis on the Baby's Day test yielded two factors: the Tension factor and the Development factor. Another principal components analysis on the childrearing environment measure identified four principal types: the overstimulating, the affectionate, the strict, and the understimulating environments.

Balleyguier also contrasted age levels. At 9 months, results showed that home-reared children were the most "uptight" of the three groups. On the other hand, day-care center children were scored as more passive when observed at the center than when seen at home. Social class did not make any difference. Children who experienced an affectionate childrearing environment were more controlled and less tense than children with an understimulating environment, who were observed as more passive. This last result can be paralleled with Baumrind's (1989) and Maccoby and Martin's (1983) data on parental attitude categories. In both cases, the children of affectionate but firm parents were considered socially competent.

The differences resulting from childcare settings found in the 9-month-olds were also found in the 2-year-olds. Home-care children were even more anxious, which corresponds, according to Balleyguier (1991), to the Terrible Twos period. The day-care center children were then more nervous at home and even more passive at the center. However, she pointed out a possible influence of the rearing setting. The affectionate style was predominant among mothers in the day-care center group, whereas the caregivers' predominant style was understimulating.

Finally, at 41–48 months, mothers' reports showed no significant differences between the three groups. Interestingly, teachers reported gender differences. Boys were more active and girls were more inhibited and submissive. This result was not confirmed by studies of social dominance by Strayer (1989), in which some girls were observed to be part of the dominant group.

These results seem to imply that children, even 9-month-olds, are quite sensitive to the quality of their environment and can adopt different behavioral strategies according to the setting they are in. This is consistent with the issue of continuity between home- and day-care that I discuss in the next section.

Balleyguier described French nurseries as "often a place where children were not stimulated very much" (Balleyguier, 1991, p. 43). She advocated better training programs for staff members to help them improve their understanding of children's needs. In Quebec, in a North American environment, things are looking somewhat different. Dumont, Provost and Coutu (1987) have demonstrated that time spent in non-university-based day-care centers is positively related— using partial correlation controlling for age—to cooperative and associative play, and negatively related to individual and self-centered activities. According to these authors, social experience is an important factor in establishing one's own social capacities and day-care centers are well suited to providing the necessary setting for this so-called "social" experience. The somewhat different findings of the two last studies suggest the importance of the social context in day-care programs and, thus, call for cross-cultural comparisons.

DISCONTINUITY BETWEEN ENVIRONMENTS

Discontinuity has often been used for referring to several dimensions of differences between the experiences of children at home and in day-care centers. The assumption underlying these differences is that differences imply discontinuity, and that discontinuity is disruptive to the development of young children (Long, Peters, & Garduque, 1985). This is consistent with the psychoanalytic (Erikson, 1963) or the ethological (Bowlby, 1969) theories of mother–child relationships, stating that discontinuity between types of care is disturbing for later socioaffective development. Unfortunately, research on the effects of day care is limited to comparing children who attend a day-care program and children who do not, without considering the daily passages between the two environments as an important variable.

Balleyguier (1991) has already shown that children change their behaviors from one setting to another. In an attempt to test empirically the influence of this daily passage between types of care, Provost, Garon, and LaBarre (1991) studied the social adjustment of preschoolers related to continuity between home and day-care centers. Over an 8-month period we coded social adjustment from free play sessions in day-care centers by observing, for each child, social participation, autonomy, and positive social expression with peers.

A global index of the difference between home and day care was computed to define *continuity*. The classification system for play objects, ESAR (Garon, 1985) was used to make an exhaustive list of play objects in each house and in the day-care center, and to determine which categories were best represented in each of these environments. A child who had play objects at home similar to those found in the day-care center received a low scores, whereas a child who lived in an environment very different from the day-care center environment received a high score on this index of continuity. Partial correlations controlling for age were computed between the difference index and the social adjustment measures. Positive relations were found between the difference index and cooperative play, associative play, autonomy, and positive expression of emotions with peers. These results imply that children with a high difference index were more likely to be observed in well-adjusted behaviors. This prompts the conclusion that some discontinuity between environments, at least as defined by play objects, may help children to develop a flexible behavioral repertoire and to facilitate the development of their social adjustment skills.

According to Provost et al. (1991), the assumption that discontinuity may be disruptive to the development of young children has to be tested at different age levels. The development of the mother–child relationship may need continuity between parental attitudes and environmental stimulations. However, this may no longer be true with preschoolers who are in the process of acquiring their autonomy and who need new stimulations as motivators to master this new developmental task.

The transition from preschool to school is another example of discontinuity in which children must adapt themselves to many different teachers and peers over a short period of time. In Quebec, a team of researchers is concerned with this transition. Because several studies have stressed the role played by adults' perceptions of the quality of their interactions with children, this team is involved in a project seeking information regarding kindergarten teachers' perceptions of day-care children (Baillargeon & Betsalel-Presser, 1988; Betsalel-Presser, Baillargeon, Romano-White, & Vineberg-Jacobs, 1989; Betsalel-Presser, Lavoie, & Jacques, 1989).

Kindergarten teachers were asked to complete a questionnaire measuring their perceptions of the capacities of adaptation and social competence of children who experienced a day-care center (Baillargeon & Betsalel-Presser, 1988; Betsalel-Presser, Lavoie, et al., 1989). The results suggest that teachers perceived these children as being able to adapt to school without major problems. Most of them (68%) also felt that day-care experience facilitates this adaptation (Baillargeon, Gravel, Larouche, & Larouche, 1989).

However, separate results for each scale must be taken into account to get a more accurate picture. On the one hand, teachers thought that children from day-care centers can manifest some interest and enthusiasm in activities and curiosity for the environment, but on the other hand, teachers perceived weaker concentration skills during organized activities in children who had experienced day-care centers.

Another important scale of the questionnaire was discipline. A majority of teachers had negative opinions about this issue. Most of them felt that children coming from day-care centers lacked discipline, did not respect the class rules, and challenged the teacher by creating their own sets of rules. Many teachers considered their work to have become more difficult because of this type of behavior. However, a small percentage of teachers did not see these difficulties and considered that these children respected the rules sooner than their only-home-reared peers because they had previously been exposed to group rules.

As for the social competence scale, teachers were generally positive in their assessment. They perceived these children as having a positive self-esteem, which was reflected in their ability to take initiative and to assume responsibilities and leadership. However, many of them displayed aggressive behaviors toward their peers. Finally, their relationships with their teacher was perceived, globally, as good.

Betsalel-Presser and her team concluded that there is a need to facilitate transition from care to education, and that this can happen only if teachers, caregivers, and parents act together toward this goal. However, there is still a need to understand the interaction that children have with these different participants.

QUALITY OF ATTACHMENT TO PROFESSIONAL
CAREGIVERS AND TO MOTHER

Few studies have been carried out to assess quality of attachment to professional caregivers, although this issue seems important if one considers the amount of time spent at the day-care center (Howes, Rodning, Galluzzo, & Myers, 1988; Sagi et al., 1985). Because children's attachment to caregivers may influence their socioemotional adaptation to a day-care center, research should take time to study children's networks of attachment relationships. This issue is also crucial for understanding the possible beneficial influence of day-care centers on certain types of children. For example, child–caregiver attachment may compensate, in certain circumstances, for insecure child–parent attachments (Goossens & van IJzendoorn, 1990; van IJzendoorn & Tavechhio, 1987).

Desbiens and Provost (1989, 1991) discussed this issue and reviewed the literature on the quality of attachment to professional caregivers. We argued that the relationship between a child and a teacher cannot be viewed as an attachment relationship in terms of the ethological control systems theory. We concluded that the commonly used assessments of attachment (i.e., the strange situation and the Q-sort), which have been validated for assessing child–mother attachment, may not adequately measure the quality of the infant–caregiver relationship. Thus, we developed a new questionnaire to assess quality of child–caregiver relationships considering the special context in which this relationship develops. The ultimate goal was to compare mother–child attachment and teacher–child relationship.

We followed the stages Waters and Deane (1985) used to develop their Q-sort test. However, our Q-set was 72 items long because we felt that a 100-item set would be too big a task for teachers to do for many children. The next step was to use this Q-set with teachers and professional observers to measure the psychometric qualities of the instrument.

A total of 22 teachers completed the set for 56 children from 3 to 5 years old twice during the year. Results show considerable psychometric qualities. The reliability score between the two sortings was good for the whole set, and consistency was also high ($\alpha = .87$, $p < .001$). The Q-sort was then divided into clusters to assess specific characteristics of the relationship. Six clusters were computed: Autonomy ($\alpha = .75$), Support ($\alpha = .60$), discipline ($\alpha = .82$), Attention ($\alpha = .54$), Social desirability ($\alpha = .77$), and Security ($\alpha = .70$).

A total of four specialists on day-care teachers' training were used to operationalize a good teacher–child relationship by sorting the items to describe the theoretically best relationship possible. The reliability of this composite was assessed by computing the mean intercorrelation among the scores. The Spearman–Brown was .90 ($p < .001$). As for Waters and Deane's Q-sort, the actual score of each child is the correlation between the 72 items as scored by the teacher and the mean score of items as scored by the specialists.

The final stages of development consisted in going back to the day-care centers, having new teachers answered the Q-set for each of the children they were in charge of, and observing their behavior with children to test the external validity. Correlations computed between behaviors and the six clusters showed considerable validity for the Q-sort.

Finally, correlations made between the attachment Q-sort from the mother and this next Q-sort from the teachers yielded an interesting and unexpected result: Analysis revealed no correlations between the two Q-sorts. Correlations between clusters of both Q-sorts are still to be computed, however.

These preliminary results imply that there is a discontinuity between the qualities of interactions the child has with his or her mother and his or her teachers. This is consistent with data from Goossens and van IJzendoorn (1990), who found that caregiver–infant attachment, as measured by the strange situation, to be independent of mother–infant attachment. Thus, children may develop different socioemotional relations with different adults. Consequently, out-of-home care may be beneficial to insecurely attached children in providing them opportunities to create secure socioemotional bonds with adults.

THE MUTUAL EFFECT OF PEERS AND SIBLINGS

This last transition was investigated by the Francophone team of Coutu, Provost, Pelletier, and Desbiens (1990), who argued that the quality of sibling relationships is seldom mentioned as a dependent variable, even though family relationships are considered to be one determinant of the development of social behavior.

The aim of our project was to compare the behavioral profile of preschool children in interaction with peers and with siblings. Two hypotheses were tested. First, social participation at home was related to social participation in the day-care center. Second, the quality of social interactions at home was compared with social competence in the day-care center. The sample included 24 children (12 girls and 12 boys) with a mean age of 54 months; all were from middle-class French-Canadian families with two children.

Observations at home were conducted during three 45-minute sessions, over a 4-month period. Each child was observed with his or her sibling and parents during a semistructured play session designed to keep all participants together. Behaviors of the focal child and of the sibling were scored using a social behavior check list. Observations at the day-care center were conducted during periods of free play. The focal child method (Altman, 1974) was used to collect each child's behavior during 2-minute sessions twice a week over an 8-month period. Children were observed in a random order determined at the onset of each session for a mean of 64 sessions. Observation scales were a modified version of Parten's (1932) Social Participation and Autonomy Scale, which was designed as a broad-band index of social adjustment in the classroom. At the end of the 8-month period, the two full-time teachers of each target child were asked to rank order their children according to a brief description of social competence. They also rated each child they supervised using the Preschool Behavior Questionnaire (Behar & Stringfield, 1974) and the Prosocial Behavior Questionnaire (Weir & Duveen, 1981). Three variables were considered for this analysis: the Anxious-Fearful and the Aggressive factors from the Behar and Stringfield's factor analysis, and the Prosocial factor from Weir and Duveen. Finally, each group member was rated on a 3-point continuum of attraction–rejection by other peers in the class (see Asher, Singleton, Tinsley, & Hymel, 1979).

In support of the first hypothesis, few cross-setting correlations were found between categories of social participation. This lack of consistency across settings may possibly be attributed to differences in the patterns of mixed-age (sibling) and same-age (peers) interactions. In addition, these results suggest that children use different behaviors according to contexts, and that broad-band measures of the quality of interactions are more advisable for a better understanding of cross-setting continuity in children's social behavior. Accordingly, the second hypothesis on quality of social interactions in both settings was well-supported by the results. For instance, the frequency of conflictual episodes with the sibling was positively associated with the frequency of aggression to peers, and negatively related to social competence with peers. Prosocial behavior at home was correlated with prosocial behavior with peers. The number of conflicts at home was negatively correlated with popularity in the peer group.

These results suggest that the quality of social competence shows a continuity across settings with all social partners. This is congruent with Hartup's (1983) suggestion that individual differences in preschool social behavior presumably reflect differences that depend, in part, on experience at home.

Coutu, Provost, and Pelletier (1991) studied the relation between the quality of sibling relationships and the experience in a day-care program. As in the previous studies, subjects were observed in three 45-minute semistructured play sessions at home in the presence of a sibling and parents. No differences were found between day-care and exclusively home-reared children on the quality of sibling interactions. However, exclusively home-reared children interacted more often with their sibling than did day-care children. These results suggest that the child-rearing setting is not a determining factor accounting for individual differences in children's social involvement with their siblings. Other factors, such as quality of child care, children's temperament, and positive family interactions, should be considered as highly determining of sibling relationships.

CONCLUSION

In this chapter, I have reviewed several dimensions of continuity and discontinuity in day-care rearing in the Francophone literature. Three aspects were considered. First, it appears that children experience setting discontinuity between home and day care, and between day care and kindergarten. Results from these studies suggest, however, that these discontinuities are not disruptive to the development of preschoolers. Children seem to experience discontinuity, also, between their relation with their mothers and their teachers, but the impact of such a discontinuity is not well documented. Finally, continuity exists between siblings and peers.

Most of the literature on day care has focused on the effects on children resulting from physical setting characteristics or adult characteristics and behaviors. The three sets of results discussed here suggest that children may, themselves, be a source of discontinuity, presenting different behaviors in different circumstances. They may alter their behavior depending on whether they are with their mothers or their teachers, so that answers to Q-sorts from the two adults are not related; they may also react to different behaviors from these two adults, who may have different views on interacting with children. They may also benefit from discontinuity between settings, and behave competently in day-care settings that are interesting simply because they are different from home. Finally, they may behave in the same way with siblings and peers, because these social partners share the same norms of social interaction.

As several reviewers (Belsky, 1988; Caldwell & Freyer, 1982; Clarke-Stewart, 1988; Long et al., 1985) have pointed out, we know little about the process of day care. As Long et al. concluded, research should observe the same children across settings to assess what kinds of discontinuities or continuities exist and what impact they really have on children's social adaptation to day care. This is crucial if we want to study further the impact of day care on children's later development.

REFERENCES

Altman, J. (1974). Observational study of behavior: Sampling methods. *Behaviour, 39*, 227–267.

Asher, S. R., Singleton, L. C., Tinsley, B. R., & Hymel, S. (1979). A reliable sociometric measure for preschool children. *Developmental Psychology, 15*, 443–444.

Baillargeon, M., & Betsalel-Presser, R. (1988). Effets de la garderie sur le comportement social et l'adaptation de l'enfant: perceptions des enseignantes de la maternelle [The effects of day-care centers on social behavior and adaptation of the child: perceptions of teachers in kindergarten]. *Revue Canadienne de l'Etude de la Petite Enfance, 2*, 91–98.

Baillargeon, M., Gravel, M., Larouche, H., & Larouche, M. (1989, March). *Day care: Language and social development in kindergarten.* Paper presented at the Conférence Nationale sur la Garde des Enfants, Winnipeg, Manitoba, Canada.

Balleyguier, G. (1979). *Test pour l'évaluation du caractère du jeune enfant et des attitudes éducatives de l'entourage* [A test for evaluating the temperament of young children and educational attitudes of adults]. Issy-les-Moulineux: Editions Scientifiques et Psychologiques.

Balleyguier, G. (1988). What is the best mode of day care for young children: A French study. *Early Child Development and Care, 33*, 41–65.

Balleyguier, G. (1991). French research on day care. In E. C. Melhuish & P. Moss (Eds.). *Day care for young children: International perspectives* (pp. 27–45). London: Routledge.

Baumrind, D. (1989). Rearing competent children. In W. Damon (Ed.) *Child development today and tomorrow* (pp. 349–378). San Francisco: Jossey-Bass.

Behar, L., & Stringfield, S. (1974). A behavior rating scale for the preschool child. *Developmental Psychology, 10*, 601–610.

Belsky, J. (1984). Two waves of day care research: Development effects and conditions of quality. In R. Ainslie (Ed.), *The child and the day care setting* (pp. 1–34). New York: Praeger.

Belsky, J. (1988). The "effects" of infant day care reconsidered. *Early Childhood Research Quarterly, 3*, 235–272.

Belsky, J., & Steinberg, L. D. (1978). The effect of day care: A critical review. *Child Development, 49*, 929–949.

Betsalel-Presser, R., Baillargeon, M., Romano-White, D., & Vineberg-Jacobs, E. (1989). La qualité de garderie affecte-t-elle la transition de l'enfant vers la maternelle? [Does the quality of day care centers affect the adaptation of children to kindergarten?]. *Apprentissage et Socialisation, 12*, 227–237.

Betsalel-Presser, R., Lavoie, C., & Jacques, M. (1989). Les enfants de la maternelle provenant des services de garde: Perception de leurs éducatrices [Children of kindergarten coming from day care centers: perceptions of their teachers]. *Revue des Sciences de l'Education, 15*, 399–432.

Bowlby, J. (1969). *Attachment and loss: Vol. 1. Attachment.* London: Basic Books.

Brunet, O., & Lézine, I. (1951). *Le développement de la première enfance* [Development in infancy]. Paris: Presses Universitaires de France.

Caldwell, B., & Freyer, M. (1982). Day care and early education. In B. Spodek (Ed.), *Handbook of research in early childhood education* (pp. 341–374). New York: Free Press.

Clarke-Stewart, K. A. (1988). The "effects of infant day care reconsidered" reconsidered: Risks for parents, children and researchers. *Early Childhood Research Quarterly, 3*, 293–318.

Clarke-Stewart, K. A., & Fein, G. (1983). Early childhood programs. In P. H. Mussen (Series Ed.) & M. M. Haith & J. J. Campos (Vol. Eds.), *Handbook of child psychology: Vol 2. Infancy and developmental psychobiology* (4th ed., pp. 917–999). New York: Wiley.

Coutu, S., Provost, M. A., & Pelletier, D. (1991, July). *Sibling relationship and mother–child attachment of day care versus home-reared children.* Paper presented at the meetings of the International Society for the Study of Behavioral Development, Minneapolis, MN.

Coutu, S., Provost, M. A., Pelletier, D., & Desbiens, L. (1990, August). *Cross contextual assess-*

ments of children's social behaviour. Paper presented at the Fourth European Conference on Developmental Psychology, Stirling, Scotland.

Desbiens, L., & Provost, M. A. (1989, March). *La construction et la validation d'un questionnaire sur la qualité de la relation éducatrice-enfant en garderie* [The construction and the validation of a questionnaire on the quality of the teacher-child relationship in day care centers]. Paper presented at the Conférence Nationale sur la Garde des Enfants, Winnipeg, Manitoba, Canada.

Desbiens, L., & Provost, M. A. (1991, October). *Validation d'un questionnaire sur la qualité de la relation enfants–éducatrice en garderie* [The validation of a questionnaire on the quality of the teacher-child relationship in day care centers]. Paper presented at the XIVth Congrés de la Société Québécoise pour la Recherche en Psychologie, Trois-Rivières, Québec, Canada.

Dumont, M., Provost, M. A., & Coutu, S. (1987, October). *Le type de participation sociale émis par l'enfant en fonction du sexe et du temps de fréquentation à la garderie* [Social participation of children in day care centers: Effects of children's age and time spent in the day care center]. Paper presented at the IXth Congrès de la Société Québécoise pour la Recherche en Psychologie, Québec City, Qc, Canada.

Erikson, E. H. (1963). *Childhood and society.* New York: Norton.

Garon, D. (1985). *La classification des jeux et des jouets: Le système ESAR* [The categorization of games and toys: The ESAR system]. Québec: Documentor.

Goossens, F. A., & van IJzendoorn, M. H. (1990). Quality of infants' attachments to professional caregivers: Relation to infant–parent attachment and day-care characteristics. *Child Development, 61,* 832–837.

Hartup, W. W. (1983). Peer relations. In P. H. Mussen (Series Ed.) & E. M. Hetherington (Vol. Ed.), *Handbook of child psychology: Vol. 4. Socialization, personality, and social development* (4th ed., pp. 103–196). New York: Wiley.

Howes, C., Rodning, C., Galluzzo, D. C., & Myers, L. (1988). Attachment and child care: Relationships with mother and caregiver. *Early Childhood Research Quarterly, 3,* 403–416.

Lézine, I. (1951). *Psycho-pédagogie du premier âge* [Psychopedagogy in infancy]. Paris: Presses Universitaires de France.

Lézine, I., & Spionek, H. (1958). Quelques problèmes de développement psychomoteur et d'éducation des enfants dans les crèches [Some issues in motor development and in education of children in day care centers]. *Enfance, 3,* 245–267.

Long, F., Peters, D. L., & Garduque, L. (1985). Continuity between home and day care: A model for defining relevant dimensions of child care. In I. E. Sigel (Ed.), *Advances in applied developmental psychology* (Vol. 1, pp. 131–170). Norwood, NJ: Ablex.

Maccoby, E. E., & Martin, J. A. (1983). Socialization in the context of the family: Parent–child interaction. In P. H. Mussen (Series Ed.) & E. M. Hetherington (Vol. Ed.), *Handbook of child psychology: Vol. 4. Socialization, personality, and social development* (4th ed., pp. 1–102). New York: Wiley.

Mermilliod, C., & Rossignol, C. (1974). Le développement de l'enfant de quatre ans est-il significatif des modes de garde antérieurs? [Does four year old children's development reflect previous settings of day care?] *Bulletin de Statistique "Santé-Sécurité Sociale", 2,* 105–131.

Parten, M. B. (1932). Social participation among preschool children. *Journal of Abnormal and Social Psychology, 27,* 243–269.

Provost, M. A. (1980). L'effet des garderies sur le développement de l'enfant [The effects of day care on children's development]. *Santé Mentale au Canada, 28,* 17–20.

Provost, M. A., Garon, D., & LaBarre, R. (1991). L'ajustement social des jeunes enfants d'âge préscolaire en fonction de la cohérence maison-garderie [Social adjustment of preschool children as function of continuity between home and day care center]. *Revue Canadienne des Sciences du Comportement, 23,* 183–194.

Strayer, F. F. (1989). Co-adaptation within the early peer group: A psychobiological study of social competence. In B. H. Schneider (Ed.), *Social competence in developmental perspective* (pp. 145–174). Genève: Kluwer Academic Publishers.

van IJzendoorn, M. H., & Tavechhio, L.W.C. (1987). The development of attachment theory as a Lakatosian research program: Philosophical and methodological aspects. In L.W.C. Tavecchio & M. H. van IJzendoorn (Eds.), *Attachment in social networks* (pp. 3–34). Amsterdam: Elsevier Science Publishers.

Waters, E., & Deane, K. E. (1985). Defining and assessing individual differences in attachment relationship: Q-methodology and the organization of behavior in infancy and early childhood. In I. Bretherton & E. Waters (Eds.), *Growing points of attachment theory and research* (pp. 41–65). *Monographs of the Society for Research in Child Development, 50,* (1–2, Serial No. 209).

Weir, T., & Duveen, G. (1981). Further development and validation of the Prosocial Behavior Questionnaire for use by teachers. *Journal of Child Psychology and Psychiatry, 22,* 357–374.

23 Parental Conceptions of Early Development and Developmental Stimulation

Colette Sabatier
Université de Rennes II

One of the most striking trends in developmental psychology is the rapidly growing research interest in parental representations of child education and child development. Parental knowledge is now considered an important aspect of adult social cognition that we must take into account in order to understand the process of child development and its variations among different subgroups (Goodnow & Collins, 1990; Miller, 1988; Sigel, 1985). Many terms have been used to describe cognition about parenting. Some refer to "ideas" (Goodnow, Cashmore, Cotton, & Knight, 1984), others to "parental beliefs" (Sigel, 1985), or "naive theories" (Ninio, 1979). There have been efforts to clarify the concept of parents' ideas or beliefs, to classify research according to their focusing aspect of parent social cognition (content or quality), and to identify the origins of these representations (Goodnow & Collins, 1990; Palacios, 1990).

In a cross-cultural perspective, Ogbu (1981) stressed the importance of studying parental beliefs. He wrote that to really understand what is going on, especially in the case of immigrant and ethnic minority groups, the variations of parental behaviors and child development have to be related not only to the specific context of the group but also to the specific theories of education that are prevalent in these groups. However, even if, following Caudill and Weinstein (1969), a growing body of research documents the cultural diversity of mother-infant interactions, I have noticed, in a review of the scientific literature on this topic (Sabatier, 1986), the paucity of empirical studies on maternal beliefs in different cultural groups compared to the increasing number of studies focusing on mother–infant relationships or caregiving practices. Four years later, in a special issue of *Child Development* on American ethnic minorities, Garcia Coll (1990) observed again that very few comprehensive studies were available about the beliefs, developmental goals, and caregiving practices during infancy of the different minority groups in the United States. The author considered this to be prejudicial to intervention programs, which consequently missed reliable information. In Canada, Berry (1986) and Bibeau (1987) concluded the same.

In the French-speaking scientific community, there has been a long tradition among human and social scientists to examine the context of education, social values, and representation about child development and education (Ariès, 1962; Boltansky, 1969; Chombart de Lauwe, 1971, 1984). Some of these studies are well known around the world. Unfortunately, outside of Bril, Zack, and Hombessa Nkounkou's (1989) study, there has been no French developmental psychological research bearing specifically on parental knowledge and beliefs. In fact, most of the research comes from the fields of ethnology, sociology, social psychology, and history, mainly in the *Ecole des Hautes Etudes en Sciences Sociales* in Paris.

In this chapter, I mainly focus on parental conceptions of early development and developmental stimulation in a cross-cultural perspective, especially in the immigration context in two Francophone host societies, Quebec and France. In the first part, I describe the Francophone perspective on the parental social representation of the child (with a special interest in infants). Subsequently, empirical data from two studies with immigrant groups—one in Quebec and one in France—are reported on and discussed within the framework of the Francophone perspectives.

PARENTAL BELIEF SYSTEMS AND THE PERCEPTION OF THE CHILD

French authors have documented how representations of young children's needs and of ways to rear them are embedded in the global cultural system of society. The well-known historian, Ariès (1962), demonstrated that the representation of the childhood period as a specific stage of human development, with its own characteristics and demands, is not universal, but is a social construction that appeared in one moment of Western history. He pointed out the emergence of a serious and authentic interest in the psyche of the child during the 17th century with two "opposite" components: love and education (mainly in the moral sense). Some people (mainly women) considered that children, with their spontaneity and gentleness, were a source of pleasure, relaxation, and tenderness for adults. Others (mainly churchmen) claimed the necessity of educating children and developing specific procedures to teach them how to behave, think, and master intellectual things. Children, said these educators, need to be directed and trained; otherwise, they will never become competent adults. In consequence, there were evident efforts to understand the minds of children so as to develop appropriate educational actions.

Badinter (1980) indicated the same evolution of ideas concerning women's maternal roles and the maternal instincts. Taking anthropological views, Devereux (1949, 1966) and Stork (1986) described the variations of ideas concerning infants; their initial vulnerability and receptivity to stimulations and to persons; and their needs of love, consideration, and education among different cultures. Within French society, Boltansky (1969) documented such differences between lower and middle urban classes, and Loux (1978) reported the specific ideas and practices of a rural population. Authors claimed that, in spite of appearances, parental beliefs of each group were not inchoate. They tried to point out the coherences and symbolic meanings, as well as the processes through which such ideas were acquired and maintained. They mainly stressed the point that naive childrearing theories were tied to the cultural systems of the groups.

According to researchers, ideas concerning childhood and education are not transmitted only by chance. Societies deliberately try to teach new ideas and societal values to everyone and to modify people's behavior through their own institutions. Stork (1986) noted that, in the Indian society, child representations and childrearing practices are registered in ancient indigenous medical (Ayurvedic) and law books (Manusmriti), which are still the spiritual source of reference for people (educated or not). Meyer (1977) demonstrated the influence of French city laws during the 18th century on family life: Children began to be isolated within the family circle and were separated from the adult group. At the same time, they acquired a special status: They lost the possibility of learning adults' roles and adults' ways of thinking through observation and interactions with the adult world. Parents were considered, henceforth, as the only adult in charge of children's education and good conduct. In spite of this, the analyses by Boltansky (1969) and by Delaisi de Parseval and Lallemand (1980) of primers (modern or not) for mothers reaffirm the deliberate training objective of social institutions. In these books, mothers largely emerged as incompetent, immature, and in need of advice, directives, and admonitions to be able to adequately fulfill their educational role.

Nonetheless, the routes of acquisition of parental representations are numerous, because people are submitted to multiple and complex influences. Chombart de Lauwe (1984) identified two main types of transmitters: those who are involved directly with children and have a moderate but realistic view of the child, and those who are not directly tied to children but have the power to influence the representation of children (e.g., lawyers, medical doctors, architects, and urbanists). It happens that, because of their distance from concrete children, the latter have a more idealistic and schematic view of children than the former. Furthermore, Chombart de Lauwe noticed that even the intervention styles of professionals are influenced by their informal personal representation of children and by ideas embedded in the specific culture of their country and their epoch.

All these variations suggest that parents' ideas are influenced by conditions other than their direct experience, and many of the ideas they hold are "social constructions" or "cultural inventions." Parents' ideas appear less self-constructed than handed-down or ready-made. In a psychological perspective, Bril et al. (1989), adopting a methodology similar to the studies of Ninio (1979) and of Keller, Miranda, and Gauda (1984), noted in three African groups and one French group the existence of specific cultural norms that underlay mothers' conceptions of child development (such as the age of onset of infant walking and talking), and the role of the environment on the acquisition of social behaviors and psychomotor abilities. This more or less explicit system of convictions, images, and rules concerning the education and socialization of the child relates to the concept of naive theories or parental belief systems. For my part, I share with Bril et al. the same interest in knowing more about the cross-cultural variations of maternal conceptions, but within the same society. My main interest concerns the adaptation and psychological development of children born and raised in immigrant or ethnic families.

CULTURAL DIVERSITY OF MATERNAL CONCEPTIONS WITHIN FRANCOPHONE SOCIETIES

With this perspective, my colleagues and I undertook two studies in two occidental French-speaking societies: France and Quebec. These countries receive many immigrants but, for historical reasons, have differing politics of integration. Montreal is a multiethnic, mostly French-speaking, Canadian metropolis. Rennes, the administrative capital of Brittany in France, has only about 10% non-French people. Nonetheless, in both cities, several community programs are offered to immigrants by ethnic associations, as well as by citizen groups or governmental institutions.

The main goal of the Montreal study was to establish an overview of the developmental niche of immigrant and Québécois babies in order to elaborate social and health programs that would be adapted to these populations. Following previous work on the methodological and ethical questions raised by cross-cultural studies (see Sabatier, 1986), we adopted a methodology that was multidimensional and multicultural. As part of the research, we interviewed 38 Haitians, 45 Québécois, and 26 Vietnamese primiparous mothers of a 3- to 9-month-old baby on their conceptions of child development and child rearing at home in their maternal language. Haitian and Vietnamese mothers were first-generation immigrants; the majority immigrated as adults and had 10 years of schooling. Other parts of the study dealt with maternal perception of temperament, physical and social organization of the environment, and mother–infant interaction around a learning task; results and details of this study are reported in a number of papers (Pomerleau, Malcuit, & Sabatier, 1991; Sabatier, Malcuit, & Pomerleau, 1989, 1990; Sabatier, Pomerleau, & Malcuit, 1989; Sabatier, Pomerleau, Malcuit, St.-Laurent, & Allard, 1990). The second study is a partial replication study in Rennes (France), focusing especially on maternal conceptions. In this study, 60 mothers of a 3- to 12-month-old baby were interviewed: 30 of them were metropolitan French, and 30 others came from circum-Mediterranean countries, French nonmetropolitan territories, Africa, and Southeast Asia (see Gueniou, Tanguy, & Sabatier, 1993).

The questionnaire constructed for the first study contained questions based on the work of Ninio (1979), Keller et al. (1984), and Frankel and Roer-Bornstein (1982). It was specifically designed to tap the particular representations of each ethnic group, while still allowing group comparison. In this sense, it respected the etic-emic methodology discussed by Berry (1989) in the framework of cross-cultural studies. The questionnaire assesses the mothers' conceptions of infant competence (milestones of development, as well as the cognitive and affective abilities attributed to infants), their expectations of infant behaviors, their beliefs concerning the role parents play in the child-rearing process, and their daily socialization practices. Some questions are also designed to capture the various sources of the mothers' information.

On the whole, these studies reveal different values and beliefs among cultural groups and illustrate the variety of maternal conceptions within Western societies. The same general differential tendencies between nonoccidental and occidental mothers were observed in both studies. Due to the heterogeneity of the samples, the method of collecting data as well as the general lower level of education in the Rennes sample and statistical differences are less numerous in the second study than in the first one, but they are in the same direction. In this chapter, only major observations are reported.

Conceptions About Infant Abilities

The most coherent patterns of differences in conceptions about infant abilities were found in the area of developmental timetables. For this, mothers had to report, as precisely as possible, the age at which they thought that infants acquire various abilities in the perceptual, cognitive, social, and motor domains. Occidental mothers expect the earliest emergence of most infant competencies, especially at the perceptuo-cognitive level. In the Montreal sample, the Québécois mothers expected infant perceptual and cognitive abilities to develop at the earliest age, but not the abilities to sit and to walk. The Haitian mothers expected earlier development of motor abilities, with the exception of crawling. The Vietnamese placed most of the milestones at the latest age. No significant differences were found for crawling, identifying objects from pictures, and giving up the pacifier, due to a large within-group variability. In the Rennes study, ethnic mothers situated the onset of hearing, understanding, thinking, and sleeping in the baby's own bedroom at later ages than did French mothers, and crawling at earlier age.

In order to gain more information concerning the possible cultural variations in maternal representations of a baby, we asked several open questions concerning their interpretations of common behaviors, such as crying and mouthing (only in the Montreal study), their images of an ideal baby, and their representations of attachment (only in the Rennes study). Mothers gave a variety of answers. On the whole, Québécois and French mothers put emphasis on affective needs and psychoaffective factors in development, whereas ethnic and immigrant mothers considered health and basic needs as their first priority. For instance, most mothers considered the infant's basic physiology (regularity of feeding and sleep, good health, infrequent unmotivated crying) as an important criteria of a "good baby." However, although the preoccupations of immigrant and ethnic mothers were on basic physiology only, and for some of them the most important thing was the facility of feeding, French and Québécois mothers also mentioned the manifestation of psychoaffective behaviors, such as smiling and playful activity, as the defining criteria of a good baby. In the same vein, although most of the mothers indicated physical needs as the main reason for crying, Québécois mothers also stressed affective needs, and the Vietnamese noted a need to communicate. In contrast with the others, Québécois mothers mentioned the mouthing of objects as a means of exploration, whereas one third of Vietnamese mothers considered hunger and the need to suck as the motivating factors for infant mouthing. Finally, in the second study, in their answers to a question concerning attachment and its appropriate maternal handling, French mothers seemed to regard their child as a partner capable of exchanges and interactions more often than ethnic mothers. They saw their role as stimulating this exchange and sharing activities with their child. Ethnic mothers, for their part, considered caregiving, protecting, and cuddling to be appropriate activities, and were not specifically centered on infant competencies.

On the other hand, when asked what abilities they wanted their infants to develop for the future, ethnic and immigrant mothers value formal education more than French mothers, either for cognitive development or for social development. For example, they valued the acquisition of social norms: kindness, good manners, social awareness, respect for parents, and the rules of life sharing (this was particularly true for the Haitian group) and stressed the importance of providing their child with a good formal education (this was particularly true for the Vietnamese mothers). French and Québécois mothers, for their part, were more sensitive to the psychoaffective domain and to cognitive aspects, such as curiosity and experimentation.

Conceptions of the Influence of Parents on Infant Development

We also asked several questions concerning the role of parents in development, especially concerning the age at which mothers should initiate specific activities, beliefs about the likelihood of accelerating some aspects of development (sitting, walking, and language development), the possibility of teaching something to 9-month-old infants, and the role of play as a factor in development. The responses to questions concerning the age at which mothers should initiate specific activities gave the most coherent pattern. It comes as no surprise that the Québécois and French mothers, who expected the appearance of infants' cognitive abilities at an earlier age, also reported an earlier age of initiation of activities than the immigrant and ethnic mothers. In the Rennes study, no statistical differences appeared in stimulation for autonomy (such as in feeding and dressing alone), but differences became evident on the issue of language stimulation (telling stories, buying books, and speaking about absent objects and persons), and to prohibition and punishment. French mothers appeared to introduce these activities earlier. In the Montreal study, some differences also appeared between the two immigrant groups. Mothers from Vietnam, for example, tend to underestimate the age of appearance of infant abilities. However, the age at which they would introduce activities did not differ greatly from the Québécois. On the other hand, Haitians, who situated two motor milestones at an age between Québécois and Vietnamese mothers, reported introducing most activities at the latest age.

Maternal responses to open questions did not yield clear-cut differences. Mothers were, in some aspects, embarrassed by our questions. Most of the time, they hesitated to say if parents have influence on their child. They stated that they could do something to influence child development, but were enable to explain which domain or in what degree. Many inconsistent and ambivalent answers were given in all groups. For example, Québécois mothers, who expressed nuances concerning their influence on motor development but were affirmative concerning language development, did not stress the fact that they can teach verbal skills to 9-month-olds as much as did the immigrant mothers, who were more skeptical concerning their influence on language development. Québécois mothers also did not report the use of verbal games, but put emphasis on psychomotor abilities.

Concerning routines and discipline, some differences appeared between groups in the Montreal study but not in the Rennes one. Vietnamese mothers reported more rigid attitudes concerning routines than Québécois and Haitian mothers. A fair number of Vietnamese mothers considered the regularity of feeding and sleeping very important. They also preferred their infant to play alone. Haitians, more than the others, thought that babies should be played with at request, and most of the mothers did not led their babies cry at night. On the other hand, the Québécois mothers initiated punishment earlier than the other two groups. However, techniques and reasons for punishment were different. More Québécois mothers reported using verbal punishment as a way to help the child to understand, whereas, in immigrants, punishment was merely considered as a way to correct the child behaviorally.

Differences in Degree of Industrialization or Differences in Culture?

These findings illustrate the variety of maternal conceptions within Western societies, but raise the question of the source of these differences. On the whole, the thoughts and beliefs expressed by the Québécois and French mothers reflect the message of the occidental developmental psychology: An infant is a competent and sociable human being who deserves to be stimulated and loved. In the Québécois and French society, as in most modern occidental cultures, it is considered important to help enhance the development of already-present perceptual and cognitive competencies. Thus, the mothers introduce certain activities from early on. On the other hand, the ethnic mothers underestimated many infant competencies, with the exception of basic motor abilities.

Some of the differences in parental goals and conceptions between Western industrialized societies and Third World countries could be related to the perceived vulnerability of the infant. In countries where the infant mortality rate is high and life is threatened, mothers are focused on their infants' survival and physical well-being more than on their psychological competencies (LeVine, 1988). Indeed, we found a number of similarities between immigrant groups in our studies that led us to consider the possibility that observed discrepancies between the Québécois group and the two immigrant groups could be related to a dichotomy between the industrialized, occidental and the nonindustrialized, nonoccidental way of life. However, groups (ethnic as well as occidental) are also quite different from each other, and each has its own distinct way of rearing children and its own vision of what the aim of their education should be.

For example, in the Montreal study, the Vietnamese mothers, just as the Haitians, stressed the importance of fostering moral and social development, but, unlike the Haitians, they did not think that parents could play a significant role in the psychoaffective development of the child. This is in keeping with the values of their culture of origin and is consistent with views on infant development. Affective needs are, indeed, considered important to Haitians and Québécois. Haitian mothers respond quickly to their infants' demands and appeared to be more laissez faire concerning the necessity of introducing stimulation and activities at an early age. In the Rennes study, although we did not analyze the data for each ethnic group because of the small number of subjects, Moroccan mothers seemed to be different from the other ethnic mothers, but shared the same maternal preconceptions concerning the onset of infant abilities.

When we compared the data of the French and of the Québécois mothers, some differences emerged. There were no differences in the onset of use of punishment, but French mothers tended to be more authoritarian, and they did not invoke explaining as a way to teach appropriate conduct, as Québécois mothers did. French mothers, more than Québécois, want their children to have regular schedules for sleeping and feeding, and concerning punishment they adopt authoritarian techniques. For their part, Québécois were less consistent, and tried to explain to their children the reasons for prohibitions. Compared to all groups, they were the only ones who credited themselves for their own judgment, experience, or natural abilities and instincts. With regard to the literature, this attitude appears to be unusual (Baranowski et al., 1983; Bril et al., 1989;

Shand & Kosawa, 1984). Two alternative interpretations are possible: It could be related to the old beliefs in maternal instinct valued by the Catholic Church before the period of the *révolution tranquille* (the silent revolution), as well as to a new attitude of autonomy regarding medical knowledge and power. Prêteur and Louvet-Schmauss (1991) have also reported differences between maternal conceptions in two occidental societies, Germany and France. They described how governmental politics and the educational goals and practices of the school systems can have an impact on maternal conceptions, especially on the representation of learning processes. However, compared to the number of studies focusing on child-care practices and maternal–child interactions, few studies document the variations of parental beliefs across several occidental countries.

LINKS BETWEEN MATERNAL REPRESENTATION AND MATERNAL ACTION

Another question left behind by research concerns the relation between representation and what happens in practice, especially in education. Much of the recent interest in parental beliefs has stemmed from the conviction that parents' conceptions about children mediate how they treat their own children. Parental beliefs and attitudes are regarded as filters through which their behavior is molded; they are interpreted as playing an important role in the mutual regulation between parent and infant. Some investigators believe that clarifying the attitude concept and the interplay of parental attitudes and behaviors will enhance our knowledge of the parent–child relationship and its effects on child development. This knowledge, they suggest, can serve as a guideline for the creation of adequate social and health programs. However, one surprising feature of the literature on parental beliefs is the paucity of empirical work done to evaluate the relationships between beliefs and behavior. In fact, determining the extent and the nature of the relationships has proven to be difficult.

Several studies document the role of maternal conception and knowledge on the organization of the environment, the maternal assessment of infant temperament, and their language stimulation (Goldring-Zukow, 1985; Luster, 1986; MacPhee, 1983; Stevens, 1988). However, many of them recognize that the links are not always direct and simple. Causality is hard to determine. Crouchman (1985) noted that even mothers who think that vision begins several days after birth, report seeing some looking and social smiles from their newborns within the first 5 days of life. Hopkins and Westra (1989) indicated that, in general, West Indian mothers expect the onset of sitting and walking at earlier ages than Indian and British mothers, but this has no direct effect to the onset of walking of their children. Moreover, the correlations between parental beliefs and parental involvement with the child (e.g., length of breast-feeding, fathers' involvement), as observed by Crouchman (1985), as well as by Ninio and Rinott (1988), suggest more an effect of the culture or the general cultural attitudes toward childrearing. The two dimensions are subjected to the same source of variation. In the Francophone scientific community, several researchers have developed ideas and frameworks in which these relationships can be examined and understood. Vandenplas-Holper (1987) referred to the theory of action to explain the link between implicit theories and behavior. The theory of action studies goal-oriented behaviors and their social purposes and functions. In this perspective, an action is seen as oriented, planned, justified, and deliberate. The concept of action also includes emotions and their socially guidance and control. If this theory can explain how beliefs can guide actions and are, in fact, one component of action, it does not explain the strength of the link and whether belief is always followed by action.

Devereux (1968) noted that the adult way of seeing children influences their character and behavior, but in a more complicated way than it appears to be. Both child-rearing practices and the related parental beliefs have to be taken into account. He then demonstrated that both Sedang and Mohave cultural groups have the same weaning practice, but, due to different representations of the child and of the mother–infant bond, outcomes in the child's development are different. Child-care practices are partly determined by social representations of the child, but they are other influences, also. Parental beliefs are adjusted in accordance with them: Parents believe in what is useful.

For Mugny and Carugati (1989), the connections between social representations of intelligence and educational action are clear, but they are not as close as one might hope. This is because the psychological structures of representation and action are different. Actions are in some ways more specific and defined than representations. Thus, the transition to action needs the production of new cognitive elaboration. A further reason lies in the actual system of communication governing the representation of intelligence. Moscovi (cited in Mugny & Carugati, 1989) identified different kinds of communication related to social (or popular) representations. In some instances, the aim of the communication is precisely the transition into action: People are told precisely what to do and how. Social desirability entails the adoption of a position and dictates specific behavior. In other situations, the ideas that are transmitted are not so specific, but entail a general attitude, making a direct connection with action probable but not necessary. In this perspective, Mugny and Carugati concluded that parental representations of intelligence may belong to the latter type: that is, linked to action in a way that it is more probabilistic than deterministic.

For our part, the multidimensional aspects of our Montreal study allowed us to trace links between expressed maternal belief systems (what mothers know and expect of infants and their development) and the actual environment they provide for their infants, and also permitted us to suggest some possible explanations. Some relations between the different elements appear to be clear. For instance, Québécois mothers, more than the others, considered mouthing as a way to explore objects. In accordance with this point of view, they appeared to allow their 9-month-old infants to mouth the objects in the learning tasks more than the mothers of the other two groups did. In the same vein, our data indicate that Québécois mothers considered infants to be competent in the affective and cognitive domains. In accordance with this belief, they reported introducing specific activities very early in order to stimulate development in this area.

In other domains, links are not easy to determine. Two examples illustrate the complexity of the relationships between beliefs and behavior. First, as mentioned previously, the Québécois babies, in contrast with those of the immigrants, were surrounded by toys, accessories, and miscellaneous objects. It is tempting to relate the differences in the physical environment of the infants to the mothers' belief concerning the course of development, as Emiliari, Zani, and Carugati (cited by Vandenplas-Holper, 1987) have done. However, the questions related to the function of play indicate that play was viewed by every mother, immigrant or not, as an important opportunity for learning, and toys were appreciated for their educational potential. Furthermore, all mothers reported that they played with their infants. In this example, maternal beliefs can hardly be an explanation for the differences observed in the organization of the physical environment. Sigel (1985) has already discussed such results. He has shown that a point-to-point correspondence between beliefs and behavior can be misleading. Other sources of influence have to be postulated: The consumer habits of occidental societies and the need to be surrounded by many objects are certainly significant factors. In addition, although all mothers recognize the importance of play and stimulation in the development of the infant (even during the neonatal period), in our society, giving toys to an infant is seen as a sign of a good parent–child relationship.

The second example bears on the relationship between maternal beliefs and teaching strategies. We have seen that both Haitian and Vietnamese mothers stress the value of social conformity. Thus, one would expect both groups of mothers to be more directive with their babies. However, at 9 months, there were differences between the two groups in the teaching tasks. Vietnamese mothers used directive behaviors with their infants and guided and restrained them more than both the Haitian and Québécois groups. We could consider, as Devereux (1966) suggested, the consonance or the coeffects of the two variables: maternal insistence on social conformity and maternal teaching strategies. Beyond simple correlations, these two variables can provide us with a more subtle understanding of the reality of maternal child-rearing practices. As Whiting and Edwards (1988) have indicated, several types of interactions can be identified. Some mothers can be conceived as teachers, some as controlling, and others as liberal. Vietnamese mother appear to fit into the first category: They value social conformity, and, at the same time, they carefully supervise their babies' actions in order to control each of their movements. Québécois mothers value individuality, mainly in the affective and cognitive domains; they give their babies free rein to explore and to mouth objects. Haitians think that it is important to give attention to the baby and to support the affective domain. At the same time, just as the Vietnamese, they value social conformity, but they are not as controlling as the Vietnamese mothers in the context of observation.

Links Between Popular and Scientific Knowledge

Finally, according to our data, ethnic mothers express confidence in the medical world and in the physician as sources of information related to their infants. They are also ready to accept advice concerning their child's development and, contrary to French and Québécois mothers, do so without any restriction. This apparently positive attitude can be seen as an indication of their adaptation to the pediatric health services offered by their host country and provide some faith in the efficiency of the intervention programs. It is consistent with the experience of people who have taken time to listen to these mothers and to adjust their intervention to the specific needs and particular communication styles of the minority mothers (Dempsey & Gesse, 1983; Lieberman & Weston, 1986; Lynam, 1985). However, this raises questions about the link between popular and scientific knowledge and the way scientific knowledge is received by people who are not familiar with it.

Among the Francophone scholars, several points of view have been adopted. According to Vandenplas-Holper (1987), popular knowledge parallels scientific theories, entailing, in its structure, the same components as scientific knowledge. Parental beliefs borrow ideas from maturationist and constructivist theories. Thus, we could conclude that it would be easy to modify parental beliefs. Massé (1991), in contrast, considered popular knowledge to evolve independently of scientific knowledge. Parents of lower socioeconomic class, even when they participate to programs and have access to scientific information, maintain their own belief systems. In these circumstances, the issue is less to evaluate the degree of scientific knowledge of parents than to know how parents interpret the parental competence professionals describe and desire. It is important to document the ecological niche of such reinterpretations, as it is also relevant to examine the links between beliefs and actual behavior. Such studies are needed before we can design appropriate intervention programs.

Boltansky (1969), for his part, considered that one way to explain the specificity of educational beliefs of lower class parents is to examine the different steps in the communication of medical knowledge. He stressed the fact that because this communication is never rational or complete, the meaning of a practice is never explained in all its dimensions. Thus, because people need to attach a meaning to a practice, they elaborate new ones. This work of reinterpretation, which is covert, surreptitious, and lengthy, has its own logic. Most of the time, people interpret unknown elements within a familiar framework of understanding. Reduction and analogy are two common procedures. The time required to integrate the new theory varies with the social distance between the receptors and the emittor, which is necessarily at the top of the hierarchy. Nevertheless, the speed of dissemination within a social class depends on the relation (affinity or disagreement) of the practice and the general belief system of the group. Consequently, most of the time, lower class parental belief systems seem to follow old-fashioned medical theories that are reinterpreted in their own framework of understanding.

Taking a very different view, Mugny and Carugati (1989) emphasized the discrepancy between popular conceptions of intelligence and Piaget's theory. They observed a multiplicity of representations, not only among the different groups, but also within groups and even within one individual. According to the authors, this is why social representations appear to be assembled out of apparently contradictory discourses. It is not a question of logical contradiction, or inadequate cognitive organization: It is a matter of complexity and richness, with a variety of discourses complementing each other in order to take account of the totality of discourses covered by the single concept of intelligence. Representations by parents and experts may come to diverge because of differences in the base of judgment, or, more specifically, in the cues, categories, or images used to form a judgment. In this perspective, they argue that popular knowledge has to be considered as a way to study child developmental processes. Other definitions of psychological competences ought to encourage specialists to take more variables into account in their analyses if they are to avoid studying mental processes in terms that have no relation to the actual social practices that create and organize them.

CONCLUSION

In this chapter, I have tried to interpret the data on the maternal conceptions of immigrant mothers living in Québec and in France within the Francophone conceptual framework. Although very few French studies, except those with a really practical objective (concerning practical school or health matters), focus on this topic, Francophone social scientists offer an original and comprehensive background.

Historians reveal the links between the representation of children and the values or ideologies of the society. Anthropologists demonstrate their intertwining. Various Francophone scholars scrutinize, using a fruitful perspective, the very specific role of representation and analyze the way the different levels of representation do, in fact, influence behavior.

Following these seminal comments, two directions for further explorations can be recommended. First, we have to consider parental knowledge as useful information in fundamental research, as well as in intervention programs. Its structure—the way it is built, transmitted, and maintained—has to be considered with particular attention. Second, in addition to the study of the links between parental beliefs and parental behaviors, we have to examine how these beliefs and child-rearing practices complement each other in order to explain parental functioning and its effect on child development.

REFERENCES

Ariès, P. (1962). *Centuries of childhood*. New York: Vintage.

Badinter, E. (1980). *L'Amour en plus* [Love in addition]. Paris: Flammarion.

Baranowski, T., Bee, D. E., Rassin, K., Richardson, C. J., Brown, J. P., Guenther, N., & Nader, P. R. (1983). Social support, social influence, ethnicity and the breastfeeding decision. *Social Sciences and Medicine, 17*, 1599–1611.

Berry, J. W. (1986, July). *Psychology in and of Canada*. Paper presented at the meeting of the Eighth International Congress of Cross-Cultural Psychology, Istanbul, Turkey.

Berry, J. W. (1989). Imposed etics–emics–derived etics: The operationalization of a compelling idea. *International Journal of Psychology, 24*, 721–735.

Bibeau, G. (1987). *A la fois d'ici et d'ailleurs: Les communautés culturelles du Québec dans leurs rapports aux services sociaux et aux services de santé* [In the same time: Here and there. The relation of the Québec cultural groups with the health and social services]. Québec: Les Publications du Québec.

Boltansky, L. (1969). *Prime éducation et morale de classe* [Primary education and moral of social classes]. Paris: Editions de l'Ecole des Hautes Etudes en Sciences Sociales.

Bril, B., Zack, M., & Hombessa-Nkounkou, E. (1989). Ethnotheories of development and education: A view from different cultures. *European Journal of Psychology of Education, 4*, 307–318.

Caudill, W., & Weinstein, H. (1969). Maternal care and infant behavior in Japan and America. *Psychiatry, 32*, 12–43.

Chombart de Lauwe, M. J. (1971). *Un monde autre: L'enfance* [A different world: Childhood]. Paris: Payot.

Chombart de Lauwe, M. J. (1984). Changes in the representation of the child in the course of social transmission. In R. M. Farr & S. Moscovi (Eds.), *Social representations* (pp. 185–209). Paris: Maison des Sciences de l'Homme.

Coll, Garcia (1990, April). Special issue on minority children. In N. B. Spencer & V. C. McLoyd (Eds.), *Child Development, 61*(2).

Crouchman, M. (1985). What mothers know about their newborns' visual skills. *Developmental Medicine and Child Neurology, 27*, 455–460.

Delaisi de Parseval, G., & Lallemand, S. (1980). *L'art d'accommoder les bébés: Cent ans de recettes française de puériculture* [The art to dress the baby: A hundred years of French childrearing recipes]. Paris: Seuil.

Dempsey, P. A., & Geese, T. (1983). The childrearing Haitian refugee: Cultural applications to clinical nursing. *Public Health Reports, 98*, 261–267.

Devereux, G. (1949). Mohave voice and speech mannerism. *Word, 5*, 268–272.

Devereux, G. (1968). *L'image de l'enfant dans deux tribus Mohave et Sedang et ses conséquences* [The child's image and its consequences in two tribes, Mohave and Sedang]. *Revue de Neuropsychiatrie Infantile et d'Hygiéne Mentale de l'Enfant, 4*,25–35.

Frankel, D. G., & Roer-Bronstein, D. (1982). Traditional and modern contributions to changing infant-rearing ideologies of two ethnic communities. *Monographs of the Society for Research in Child Development, 47* (4, Serial Nr. 196).

Garcia Coll, C. T. (1990). Developmental outcome of minority infants: A process-oriented look into our beginnings. *Child Development, 61,* 270–289.

Goldring-Zukow, P. (1985). *Folk theories of comprehension and caregiver practices in a rural-born population in central Mexico.* Unpublished manuscript, University of California, Los Angeles.

Goodnow, J. J., Cashmore, J., Cotton, S., & Knight, R. (1984). Mothers' developmental time-table in two cultures. *International Journal of Psychology, 19,* 193–205.

Goodnow, J. J., & Collins, W. A. (1990). *Development according to parents: The nature, sources and consequences of parents' ideas.* Hillsdale, NJ: Lawrence Erlbaum Associates.

Gueniou, I., Tanguy, F., & Sabatier, C. (1993). Les conceptions des mères des minorités ethniques de Rennes (immigrées et ressortissantes des Dom-Tom) à propos du développement du tout-petit [The maternal conceptions of infant development among ethnic minorities living in Rennes]. *Proceedings of the Xième Colloque du Groupe francophone d'étude de l'enfant jeune.* Laboratoire de psychologie de l'éducation. Université Rennes 2. France.

Hopkins, B., & Westra, T. (1989). Maternal expectations and motor development: Some cultural differences. *Developmental Medicine and Child Neurology, 31,* 384–390.

Keller, H., Miranda, D., & Gauda, G. (1984). The naive theory of the infant and some maternal attitudes: A two-country study. *Journal of Cross-Cultural Psychology, 15,* 165–179.

LeVine, R. A. (1988). Human parental care: Universal goals, cultural strategies, individual behavior. In R. A. LeVine, P. M. Miller, & M. M. West (Eds.), *Parental behavior in diverse societies* (pp. 3–12). San Francisco: Jossey-Bass.

Lieberman, A. F., & Weston, D. (1986, August). *Preventive intervention with anxiously attached Latino infants and their mothers.* Paper presented at the annual meeting of the American Psychological Association, Washington, DC.

Loux, F. (1978). *Le jeune enfant et son corps dans la médecine traditionnelle* [The young child and his body in the traditional medicine view]. Paris: Flammarion.

Luster, T. (1986, May). *Influences on maternal behavior: Child-rearing beliefs, social support and infant temperament.* Paper presented at the International Conference on Infant Studies, Los Angeles.

Lynam, M. J. (1985). Support networks developed by immigrant women. *Social Science and Medicine, 21,* 327–333.

MacPhee, D. (1983, April). *What do ratings of infant temperament really measure?* Paper presented at the biennial meeting of the Society for Research in Child Development, Detroit, MI.

Massé, R. (1991). La conception populaire de la competence parentale [Popular conception of parental competence]. *Apprentissage et Socialisation, 14,* 279–290.

Meyer, P. (1977). *L'enfant et la raison d'état* [The child and the logic of the State]. Paris: Seuil.

Miller, S. A. (1988). Parents' beliefs about children's cognitive development. *Child Development, 59,* 259–285.

Mugny, G., & Carugati, F. (1989). *Social representations of intelligence.* Cambridge: Cambridge University Press.

Ninio, A. (1979). The naive theory of the infant and other maternal attitudes in two subgroups in Israel. *Child Development, 50,* 976–980.

Ninio, A., & Rinott, N. (1988). Fathers' involvement in the care of their infants and their attributions of cognitive competence to infants. *Child Development, 59,* 652–663.

Ogbu, J. U. (1981). Origins of social competence: A cultural-ecological perspective. *Child Development, 52,* 413–429.

Palacios, J. (1990). Parents' ideas about the development and education of their children: Answers to some questions. *International Journal of Behavioral Development, 13,* 137–155.

Pomerleau, A., Malcuit, G., & Sabatier, C. (1991). Child-rearing practices and conceptions in three cultural groups of Montréal: Québécois, Vietnamese, Haitian. In M. H. Bornstein (Ed.), *Cultural approaches to parenting* (pp. 45–68). Hillsdale, NJ: Lawrence Erlbaum Associates.

Prêteur, Y., & Louvet-Schmauss, E. (1991). Conceptions éducatives parentales vis à vis de l'ap-

314   SABATIER

prentissage de la lecture chez l'enfant d'âge préscolaire: Etude comparative selon deux systèmes socio-culturels et politiques (RFA et France) [Parental childrearing conceptions of reading learning processes of preschoolers. Comparative study between Germany and France]. *Enfance, 45,* 83–97.

Sabatier, C. (1986). La mère et son bébé: Variations culturelles. Analyse critique de la littérature [Mother and infant: Cross-cultural variations. A critical review of literature]. *International Journal of Psychology, 21,* 513–553.

Sabatier, C., Malcuit, G., & Pomerleau, A. (1989, July). *Haitian, Quebec and Vietnamese mother's instructional interactions with their 9-month-old babies.* Poster presented at the biennial meeting of the International Society for the Study of Behavioral Development, Helsinki, Finland.

Sabatier, C., Malcuit, G., & Pomerleau, A. (1990, May). *A cross-cultural study on temperament: A tentative interpretation of the influence of culture and some aspects of the daily life.* Poster presented at the International Conference for Infant Studies, Montreal, Quebec, Canada.

Sabatier, C., Pomerleau, A., & Malcuit, G. (1989, April). *The cultural context of development in 9-month-old babies: A comparison of Haitians, Québécois and Vietnamese.* Poster presented at the biennial meeting of the Society for Research in Child Development, Kansas, City, MO.

Sabatier, C., Pomerleau, A., Malcuit, G., St.-Laurent, C., & Allard, L. (1990). Comment les mères montréalaises se représentent-elles le développement du nourisson? Une comparaison de trois cultures [Montreal mothers' representation of infant development. A comparative study between three ethnic groups]. In S. Dansereau, B. Terrisse, J.-M. Bouchard (Eds.), *Education familiale et intervention précoce* (pp. 87–102). Montréal: L'Agence d'Arc.

Shand, N., & Kosawa, Y. (1984). Breast-feeding as cultural or personal decision: Sources of information and actual success in Japan and United States. *Journal of Biosociological Science, 16,* 65–80.

Sigel, I. E. (1985). *Parental belief systems: The psychological consequences for children.* Hillsdale, NJ: Lawrence Erlbaum Associates.

Stevens, J. H., Jr. (1988). Shared knowledge about infants among fathers and mothers. *Journal of Genetic Psychology, 149,* 515–525.

Stork, H. (1986). *Enfances indiennes: Etude de psychologie transculturelle et comparée du jeune enfant* [Indian infancy. A cross-cultural and comparative study of infancy]. Paris: Le Centurion.

Vandenplas-Holper, Ch. (1987). Les théories implicites du développement et de l'éducation [Implicit theories of development and education]. *European Journal of Psychology of Education, 11,* 17–39.

Whiting, B. B., & Edwards, C. P. (1988). *Children of different worlds: The formation of social behavior.* Cambridge, MA: Harvard University Press.

24

Representational and Communicative Processes in the Social Construction of Early Temperament

Teresa Blicharski
Université de Franche Comté

France Gravel
Université du Québec à Montréal

Marcel Trudel
Université du Québec à Abiti-Tamissquemingue

In North America, psychological theories about the origins of personality and the nature of early social development have generally stressed the central roles of child-rearing practices, parental attitudes, and interpersonal relationships as the primary determinants of children's emerging social, emotional, and cognitive styles (Ainsworth, 1969; Maccoby & Martin, 1983). More recent views about early learning usually acknowledge that children impose some limits on their own socialization experience, and thus, modern models usually reformulate classic concerns about early parenting in terms of the facilitative roles of adults, who furnish the necessary "scaffolding" for children's emerging psychological skills (Bruner, 1975; Nelson, 1975; Olson, Bates, & Bayles, 1984).

In contrast, biologically oriented theories of social growth have stressed the importance of early differences in temperamental dispositions, arguing that developmental processes are governed, to a large extent, by immutable genetic forces, by factors that lead to the emergence of basic traits resistant to modulation by fluctuations in experiential events (Bertenthal, 1991; Buss & Plomin, 1984; Scarr-Salapatek, 1976). Although these latter researchers admitted that situational factors might influence some forms of adaptation, they insisted that more basic biological and physiological variables are directly associated with individual differences in early temperamental characteristics, with subsequent mental or cognitive development, and, finally, with more long-term emotional and social adjustment (Bates, Bretherton, & Snyder, 1988; Cairns, 1991; Lerner, 1991; Thomas & Chess, 1977).

FRENCH STRUCTURALISM AND THE ANALYSIS
OF EARLY TEMPERAMENT

In France, perhaps because of the relatively later emergence of psychology as an independent discipline, the importance of psychoanalytic perspectives in psychology or the greater recognition of medical concerns for developmental research, early temperamental traits were theoretically linked to hypothesized differences in underlying constitutional dispositions and primary physiological processes (Balleyguier, 1989). Initially, *infant character* and *early temperament* were used interchangeably as labels for the behavioral expression of somatic and constitutional dispositions. From this quasimedical vantage point, constitutional differences were understood to reflect differences in individual heredity. In 1934, Wallon discussed affective components of infant personality in terms of maturational variation in emerging processes of hierarchically ordered nervous centers. Le Senne (1945) was among the first to try to distinguish between infant temperament and infant character. The former was limited to constitutional and somatic dispositions, whereas the latter included more general behavioral dispositions shaped by early experience. The conception of temperament as constitutionally fixed and anchored in family heredity was brought into question when researchers began to examine experimentally modes of early adaptation rather than document individual differences in reactive dispositions (Piaget, 1967, 1981).

In later studies of infant differences, feeling and acting emerged as central constructs in French discussions of early temperament (Berger, 1950). Both Piaget's and Wallon's theories remained influential in this new wave of empirical studies on early socioaffective development. Temperament researchers continued to employ the terms of *characterology* or *temperament,* but began to examine how early individual differences might relate to issues of early self–other differentiation and emerging sociocognitive development. For example, in a series of longitudinal assessments, Malrieu (1952) elaborated procedures for the identification of tonicomotor styles as core processes for differentiation of early temperament. Subsequent studies identified atonic and hypertonic children using standardized tests and attempted to relate these early characteristics to later behavioral adaptation and to school adjustment (de Ajuriaguerra, Harrisson, & Lézine, 1967; Soussignan, Koch, & Montagner, 1988).

In contrast with contemporary American research, the primary preoccupations of modern French scientists continues to center on variation in the structure of early individual behavior, rather than on modes of joint adaptation or the contents and meanings of early social exchange (Balleyguier, 1989; Montagner et al., 1977; Nadel-Brulfert & Baudonnière, 1982; Naud, 1991; Strayer & Moss, 1990). The rationalist, structuralist tradition, when applied to ,studies of behavioral development, encourages a rigorous description of micromodulation in motor activity as evidence for variations in underlying physiological processes. Unfortunately, in temperament research, the role of the social environment has less often been seen as a central part of the dynamic developmental system, a part that is essential for subsequent differentiation of social and cognitive processes. Instead, external socializing influences have more often been considered as part of the larger context—the external ecosystem—which imposes varying constraints on different types of children (Montagner et al., 1977).

In spite of their apparently different historical perspectives on early temperament, modern French and American behavioral scientists converge in the conviction that facilitative functions of adult behavior, in conjunction with patterns of child adjustment, must be viewed as prime movers of social, emotional, and mental growth (Bates et al., 1988; Balleyguier, 1989). Since the 1980s, researchers have begun to emphasize the important role of the child as an agent in the developmental process. Adopting a constructionist perspective, scientists have begun to examine early behavioral styles as central to an understanding of the child's role in shaping his or her immediate experience and subsequent development.

Since the late 1970s, researchers at the *Laboratoire d'Ethologie Humaine* in Montreal have studied the development of early behavior from a theoretical perspective in which individual growth is seen as a natural part of short-term adjustment to the immediate social world. Our preoccupation with observing children's actions in natural settings has led us to a reformulation of a biosocial model of behavioral selection during early development. From this perspective, both mental and physical actions of the young child are seen as by-products of strategic adaptation to specific constraints imposed by familiar social partners. Like other contemporary approaches in the behavioral sciences, a biosocial view acknowledges the continuing interaction between biological and experiential factors throughout the course of individual development. However, it places greater emphasis on the role of other social agents as a constraining force in individual adjustment (Strayer & Moss, 1989; Trevarthen, 1980). This biosocial approach assumes that social settings serve as primary forces canalizing the phenotypic expression of genetic potential. From this perspective, the analysis of early development of children's mental and physical adaptation, cannot be complete without a detailed consideration of organizational features that characterize the early social relations and the stable group settings within which individual growth and development take place (Valsiner, 1987).

BEHAVIORAL TYPOLOGY AND DEVELOPMENTAL SELECTION

Although modern researchers generally endorse an interactionist approach in the study of structure–process relationships during early development, the interactionist view is articulated somewhat differently by psychologists studying social development and behavioral biologists studying biosocial processes of adaptation. First, in studies of social development, coaction between partners is considered to be the driving force behind early growth in competence. In this type of research, individual experience is directly linked to aspects of social interaction with familiar partners (Trevarthen, 1980, 1983; Vygotsky, 1962), and individual understanding of reality is negotiated during the course of interaction with others (Winegar, 1988). The meaning of experience is co-constructed, and structural changes in the nature of communication are associated with social processes in which the actions of both partners are equally important (Strayer, Moss, & Blicharski, 1989). Studies in behavioral biology consider coactive processes at multiple levels in a systemic view of mutual influences among genetic, physiological, psychological, and social variables (Cairns, 1991; Gottlieb, 1991; Thelen, 1989).

In both disciplines, the accent is on what and how things develop. During the course of ontogeny, the initially diffuse behavioral potential of the child is structured by experience that leads to the emergence of progressively more mature traits. Although some stress the importance of the environment or physiology, others are more concerned with individual agency or social interchange. However, often such constructive approaches neglect the counterbalancing effects of behavioral selection and restriction of initial developmental potential. More specifically, a selectionist view supposes that, in the course of acquiring of an adaptive characteristic, alternative modes of functioning become increasingly less accessible to the individual. Although human plasticity is such that some acquired characteristics are changeable to some extent, the general process points in the direction of lost potential in the service of optimizing adaptive functions (Baldwin, 1897; Edelmann, 1987; Wallon, 1934). The concept of experiential canalization suggests that past experience constrains the possible range of reaction in specific developmental contexts. Particularities of past experience, encoded either in physiological functions or in mental representations of events, orient children toward different developmental pathways. Each successive experience progressively canalizes the ontogenetic trajectory.

Selective forces operate on individual, social, and physiological planes throughout development. Such individual selective processes are responsible for variability in the population, delineating homogeneous subgroups that display similar behavioral styles, individual characteristics, and experiential norms. At the level of the population, the apparent uniqueness of individual experience is attenuated by communalities of genetic, cultural, and ecological constraints. Children share a variety of predispositions that establish the range of individual differences in biological structures. On a sociocultural level, similarity of social roles and functions across human societies provides additional constraints on the reaction range within our species. Such genetic and experiential norms contribute to the emergence of stable individual differences that serve as differentiating boundaries between groups and cultures, while circumscribing groups of individuals who display similarities in behavioral expression and other developmental processes. It has been assumed that all known temperament types exist in all cultures, but methodological hurdles involved in intercultural research suggest that empirical enquiry into temperament types remains preliminary, and assumptions about the universality of characteristics remain hypothetical and potentially controversial (Angleitner & Riemann, 1991; Kohnstamm, 1989).

The conceptualization of the ontogenetic process as a form of behavioral canalization can be traced historically to Waddington (1942) and Holt (1931), and, still further, to Baldwin (1897), who was a major influence on the theoretical views of both Piaget and Wallon. For Baldwin, social interaction was not only characteristic of the human child, but also provided an important tool for ensuring survival of individuals and of the social species as a whole. He believed that recurrent combination of particular types of actions and responses during interaction with familiar others facilitates the emergence of qualitatively distinct social styles. The resulting diversity in behavioral styles can be linked to processes of ontogenetic selection that ultimately provide the source for evolutionary change within a given population (Cairns, 1991; Cairns & Hood, 1983; Edelmann, 1987; Strayer, 1990). Certain concepts, such as selection, plasticity, phenotypic range, and diversity, that have been central in behavioral biology are becoming increasingly important in psychological studies of developmental processes, and representational experience is of increasing concern for biological studies of early ontogeny.

In order to respond empirically to this tapestry of variables, associations, and developmental trajectories, we have chosen to adopt a descriptive typological approach while centering our attention on two fundamental aspects of individual differences in development: child temperament and mother–child information exchange during play. Early temperament has often been considered to be a relatively stable personality structure related in complex ways to genetic underpinnings, and represents, conceptually, the structure in our structure–process analysis (Buss & Plomin, 1984; Rothbart & Derryberry, 1981; Strelau & Angleitner, 1991). The convergent analysis of early temperamental characteristics in relation to patterns of mother–child interaction during spontaneous play offers important information about developmental processes shaping individual diversity in behavioral styles or, in other words, how constitution is associated with experience.

Since Schneirla's theoretical position, which emphasized behavioral development guided by dynamic meshing of innate and acquired characteristics, researchers of early temperament have generally adopted an interactive approach to early personality formation (Buss & Plomin, 1975, 1984; Rothbart & Posner, 1985; Schneirla, 1965/1972). Current debates in temperament research often focus on the issue of dynamic versus stable nature of early individual differences and the relationship of basic characteristics to other variables, such as language (Bates et al., 1988), cognition (Thomas & Chess, 1989) and social context (Trudel, 1988). Early on, findings from research on temperament were used, and they are still very useful, in child clinical evaluations. The goodness-of-fit model of Thomas and Chess (1977) accentuated the contribution of the child's temperamental characteristics to the social dynamics within the family, whereas other research evaluated how difficult temperament types affect child-rearing and child-care practices (Bates, Maslin, & Frankel, 1985; Carey & McDevitt, 1978). In parallel, in both Europe and North America, school psychologists have evaluated temperament in the educational setting (Balleyguier, 1989; Maziade, Côté, Boutin, Bernier, & Thivierge, 1987).

Children's temperament characteristics have most often been assessed using clinical interviews (Thomas & Chess, 1977) or parental questionnaires (Fullard, McDevitt, & Carey, 1984). In the past, naturalistic observation methods have usually been employed in order to validate questionnaire findings (Bates, 1989; Balleyguier, 1989). More recently, researchers have began to assess individual differences in temperamental characteristics using observational methods in laboratory settings (Goldsmith & Rothbart, 1991; Sameroff, Seifer, & Barocas, 1983). In our research, given our reliance on questionnaire assessments of temperament, it is important to note that the typological classification we propose is based on maternal conceptions and interpretations of children's emerging personalities. Although some temperament traits, such as activity level or mood, might readily be observed directly, others, like adaptability, persistence, or sensitivity, require greater familiarity over long periods, which renders direct observation impractical for researchers. For the purposes of this study, the temperament measure we have chosen represents maternal conceptualization of the child's disposition or style. These maternal representations are useful in two ways. First, as the child's privileged social partner, the mother's opinion of her child reflects a history of intimate interaction. Second, maternal conceptions about the child might influence her actions and thus indirectly contribute to changes in the child's behavior.

A PSYCHOBIOLOGICAL STUDY OF EARLY BEHAVIORAL STYLES

In our research program, we have investigated the family environment as a potential source of constraint and facilitation of children's early social styles and individual development (Blicharski & Strayer, 1991; Strayer & Moss, 1989). The MADEQ project (*Milieux d'Adaptation et du Développement des Enfants Québécois*) generated longitudinal information about mother–child interaction in the home environment (Strayer, 1982). The subjects in this project were drawn from a population of middle-class Québécois families residing in Montreal. Video records of mother–child interaction and a number of indirect measures were gathered every 6 months between the child's first and third birthdays.

In our longitudinal project, mothers responded to a translated version of the

Toddler Temperament Scale (TTS; Fullard, McDevitt, & Carey, 1978), when their children were 18 and 30 months old. The descriptive items correspond to nine temperament traits: activity, regularity, approach, adaptability, intensity, mood, persistence, distractibility, and threshold. Factor analyses yielded three distinct factors that were associated with the easy–average–difficult construct. Children whose individual temperament factor scores were on the extreme ends of the scale were identified as either *easy* or *difficult,* whereas the larger central group was identified as *average.* Furthermore, reduction of components in the factorial structure at 3 years indicated general trait consolidation as a function of age (Trudel, 1988). In another study, the relationship between temperament and early socialization experience was examined. Home-reared and day-care children differed clearly in the trait scores that were associated with the difficult-child construct (Trudel, Strayer, Jacques, & Moss, 1991).

In measuring the cognitive interactive processes of mother–child interaction, we have adopted a co-constructive approach to intellectual development. Vygotsky (1962) suggested that individual cognitive functioning is ultimately a product of more basic cultural processes involving the transfer of information between active social agents. In our study, we observed mother– child representational tactics in order to assess the co-constructed process directly. Observers noted all instances of eight basic problem-solving tactics used by their respective focal subjects (i.e., mother or child). *Identification* was coded when the focal subject labeled or identified an object. *Subgoal* was coded each time the subject accomplished, stated, or asked about an intermediate stage of the task activity. *Perceptual cue-highlighting* referred to tactics that describe physical or sensory aspects of objects or persons. *Functional* or *contextual cue-highlighting* re-grouped actions related to the exploration of functional or contextual associations among objects or events. A global distancing category regrouped four distinct tactics. *Distancing* was recorded whenever the focal subject identified or asked about the overall aim of the activity; when the tactic involved a comparison of current activities or objects with elements not present in the immediate context of the interaction; when the speaker evaluated past action and its relationship to the current state of affairs; or when the subject anticipated the impact of a proposed action on the attainment of a goal or subgoal. Finally, *social regulation* was evaluated using three categories: approval, disapproval, and task orientation, in which either individual attempts to orient the partner's attention to the ongoing activity (Strayer, Moss, & Blicharski, 1989).

In preliminary research, Blicharski, Moss, and Strayer (1985) found significant age and socialization effects in the use of a variety of verbal and nonverbal problem-solving tactics by 2-year-old children. Age of entry into early day care was associated with a more rapid emergence and more complex coordination of elementary problem-solving skills. In a second series of studies, differences in these children's representational activity were examined as a function of the quality of the primary attachment relationship and of early day-care experience

(Blicharski, LaFerté, & Strayer, 1989; Strayer & Moss, 1989; Strayer et al., 1989). Results indicated that both security of attachment and early social experience were positively correlated with developmental rates of various problem-solving tactics. Secure dyads displayed behavioral exchanges such that the use of cognitive distancing tactics by one partner was followed by a distancing response from the other with greater frequency. Similar distancing initiatives by partners in insecure dyads led to social-regulation responses. Results from these studies supported the view that the emergence of problem-solving strategies is a socially constructed process, and actions of both partners contribute to changes in children's cognitive development (Vaugn, Strayer, Jacques, Trudel, & Seifer, 1991).

Global aspects of mother–child representational tactics used during play at home were also evaluated in terms of the *easy–difficult* dimensions of child temperament at both 18 and 30 months. Hourly rate use of four types of information-exchange strategies were examined separately for children and for mothers; these included action tactics, object references, cognitive distancing, and social regulation (Strayer et al., 1989). Repeated measures analyses of variance (age × *easy–difficult* classification and gender) were performed on the two sets of observational data (Gravel & Lapointe, 1990). Although there were no significant associations between child temperament and children's use of these global measures, children classified as more difficult consistently received fewer regulatory directives from their mothers at both ages. At 18 months, *easy* girls received more social regulation from their mothers than children from the other two temperament types. However, at 30 months, *average* boys witnessed maternal regulatory activity most often. Taken together, these findings provided initial evidence for a possible link between indirect measures of child temperament and observational indices of information exchange during mother–child play.

DIVERSITY IN TEMPERAMENTAL PROFILES

In reviewing these results in light of our biosocial perspective, two problems became apparent. First, the classification of children into *easy, average,* and *difficult* hides diversity in temperamental profiles. Second, the lack of significant associations between temperament classification and children's use of cognitive tactics might have been an artifact of the global nature of our behavioral classification. Because more detailed data were available, we were able to investigate this hypothesis. Furthermore, the social regulation category regrouped three quite diverse tactics noted by the observers. These included approval, disapproval, and task orientation. Given the significant findings on maternal regulatory activity, we needed to determine whether the less difficult children received more approval, more disapproval, or more orientations to task.

As analytic tools, descriptive typologies have frequently been used in etholog-ical, biological, and ecological investigations. The general goal involves classi-fying species, individuals, or behaviors into natural subgroups that can be char-acterized as highly similar across a set of relevant, and usually empirically derived, descriptors (De Ghett, 1978; L. Legendre & P. Legendre, 1985). In our study, the descriptive typological approach was used specifically to delineate developmental trajectories for subgroups of children who seemed to be similar in their temperament profiles between 18 and 30 months. For example, Naud (1991) identified subgroups of children at both 18 and 30 months showing distinct temperament profiles by using cluster analyses of the nine temperament traits. Contrasting the resulting child clusters on a number of socioaffective measures of mother–child interaction, Naud reported associations between chil-dren's and mother's affective tone, dyadic engagement, and the cluster classifica-tions. Some of the results remained stable at the two ages. From a biosocial perspective, the clustering technique seemed more adequate in accounting for diversity in the sample than the traditional *easy–difficult* dichotomy. However, because the main focus of Naud's study was on socioaffective dimensions of mother–child interaction, little attention was given to actually describing the ways that the clusters of children differed in their temperament characteristics. Guided by questions raised in these earlier studies, we undertook a series of analyses that we hoped would clarify our understanding of the relation between children's temperament structures and observable processes in mother–child in-formation exchange.

From the original longitudinal project, temperament data were available at both 18 and 30 months for 50 children (27 girls, 23 boys). The objective of the primary analyses was to identify temperament types by classifying children who were perceived in similar ways by their mothers on the nine temperament traits across this 1-year period. The clustering procedure, which took into account both the 18- and 30-month data (9 variables at 2 ages) revealed five subgroups of children differing significantly in temperamental profiles. Figure 24.1 illustrates the cluster solution. Children regrouped in cluster E; and the two children who appeared to be unique could not be considered in descriptive analyses because of their small number. However, it is possible that these outliers represent other coherent temperament types, which would emerge if a larger sample of children were available for classification.

Repeated measures analyses of variance (cluster membership × age) were used to determine the contribution of each of the nine traits, at either age level, to cluster differentiation. In general, all nine traits differentiated the four tempera-ment types at both 18 and 30 months. Stable main effects of temperament classification were apparent for eight of the nine traits. The Intensity trait con-tributed to cluster differentiation only when considered in interaction with age. Main effects for age indicated that as children grow older, they are perceived as

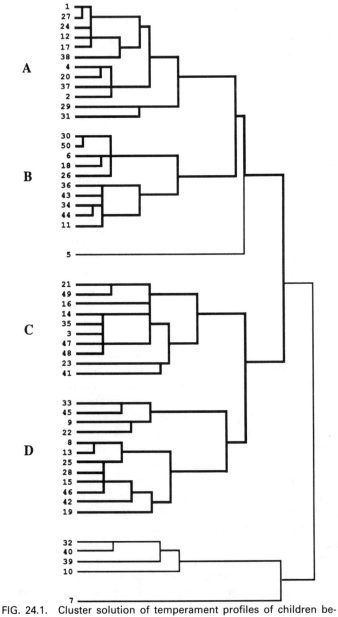

FIG. 24.1. Cluster solution of temperament profiles of children between 18 and 30 months.

more adaptable, more irregular, and more persistent, and show higher threshold scores. However, they are seen as less active at 30 months than they were at 18 months.

Children in the first cluster (A) were characterized as most approaching, most moody, most distractable, most active, and most irregular at both age levels. They were also described as the least persistent and showed the lowest scores on the threshold trait. It appeared that mothers of Cluster A children held extreme conceptions of their children's temperaments. This particular combination of scores on traits describing Cluster A children corresponds to the "difficult child" construct. Temperament profiles of children in Cluster B were differentiated from the other three types in being described as most adaptable, most regular, and least active. The characterization of Cluster B children corresponds to the "easy child" construct. Children in Cluster C were described as least distractable and most persistent by their mothers at both ages. These children were characterized by their mothers as attentive, perseverant, and adapted to learning. Finally, mothers described Cluster D children as least approaching, least adaptable, best humored, and with highest threshold scores of the four groups at both ages. Furthermore, these children were portrayed as most intense at 18 months and least intense at 30 months. This age change in the attribution of children's intensity might reflect important life events occurring during this period. In general, Cluster D children were portrayed as shy, sensitive, and happy.

Our second set of analyses examined possible associations between temperament classifications and mother–child information-exchange tactics during play at home at both ages. Observational data were available for 32 mother–child dyads from the preceding sample; 11 Cluster A, 6 Cluster B, 7 Cluster C, and 8 Cluster D children provided both the temperament and observational data. Hourly rate indices were calculated for each tactic for both children and mothers. Hourly rate measures were chosen because these indices remain sensitive to differences in interactive involvement while controlling for possible variations in the duration of video segments. Repeated measures analyses of variance were used to investigate whether particular temperament profiles were associated with differences in either children's or mothers' cognitive styles across this 1-year period. In general, with age children increased their hourly rate of total representational activity, only reducing their use of task orientation at 30 months. Mothers' hourly rates of tactics use in interaction was also affected by their children's age. As the children became more competent in social action and object use, mothers engaged in less overall representational activity. In general, only maternal distancing tactics increased at 30 months.

When we examined the interaction between temperament classification and hourly rates of representational tactics, results indicated significant differences between groups at 18 months, as well as some age × temperament-type interactions. At the younger age, clusters differed in their use of total representational activity, particularly in hourly rate of use of subgoals, identifications, and disapproval tactics. Analyses of maternal data revealed a similar trend. Mothers also differed the most in their total rate use of tactics when their children were 18 months old. Mothers of children showing particular temperament types differed in their hourly rate use of subgoals, functional cues, and approval, at the younger age.

Children in Cluster A were portrayed as extreme on most temperament traits, including activity level. At 18 months, children in Cluster A showed the lowest rates of total representational activity. At 30 months, they showed the highest frequencies of labeling, a tactic characteristic of the younger age. Because frequent use of representational tactics indicates persistent attention to the task, these children's low rates of tactics use suggest that they were not attending to the object play during the videotaped home visit, possibly being distracted by other interests. On the interactive plane, mothers of Cluster A children showed the lowest rates of functional cues, approval, and distancing tactics at 18 months. The mothers' infrequent use of these facilitative tactics is consistent with their children's behavior and with their own characterization of the children as "difficult."

Cluster B children seemed easier for the mothers: most adaptive and regular, least active and least intense in their temperament. During interaction, these children used object labeling the most at 18 months and the least at 30 months. In parallel, their mothers seemed highly engaged in object play at 18 months, using more total tactics than other mothers. However, at 30 months these mothers were the least approving. In this cluster, child behavior seemed to be related to maternal didactic involvement.

Children in Cluster C were described as least distractable and most persistent by their mothers at both ages. These children were most engaged in object activity at 18 months, using higher hourly rates of subgoals than the other groups. They also used more disapproval than other children at the younger age. The infrequent use of labeling at 18 months by Cluster C children indicates that their persistent, concentrated play was not accompanied by object identification. The mothers of Cluster C children also did not use nominal tactics at the younger age, indicating some synchrony in their interaction. At 30 months, these mothers show the highest total hourly rates of tactics use. They engaged in more functional cues, more distancing, more approval, and more identification than the other mothers at the older age.

Finally, the least approaching, least adaptive, highly reactive, and good humored Cluster D children did not show any particular profile of tactics use. Hourly rate use of representational activity remained close to the sample mean, neither particularly high nor low on any category. Mothers of Cluster D children used representational tactics least often in object play at both ages. Therefore, the children's nonapproaching attitude was paralleled by maternal noninvolvement in structuring of the play interaction, especially at 30 months.

CONCLUSION

In general, our results support the argument that there is a fundamental connection between individual personality development and socially embedded representational experience. However, the relationship between temperamental characteristics and representational activity profile is complex, and is better understood as a co-constructive process involving social canalization of individual styles.

Our typological approach yielded four subgroups of children who were differentially characterized by their mothers. Although the *easy* and *difficult* child types were clearly identified by our procedure, the attentive and persistent Cluster C children and the shy and sensitive Cluster D children do not fall easily into the traditional construct. Our findings also indicate that dyadic play in the home environment is affected by children's temperamental dispositions. Both the children and their mothers differed as a function of child temperament classification. Regarding questions about maternal regulatory activity raised by previous studies, it appears that mothers of difficult children showed the lowest rates of approval at 18 months. Mothers of children classified as *easy* used the highest frequencies of representational tactics at both ages, but used approval least at 30 months. It is interesting to note that greater differences between the groups were evident at the younger age level, a result that supports a socialization view of behavioral style and the emerging stability of early temperament (Trudel, 1988). Mothers appear to adjust their communicative tactics in relation to their type of child. Most importantly, their behavior appears consistent with their interpretation of their child's character.

Social experience has been addressed in past studies of temperament. However, most researchers use socialization measures as grouping variables for analyses of variance, rarely assessing children's social interaction through direct observation (Rutter, 1987, 1989). Although some argue that temperament profiles are associated with the quality of parent–child relationship, the relationship itself is often evaluated using questionnaires or laboratory data (Vaughn, Strayer, Jacques, & Trudel, 1990). The biosocial approach that guided our observational assessment of child temperament and interactive processes yielded a coherent portrait of the diversity in child temperament and play tactics. The generalizability of our findings to other groups can only be assessed through further data collection. However, it is important to note that, even with a restricted sample, four clearly distinguishable temperament types were identified. Given that selective forces shape the course of development through both social and biological experience, we would predict a still greater diversity in temperamental profiles and interactive styles if data were available for a larger sample of children.

Although child temperament has often been described as a dynamic structure, empirically, information from questionnaire data can, at best, be considered as shadows on the cave wall, representing elusive forms that are difficult to describe precisely with existing methods within the ethical boundaries of science. According to guidelines in the literature, temperament should be evaluated by convergent measures from descriptions by parents and independent observers, as well as from direct observation of the child in various contexts (Goldsmith et al., 1987). Furthermore, endogenous factors, such as child health, or genetic and physiological givens, are considered as central in personality development. If we take these guidelines seriously, then the temperament construct is probably best understood as a complex mental representation rather than a tangible organic structure. Nevertheless, such a representation, in the minds of either parents or developmental researchers, may serve as a potentially useful tool for understanding and facilitating child adaptation.

ACKNOWLEDGMENTS

The research presented in this chapter was funded by grants from the *Spencer Foundation*, the *Conseil de Recherche en Sciences Humaines du Canada*, and the *Fonds pour la Formation de Chercheurs et l'Aide à la Recherche*. We are especially grateful to Fred Strayer, Director of the *Laboratoire d'Ethologie Humaine*, who has been the driving force behind the concepts and methods presented. We also graciously thank Brian Vaughn and Terry Winegar for their constructive criticism and encouraging comments throughout the preparation of this chapter.

REFERENCES

Ainsworth, M.D.S. (1969). Object relations, dependency and attachment: A theoretical review of the infant–mother relationship. *Child Development, 40*, 969–1025.

Angleitner, A., & Riemann, R. (1991). What can we learn from the discussion of personality questionnaires for the construction of temperament inventories? In J. Strelau & A. Angleitner (Eds.), *Explorations in temperament: International perspectives on theory and measurement* (pp. 191–204). New York: Plenum.

Baldwin, J. M. (1897). *Social and ethical interpretations in mental development*. London: Macmillan.

Balleyguier, G. (1989). Temperament and character: The French school. In G. A. Kohnstamm, J. E. Bates, & M. K. Rothbart (Eds.), *Temperament in childhood* (pp. 597–606). New York: Wiley.

Bates, J. E. (1989). Applications of temperament concepts. In G. A. Kohnstamm, J. E. Bates, & M. K. Rothbart (Eds.), *Temperament in childhood* (pp. 321–355). New York: Wiley.

Bates, J. E., Bretherton, I., & Snyder, L. (1988). *From first words to grammar: Individual differences and dissociable mechanisms*. Cambridge, England: Cambridge University Press.

Bates, J. E., Maslin, C. A., & Frankel, K. A. (1985). Attachment security, mother–child interaction, and temperament as predictors of behavior problem ratings at age three years. In I. Bretherton & E. Waters (Eds.), *Growing points in attachment theory and research. Monographs of the Society for Research in Child Development* (Serial No. 209, 167–193).

Berger, G. (1950). *Traité pratique d'analyse du caractère* [Practical treatise for the analysis of character]. Paris: Presses Universitaires de France.

Bertenthal, B. I. (1991). A systems view of behavioral canalization: Theory and commentary. *Developmental Psychology, 27,* 3.

Blicharski, T., Laferté, L., & Strayer, F. F. (1989, May). *Contingencies in information exchange during mother–child problem-solving.* Poster presented at the meeting of the Society for Research In Child Development, Kansas City, MO.

Blicharski, T., Moss, E., & Strayer, F. F. (1985, July). *Cognitive tactics in child–mother interaction.* Poster presented at the International Society for the Study of Behavioral Development, Tours, France.

Blicharski, T., & Strayer, F. F. (1991). *A cross-cultural study of contextual constraints on the development of language and communication.* Grant proposal to the Conseil de Recherche en Sciences Humaines, Canada.

Bruner, J. S. (1975). The ontogeny of language acts. *Journal of Child Language, 2,* 1–19.

Buss, A. H., & Plomin, R. A. (1975). *A temperament theory of personality development.* New York: Wiley.

Buss, A. H., & Plomin, R. A. (1984). *Temperament: Early developing personality traits.* Hillsdale, NJ: Lawrence Erlbaum Associates.

Cairns, R. B. (1991). Multiple metaphors for a singular idea. *Developmental Psychology, 27,* 23–26.

Cairns, R. B., & Hood, K. E. (1983). Continuity in social development: A comparative perspective on individual difference prediction. In P. B. Baltes & O. G. Brim (Eds.), *Life-span development and behavior* (Vol. 5, pp. 301–358). New York: Academic Press.

Carey, M. C., & McDevitt, S. C. (1978). Revision of the Infant Temperament Questionnaire. *Pediatrics, 61,* 735–739.

de Ajuriaguerra, J., Harrisson, A., & Lézine, I. (1967). Etude sur quelques aspects de la réactivité émotionnelle dans la première année [Study of aspects of emotional reactivity during the first year]. *Psychiatrie de l'Enfant, 10,* 293–380.

De Ghett, V. J. (1978). Hierarchical cluster analysis. In P. W. Colgan & Smith (Eds.), *Quantitative ethology* (pp. 116–143). Kingston, Ontario: Queen's University Press.

Edelmann, G. M. (1987). *Neural Darwinism: The theory of neuronal group selection.* New York: Basic Books.

Fullard, W., McDevitt, S. C., & Carey, W. B. (1978). *The Toddler Temperament Scale.* Unpublished manuscript, Temple University, Department of Educational Psychology, Philadelphia.

Fullard, W., McDevitt, S. C., & Carey, W. B. (1984). Assessing temperament in one- to three-year-old children. *Journal of Pediatric Psychology, 9,* 205–216.

Goldsmith, H. H., Buss, A. H., Plomin, R., Rothbart, M. K., Thomas, A., Chess, S., Hinde, R. A., & McCall, R. B. (1987). Roundtable: What is temperament? Four approaches. *Child Development, 58,* 505–529.

Goldsmith, H. H., & Rothbart, M. K. (1991). Contemporary instruments for assessing early temperament by questionnaire and in the laboratory. In J. Strelau & A. Angleitner (Eds.), *Explorations in temperament: International perspectives on theory and measurement* (pp. 249–272). New York: Plenum.

Gottlieb, G. (1991). Experiential canalization of behavioral development: Theory. *Developmental Psychology, 27,* 4–13.

Gravel, F., & Lapointe, P. (1990, April). *The role of temperament in mother–child problem solving.* Poster presented at the International Conference on Infant Studies, Montreal, Quebec, Canada.

Holt, E. B. (1931). *Animal drive and the learning process* (Vol. 1). New York: Holt.

Kohnstamm, G. A. (1989). Historical and international perspectives. In G. A. Kohnstamm, J. E. Bates, & M. K. Rothbart (Eds.), *Temperament in childhood* (pp. 557–566). New York: Wiley.

Legendre, L., & Legendre, P. (1985). *Numerical ecology* (Vol. 1). Montréal: Masson, Presses de l'Université du Québec.

330   BLICHARSKI, GRAVEL, TRUDEL

Lerner, R. M. (1991). Changing organism–context relations as the basic process of development: A developmental contextual perspective. *Developmental Psychology, 27*, 27–32.

Le Senne, R. (1945). *Traité de caractérologie* [Treatise of characterology]. Paris: Presses Universitaires de France.

Maccoby, E. E., & Martin, J. (1983). Socialization in the context of the family: Parent–child interaction. In P. H. Mussen (Series Ed.) & E. M. Hetherington (Vol. Ed.), *Handbook of child psychology: Vol. 4. Socialization, personality, and social development* (4th ed., pp. 1–102). New York: Wiley.

Malrieu, P. (1952). *Les émotions et la personnalité de l'enfant* [Child emotions and personality]. Paris: Vrin.

Maziade, M., Côté, R., Boutin, P., Bernier, H., & Thivierge, J. (1987). Temperament and intellectual development: A longitudinal study from infancy to four years. *American Journal of Psychiatry, 114*, 144–150.

Montagner, H., Henry, J. C., Lombardot, M., Benedini, M., Restoin, A., Bolzoni, D., Moyse, A., Humbert, Y., Durand, M., Burnod, J., Nicolas, R. M., & Rosier, M. (1977). Etudes éthophysiologiques de groupes d'enfants de 14 mois à 5 ans à la crèche et à l'école maternelle [Ethophysiological studies of children between 14 months and 5 years of age in day-care settings]. *Psychologie Médicale, 9*, 2075–2112.

Nadel-Brulfert, J., & Baudonnière, M. (1982). The social function of reciprocal imitation in 2-year-old peers. *International Journal of Behavioral Development, 5*, 95–109.

Naud, J. (1991). *Caractéristiques individuelles et régulation socio-affective à la fin de la prime enfance* [Individual characteristics and socioaffective regulation at 30 months]. Unpublished doctoral thesis. Université du Québec à Montréal, Canada.

Nelson, K. (1975). Structure and strategy in learning to talk. *Monographs of the Society for Research in Child Development*, No. 38 (Serial No. 149).

Olson, S. L., Bates, J. E., & Bayles, K. (1984). Mother–infant interaction and the development of individual differences in children's cognitive competence. *Developmental Psychology, 20*, 166–179.

Piaget, J. (1967). *Biologie et connaissance: Essai sur les relations entre les régulations organiques et les processus cognitifs* [Biology and knowledge: Essay on the relationship between organic regulation and cognitive processes]. Paris: Gallimard.

Piaget, J. (1981). *Intelligence and affectivity: Their relationship during child development*. Palo Alto, CA: Annual Reviews.

Rothbart, M. K., & Derryberry, D. (1981). Development of individual differences in temperament. In M. E. Lamb & A. L. Brown (Eds.), *Advances in developmental psychology* (Vol. 1, pp. 37–86). Hillsdale, NJ: Lawrence Erlbaum Associates.

Rothbart, M. K., & Posner, M. I. (1985). Temperament and the development of self-regulation. In L. C. Hartlage & C. F. Telzrow (Eds.), *The neuropsychology of individual differences: A developmental perspective* (pp. 93–123). New York: Plenum.

Rutter, M. (1987). Continuities and discontinuities from infancy. In J. D. Osofsky (Ed.), *Handbook of infant development* (pp. 1150–1198). New York: Wiley.

Rutter, M. (1989). Temperament: Conceptual issues and clinical implications. In G. A. Kohnstamm, J. E. Bates, & M. K. Rothbart (Eds.), *Temperament in childhood* (pp. 463–479). New York: Wiley.

Sameroff, A. J., Seifer, R., & Barocas, R. (1983). Impact of parental psychopathology: Diagnosis, severity, or social status effects? *Infant Mental Health Journal, 4*, 236–249.

Scarr-Salapatek, S. (1976). Genetic determinants of infant development: An overstated case. In L. Lipsitt (Ed.), *Developmental psycho-biology: The significance of infancy* (pp. 59–79). Hillsdale, NJ: Lawrence Erlbaum Associates.

Schneirla, T. C. (1972). Aspects of stimulation and organization in approach–withdrawal processes underlying vertebrate behavior development. In L. R. Aronson, E. Tobach, D. S. Lehrman, &

J. Rosenblatt (Eds.), *Selected writings of T. C. Schneirla* (pp. 344–412). San Francisco: W. H. Freeman. (Original work published 1965)

Soussignan, R., Koch, P., & Montagner, H. (1988). Cardiovascular and behavioral changes in children moving from kindergarten to elementary school. *Journal of Child Psychology and Psychiatry, 29*, 321–333.

Strayer, F. F. (1982). *Groupe de Recherche sur les Milieux d'adaptation et le Developpement des Enfants Québéquois* [Research group for the study of contexts of adaptation and development of children in Québec]. Unpublished manuscript.

Strayer, F. F. (1989). Co-adaptation within the peer group: A psychobiological study of early competence. In B. Schneider, G. Atilla, J. Nadel, & R. Weisman (Eds.), *Social competence in developmental perspective* (pp. 145–173). Dordrecht, Netherlands: Kluwer.

Strayer, F. F., & Moss, E. (1989). The co-construction of representational activity during social interaction. In M. H. Bornstein & J. S. Bruner (Eds), *Interaction and human development* (pp. 173–196). Hillsdale, NJ: Lawrence Erlbaum Associates.

Strayer, F. F., Moss, E., & Blicharski, T. (1989). Bio-social bases of representational activity during early childhood. In T. Winegar (Ed.), *Social interaction and the development of children's understanding* (pp. 78–93). Norwood, NJ: Ablex.

Strelau, J., & Angleitner, A. (1991). Temperament research: Some divergences and similarities. In J. Strelau & A. Angleitner (Eds.), *Explorations in temperament: International perspectives on theory and measurement* (pp. 1–12). New York: Plenum.

Thelen, E. (1989). Self-organization in developmental processes: Can systems approaches work? In M. R. Gunnar & E. Thelen (Eds.), *Minnesota Symposia on Child Psychology: Vol. 22. Systems and development* (pp. 77–117). Hillsdale, NJ: Lawrence Erlbaum Associates.

Thomas, A., & Chess, S. (1977). *Temperament and development.* New York: Brunner/Mazel.

Thomas, A., & Chess, S. (1989). Temperament and personality. In G. A. Kohnstamm, J. E. Bates, & M. K. Rothbart (Eds.), *Temperament in childhood* (pp. 249–261). New York: Wiley.

Trevarthen, C. (1980). Neurological development and the growth of psychological functions. In J. Sants (Ed.), *Developmental psychology and society* (pp. 51–84). London: Macmillan.

Trudel, M. (1988). *Perspective bio-sociale sur le tempérament durant la prime enfance* [Bio-social perspective on temperament during early childhood]. Unpublished doctoral thesis, Université du Québec à Montréal, Canada.

Trudel, M., Strayer, F. F., Jacques, M., & Moss, E. (1991). Influence de la socialisation précoce en garderie sur le tempérament de l'enfant à deux ans [Influence of early socialization in day-care on children's temperament at two years of age]. *Apprentissage et Socialisation, 14*, 105–115.

Valsiner, J. (Ed.). (1987). *Culture and development of children's actions.* Chichester, England: Wiley.

Vaughn, B. E., Strayer, F. F., Jacques, M., Trudel, M., & Seifer, R. (1991). *Maternal descriptions of two- and three-year-old children: A comparison of Attachment Q-sorts in two socio-cultural communities. International Journal for the Study of Behavioural Development, 14*, 249–271.

Vygotsky, L. S. (1962). Thought and language (E. Hanfmann & G. Vaker, Trans.). Cambridge, MA: MIT Press.

Waddington, C. H. (1942). Canalization of development and the inheritance of acquired characters. *Nature, 150*, 563–564.

Wallon, H. (1934). *Les origines du caractère chez l'enfant* [The origins of character in children]. Paris: Boivin.

Wertsch, J. V. (1984). The zone of proximal development: Some conceptual issues. In B. Rogoff & J. Wertsch (Eds.). *Children's learning in the zone of proximal development* (pp. 7–18). San Francisco, CA: Jossey-Bass.

Winegar, L. T. (1988). Children's emerging understanding of social events: Co-construction and social process. In J. Valsiner (Ed.), *Child development within culturally structured environments* (pp. 3–27). Norwood, NJ: Ablex.

25 The French Tradition From the American Perspective

Bettye Caldwell
University of Arkansas for Medical Sciences

Serving as a discussant for this exciting group of chapters fills me with a poignant sense of loss, as it makes me aware of just how provincial most American behavioral scientists are. Although I am a devout Francophile, one who can struggle through a paper written in French with a minimum of assistance, I simply don't have access to the work of authors of the chapters in this section, unless, of course, they publish in American journals, as several of these authors have, or unless one is fortunate enough to be on a reprint exchange list, as I used to be with Therese Gouin-Décarie and Irène Lézine—two scientists whose work is quoted in this series. But most of the studies discussed by the authors were new to me, and I should have known about the work. Thus, it is clear that a major lesson to be learned from all the papers in this book is that it is time for American investigators to end their scientific isolationism, acting as though all the relevant literature that needs to be referenced in any research area is to be found in American journals written in the language we have convinced ourselves was used when the command came down to "Let there be light."

A reading of these chapters stimulates many reactions. However, keeping with my assignment of brevity, I shall limit my comments to three areas: (a) Francophone recognition of the changing nature of early socialization; (b) the laudatory biosocial orientation of much of the research; and (c) and the acceptance of research as an arm of public policy.

THE CHANGING NATURE OF EARLY SOCIALIZATION

Three chapters in this section (by Pêcheux and Labrell; by Pierrehumbert and Fivaz-Depeursinge; and by Provost) bear testimony to the recognition by these investigators that there has been a *paradigm shift* in early socialization throughout all the industrialized world and much of the developing world. This shift has been necessitated by the dramatic increase in the percentage of mothers with young children who are in the labor force. As different countries rarely use the same age cuts for their demographic surveys, it is difficult to compare the 75% of French mothers with children younger than 2 years old working full-time with the 54% of American mothers with children younger than 1 year in the work force. Even so, on cannot escape the conclusion that the norm for early child rearing has now shifted from the (perhaps mythological) exclusivity of a dyadic relationship to at least triadic, if not polyadic, relationships.

There have been a few studies in America that recognized the necessity of considering nonmaternal attachment as a developmental experience of consequence on its own (e.g., Howes, Rodning, Galluzo, & Myers, 1988). In general, however, attachments to persons other than the mother—even the father—have been held up to the prism of infant–mother attachment to see what colors might radiate forth from it. In general, that attachment in the American literature (and in articles written for parent consumption) is still considered prototypical, necessary as a baseline for all other attachments, and, in some analyses (e.g., Belsky, 1986), vulnerable and at the mercy of early child care arrangements that deviate from the formula for the previous paradigm—namely, full-time maternal care.

It is refreshing to find in the Francophone studies full-scale recognition of the importance of all the other attachment assignments that the human infant has—to the father, to alternative caregivers (sometimes more than one simultaneously or sequentially), and to siblings and other family members. Findings that these may be either continuous or discontinuous (see the chapter by Provost), or possibly complementary or compensatory (see the chapter by Pierrehumbert and Fivaz-Depeursinge), represent a step forward in our understanding of the inevitable complexity of such relationships. And the evolution of these different patterns (undifferentiated at 6 months, essentially unrelated at 24 months) traced longitudinally by Pierrehumbert and Fivaz-Depeursinge needs to be noted by all American investigators. The conceptualization of variables in such research represents an important theoretical advance in the study of early socialization.

A MORE SUBSTANTIAL BIOSOCIAL ORIENTATION

Most American investigators pay lipservice to the importance of linking biological and social factors in our attempts to understand human development. But for most of us it is rarely more than a sentence or two included near the end of an article. Actually, to many of us this point of view is, deep within our psyches, positively unAmerican. We forgave Piaget for his repeated assertions that he was really a biologist or an epistemologist, perhaps only because it was easy to forget about it while digesting many pages of descriptions of Laurent or Jacqueline. But even that was not easy.

The re-emergence of temperament as an important variable in socialization research is encouraging; one also finds this in America, as evidenced by a number of new measurement instruments such as those by Achenbach, Edelbrock, and Howell (1987), and Carey and McDevitt (1978). However, its use as a major variable by Blicharski, Gravel, and Trudel (this volume) fits more comfortably into the authors' theoretical framework than is often the case in American research. Nonetheless, I was a bit disappointed after being so drawn into the rationale for attention to the variable to find that "easy, average, and difficult" were the only categories they found useful in their analysis. Hopefully, on both sides of the Atlantic we shall do a better job in the future of meaningfully including biological variables in child development research. In the on-going National Institute of Child Health and Human Development (NICHD) Study on Early Child Care we are including child temperament as a moderating variable. Our instrumentation is no more sophisticated than that being used in the France and Quebec study, and perhaps our classification will offer no more than the three obvious options open to those investigators. However, even without clear methodological advances, such an attempt represents a conceptual improvement over previous research.

POLICY-RELEVANT RESEARCH AGENDA

It was especially encouraging to read in the paper by Pêcheux and Labrell that "researchers in France are civil servants and have to meet the State concerns." American investigators should also take note of the reminder that Wallon, in this country, hardly more than a footnote in a book on the history of psychology, played a key role in France "not only as a scientist, but as a citizen and a militant." In this country a few scientists have played that role—at least the citizen part and occasionally the militant (and unpopular) part of the role. People like Urie Bronfenbrenner, Ed Zigler, Jim Gallagher, and Susan Gray come immediately to mind as good examples of citizen-scientists. When the data warranted action, these people were willing to try to influence policy and catalyze action. And both the science and the public welfare have benefitted from their efforts.

The area of day-care research cited in the Pêcheux and Labrell paper is a good example of the rallying of research attention to a demographic trend. But again, France was far ahead of this country. They tell us that as far back as 1966 French scientists were on the *qui'vive* to make certain that day care did not harm children and could be a positive experience for them. At that time, only a few brave Americans were either aware of or concerned about the issue, and most of us who were (e.g., Caldwell & Richmond, 1964; Robinson, 1968) were either patronized or criticized for our efforts. Now, fortunately, there is almost a bandwagon effect as day care research has been identified as the "in" topic. Improve-

ments in conceptualization and methodology are sure to result from this acceptance of the fact that social issues can legitimately drive research efforts.

REFERENCES

Achenbach, T. M., Edelbrock, C. S., & Howell, C. T. (1987). Empirically based assessment of the
behavior/emotional problems of 2- and 3-year-old children. *Journal of Abnormal Child Psycholo-
gy, 15*, 629–650.
Belsky, J. (1986). Infant day care: A cause for concern? *Zero to Three, 6*, 1–7.
Caldwell, B. M., & Richmond, J. B. (1964). Programmed day care for the very young child: A
preliminary report. *Journal of Marriage and the Family, 26*, 481–488.
Carey, M. C., & McDevitt, S. C. (1978). Revision of the Infant Temperament Questionnaire.
Pediatrics, 61, 735–739.
Howes, C., Rodning, C., Galluzo, D. C., & Myers, L. (1988). Attachment and child care: Rela-
tionships with mother and caregiver. *Early Childhood Research Quarterly, 3*, 403–416.
Robinson, H. B. (1968). The Frank Porter Graham Child Development Center. In L. Dittman (Ed.),
Early child care: The new perspectives (pp. 302–312). New York: Atherton Press.

26

Interaction and Development: Francophone, Anglophone, and Germanophone Perspectives?

Hellgard Rauh
Free University of Berlin

Reading the five chapters in this section on interaction and development, equipped with the helpful introduction by Pêcheux and Labrell, not only gave me new insights into Francophone approaches to developmental psychology, but also put into a new light the culturally and philosophically rooted scientific predelications of my own language community as compared to the Francophone and the Anglophone worlds.

As a first step, I compared the topics in this book, in particular in the section on interaction and development, with the paper and poster titles of the Francophone participants at the 1992 European Conference on Developmental Psychology (see Palacios, 1992) and found a remarkable overlap. It appears that the research topics selected for this volume are, in fact, representative of recent Francophone developmental psychology of the infancy and early childhood period. This early period seems to be most attractive for Francophone developmental psychologists altogether.

The reader used to American research papers may be somewhat puzzled by the wide avenue that Francophone scientists take to introduce and to discuss their research. They easily shift between disciplines—philosophy, sociology of cultures, psychoanalysis, and biology—as well as between theories, models, empirical observations, and clinical insights. Except for Provost, whose chapter represents a North American rather than a Francophone style (straightforward, linear, and without philosophical and interpretive excursions), most authors seem to use their empirical research approaches and results as secondary to their general discussion, an attitude they share with many other continental Europeans. The greater emphasis on facts rather than on theories, in contrast, seems to be the typical Anglo-American approach. Both approaches are rooted historically in different philosophical lines of thought: rationalism and empiricism.

Under the heading "Interaction and Development," I expected psychological research results on social development in infancy and childhood. What I actually read, however, could be more properly characterized as a social psychology of development. While typical also for most of the research topics, this shift in emphasis most properly reflects the theoretical and methodological approaches. Sociology and social psychology, in fact, are the fields within the social sciences in which French scientists have been most influential internationally.

Three major topics are addressed in the five chapters. First, there are processes of mother–infant or father–infant interaction, such as mutual attention monitoring, cueing, highlighting, and distancing as examples of cognitive regulatory behaviors, and approving/disapproving, task orienting, and even teasing as examples of social regulatory behaviors (Pêcheux & Labrell; Blicharski, Gravel, & Trudel). Second, the dynamics of and changes in social relations are discussed within families (dyadic and triadic), across settings (home and day care), or during a setting transition (home to day care; day care to kindergarten), including adult–infant attachment, as well as peer relations (Pierrehumbert & Fivaz-Depeursinge; Provost). Finally, the social construction of parental conceptions of the child's personality, of developmental milestones, and of proper developmental stimulation (Blicharski et al.; Sabatier) were presented. Although these topics may have been dealt with by any author outside the Francophone world, the particular Francophone approach appears to be quite unique.

VIEWS ON SOCIAL DEVELOPMENT
AND INTERACTION

The Origins of Social Behavior

For the Francophone authors, it seems obvious that the infant is social from birth on and that he or she can live and develop only within social relations and by social interaction. Social relations, in their conceptions, are so fundamental to human development that some place their origin already in the fetal period (see Pierrehumbert & Fivaz-Depeursinge).

In contrast, there has been a long discussion in the United States about the age from which infants or toddlers are capable of "truly" social behaviors (Hartup, 1983; see Rauh, 1987b). In this conception, the infant is born with behaviors or operants that are nonsocial or, at best, neither social nor nonsocial, and becomes social only as a result of learning, rearing, and teaching in the interaction with a competent adult person (Gewirtz, 1969). Occasionally, the term *socialization* seems to carry overtones of normative moral behavior.

Germanophone conceptual inclinations could be placed between the Francophone and American approaches in this discussion and seem to have been influenced by Lorenz (1965), as well as by Bühler (1927) and Hetzer (1967). In their conceptions, the infant is born with some social or protosocial competencies necessary for eliciting social interaction and, thus, for survival, on which he or she may build more complex behaviors with development (Bischof, 1989; Keller, 1989; Lamb & Keller, 1991; Markefka & Nauck, 1992; M. Papousek & H. Papousek, 1991; Rauh, 1987a, 1987b, 1987c). These behaviors are thought of as being rooted in approach and avoidance tendencies, as possibly instinctive in origin, and, at the same time, as emotional, motivational, and motoric in nature; they are paralleled by "intuitive parenting" behaviors of the adult interaction partner that optimally match the infant's growing capabilities, social as well as nonsocial. These "natural" social tendencies of infant and parent may get damaged under adverse circumstances. Both theoretical and research approaches are endebted to ethological approaches (Lamb & Keller, 1991) that is to the Lorenz and Eibl-Eibesfeldt schools (Eibl-Eibesfeldt, 1986; Lorenz, 1965), as well as to the Tinbergen branch (Tinbergen, 1951), with its prominent developmentalists in the United Kingdom (Schaffer, 1984, 1987; Trevarthen, 1979).

Processes of Interaction

In the Francophone conception, individual experience results from social interactions with familiar partners (Blicharski et al.). Early social interaction is described as spontaneous infantile shifts and swings in motor tonicity and emotional arousal in need of sensitive regulation by an adult partner. Interaction is therefore built on proximal contacts between child and caregiver, on close bodily contact, posture changes, and gaze. From this *dialogue tonique,* from the emotional–tonic interchanges and regulations, temperamental characteristics as well as cognitions and representations of self and of other originate. The main developmental forces, instead of environment and physiology, are the coaction between partners, individual agency, and social interchange. Even individual understanding of the reality results from negotiation during the course of interaction—a sociological conception of socialization also advanced by Weinstein (1969): Meaning is the result of co-construction. Even structural changes occur primarily via social processes.

The unit of study, therefore, is the dyad, and not two independent persons and their socially directed actions. The basic idea seems to be that social behavior does not emanate from individuals; rather, individuals are integral parts of relationships. It is the interactions and relations that are the focus of analysis, and not the persons (there is no *bébé,* but only a nursing couple; see Pierrehumbert & Fivaz-Depeursinge). Accordingly, they prefer observations in quasinatural (even clinical) situations. The focus is on intraindividual variations over time in the micromodulation of motor activity and affect, in attention-focusing strategies, and in the sequential organization and timing of dyadic interaction.

The concepts used for characterizing dyadic interactions and relations also are not to be applied to individuals, but are framed in linguistic, communicative, or sociological terms, such as *proxemics, consensual, conflicting,* or *paradoxical* engagement; alliance or misalliance (Pierrehumbert & Fivaz-Depeursinge). These concepts, for their part, do not relate to realities to be discovered, but are introduced as metaphors that organize the ideas of the observer.

In the Francophone conceptions presented, the course of development seems to go from diffuse to articulate, from potential to realized, especially with regard to the evolution of interindividual differences (Blicharski et al.). Even in their biosocial model, the selective forces—the interplay between genetic and experiential norms—act in a way similar to sociological factors: They produce stable interindividual differences and create boundaries between groups and cultures. The biological concept of "canalization" (Waddington, 1957), in their interpretation, has been cast into a dynamic sociopsychological term, the "experiential canalization" with diffuse and plastic potential characterizing the beginning of development, and individual differences, as optimized adaptive functions, by lost adaptive potential at the culmination of development, a concept recently taken up in gerontology by Paul Baltes (Baltes, Dittman-Kohli, & Dixon, 1984).

Although American infant researchers also study caretaker–infant interaction, their approaches differ markedly from the Francophone ones presented in this volume. They are interested in the detection of early interindividual differences in both infants and mothers (e.g., Bornstein & Krasnegor, 1989). Therefore, both partners and their behaviors are analyzed separately as much as possible. Situations chosen for analysis are as close to experimental settings as is feasible in order to control for additional influences. Furthermore, there seems to be a clear preference for distal receptors: Vision and hearing, or vocal/verbal and visual stimulation. This preference seems to be rooted in cultural and religious convictions. American mothers, for instance, seem to be used to placing their infants opposite to them in an infant seat already in the earliest months (a position little suited for body contact between partners), and this position was taken up by infant researchers as "naturally occurring" and as optimal for studying face-to-face interaction. Taking together all facets—the body distance between infant and mother, the preference for distal at the expense of proximal stimulation, the "teaching" arrangement of the daily play situation, and the separate analyses of maternal and infant contributions to the interaction—they all seem to be related to the implicit conviction that the child has to be reared and taught from early on in order to become an adapted member of the society.

There has been little psychological research with infants in German-speaking countries (Keller, 1989; Lamb & Keller, 1991; Markefka & Nauck, 1992), and most longitudinal studies today are still adjuncts to pediatric research. Although ideas of early infant stimulation borrowed from the United States may be fashionable in some educated families, there is a general "Continental" reluctance to interfere too early in the natural course of development. Accordingly, the terms *teacher* and *school* are not used for professionals or institutions dealing with children under 6 years of age. It took a long time for infant seats to be introduced in young German families: Infants either sat on their mothers' laps or "entertained" themselves in their beds or in a playpen. Social play between parent and child as a regularly arranged daily routine seems to enter only later in the 1st year, when the baby can handle toys; if parents are interested in early stimulation, they introduce gymnastics or arrange "play dates" with peer infants. In spite of U.S. research influences and a tendency, as in the United States, to analyze parental and infantile contributions to interaction and development separately, there seems to be a preference in the German-speaking research community to study universal or general developmental changes over time rather than searching for early stable interindividual differences, and to attribute to the child a considerable portion of agency and exploration into the social and nonsocial world as motors of his or her further development.

The role attributed to the father in Francophone research may also illuminate the culturally based differences in research approaches. Pêcheux and Labrell elaborated interactive behavior expressed particularly by fathers, which they term *non-conventional play* or *teasing,* providing playful destabilization of the infant's emotions. This behavior is probably also genuine to German and American fathers, but to date, it has not been positively valued by either infant researchers in these countries or by the social community. In their research, Pêcheux and Labrell, however, present paternal teasing behavior as an important cultural component and as a developmental challenge to the child. Taking this point of view, playful teasing might be a mode of socialization that has been undervalued or misinterpreted by researchers of other cultural backgrounds.

Social Relations

Besides social interaction, social relations are units of analysis in the Francophone research on infancy and early childhood presented in this volume. Early social relations have become a topic of interest at the international level rather recently; in addition to parent–child relationships, peer relationships, friendship relationships, and sibling relationships have been differentiated. Mostly, it is interaction in these relationships or differences in interaction between these relationships that are the focus of these studies, and only rarely is the question raised regarding how the developing child becomes psychologically able to handle several social relations simultaneously. This is what makes the contribution of Pierrehumbert and Fivaz-Depeursinge, as well as that of Provost, so interesting and provocative.

Pierrehumbert and Fivaz-Depeursinge offer two contradictory lines of development in their chapter, however: a developmental progression from dyads to triads or even more complex relationships, and the development from triadic relationships to dyadic ones. The first line of progression is exemplified by the

342   RAUH

first relationship of the infant with his or her mother (a dyadic relationship), which soon extends to a triadic relation by including the father.

This relation mother–father–child, they contend, is more than the addition of a third person to the established mother–child dyad. The sheer physical or psychological presence of the father, as has frequently been studied in the United States as representative of triadic relations, and the father's active participation in the triadic interaction are not the same for the child. The infant's gaze behavior, for example, is dependent on the communicative body language of both parents physically present in the system. Although dyadic interactions with mothers and fathers differ and, for the infant, occur mostly sequentially, they will, with time, collapse into one complex family relationship.

For most Francophone infants, a second setting with new relationships is added during the 2nd year of life in the form of day care. Pierrehumbert and Fivaz-Depeursinge in France, and Provost in Canada, observed and compared attachment and social participation in both settings, home and day care, as well as during transitions from one setting to the other, in the simultaneous confrontation of the child with attachment figures from both settings, mother and caretaker.

They conclude that, in the 2nd year of life, infants seem at first to keep the two settings—family and day care—separate, with their persons and attachment figures, but soon they are able to integrate into the dyadic relationship first peers, and later, also, the attachment person from the other setting. The developmental sequence would be: relation exclusion, relation splitting, relation withdrawal, relation integration. They suggest, therefore, that the adult caregivers help the child integrate the complex relationships by the adults trying to represent internally the triadic relationship—referring to Bowlby's internal working model (Bowlby, 1973). The observations of Provost are worth pursuing: It seems that toddlers and young children carry over from one setting to the other (at home with siblings and in day care with peers, and later, in preschool) not so much quantitative but qualitative characteristics of their social behavior. In terms of integrating settings and relationships, similarity between settings seems to suit the younger children best, whereas older preschool children seem to benefit from relative dissimilarity of settings, although it remains somewhat unclear what behaviors of the child signal the benefit. Provost warns that behaviors to be chosen as indicative dependent variables, such as prosocial and antisocial behavior or attachment, may have to vary with the age of the child.

The second line of thought, presented by Pierrehumbert and Fivaz-Depeursinge, refers to historical and cultural changes as an evolution from global to differentiated or from triadic via dyadic to monadic relationships, dyadic relationships being a higher, more abstracted, and more differentiated form of relationship than triadic ones. The modern nuclear family, especially the single-parent family, are representative examples of more abstract forms of relations in this evolution. In the same chapter, the opposite interpretation of historical evolution is also presented, namely, from the traditional family as a dyadic relationship for the infant (with father and mother being taken as one), to the inclusion of a second, extrafamilial, setting, so this issue certainly needs a more highly scrutinized theoretical and empirical analysis.

There has been little research outside France comparable with this approach to the infant's development in handling and understanding relationships. The earliest reports on developing peer relationships in infants are probably the studies by Bühler (1927) and Klein and Wander (1933) of the Vienna School (see Rauh, 1987b). Except for Youniss (1980), who came from a Piagetian tradition, and who differentiated the psychological meaning of symmetrical and asymmetrical social relations for the social-cognitive development of the child, it has been mostly Judy Dunn in the United Kingdom (now in United States) who studied sibling relationships in infancy and compared them to other peer relationships (Dunn, 1983; Dunn & Kendrick, 1982; Dunn & Stocker, 1989). Krappmann (1989) and Oswald (Krappmann & Oswald, 1990) in Berlin, who were originally sociologists, carefully studied the development of peer group and role relationships (school mates, friends, close friends) via longitudinal natural observations and interviews with schoolchildren. The differentiation of family relationships, particularly the changes in relationships with the advent of the second child, are the focus of Kreppner's (1989) longitudinal study in Berlin.

These topics cross over the disciplinary boundaries between developmental psychology and sociology; and it appears that both sociologists who become developmental psychologists and developmental psychologists who become sociologists are engaged with these interesting issues. Still, scientific knowledge in this area is scarce, and it is my hope that the provocative thoughts and observations of the authors in this volume will advance the field.

Social Construction of Parental Conceptions of Child and Development

With respect to issues of childhood, Ariès (1965, 1975) is, next to Piaget, probably the Francophone thinker best known internationally. His major message was that childhood is a cultural construction, and that children at any time in history and in any cultural setting have been treated according to the representations of childhood held by their parents in their societies.

It seems that parental representations of childhood and their cultural variations is a major topic of Francophone sociopsychological and developmental research, here represented by Sabatier's contribution, but also permeating most of the other chapters. Sabatier refers to the long tradition of sociology, social psychology, and history in France, and pays credit to these sources. She studied and compared the ideas and values that Canadian and French mothers of infants on one side and immigrant mothers in France and in Canada on the other side hold with regard to developmental milestones, proper care, stimulation, child-rearing methods, and reliable sources of information. Although the assessment instruments were not totally compatible across samples, and although some immigrant mothers seemed puzzled by the "strange" questions of the investigators, several important research questions arose from these exploratory studies: What are the processes by which cultural knowledge and cultural values about child development and child rearing are transmitted? By what processes are they transformed? To what extent are developing maternal conceptions influenced by the mother's experiences with her individual child, and to what degree do they influence her interaction with her infant? To what degree are maternal social representations of child development and proper child stimulation the expression of variations in cultural values or, rather, dependent on the degree of industrialization and wealth? Finally, what is the relationship between scientific knowledge and lay conception: Are there common roots? Do they influence each other? Or are they totally separate worlds?

The study of the formation of psychological concepts in children and adults has become prominent in the recent years, often related to aspects of cognitive development and of theory of mind. In this Francophone presentation, however, the relationship to sociological thought seems to be particularly close, including a sensitivity for social relations constituted by the interview situation itself (Blicharsky et al).

PSYCHOLOGICAL CONCEPTIONS OF DEVELOPMENT

Developmental variables and processes can be viewed from various perspectives and in very different ways, rendering developmental psychology into a multidisciplinary or even interdisciplinary endeavor.

If the person is conceived of as a psychobiological member of the species *homo sapiens,* then universal behaviors and functions thought to be endogenous to the repertoire of the human, or genetic variations or habitat adaptations of this repertoire, are observed and analyzed. Accordingly, theories and methods are akin to those in biology, physiology, and ethology. This approach is widespread in Anglophone and German developmental research in infant development, especially with regard to motor and mental functions or structures (including the Piagetian kind of research), and the development of basic emotions and emotional milestones, including attachment.

In a second kind of approach, the person is conceived of as a member of a social group whose course of development can be characterized as changes occurring through social tasks and social roles. Theories, concepts, and methods are then related to those in social psychology and sociology. Topics, such as social status, social roles, sense of identity, and self-concept; developmental events, such as interaction, communication, and social conflict; and developmental contexts, such as setting, setting transitions, role changes, and developmental tasks, are typical for this approach. Research on adolescent development is usually dominated by this approach.

At a third level, the person is conceived of as a reflector of his or her own development. The units of analysis are the person's mental constructions of his or her own life and biography and his or her ideas of the social world. The main idea is that the person's conceptions of self and others not only change with development in an ordinary way, but also influence his or her behavior in many ways, and give consistency and stability to that behavior and its developmental course. Accordingly, the view from inside the person and the personal constructs are the units of behavior, and the major methods are interrogations and interviews. Accordingly, conceptions of development from this point of view are most characteristic of approaches to adult development, but they may go downward also into adolescent and to even younger ages (in theory of mind approaches). Typical topics are concepts of self and others, of values and morality, of social institutions, and of one's own life course or biography, but also topics such as stress and coping. Individual differences are usually of more interest to the investigators than are general or universal lines of development. Theories and methods are related to the historical sciences and the humanities.

It appears to me that even in cases where German and Anglo-Saxon investigators would relate to the first level, or a biological approach, as in early parent–infant communication, attachment, or early cognition, Francophone researchers tend to refer to models and methods according to the second, or sociological approach: the infant conceived of as a partner within a social relationship—even in cognition they refer to attentional processes within dyadic communication—with individuation resulting from social interaction. With regard to maternal conceptions, Francophone research at first glance seems to be related to the third approach, but even here, it remains sociological or sociopsychological in many respects.

SOME INSIGHTS INTO CULTURAL DIFFERENCES

I now take up the issue brought forward by Sabatier, and to some degree elaborated by Pêcheux and Labrell, regarding to what extent lay conceptions and scientific preconceptions and predelications in the selection of topics and the preference for models, theories, and the evaluation of empirical results, are influenced by the culture in which one lives. This issue cannot be discussed in full, but a few points may be highlighted. The first issue is: What aspects of infant behavior and development are typically seen as important for study and worth special attention by which country? Toys as the concrete expression of the cultural conceptions of play may be indicative in this. The second issue is the value attributed to early day care in the different cultures.

Toys typical of Germany would probably be solid wooden toys, even for infants. They are basic in form and color, and are constructed in such a way that the infant will investigate them and, by exploring their basic characteristics, (i.e., by more and more directed actions), will learn about the "real" world. This exploration is usually not dependent on the help of or the interaction with an adult. In the German lay perspective, as well as implicitly in the German research perspective, the infant develops, to a great deal, from his own potential for development, cognitive as well as emotional, communicative, and social. Related to an ethological approach, the child is equipped with basic abilities, social or other, and so is the adult. Optimal communication, for instance, occurs as a match between the infant's communication pattern and the interacting adult's "intuitive" motherese (Keller, 1989; Lamb & Keller, 1991). Child rearing should take care not to disturb or distort these abilities in the child. Even the term *Kindergarten* implies the image of watering a flower that grows by itself.

The toy market for infants is also replete with toys from the United States, but these are totally different from German toys. They do not necessarily represent the "real" world, but rather, are funny in form and color, often clearly *kitschig* (cf. Kitsch, in English). It seems to be enough that they are fun to act on and that by some action they produce a funny effect. These effects are more or less randomly combined with the toys, and, in contrast to German toys, are not supposed to introduce the child to the inner structure of that particular basic object. With typical American toys, the infant starts to learn particular functions very early: pulling strings, pushing buttons, and turning knobs that bring surprise effects. German toys, in contrast, are supposed to represent basic principles or to be a means for exploring reality. No funny effect is necessary; the information lies in the object, its form, color, texture, Gestalt, and aesthetics.

From France, no particular kinds of infant toys are known. If close bodily contact, tension regulation, interaction, and communication are the bases for early development, toys obviously do not have such a prominent place. What has been exported from France, instead, is a more humane entrance into the world (Leboyer, 1974), and the image of sensitive caressing of the newborn baby in close bodily contact.

Whereas stimuli provided by the adult seem to be the basis of knowledge in the Anglo-Saxon infant world, insights are what German babies are to win by active discovery, and French infants seem to learn by regulating their emotions, at first with the help of an adult, then by themselves and in social interaction.

The second issue, related to the view of toys and of infant exploratory behavior, is the value attributed to early day care in the respective cultures. There seems to be a major difference in how these societies at large perceive their responsibilities for their youngest members. In France, as Pêcheux and Labrell write, the state, by tradition, is morally and financially responsible for solutions to the problems of infancy. Not only physical, but also psychological, care and educational standards, even for infants, seem to be the responsibility of the state. Accordingly, research is tied to institutional care with respect to research subjects available, to topics selected (peer interaction, coping with early entrance into day care), and to the evaluation of results (for the emphasis on the positive effects of day care, see Pierrehumbert & Fivaz-Depeursinge, and Provost). The more positive attitude toward day care of more highly educated parents in France may be paralleled by data from Sweden, but not necessarily by data from Germany or the United States. Behavioral difficulties that could be interpreted as negative effects of early day-care attendance, such as discipline and attention problems, seem to be downplayed and are not fully outweighed by more social participation (see Provost).

In contrast with France, in the former West Germany, only 0.5% of the children under 3 years of age had a chance of getting a place in a day-care center. Most of these places were restricted to parents in particular financial or social need. Even in the West side of Berlin, where 20% of the children under 3 could find day-care places, parents reported as one of their major stresses their discussions with friends and relatives on whether a few hours a day of institutional day care could be of harm to their infants (Rauh & Ziegenhain, 1992). In East Germany, most children over 12 months attended day-care centers, usually 8 hours a day and longer. Although entry age into day care was already postponed by successive laws before unification, with unification the discussion of risks of damage by day care have intensified. The general view at the state level seems to be that for the first 3 years, the child's upbringing is fully the responsibility of his or her parents, with semiofficial agencies (churches, social agencies) offering subsidiary help if families are in need or deficient. Accordingly, there is little German psychological infancy research, unless it is combined with pediatric concerns. Under 3, a child seems to be the private property of his or her family.

In the United States, for social reasons, the state has felt partially responsible, even for the very young child, since the 1960s; day care and preschool attendance is recommended and supported, especially as compensatory education, to prevent later school failures or behavioral problems in children at psychosocial and medical risk. Consequently, curricula were even developed for infants in order to improve their learning. Optimizing cognitive or sensate stimulation was seen as a buffer against developmental deviations. It seems, seen from outside the United States, that part of the implicit aim of the U.S. infancy research of mother–child interaction, in contrast to the aims in France, was to optimize mother–child interaction by making it more effective, to improve quality when quantity (for lack of time, due to increased participation in the labor force) is reduced. Educationally valuable mother–child interaction seems to be a priority topic.

These are only cultural "flavors." In any of the countries mentioned, of course, there are tendencies, and there is research that does not conform to these biases. It seems worthwhile, however, to reflect on them from time to time. The confrontation with Francophone infancy research in such a concentrated form in this volume may stimulate such reflections even of one's own implicit biases.

REFERENCES

Ariès, P. (1965). *Culture of childhood.* New York: Knopf.

Ariès, P. (1975). *Geschichte der Kindheit* [History of childhood]. München: Hauser.

Baltes, P. B., Dittmann-Kohli, F., & Dixon, R. A. (1984). New perspectives on the development of intelligence in adulthood: Toward a dual process conception and a model of selective optimization with compensation. In P. B. Baltes & O. Brim (Eds.), *Life-span development and behavior* (Vol. 6, pp. 33–76). New York: Academic Press.

Bischof, N. (Ed.). (1989). *Das Rätsel Ödipus* [The puzzle about Oedipus]. München: Piper.

Bornstein, M. H., & Krasnegor, N. A. (Eds.). (1989). *Stability and continuity in mental development.* Hillsdale, NJ: Lawrence Erlbaum Associates.

Bowlby, J. (1973). *Attachment and loss: Vol. 2. Separation.* New York: Basic Books.

Bühler, C. (1927). Die ersten sozialen Verhaltensweisen des Kindes [The first social behaviors of the infant]. *Quellen und Studien zur Jugendkunde, 5,* 1–102.

Dunn, J. (1983). Sibling relationships in early childhood. *Child Development, 54,* 787–811.

Dunn, J., & Kendrick, C. (1982). *Siblings: Love, envy and understanding.* Cambridge, MA: Harvard University Press.

Dunn, J., & Stocker, C. (1989). The significance of differences in siblings' experience within the family. In K. Kreppner & R. M. Lerner (Eds.), *Family systems and life-span development* (pp. 289–302). Hillsdale, NJ: Lawrence Erlbaum Associates.

Eibl-Eibesfeldt, I. (1986). *Die Biologie des menschlichen Verhaltens: Grundriß der Humanethologie* [The biology of human behavior: Human ethology, an outline]. München: Piper.

Gewirtz, J. L. (1969). Mechanisms of social learning: Some roles of stimulation and behavior in early human development. In D. A. Goslin (Ed.), *Handbook of socialization theory and research* (pp. 57–212). Chicago: Rand McNally.

Hartup, W. W. (1983). Peer relations. In P. H. Mussen (Series Ed.) & E. M. Hetherington (Vol. Ed.), *Handbook of child psychology: Vol. 4. Socialization, personality, and social development* (4th ed., pp. 103–196). New York: Wiley.

Hetzer, H. (1967). *Zur Psychologie des Kindes. Werke und Abhandlungen.* (J. P. Ruppert, Ed.). [On the psychology of the child. Research publications and essays]. Darmstadt, Germany: Wissenschaftliche Buchgesellschaft.

Keller, H. (Ed.). (1989). *Handbuch der Kleinkindforschung* [Handbook of infancy research]. Berlin: Springer.

Klein, R., & Wander, E. (1933). Gruppenbildung im zweiten Lebensjahr [Group formation in the second year of life]. *Zeitschrift für Psychologie, 128,* 257–280.

Krappmann, L. (1989). Family relationships and peer relationships in middle childhood: An exploratory study of the associations between children's integration into the social networks of peers and family development. In K. Kreppner & R. M. Lerner (Eds.), *Family systems and life-span development* (pp. 93–104). Hillsdale, NJ: Lawrence Erlbaum Associates.

Krappmann, L., & Oswald, H. (1990). Sozialisation in Familie und Gleichaltrigenwelt. Zur Sozialökologie der Entwicklung in der mittleren Kindheit [Socialization in the family and in the peer world. A social ecology of middle childhood]. *Zeitschrift für Sozialisationsforschung und Erziehungssoziologie, 10,* 147–162.

Kreppner, K. (1989). Linking infant development in-context research to the investigation of life-span family development. In K. Kreppner & R. M. Lerner (Eds.), *Family systems and life-span development* (pp. 33–64). Hillsdale, NJ: Lawrence Erlbaum Associates.

Lamb, M., & Keller, H. (Eds.). (1991). *Infant development: Perspectives from German-speaking countries.* Hillsdale, NJ: Lawrence Erlbaum Associates.

Leboyer, F. (1974). *Der sanfte Weg ins Leben.Geburt ohne Gewalt.* [The gentle way into life. Birth without violence]. München: Desch.

Lorenz, K. (1965). *Über tierisches und menschliches Verhalten: Gesammelte Abhandlungen* [About animal and human behavior. Collected essays]. München: Piper.

Markefka, M., & Nauck, B. (Eds.). (1992). *Handbuch der Kindheitsforschung* [Handbook of childhood research]. Neuwied, Germany: Luchterhand.

Palacios, J. (1992, September). Programme and abstracts of the Fifth European Conference on Developmental Psychology in Seville, Spain. University of Seville.

Papousek, M., & Papousek, H. (1991). Early verbalizations as precursors of language development. In M. E. Lamb & H. Keller (Eds.), *Infant development: Perspectives from German-speaking countries* (pp. 299–328). Hillsdale, NJ: Lawrence Erlbaum Associates.

Rauh, H. (1987a). Frühe Kindheit [Early childhood]. In R. Oerter & L. Montada (Eds.), *Entwicklungspsychologie* [Developmental psychology]. (pp. 131–203). München: Psychologie Verlags Union.

Rauh, H. (1987b). Social development in infant peers. In H. Rauh & H. C. Steinhausen (Eds.), *Psychobiology and early development* (pp. 257–273). Amsterdam: North-Holland.

Rauh, H. (1987c). Verhaltensausstattung und erste Anpassungsleistungen des Säuglings [Behavioral equipment and first adaptational accomplishments of the young infant]. In C. Niemitz (Ed.), *Erbe und Umwelt: Zur Natur von Anlage und Selbstbestimmung des Menschen* [Inheritance and environment: About the nature of biological heritage and self-determination of man]. (Vol. TB Wissenschaft 6, pp. 174–199). Frankfurt/Main: Suhrkamp.

Rauh, H., & Steinhausen, H. C. (Eds.). (1987). *Psychobiology and early development*. Amsterdam: North-Holland.

Rauh, H., & Ziegenhain, U. (1992). *Frühkindliche Anpassung. Vorläufiger Abschlußbericht des DFG-Projektes Ra 373/5-1 and 5-2* [Adaptation in infancy. Preliminary research report of a project supported by a German Science Foundation research grant to the first author]. Unpublished manuscript, Free University Berlin, Institute of Psychology, Department of Educational Sciences.

Schaffer, H. R. (1984). *The child's entry into a social world*. London: Academic Press.

Schaffer, H. R. (1987). The social context of psychobiological development. In H. Rauh & H. C. Steinhausen (Eds.), *Psychobiology and early development* (pp. 239–255). Amsterdam: North-Holland.

Tinbergen, N. (1951). *The study of instinct*. London: Oxford University Press.

Trevarthen, C. (1979). Instincts for human understanding and for cultural cooperation: Their development in infancy. In M. V. Cranach, K. Foppa, W. Lepenies, & D. Ploog (Eds). *Human ethology: Claims and limits of a new discipline* (pp. 530–594). Cambridge, England: Cambridge University Press.

Waddington, C. H. (1957). *The strategy of genes*. London: Allen & Unwin.

Weinstein, E. A. (1969). The development of interpersonal competence. In D. A. Goslin (Ed.), *Handbook of socialization theory and research* (pp. 753–775). Chicago: Rand McNally.

Youniss, J. (1980). *Parents and peers in social development: A Sullivan–Piaget perspective*. Chicago: Chicago University Press.

Author Index

Neisser, U., 29, *32*
Nelson, C. A., 84, *89*
Nelson, K., 208, 210, 215, *223, 224,* 231, *239,* 315, *330*
Netchine-Grynberg, G., 256, *266*
Nguyen-Xuan, A., 143, *146*
Nicolas, R. M., 316, 317, *330*
Nicolet, M., 150, *165*
Ninio, A., 112, *114,* 299, 302, 303, 307, *313*
Noirot, E., 6, *11,* 18, 20, *30*
Norvez, A., 257, *266*

O

Ogbu, J. U., 299, *313*
Ogino, M., 260, *264*
Ohr, P. S., 57, *73*
Oléron, P., 133, *146*
Oller, D. K., 192, 194, 200, *205*
Olson, S. L., 315, *330*
Oppenheim, R. W., 2, *11*
Orlansky, M. D., 208, *224*
Orsini-Bouichou, F., 134, 137, 140, 141, *145, 146*
Oser, F., 150, *165*
Oswald, H., 343, *348*

P

Paden, L., 59, *73*
Paillard, J., 28, *32*
Palacios, J., 299, *313,* 337, *348*
Paour, J. L., 134, 135, 138, 141, *146, 147*
Papoušek, H., 70, *73,* 93, *95,* 123, 124, *131,* 339, *348*
Papoušek, M., 70, *73,* 123, 124, *131,* 339, *348*
Parke, R. D., 262, *267,* 270, 272, 276, *283, 284*
Parmelee, A. H., 62, *74*
Parrinello, R., 60, 61, *74*
Parten, M. B., 294, *297*
Pascalis, O., 39, *52*
Pascual-Leone, J., 139, *147*
Pêcheux, M. G., 80, *90,* 260, 263, *264, 265, 266*
Pedersen, F. A., 275, *284*
Pegg, J. E., 193, *206*
Peiper, A., 18, *32*
Pierret, M., 157, *166*
Pelletier, D., 293, 295, *296*
Pennington, B., 186, *189*

Pepler, D. J., 262, *266*
Peretz, I. P., 36, *49*
Perkins, G. H., 78, *88*
Perret-Clermont, A. N., 7, *12,* 136, *147,* 150, *165,* 168, 169, *170*
Perris, E. E., 23, 27, *32*
Peters, D. L., 290, 295, *297*
Peters, M., 36, *52*
Petersen, S. E., 42, *52*
Pezé, A., 185, *188*
Phelps, M. E., 48, *50*
Piaget, J., 2, 4, 5, 8, *12,* 20, *33,* 78, 86, *89, 99,* 103–105, 108–111, *116,* 119, 128, *132,* 133, 136, 138, *147,* 149, 151, 152, 155, 162, *165,* 177, 186, *188,* 207, *224,* 271, *284,* 316, *330*
Piatelli-Palmarini, M., 207, *224*
Pieraut-LeBonniec, G., 36, *50*
Pierrehumbert, B., 278–281, *284*
Pietrzyk, U., 48, *53*
Pinard, A., 103, *114, 116,* 134, 135, 137, 141, *146*
Pineau, A., 81, *89, 90,* 141, *147*
Pinker, S., 80, *89*
Pinol-Douriez, M., 258, *267*
Plancherel, B., 278, 279, *284*
Plomin, R. A., 315, 319, 328, *329*
Poirier, C., 84, *89*
Pomerleau, A., 57–59, 62, 63, 65–67, *73,* 302, *313, 314*
Posner, M. I., 37, 42, 43, 45, 46, *52,* 55, 62, *74,* 319, *330*
Poulin-Dubois, D., *16,* 107, *116,* 121, *131,* 209, 213–218, 220, *224*
Pouliot, T., 121, *131*
Power, T. G., 262, *267,* 272, *284*
Prechtl, H. F. R., 18, *33,* 93, *95*
Pressley, M., 236, *238*
Prêteur, Y., 307, *313*
Preyer, W., 119, *132*
Priel, B., 126, 127, 129, *132*
Provost, M. A., 287, 290–293, 295, *296, 297*

Q

Quinn, P. C., 83, *89,* 210, *224*

R

Rabain-Jamin, J., 259, *267*
Rahn, C. W., 260, *264*
Ramsay, D. S., 36, *52*

van de Veer, R., 167, *170*
Van Geert, P., 248, 251, *252*
van Harreveld, A., 48, *51*
van Kleeck, M. H., 45, *53*
van Ijzendoorn, M. H., 279, *284*, 292, 293, *298*
Vandenberg, B., 113, *117*
Vandenplas-Holper, Ch., 151, 154, 155, 157, 160, 162, 163, *164, 165, 166,* 308–310, *314*
Vaughn, B. E., 322, 327, *331*
Verba, M., 138, 142, *144, 147,* 184, *188,* 211, *224*
Vietze, P. M., 63, *74*
Vigorto, J., 83, *88*
Vihman, M. M., 192, 197, 199–201, *204, 206*
Vineberg-Jacobs, E., 291, *296*
Vinh-Bang, 138, *147*
Vinter, A., 93, *95*
Visier, J. -P., 259, *266*
Visser, J. H. A., 94, *95*
Viviani, P., 192, *206*
Voelin, D., 149, 163, *164*
Volterra, V., 208, 220, *221*
von Hofsten, C., 17, 18, 23, *33*
von Noorden, G. K., 48, *51*
Vurpillot, E., 80, *90*
Vygotsky, L. S., 167, *170, 179, 189,* 242, 318, 321, *331*
Vyt, A., 122, 127, *132*

W

Wachs, T. D., 59, *74*
Waddington, C. H., 319, *331,* 340, *348*
Walker, A., 78, 81, *88*
Walker, R. A., 48, *52*
Wall, S., 278, 280, *283*
Wallace, C. S., 36, *51*
Wallon, H., 3, 9, *12,* 18, 21, *33, 34,* 36, *53,* 119, 125, *132,* 177–181, 183, 184, 186, *189,* 255, 257, *267,* 318, *331*
Wander, E., 343, *348*
Waters, E., 278, 280, *283, 298*

Watson, J. S., 60, *73*
Waxman, S. R., 221, *225*
Weinstein, E. A., 339, *348*
Weinstein, H., 299, *312*
Weir, T., 294, *298*
Weiss, M. J., 28, *34*
Wellman, H. M., 107, 110, *117*
Werker, J. F., 193, *206*
Werner, J. S., 56, 66, *73*
Wertheim, E., 274, *285*
Wertsch, J. V., *170, 331*
Weston, D., 310, *313*
Westra, T., 307, *313*
White, B. L., 23, *34*
Whiting, B. B., 309, *314*
Widmer-Robert-Tissot, C., 182, *189,* 256, *267*
Wieman, L. A., 192, *205*
Williams, M., 109, *116*
Winegar, L. T., 318, *331*
Winnicott, D., 258, *267*
Winnicott, D. W., 269, 270, *285*
Winnykamen, F., 138, 142, *144, 148,* 150, *166*
Wishart, J. G., 105, *117*
Wolf, K. M., 5, *12*
Woodson, R., 181, *188*
Wu, P. Y. K., 38, *51*

Y

Yarrow, L. J., 63, *74*
Young, A. W., 37, *51*
Young, G., 36, *53,* 109, *117*
Youniss, J., 343, *348*

Z

Zack, M., 300, 302, 306, *312*
Zahn-Waxler, C., 280, *284*
Zazzo, R., 4, 9, *12,* 119–121, 124, 125, *132,* 179, 181, *189*
Zeigenhain, U., 347, *348*
Zelazo, P. R., 28, *34,* 58, 61, 64, 65, *73, 74*
Zetterstrom, R., 192, *204*

Subject Index

A

Accommodation, 2, 136, 149, 263
Acoustic spectral characteristics of speech, 194
Action(s)
  coordination of, 17–18, 94
  development of, 25
  functional, 17, 27–29
  joint, 111, 152, 157
  motor, 76
  synergistic, 20, 25
  tutoring, 152, 159, 161
  visual, 20–22
Action–effect sequences, 123
Adaptation
  early modes of, 316
  joint, 316
  transitory, 177, 247
Affective symbiosis, 8, 178, 181–182
Agrammatical statements detection, 233
Alliance, 274–275
Allocentrism, 129
Appropriation, 125
Assimilation, 2, 136, 149
Asymmetric Tonic Neck Reflex, 21, 92
ATNP (*see* Asymmetric Tonic Neck Reflex)
Attachment, 105, 271, 273
  influence of day care on, 279–280, 292–293, 334

problem-solving skills consequences, 321–322
  social responsiveness consequences, 280
Attachment Q-sort method, 292–293
Attention, 55, 63, 123
  in Down syndrome infants, 62
  focused, 63
  focusing, 56, 58, 67, 260–261
  functional explanation, 65–71
  maintenance, 56, 60, 64, 67
  in premature infants, 62
  sustained, 63, 123
  termination, 56
Awareness
  metalinguistic, 234
  of self, 119, 125, 180
  of social position, 183

B

Babbling, 192–195, 199, 249–250
  canonical, 202
Behavior
  attunement, 28
  canalization, 10, 318–319, 340
  goal-oriented, 17
  epilinguistic, 8, 248
  exploratory, 20–21, 59
  hierarchical architecture, 3
  intermodal organization, 18